NECESSARY EVILS

This book is about amnesties for grave international crimes that states adopt in moments of transition or social unrest. The subject is naturally controversial, especially in the age of the International Criminal Court. The goal of this book is to reframe and revitalize the global debate on the subject and to offer an original framework for resolving amnesty dilemmas when they arise. Most existing literature and jurisprudence on amnesties deal with only a small subset of state practice and sidestep the ambiguity of amnesty's position under international law. This book addresses the ambiguity head on and argues that amnesties of the broadest scope are sometimes defensible when adopted as a last recourse in contexts of mass violence. Drawing on an extensive amnesty database, the book offers detailed guidance on how to ensure that amnesties extend the minimum leniency possible, while imposing the maximum accountability on the beneficiaries.

Mark Freeman is Director of External Relations with the International Crisis Group. Based in Brussels, he is coauthor of *International Human Rights Law*, the first comprehensive Canadian textbook on the subject, and author of *Truth Commissions and Procedural Fairness* (Cambridge University Press), which was awarded the American Society of International Law's Certificate of Merit in 2007.

NECESSARY EVILS

AMNESTIES AND THE SEARCH FOR JUSTICE

Mark Freeman

CAMBRIDGE
UNIVERSITY PRESS

CAMBRIDGE UNIVERSITY PRESS
Cambridge, New York, Melbourne, Madrid, Cape Town, Singapore,
São Paulo, Delhi, Dubai, Tokyo

Cambridge University Press
32 Avenue of the Americas, New York, NY 10013-2473, USA

www.cambridge.org
Information on this title: www.cambridge.org/9780521895255

First published 2009

Printed in the United States of America

A catalog record for this publication is available from the British Library.

Library of Congress Cataloging in Publication data

Freeman, Mark, 1968–
Necessary evils : amnesties and the search for justice / Mark Freeman.
 p. cm.
Includes bibliographical references and index.
ISBN 978-0-521-89525-5 (hardback)
1. Amnesty. 2. International offenses. 3. Transitional justice. I. Title.
K5132.F74 2009
345'.077 – dc22   2009022601

ISBN   978-0-521-89525-5 Hardback

Whoever destroys a soul, it is considered as if he destroyed an entire world. And whoever saves a life, it is considered as if he saved an entire world.

– *JERUSALEM TALMUD*, SANHEDRIN 4:8 (37a)

Contents

Final Considerations: On the Perennial Contestation of Amnesties

Preface

This book is about amnesties adopted, reluctantly and in contexts of mass violence, for serious crimes under international law. The subject is naturally controversial. My intention in writing the book is merely to contribute to the debate, not to resolve it. The issue belies any neat solution.

More than any other measure, it is amnesty that constitutes the lightning rod – the hot-button issue – for individuals and groups dedicated to the fight against impunity. In that respect, the subject offers an important lens through which to understand the almost-seismic legal-political shift that has taken place in the global fight against impunity since the end of the Cold War – from the establishment of ad hoc international and hybrid criminal tribunals to the creation of the permanent International Criminal Court, the emergence of truth and reconciliation commissions, and the adoption of a formal UN position on amnesties that reverses the institution's long-standing prior practice.

My intention with this book is to be polemical. I believe some of my colleagues in the global fight against impunity have been moving too quickly toward closure of the amnesty debate. As someone who has chosen a professional career in human rights, and has advised on the question of amnesty in more than a dozen states, I have long been troubled by this premature push to close the debate. The fact is that there are many fundamental questions concerning amnesty that remain unresolved and that require debate. Yet the book would have little value if it only raised questions. Therefore, throughout the text, the reader will find concrete suggestions about how to reconcile the legal and policy tensions that are endemic to the question of amnesty. The goal is to nurture a debate that will have practical results.

My hope is that the book will find an audience beyond the legal profession. The legal perspective is only one among many, and yet it has dominated amnesty debates thus far. Unless more voices are added to the debate, crucially important and different perspectives will be absent. Georges Clemenceau famously said that war is something too serious to be left to the military. Similarly, amnesty is too serious to be left to the legal profession.

I also wish for this book to find an audience beyond elite policy circles. Persons outside of such circles are almost certainly unaware of the radical normative and institutional changes of recent years that have turned the generally positive image of amnesty into a generally negative one. As a result, there may be a gap between the new rules and the commonsense perspective of the broader global public, including in countries where amnesty may be a necessary last recourse.

There has been much scholarship on amnesties in recent years, although there are relatively few book-length treatments of the subject. My intention is not to repeat what others have already said. However, it is necessary to cover some familiar ground, taking into consideration the broader audience that this book seeks to reach and the fact that not many people read, for example, the numerous legal journals in which the debates on amnesty have been, in equal parts, illuminating and passionate.

The research for this book originated several years ago when I began a project that involved the creation of a significant amnesty database. The database grew over the years and today includes nearly six hundred human rights–related amnesty texts, thanks to the support of many friends and colleagues, most notably Louise Mallinder and Jorge Errandonea. It was always my belief that such a database was necessary to ensure "smart" amnesty outcomes or outcomes based on deep comparative and technical knowledge of all the possible negative and positive amnesty design choices. I also wanted to avoid engaging in the error common to some of the legal literature and jurisprudence on amnesties, which involves making broad conclusions on the topic on the basis of the same small cluster of amnesty laws and cases taken from Latin America, South Africa, and Sierra Leone. Still, I am aware that my own amnesty database is far from complete. There are undoubtedly hundreds more amnesties than have been identified to date.

Although it is important, comparative expertise on amnesties is no guarantee of smart outcomes in and of itself. Expertise in mediation, international law, and military strategy could be just as important in some situations or, indeed, more so. At the same time, expertise on amnesty legislation can help avoid foreseeable mistakes and ensure that amnesties are appropriately limited to maximally preserve future justice options. In that respect, I wish to underline that this book is ultimately less about amnesties than about the art of the pursuit of justice. It is about the art of balancing the demands of law with the human and political realities of particular contexts, while always placing a premium on justice in the broadest sense of the term.

The book is divided into two main parts. Drawing from a wide cross section of primary and secondary sources, Part I explains what amnesties are (and are not), why they tend to be viewed as inimical to the fight against impunity, and how international law treats them. It also explores the impact of the International Criminal Court on current debates and the merits of the UN Secretariat's evolving position on what crimes should be barred from future amnesties. Seeking to replace the current ad hoc approach to amnesty negotiation, Part II presents an original methodology for the design of amnesties to help limit the harm they cause to the international rule of law and victims' rights. The discussion includes argument on why amnesties should be adopted only as a last recourse, as well as a detailed presentation on design options for the content of an amnesty. The design options aim to ensure that amnesties pursue a legitimate end, are minimally entrenched in the domestic legal system, confer the minimum amount of leniency on the beneficiaries, impose the maximum conditions on them, and offer the greatest likelihood of being effectively administered.

Also included are an introductory chapter that presents several of the book's underlying themes, arguments, and dilemmas and a concluding chapter that explores different aspects of the contestation of amnesties, following their adoption. The book is complemented by appendices of primary source materials on amnesties, including excerpts from international instruments and selected jurisprudence. There is also a glossary of common abbreviations and legal terms, although the reader will note that I use a number of terms without defining them, such as *human rights crimes*, *international community*, *peace*, *democracy*, and many more. Each of these terms can be dissected and parsed in various ways. I would ask the reader simply to adopt the commonsense or everyday meaning of these terms, except where the text specifies otherwise. *Amnesty* is the only term I will devote significant time to defining.

There was a time when it was considered taboo to say too much about amnesties out of fear that the world's villains would seek to use the information to their own nefarious ends. Happily, that taboo has been overcome. Almost everything to be known about amnesties is now in the public domain where it belongs, and I know of no evidence demonstrating that amnesty outcomes have worsened as a result. Indeed, the opposite may have happened – amnesty scholarship and databases may be serving to refine and improve amnesty outcomes. At the same time, there remains much to debate and learn. This book represents my attempt to contribute to that debate by presenting some new questions and ideas on what is at stake and on how to bridge the perceived divide between amnesties and the cause of justice.

Brussels
June 2009

Acknowledgments

Like most books, this one benefited immensely from the contributions of family, friends, and colleagues. I would first like to express my heartfelt gratitude to Drazan Djukic, Jorge Errandonea, Marieke Vlaemynck, and Anatoly Vlasov, each of whom contributed extensive and superb research and editorial assistance at different stages of the manuscript's preparation. I am indebted to all of them.

I also would like to express my sincere gratitude to Luc Huyse, Kate Carey, Louise Mallinder, Michael J. Nesbitt, Max Pensky, Joanna Quinn, Tyrone Savage, Leslie Vinjamuri, and Gwen K. Young, for having read and commented on the full manuscript. Their insights and feedback were crucial in making this a better book. I am similarly grateful to Reed Brody, Phil Clark, Gibran van Ert, Dadimos Haile, Pierre Hazan, Antje Herrberg, Sonia Herrero, Larry May, Julie Ringelheim, Martien Schotsmans, Ron Slye, and Géraldine de Vries for their very helpful comments on Part I of the manuscript.

My research for this book began many years ago when I first joined the International Center for Transitional Justice, and I remain appreciative of the early support and many stimulating conversations I had with colleagues while there.

I also extend my sincere thanks to John Berger at Cambridge University Press for his encouragement and patience throughout the writing process, and to Katherine Faydash, Peggy Rote, and Eleanor Umali for their excellent editorial support.

Finally, I wish to thank Annamie, Malachai, and Jonas for putting up with my many long days and nights typing away at the computer. It is to them and to my parents, David and Claire, that I dedicate this book.

Abbreviations and Legal Terms

ACHR	the American Convention on Human Rights, OAS Treaty Series No. 36, 1144 U.N.T.S. 123, entered into force July 18, 1978
aut dedere aut judicare	the duty to extradite or prosecute
CAT	the Convention against Torture and Other Cruel, Inhuman or Degrading Treatment or Punishment, General Assembly Resolution 39/46, U.N. GAOR, 39th sess., Supp. No. 51, at 197, UN doc. A/39/51 (1985), entered into force June 26, 1987
de jure	in or concerning law
ECHR	the European Convention on Human Rights and Fundamental Freedoms
ECOSOC	the UN Economic and Social Council
force majeure	an extraordinary event or circumstance beyond one's control
Geneva Conventions	the four Geneva Conventions of August 12, 1949: Geneva Convention for the Amelioration of the Condition of the Wounded and Sick in Armed Forces in the Field, 75 U.N.T.S. 31; Geneva Convention for the

	Amelioration of the Condition of Wounded, Sick and Shipwrecked Members of Armed Forces at Sea, 75 U.N.T.S. 85; Geneva Convention relative to the Treatment of Prisoners of War, 75 U.N.T.S. 135; and Geneva Convention relative to the Protection of Civilian Persons in Time of War, 75 U.N.T.S. 287
Genocide Convention	the Convention on the Prevention and Punishment of the Crime of Genocide, General Assembly Resolution 260 A (III), adopted December 9, 1948, 78 U.N.T.S. 277
ICC	the International Criminal Court
ICCPR	the International Covenant on Civil and Political Rights, General Assembly Resolution 2200 A (XXI), adopted December 16, 1966, U.N. GAOR, 21st sess., Supp. No. 16, at 52, UN Doc. A/6316 (1967)
ICESCR	the International Covenant on Economic, Social, and Cultural Rights, General Assembly Resolution 2200 A (XXI), adopted December 16, 1966, U.N. GAOR, 21st sess., Supp. No. 16, at 49, UN Doc. A/6316 (1967), 993 U.N.T.S. 3
ICJ	the International Court of Justice
ICJ Statute	the Statute of the ICJ, which is contained within the UN Charter
ICTR	the International Criminal Tribunal for Rwanda
ICTY	the International Criminal Tribunal for Yugoslavia
ILC	the International Law Commission
jus cogens	a peremptory international norm from which no derogation is ever permitted
lex specialis	(or *lex specialis derogat legi generali*) means the rule of international legal interpretation according to which a specific law governing a subject takes precedence over a general law governing the same subject
locus standi	the right to bring a legal action
mutatis mutandis	with the necessary changes being made
ne bis in idem	the right not to be tried or punished for a crime for which the person already has been convicted or acquitted
OAS	the Organization of American States

obiter	(or *obiter dictum*) means an aside or a remark by a judge or court that is superfluous to the determination of the case
opinio juris	the belief that an action was carried out because it was obligatory to do so
proprio motu	by one's own initiative
Protocol I to the Geneva Conventions	Protocol Additional to the Geneva Conventions of August 12, 1949, and relating to the Protection of Victims of International Armed Conflicts (Protocol I), June 8, 1977, 1125 U.N.T.S. 3
Protocol II to the Geneva Conventions	Protocol Additional to the Geneva Conventions of August 12, 1949, and relating to the Protection of Victims of Non-international Armed Conflicts (Protocol II), June 8, 1977, 1125 U.N.T.S. 609
ratione loci	the territorial scope
ratione materiae	the subject-matter scope
ratione personae	the personal scope
ratione temporis	the temporal scope
Refugee Convention	the Convention Relating to the Status of Refugees, Geneva, July 28, 1951, 189 U.N.T.S. 150, entered into force April 22, 1954, as amended by the subsequent Protocol Relating to the Status of Refugees, January 31, 1967, 606 U.N.T.S. 267
res judicata	a matter that already has been adjudicated
Rome Statute	the Rome Statute of the ICC, July 17, 1998, UN Doc. A/CONF.183/9, reprinted in 37 I.L.M. 999 (1998)
Slavery Convention	the Slavery Convention (1926), 60 L.N.T.S. 253, as amended by the subsequent Protocol Amending the Slavery Convention, signed at Geneva on September 25, 1926 (1955), 212 U.N.T.S. 277
UDHR	the Universal Declaration of Human Rights, General Assembly Resolution 217 A (III), UN Doc. A/810 (1948)
UN Charter	the Charter of the United Nations, June 26, 1945, 59 Stat. 1031, T.S. 993
Vienna Convention	the Vienna Convention on the Law of Treaties, UN Doc. A/CONF. 39/27 (1969)

Opening Considerations: On the Perennial Relevance of Amnesties

There are few issues of law and policy as complex and divisive as the question of when and whether to grant amnesties for atrocities. Across the centuries and across the globe, the issue has been faced on innumerable occasions. Yet there is something particular about how it has been confronted in the past several decades that is unlike prior eras. In my view, that "something" has at least two parts: first is the rise of international human rights and international criminal law, which have abridged the scope of state sovereignty and made it impossible to see the amnesty issue in purely political terms; second is the emergence of global information and communications technologies, which have made it easier to mobilize international opinion and action about national traumas that give rise to amnesty dilemmas. These two developments make the resolution of the amnesty question a fundamentally different undertaking from earlier times.

Yet even within this modern era of international law and technological advances, at least two distinct periods can be identified. For simplicity's sake, we could describe these as the amnesty-approval period and the amnesty-disapproval period. These periods are neatly captured in the pioneering work of Louis Joinet, an influential French magistrate and international law expert.

Joinet's part in the story begins in 1983. In that year, the UN Sub-Commission on Prevention of Discrimination and Protection of Minorities, "having become aware of the importance that the promulgation of amnesty laws could have for the safeguard and promotion of human rights and fundamental freedoms," requested Joinet (at the time a UN human rights special rapporteur) to prepare a technical study on the topic.[1] His final report, issued in 1985, was in its day the most sophisticated and detailed comparative work on the subject.[2] Although published before the age of the Internet and seldom cited today, it remains a valuable academic reference on the question of amnesty.

In 1991, a mere six years after the publication of that study, the same UN Sub-Commission asked Joinet to undertake a different study on human rights.[3] On this occasion, the study was expected to show how amnesties contributed to impunity rather than to the safeguard of human rights.

At the beginning of the report that Joinet prepared in response to the Sub-Commission's second request, he offered his own reflections on the dramatic shift of perspectives on the amnesty issue that had occurred in such a short period.[4] He did so by dividing the "origins of the campaign against impunity" into four stages. He labeled the 1970s as the first stage, when "nongovernmental organizations, human rights advocates and legal experts," in particular in Latin America, argued for amnesty for political prisoners and found it to be "a topic that could mobilize large sectors of public opinion, thus gradually making it easier to amalgamate the many moves made during the period to offer peaceful resistance to or resist dictatorial regimes."[5] Focusing again on Latin American experiences, Joinet described the 1980s as the second stage, when amnesty "was more and more seen as a kind of 'down-payment on impunity' with the emergence, then proliferation, of 'self-amnesty' laws proclaimed by declining military dictatorships anxious to arrange their own impunity while there was still time."[6] He proceeded to describe the first few years after the fall of the Berlin Wall as the third stage, characterizing it as one "marked by many processes of democratization or return to democracy along with peace agreements putting an end to internal armed conflicts" in which questions of impunity constantly arose.[7] Finally, Joinet labeled the period starting with the 1993 Vienna World Conference on Human Rights as the fourth stage, "when the international community realized the importance of combating impunity."[8]

As it turned out, even more dramatic shifts were on the immediate horizon in the years that followed the UN Sub-Commission's request to Joinet. Particularly significant were the creation of international tribunals for the former Yugoslavia and Rwanda, the taking up by the UN Secretariat of a formal position on the subject of amnesty, and the adoption of the 1998 Rome Statute of the International Criminal Court (ICC). One could describe the latter event in particular as the marker of a fifth stage in the global fight against impunity. We are still in that stage.

This fifth stage in the anti-impunity struggle is turning out to be the most interesting of all, although it is also full of challenges concerning the issue of amnesty. For one thing, the amnesty bar is higher now than it has ever been. There are many international lawyers and human rights defenders who categorically reject certain kinds of amnesties, in particular ones that would grant immunity to perpetrators of war crimes, crimes against humanity, and genocide.

Another challenge is that, as a result of the Rome Statute and other significant developments in international criminal law and practice, amnesty outcomes are no longer within any individual state's or institution's control. That may have been the case in prior decades as well, inasmuch as one country's amnesty cannot bind the courts of another. Yet there is a significantly heightened zone of uncertainty today, both because of the existence of the ICC and because of the increased recourse to foreign courts under principles such as universal jurisdiction.

A further challenge linked to this fifth stage is the apparent contradiction between the ethos of amnesty disapproval and the continuing global admiration for South Africa's Truth and Reconciliation Commission (TRC) and its watershed experiment in the amnesty realm. South Africa is widely and properly regarded as one of the paradigmatic cases of a recent and successful transition out of violent conflict and abusive rule. A key institution in that transition was the TRC, which had the authority to grant individual amnesties to perpetrators of crimes of extreme brutality. While there were many shortcomings in the South African process, as in any transitional justice process, the TRC succeeded in ways that most other societies can only dream about. Even the most amnesty-averse international lawyers grudgingly acknowledge its significant social impact, despite the fact that the TRC's amnesty scheme facially contradicts the emergent view on amnesties espoused by, among others, the UN Secretariat.[9]

What this contradiction also highlights is a tension between international criminal law on the one hand and transitional justice on the other hand. The latter was underdeveloped almost everywhere but for Latin America until the experience of the South African TRC. Thus, to the extent that the South African model became the globally emblematic case of transitional justice – of "justice within constraints" – we ended up in this unexpected, almost accidental situation, in which the tolerance for amnesty was receding just as the interest in transitional justice was gathering speed.[10] Indeed, in the ensuing years after the TRC's work had ended, many in the field of transitional justice came to see the South African model in a different light or, to be precise, in a rather skeptical and sometimes even negative light. In the end, we have arrived at a situation in which the model that rightly or wrongly inspired so many around the world – and undeniably continues to do so – no longer appears acceptable. Ultimately, it has been the permanent ICC and not the temporary South African TRC – groundbreaking though it was – that has come to define the fifth stage in the global fight against impunity.

The full implications of these myriad sudden, simultaneous, and contradictory shifts in global law and policy are still being parsed. For now, what one can say for certain is that it is a difficult time to be a peacemaker. There is less flexibility to cut a deal and less certainty about whether a deal will satisfy those in the international community whose opinions greatly matter, not least the ICC Prosecutor and the UN Secretary-General. Amnesty is like a contraband product now, such that everyone dealing with it is taking a risk.

However, amnesty has not left the scene, and reports of its death are, to paraphrase Mark Twain, exaggerated. Amnesties are as prevalent today as at any time in modern history, as a recent comprehensive work demonstrates.[11] We are no more at the end of amnesties than we are at the "end of history."[12] Circumstances leading to the invocation of amnesties still abound and will continue to do so as long as there are rebels negotiating the laying down of arms or repressive leaders negotiating the terms of their departures. As Professor Max Pensky notes: "It's doubtful whether any successful democratic transition has ever managed to refrain entirely from deviating from the rule of law in the pursuit of democratically legitimate outcomes: you play the cards you've been dealt in such transitions, and flexibility – including a high tolerance for not-quite-clean policy – may be a *sine qua non* for the efficient domestic politician."[13] Professor Ron Slye similarly comments:

> Even as the international criminal justice system expands, states continue to turn to amnesties as the mechanism of choice to address systematic violations of human rights and to facilitate their own political transitions after a period of state-sponsored terrorism. Amnesties of one form or another have been used to limit the accountability of individuals responsible for gross violations of human rights in every major political transition in the twentieth century.[14]

Yet the continued recourse to amnesty as a tool for dealing with periods of extraordinary war and violence is not linked to the presence of political constraints alone. In earlier centuries, amnesties were adopted more in the original sense of the term: *amnesty* derives from the Greek word *amnēstia*, which means "to cast into oblivion." Amnesty in this original sense was a tool to wipe the slate clean, erase, or bury the memory of certain past events so as to focus on the future. Such amnesties were about mercy as well as pragmatism. The idea was to make a fresh start with former enemies. Amnesty in this early sense was a tool of social rebuilding, of imposing a rupture with the past so as to mend broken relationships that would need to continue into the future.

Admittedly, there are several historical cases in which this traditional form of amnesty was not used. Perhaps the best known of these is the case of Germany, which was economically and politically punished rather than forgiven at the end of the First World War – a fact that is often cited as a major contributor to the rise of Nazi Germany. The watershed trials of the Nuremberg tribunals at the end of the Second World War, which helped crystallize a new set of European values and legal standards, surely constitute another important exception. However, up until the 1990s, the practice of turning the page appears to have dominated state practice through history, especially in contexts in which there was neither a clear winner nor a clear loser.

Is such an approach without merit? Is there any wisdom or validity left in the ideas of letting bygones be bygones and closing the book on the past as a pragmatic means of restoring order and stability? Does mercy in the legal form of amnesty remain an acceptable form of statesmanship? Or does today's emphasis on the need to prosecute eclipse the space for any grand gestures of national unity and reconciliation? Does it prevent today's responsible leaders from saying, "Though you have harmed us terribly, for the sake of the future we will leave you alone?"[15]

The truth is that such questions are difficult to answer in the affirmative – particularly in an era dominated by the European project of an international order where, as Robert Kagan writes, "international law and international institutions matter more than the power of individual nations, where unilateral action by powerful states is forbidden, where all nations regardless of their strength have equal rights and are equally protected by commonly agreed-upon international rules of behavior."[16] An affirmative answer to such questions also is complicated by the new institutional reality of the ICC and the uncontrollable threat of trials by it or by foreign courts exercising criminal jurisdiction over cases involving atrocities committed in other states.

The idea of political mercy through amnesty also is difficult to reconcile with the apparent "norms cascade" that has substituted mercy for accountability when it comes to dealing with past atrocities.[17] And yet the value of mercy remains in keeping with many of the world's most influential religious teachings. As Robert Parker explains, "[A]mnesty is a concept wrought with contradictions and paradoxes: on the one hand, it conjures feelings of benevolence and virtue that are extolled by the religious and cultural traditions of most societies; on the other, it contradicts the rule of law and seems to violate basic notions of justice."[18]

To be sure, no one ever should call on victims or their families to forgive that which is unforgivable.[19] However, who can deny the power of the great political leaders that rise above their own experience as victims and adopt the language and habits of mercy and reconciliation as a means of nation building? As Alex Boraine notes of Nelson Mandela:

> From the day of his release to now, he has focused on the need to come to terms with the past, but always with a readiness to forgive and to move on. It is not merely words that he uses, powerful as they are, but in his actions of reaching out to the very people who had him put in jail, who had kept him there, who had decimated his own past, who were responsible for torture and deprivation, detention without trial, mass removals, and so on. He stretched out a hand of reconciliation and friendship.[20]

The fact is that for one reason or another throughout history, people have managed – against all odds – to cope with their traumatic memories and find ways to live with the murderers in their midst, even when the result is nothing more than peaceful but superficial coexistence.[21] For societies to regenerate after mass violence or genocide, there may, in fact, be no other choice. It is possible that societies rebuild themselves as much on account of what they are able to overlook – or feel required to overlook – as what they are unable to forgive.[22] Indeed, if individuals have a right to truth, then they also have a right, if ability and willingness are present, to try to forget. People can never be forced to forget certain events, but they have every right to choose not to look back, or to at least leave the past behind in their daily lives.[23]

The encouraging news is that, in the aftermath of widespread atrocities, the choice is no longer misunderstood as a binary one between mercy and accountability or impunity and justice. The field of transitional justice has highlighted that there is actually a broad spectrum of choices available to respond to such situations, including formal and informal nonjudicial and quasi-judicial mechanisms such as truth commissions, victim reparation programs, and institutional reform measures. Yet we should continue to recognize that the scale of past abuses, and constraints in the balance of power, invariably will require elements of both impunity and justice.

These observations are all linked to larger debates that persist about how societies can or must deal with their past. Put simply, we are still struggling with the tension between the demands of law and the impediments of reality, and with the tension between the need to remember and the need to overlook. In this debate, especially as it concerns amnesty, there are many valid viewpoints, and not only legalist and realist ones. The fact is that, when it comes to amnesty, there is much more ambiguity in the legal realm than many legalists are prepared to acknowledge, and there is much less empirical certainty about amnesty's benefits than many realists are ready to concede.

Although the divergent viewpoints of legalists and realists are impossible to fully reconcile, this book proposes several areas where common ground can be reached. It does so, in part, by suggesting the avoidance of red lines and by recommending instead a set of public interest principles and values that can be balanced in sensible ways in specific contexts at particular points in time. It is only in this way that one can hope to achieve a proper weighing of facts, law, and policy in a case at hand. Any other choice precipitates a return to the usual divide, in which one side insists that justice must step back when it directly and significantly threatens the prospects of peace or an end to despotic rule, and the other side insists that amnesty for mass atrocities is a red line that one cannot cross, irrespective of the human consequences.[24]

We should also recognize, however, that these differing positions reflect differing priorities in the context of a fragile negotiation: peace and political transition for some, and justice for others. And one's priorities, of course, shape one's positions. At the same time, priorities are not fixed. For example, a person may place general value on justice, but if he or she suddenly had to choose between survival and justice, this would undoubtedly affect the way that person values justice. This is not a small point. Persons who wish to take rigid stands on amnesty have a responsibility to grapple with the issue from as many different vantage points as possible: the family of a missing person craving to know the fate of a loved one, the torture survivor who rightly insists on justice and reparation without delay, the child soldier who wishes to be forgiven for his crimes and reunited with his family, the sex slave who wants the horror of her circumstances to end no matter what the social cost, and so forth.

Imagining oneself in a variety of circumstances does not make things any easier. But that is precisely the point. There are no obvious or cost-free answers to the amnesty dilemma. Professor Dan Markel captures the predicament well by asking the following questions:

> Imagine that we had to decide between general amnesty, on the one hand, and retribution at the risk of civil war, on the other – from relative positional ignorance, namely, not knowing whether we would be perpetrators, victims, or family members of victims.... The problem with this hypothetical contract is that we still have to engage in prediction and value assessment: Is the civil war certain? Will we all die or just some of us? Will a life with no promise of retribution be worth living?[25]

For many years, I have engaged classes with an equally abstract dilemma. I begin by listing various public goods on the board: justice, truth, reparation, institutional reform, democracy, public security, economic development, and reconciliation. I then ask the class to create a hierarchical list of the goods that will best ensure the prevention of atrocities after a period in which they have occurred on a massive scale. The answers naturally run the gamut. Yet there is one thing that never varies: public security always ranks at the top of the list.[26]

I mention this to raise a final issue, which concerns my own bias in writing this book. I rank public security at the top of the list, too. Where public security and the human rights related thereto are jeopardized on a mass scale by the threat of prosecution, in my opinion, the protection of them should prevail. Indeed, for me, the thought of living with impunity is insignificant compared with the thought of living with open, armed conflict or state terror. As a human rights advocate, I am repulsed by the idea of impunity for perpetrators of heinous atrocities. Yet because I consider the human rights related to public security paramount – not least the right to life itself – my repulsion for war and tyranny is greater.

My repulsion for impunity also leads me to this position. Impunity at the national level is at its peak in times of war and tyranny, when the ability or willingness to deliver justice for atrocities is largely absent. Granted, it will always be maddening to forego formal justice concerning people responsible for vicious crimes of any sort. Yet I believe there is a powerful case to be made in both human rights and ethical terms for ceding that right in extreme circumstances. Such a case is powerful even if the only peace that can be guaranteed is a negative peace (absence of direct and violent conflict) with no certainty of being followed by a positive peace (absence of indirect and structural violence).[27] The fact is that even incomplete forms of peace and security are necessary to create the conditions for a society in which there is both freedom from want and freedom to live in dignity.[28]

To be sure, I continue to believe that one's default orientation always should be to do justice. It is important to insist on the state obligation to prosecute, and there is indeed no inherent reason why justice and peace efforts cannot work together in a mutually reinforcing way, as is the case to some degree in places such as Colombia and Sierra Leone. Likewise, I continue to believe that, as a general rule, amnesties must not cover serious human rights crimes. Such crimes should be prosecuted to the maximum extent possible. Yet I hold fast to the importance of exceptions and the notion of the last recourse. In that respect, I always am ready to defend amnesties of the widest possible scope provided that they are necessary, *stricto sensu*. That viewpoint may be at odds with certain prevailing accounts of international legal standards, but I, for one, could never oppose an amnesty on the basis of law alone. That would be legalism of the worst sort.[29] In a world still full of uncontrolled violence and misery, the concept of the last recourse remains vital to building a fairer and safer world. So I argue in favor of keeping the standards high and clear but also of remaining flexible in the application so as to be responsible in the decision.

As this book will demonstrate, the issue of amnesty is full of unavoidable paradoxes and agonizing choices. Advances in law cannot alter that. And legal advances cannot overturn history. They cannot disprove that amnesties of the widest possible scope adopted in countries such as Spain, Brazil, and Mozambique have accompanied – rather than impeded – gradual and sustained improvements in democracy, peace, human rights, and the rule of law. That is a simple fact.

Yet it is also the case that, in the amnesty arena, there is much room for improvement. The history and practice of amnesties is full of bad models. What we need most of all, to ensure improved amnesty outcomes in the future, is a wider and more sober debate based on a better understanding of what is at stake in theoretical, legal, and practical terms. This book is meant as one contribution to that goal.

PART I

The Debate on Amnesties

1. INTRODUCTION

This part of the book offers an extended analysis of the law and policy considerations concerning amnesties that encompass human rights crimes. It begins with technical analysis and then becomes more polemical. The goal is to deepen debate on both the overt and underlying complexities of the topic, bringing new issues to the fore and reexamining old issues through a different lens. It is the gray areas that are of special interest in this field and the areas where the most important debates still need to occur.

The discussion comprises five sections. The first section offers a definition of the term *amnesty*, including analysis of its distinctive features as a legal instrument. For purposes of conceptual clarity, comparisons will be made between amnesties and other legal instruments that have the effect of displacing individual criminal accountability, including pardons, statutes of limitation, and the various types of standing immunities recognized in treaties and domestic legislation. By understanding the specificity of amnesty as a legal instrument, the subsequent analyses are situated in their proper technical context.

The second section offers an assessment of amnesty in the context of the fight against impunity, a theme introduced in the book's opening considerations. Here the analysis expands considerably, beginning with an examination of the specific ways in which amnesties fit within the field of transitional justice. This is followed by discussion of various methodological errors that commonly arise in the evaluation of the effects of amnesties, including the presence of selection bias and optimism bias. A central assertion throughout the section is that amnesty's relation to the fight against impunity has been miscast in recent years. Amnesty is not necessarily the antithesis of criminal justice or of transitional justice, and its purported negative effects on stability and the rule of law are open to question.

The third, and longest, section provides an analysis of amnesties in relation to the transitional justice obligations of states regarding human rights violations and international crimes. It begins with a review of the various treaty and nontreaty sources related to the subject of amnesty, as well as some of the main trends in the jurisprudence. It then offers an alternative legal account of amnesty, one that goes beyond the question of prosecution and focuses on the countervailing state obligations to prevent and suppress human rights violations. The section also includes a discussion of various legal defenses to state breaches of international law, and of relevant limitation and derogation clauses contained in human rights treaties. Drawing on the legal principle of harmonization, the section concludes with a proposed framework for reconciling the divergent strands of international law in a manner that balances the goals of ending violations, facilitating peace and security, and preserving transitional justice options.

The fourth section examines the relevance of the International Criminal Court (ICC), and the Rome Statute framework as a whole, on amnesty options. The mere existence of the ICC affects the calculus of any state-sponsored leniency arrangement and therefore must figure in any comprehensive evaluation of how to resolve amnesty dilemmas in the years to come. Accordingly, the section encompasses considerations about the impact of the ICC's existence and mandate, as well as analysis of the most pertinent provisions of the Rome Statute. The discussion also includes a brief analysis of the ICC's role in Uganda, its first country situation, where the subject of amnesty – and the tensions between peace and justice more generally – was at the hub of a larger international debate.

The fifth, and final, section takes a detailed look at the evolving position of the UN Secretariat on amnesties, raising questions about certain of its risks and assumptions. The discussion primarily focuses on policy questions about the UN position, presenting the arguments both for and against the current stance. The analysis reveals a number of reasons for being skeptical about the wisdom and efficacy of the current position in achieving positive human outcomes for states in situations of fragility, and concludes by offering several possible alternative formulations of the position.

By the end of the discussion, it ought to have become clear why the debate on amnesty continues to be controversial. The subject is one on which it always will be difficult to remain neutral – especially when, as is so often the case, the interests of peace and justice must compete for priority. Yet finding principled solutions to situations as complex as those in which the worst amnesty dilemmas arise requires degree of openness and sangfroid. Precisely for that reason, a central goal of this first part of the book is to help situate the amnesty issue in a broader framework that shows what is truly at stake for everyone. Too often, the subject of amnesty has been distorted through oversimplification. By revealing a broader account of the challenges, and by proposing practical means for reconciling competing interests, a more just and context-specific resolution of amnesty dilemmas comes within reach.

2. DEFINING AMNESTY

Amnesty is a term for which there is insufficient clarity or precision about its definition. The *Oxford English Dictionary* defines it as follows: "An act of oblivion, a general overlooking or pardon of past offences."[1] *Black's Law Dictionary* uses the following definition: "A sovereign act of forgiveness for past acts, granted by a government to all persons (or to certain classes of persons) who have been guilty of crime or delict, generally political offences – treason, sedition, rebellion, draft evasion – and often conditioned upon their return to obedience and duty within a prescribed time."[2] In *Amnesty for Crimes in International Law and Practice*, Professor Andreas O'Shea defines the term as "immunity in law from either criminal or civil legal consequences, or from both, for wrongs committed in the past in a political context."[3] In *Amnesty in International Law*, Professor Ben Chigara argues that amnesties are "laws [that] purport to extinguish legal liability of agents of a prior regime alleged to have violated basic human rights of individuals."[4]

In my view, none of these definitions adequately captures all of the key features of amnesty. In particular, none of them is sufficiently broad to cover the diverse types of amnesty contexts, structures, and functions that are observable in state practice. In this respect, consider the following:

- Some amnesties are given to correct past injustices (e.g., *Morocco 1994*)[5] and others to entrench impunity (e.g., *Chile 1978*).[6]
- Some are given in postconflict contexts (e.g., *Croatia 1996*),[7] others in midconflict contexts (e.g., *Guatemala 1983*),[8] and others in nonconflict contexts (e.g., *Portugal 1974*).[9]

- Some extinguish liability for the most serious human rights offenses (e.g., *Peru 1995*),[10] while others extinguish liability only for less serious offenses (e.g., *Democratic Republic of the Congo 2003*).[11]
- Some are given to encourage lower-level combatants to break rank (e.g., *Uganda 2000*),[12] while others are conceded as part of a pacted transition (e.g., *Uruguay 1986*).[13]
- Some are democratically adopted as laws by the legislative branch (e.g., *South Africa 1995*),[14] while others are imposed unilaterally by the executive branch (e.g., *Zimbabwe 1988*)[15] or negotiated in peace accords (e.g., *Sierra Leone 1999*).[16]
- Some apply only to state agents (e.g., *France 1962*),[17] others only to non-state actors (e.g., *Colombia 2003*),[18] and others to both state and non-state actors (e.g., *El Salvador 1992*).[19]
- Some amnesties are accompanied by commitments to formal transitional justice measures (e.g., *Aceh/Indonesia 2004*),[20] while others are not (e.g., *Angola 2002*).[21]
- Some are unconditional in nature (e.g., *Mozambique 1992*),[22] while others impose numerous preconditions (e.g., *Algeria 1999*).[23]

The difference between certain amnesties is so vast, in fact, that it is almost nonsensical to compare them. A corrective amnesty passed in good faith by a democratically elected government is, for example, on a completely different moral and legal plane from a general and unconditional self-amnesty adopted without public debate by an authoritarian regime. In short, no two amnesties – and no two contexts of amnesty – are exactly alike.[24]

It is possible, nevertheless, to provide a functional definition of amnesty. In this book, the following definition is used:

> Amnesty is an extraordinary legal measure whose primary function is to remove the prospect and consequences of criminal liability for designated individuals or classes of persons in respect of designated types of offenses irrespective of whether the persons concerned have been tried for such offenses in a court of law.

In my view, this definition is sufficiently broad to cover the full diversity of amnesty models. It is also broad enough to cover so-called pseudo-amnesties. Pseudo-amnesties are legal measures that have the same juridical effect as amnesties but are drafted in a disguised form and given titles that explicitly omit the word *amnesty*. The Argentine Law on Due Obedience is a good example of such a measure.[25] This law created an irrebuttable presumption that public officials exercising nonleadership positions were all "following orders" and thus exempt from criminal responsibility for their offenses (with the exception of kidnapping of minors, rape, and appropriation of real property).

This book's definition of amnesty is also sufficiently narrow to avoid common confusion, or false equations, with analogous yet different types of leniency measures. For example:

- The definition enables differentiation from *pardons*, which are acts of legal leniency that remove only the consequences but not the prospect of adverse court proceedings. In other words, pardons apply exclusively to persons who already have been convicted of the relevant offense. Although the underlying judgment normally remains in place in the event of a pardon, the convicted person is released from prison by means of it.[26] By contrast, amnesties apply prejudgment to shield persons from the process and consequences of legal judgment. Similar to a pardon, though, an amnesty law may simultaneously apply to convicted persons, thereby bringing an end to the consequences of legal judgment. Unlike pardons, however, amnesties tend to apply only to classes or categories of persons, whereas pardons tend to apply on an individual or case-by-case basis. Despite these differences, amnesties sometimes are mistakenly described or legislated as pardons, and vice versa.[27] As with amnesty, the issue of pardons is a gray area of international law. Among other things, there is no explicit multilateral treaty-based prohibition or discouragement of pardons.[28]
- The above definition of amnesty also facilitates differentiation with various types of *reduced sentence measures*, whether of a case-based nature (e.g., an individual's sentence is commuted for reasons related only to his or her case) or a class-based one (e.g., an individual's sentence is commuted because of his or her membership in an eligible class of offenders). Amnesties differ from reduced sentence schemes in at least two ways. First, as with pardons, reduced sentence measures apply only after judgment, whereas amnesties can apply to persons in both prejudgment and postjudgment situations. Second, unlike amnesties, reduced sentence measures – like plea bargains – lower but do not eliminate legal responsibility, meaning that the persons concerned by the measure are actually the objects of a criminal sentence.
- This book's definition of amnesty also enables distinctions vis-à-vis *statutes of limitations*, also known as prescription periods. These statutes stipulate the maximum period of time by which legal action needs to be taken against persons responsible for designated offenses; failing that, the possibility of adverse legal action by individuals or the state expires.

Inasmuch as a statute of limitations forecloses the possibility of conducting judicial proceedings, it is similar to certain types of amnesties. However, unlike an amnesty, a statute of limitations is a form of standing legislation rather than a one-time (i.e., extraordinary) legal measure. In that respect, such statutes are of a different juridical character.[29] Statutes of limitation also operate differently from amnesties in that their primary legal function is to preserve, not extinguish, the possibility of justice. Expiration of the right to justice occurs only after a significant amount of time has passed, and the time frame for expiration varies according to the crime.[30]

- The foregoing definition also takes account of the differences between amnesties and *status-based legal immunities*, which are legal measures that bar adverse legal proceedings against certain categories of persons on account of their official status or legal personality. Examples of such immunity include judicial immunity, parliamentary immunity, diplomatic immunity, head-of-state immunity, and UN immunity.[31] Unlike amnesties, these types of immunity take the form of treaties or standing legislation. They are not one-time legal actions adopted in exceptional circumstances. An additional distinction with status-based immunities is that there is no presumption, implicit or explicit, that crimes have been or will be committed by the persons who benefit from the immunities. With amnesties, by contrast, there is an implied presumption that crimes have been committed.
- Finally, this book's definition of amnesty enables a clear distinction with *prosecutorial immunity*. The latter is a grant of immunity, either full or partial, made to an individual by a prosecutor in exchange for his or her testimony in a trial. Whereas amnesties tend to apply to classes or categories of persons, grants of prosecutorial immunity apply only on a case-by-case basis. In addition, unlike amnesties, the primary purpose of prosecutorial immunity is to obtain convictions in the trial of third parties.[32] A similar purpose does not exist, as a rule, in the case of amnesties.

It is furthermore worth noting that this book's definition of amnesty differs in four important respects from other definitions in use. First, it omits the attribution of any amnesiac function to amnesties. As amnesty expert Louise Mallinder notes, "[T]he traditional conception of amnesty as 'amnesia' is increasingly becoming outdated. Instead, states are finding innovative ways to address past crimes without burying the truth or enforcing widespread retributive justice."[33] The case par excellence of such an amnesty is, of course, the South African Truth and Reconciliation Commission legislation, which allowed individuals to apply for full amnesty on condition of providing full disclosure of their responsibility for eligible crimes. Concerning that case, Jessica Gavron notes, "The amnesty was conceived, in part, to facilitate the recording of the truth rather than the denial of the past, thus the traditional association of amnesty with amnesia is inverted."[34] This book's definition of amnesty is sufficiently flexible to conform to this more modern sense of the term without contradicting its original amnesiac sense.

Second, some definitions provide that amnesty is applicable only to past crimes, in the sense of crimes committed prior to the enactment of the amnesty.[35] This appears to be the case for a majority of amnesties. However, it is not the case for all of them. For instance, there are many examples of defection-oriented amnesties, which are amnesties issued during conflict as a device to encourage rebels, paramilitaries, or terrorist organizations to abandon their cause, disarm, and demobilize. By design, such amnesties do not apply only to past crimes. In countries such as Uganda, Algeria, Colombia, and Afghanistan, such amnesties have been adopted, in each case allowing access to the law's benefits for eligible offenses committed after the amnesty's entry into force.[36] Such laws are thus open ended – they assume that violations will occur after the date of the law's promulgation, yet they offer amnesty for the violations nonetheless.[37] This book's definition is broad enough to encompass such forms of amnesty.

Third, while the normal intention of amnesty is to permanently extinguish legal liability rather than temporarily remove it, there are many examples of amnesties that impose explicit conditions of retention on the law's beneficiaries. A classic example is an amnesty law that makes nonrecidivism a condition for retaining its benefits, which means that the commission of a new crime triggers the cancellation of the original amnesty's benefits for the individual concerned as well as prosecution for both the new offense and the original one.[38] According to one view, the inclusion of such a condition takes the legal measure out of the amnesty realm because the juridical effect is to suspend rather than extinguish criminal responsibility.[39] However, this view seems mistaken. There is still extinguishment of criminal responsibility, just of a conditional sort. Indeed, an amnesty based on conditional extinguishment remains a form of amnesty, just as conditional release from prison remains a form of release from prison. In other words, the amnesty remains in place whether or not the condition materializes.

Fourth, a number of definitions of amnesty focus on its political character. In his seminal 1985 study, Louis Joinet describes amnesty as "the juridical expression of a political act."[40] Max Pensky similarly describes amnesty as a "a sovereign act ... demonstrating the (usually executive) power to effect significant alterations in the normal application and range of the domestic criminal law in order to bring about a politically desirable effect."[41] Such characterizations of amnesty are appropriate when it comes to amnesties of the sort focused on in this book. Yet there are various other types of amnesty – such as tax amnesties and amnesties aimed at improving conditions in congested national prisons – for which the character is usually of a legal-bureaucratic nature, thus rendering inapposite their classification as "political."[42] This book's definition is broad enough to include such nonpolitical amnesties.

A final point on the term amnesty concerns the tendency, in literature and in practice, to use it too loosely. For example, one often encounters references to *de facto amnesty*, a term commonly used to describe a situation in which there is impunity in practice, notwithstanding the absence of a legally-enacted amnesty law that would prevent national prosecutions.[43] The expression is misleading because one of the definitional elements of an amnesty is that it is a legal (i.e., de jure) measure. Thus, while it makes perfect sense to discuss and condemn the reality of impunity, the use of the term *de facto amnesty* creates conceptual confusion.[44] Similarly, one can find references to *blanket amnesty*, which refers to an amnesty that is unlimited or unconditional or both. Because this term is used inconsistently to refer to different types of amnesties (i.e., to amnesties that are unlimited or unconditional or both), it is not used in this book. Last, it is important to note that not every amnesty is a pure amnesty. For instance, there are several amnesty laws that provide full legal immunity for specific categories of offenders or crimes but only reduced sentences for other categories of offenders or crimes.[45] One could perhaps classify such legal measures as a subcategory of amnesties: hybrid amnesties.[46]

With all of these distinctions in mind, we now turn to a first aspect of the larger debate: the place of amnesties in the global struggle against impunity.

3. AMNESTIES AND THE FIGHT AGAINST IMPUNITY

As previously explained, this book does not examine the full range of amnesty types but instead focuses on those adopted, reluctantly and in contexts of mass violence, for serious crimes under international law. In this respect, the focus is on amnesties perceived to be in tension with the global fight against impunity and more particularly with the new field of transitional justice. Professor Ruti Teitel usefully refers to such amnesties as "transitional amnesties."[47]

The first part of this discussion deals with the relation between amnesty and the goals and mechanisms of transitional justice, in particular that of criminal prosecution. The second part expands the analysis by looking at when and how amnesty may be defended as the lesser of two evils, and by considering the limits of what trials can achieve according to their own internal logic. The third part explores methodological issues related to evaluations of the long-term impact of amnesties on the fight against impunity.

3.1 Transitional justice and amnesty

Transitional justice is a multidisciplinary field of research and practice linked to the fight against impunity and the broader domains of human rights and conflict resolution.[48] Although its historical roots trace back to Nuremberg and earlier, the term *transitional justice* did not enter the modern political lexicon until shortly after the Cold War.[49]

Transitional justice focuses on the challenge of confronting legacies of mass abuse. Its methods and approaches typically apply in societies in transition from war to peace, or from authoritarian rule to democracy, in which strong societal trends have created a window of opportunity for political and social transformation. They can sometimes apply to other situations as well, including well-established democracies dealing with earlier legacies of abuse.

Naturally, every postconflict or democratic transition context is unique in economic, political, social, and cultural terms, as well as in terms of the path of transition. Consider, for example, the vast differences in the national transitions that occurred in South America in the 1980s, as compared to those in Eastern and Central Europe after the collapse of the Soviet Union, as compared to those in southern Africa after the end of the apartheid era. Notwithstanding the diversity across these and other examples, there is at least one feature that all such contexts hold in common: the existence of legacies of mass abuse. In such contexts, the demand for justice is typically at or near its highest point, whereas the possibility of delivering justice – in any degree proportionate to the scale of the crimes – is typically at or near its lowest point. Incomplete justice – the so-called impunity gap – is not merely likely in transitional contexts. It is a virtual guarantee. For when crime becomes the rule, as is the case during any period of repression or armed conflict, no justice system can adequately cope with the fallout – least of all one in a state of transition and fragility. In such contexts, therefore, nonjudicial measures such as truth commissions, victim reparation programs, and security system reforms ought to accompany trials. These measures constitute the main mechanisms of transitional justice.

Unlike in the past, today there is an expectation – albeit not a universal one – that societies must face their past national traumas. Since at least the end of the Cold War, the question has been gradually changing from whether to face the past, to when and how to face the past – and, importantly, with what international involvement.[50] In responding to the challenge, transitional justice offers a practical set of tools to potentially assist a society seeking to morally regenerate itself through a confrontation of the worst abuses in its modern history. While the tools of transitional justice derive from a universal human rights framework, the field is characterized by a search for solutions balancing universal claims with local realities that test the limits of those claims. For this reason, the theory and practice of transitional justice emphasize the need always to tailor policy to match local conditions.

Amnesty is, of course, a transitional justice issue. However, amnesty generally is not considered a transitional justice mechanism. If anything, an amnesty of the sort adopted in a transitional context usually is considered a direct impediment to transitional justice, especially to the holding of criminal trials. Depending on its content, and depending on the nature of the surrounding legal system, amnesty also may be considered a direct bar to judicially-established truth and compensation.[51]

Yet the paradox of amnesty is that it also can form an integral element of a transitional justice mechanism – for example, by incorporation in a truth commission's mandate. Amnesty also can be a functional precondition for establishing conditions conducive to transitional justice – for example, by catalyzing or facilitating a gradual transition away from terror and impunity and toward good governance and human rights (e.g., *Uruguay 1986* amnesty).[52] In such cases, one reasonably may characterize amnesty's relation to transitional justice positively. Rather than be cast as the antithesis of transitional justice, amnesty becomes its enabler by potentially helping to pave the way at the national level for increased truth, reparation, and reform with respect to past violations, and for increased democracy, peace, and justice in the long term.[53] To be sure, there is no certainty that such an amnesty will have a salutary effect.[54] The point is that in many cases amnesty may have such an effect. In the same vein, it is important to stress that a preference for peace or democracy as first steps in a transitional sequence does not necessarily imply that justice is a lower priority. As Moses Okello observes:

> [S]equencing should be distinguished from prioritization. If the preferred sequencing is peace followed by justice, this in no way signals that justice is a lower priority than peace – quite the opposite, in fact. Whichever way you look at it, trying to ensure that the environment is conducive for a comprehensive pursuit of justice . . . is definitive proof that you want real justice to be done.[55]

In any event, what is certain is that amnesty's relation to transitional justice remains highly controversial.[56] This is principally because of the negative impact of amnesties on the achievement of the aims of criminal prosecution.

The International Criminal Tribunal for Rwanda's judgment in the case of *Prosecutor v. Laurent Semanza* provides a useful articulation of these aims, each of which is the object of subsequent discussion.[57] (This discussion is necessarily in a summary form. Each of the aims is the subject of a vast literature in its own right, encompassing law, criminology, penology, normative ethics, and many other disciplines.[58])

- *Retribution.* Persons responsible for criminal acts should be punished. This retributive premise underpins any system of criminal justice. Hence, by removing the possibility of punishment, amnesties are viewed as preventing the retribution that a society needs to correct the social imbalance created by the crime. As Max Pensky notes, "[F]ailure to punish is itself an injustice. The injustice of the criminal act is doubled by the injustice of the state authority in failing to fulfill its retributive duties."[59] An amnesty that ousts the prerogative of courts to try the worst crimes also contradicts the related principle that for every crime there must be a proportionate punishment. In short, amnesties achieve the functional opposite of retribution. Rather than punish the perpetrator, they give him or her legal peace of mind before the country's courts.

- *Deterrence.* There are two kinds of deterrence in criminal law: specific and general.
  - Specific deterrence refers to the idea that the individual responsible for a crime must be punished to deter him or her from reoffending. The idea is that if such an individual lacks a reason to fear judgment and sentencing, he or she will continue engaging in criminal behavior.[60] Most amnesties, therefore, are viewed as undermining specific deterrence. Yet not every amnesty is inherently at odds with specific deterrence. An amnesty that makes nonrecidivism a condition of retaining its benefits would, for example, be logically and functionally consistent with the goal of specific deterrence.[61] In addition, there are doubts about the theory of specific deterrence in relation to persons who order or commit atrocities in contexts of mass violence. As Professor Mark Drumbl notes, "[D]eterrence is based on the essentially unproven assumption of perpetrator rationality in the chaos of massive violence, incendiary propaganda, and upended social order."[62] That is, the people who arguably most belong before a court may in fact fear it little at all, as compared to the fear of being captured, tortured, and killed, or being stripped of ill-gotten wealth. In addition, as Charles Trumbull observes, in civil war and insurgency contexts many perpetrators are motivated by an ideology and thus less likely

to weigh the costs and benefits of their actions before committing a crime or to view the risk of incarceration as exceeding the benefit of committing the crime.[63] The implication of all this for amnesty practice is direct: where there is diminished fear of punishment, the allure, and thus the effectiveness, of amnesty is correspondingly diminished.[64]

- General deterrence is the corollary of specific deterrence. It refers to the idea that an individual responsible for a crime must be punished to send a strong message to others in society that crimes result in legal punishment, thus deterring the rest of society from committing similar acts.[65] On its face, an amnesty appears to directly contradict this objective. Yet in a context of mass violence, it may be unrealistic to expect a small number of targeted prosecutions to have a major effect in general deterrence terms, as we learned from the increases in violence that occurred in places such as the Western Balkans and Sudan after the issuance of international arrest warrants.[66] Moreover, claims of general deterrence are notoriously difficult to measure. As crime and conflict prevention experts regularly observe, it is very hard to prove that a particular policy measure – a trial; a truth commission; a demobilization scheme; etc. – caused something not to happen.[67]

- *Stigmatization.* Another reason why states prosecute serious offenders is to stigmatize or bring social shame on them. In that respect, amnesty appears to send a social signal opposite to the one that is normally desirable. Yet such a concern is not present in the case of an amnesty that is preconditioned on individual application and the public disclosure of one's crimes.[68] In addition, stigmatization through amnesty can work in the opposite sense: sometimes amnesty is opposed by those who one would most expect to be seeking it, because amnesty implies personal responsibility for past crimes.[69]

- *Rehabilitation.* Although it is an ancient controversy and a disputed notion in criminology literature, the idea that punishment facilitates the rehabilitation of the offender is often present in criminal law and practice. By eliminating the possibility of punishment, and thus eliminating a possible means for the offender's reformation, amnesty is considered inimical to the goal of rehabilitation. However, the prospect of moral redemption for persons who have perpetrated extreme acts of violence on a mass scale is far from certain.[70] The prospect of rehabilitation appears similarly uncertain when it comes to persons whose offenses were committed on the basis of strong political, religious, or class convictions.[71] In addition, an amnesty process conditioned on any combination of confessions, apologies, compensation, and community service could contribute to the offender's rehabilitation rather than undermine it.[72]

- *Protection of society.* A practical reason for bringing persons to justice is to remove them, through sentencing, from free circulation in society – a concept also sometimes called incapacitation. The protection of society is, of course, a principal reason societies build and maintain prisons in the first place. In that respect, amnesties that prevent offenders from going to prison and potentially release convicts into society before the end of their sentences, are in direct tension with this goal of criminal justice. However, it should be noted that incapacitation of offenders can be achieved by various means, not only by incarceration. Even an amnesty can be conditioned on any combination of disarmament, exile, relocation to remote parts of the country, and ongoing state monitoring and supervision of the individual from whom the society requires protection.[73]

- *Public confidence in the rule of law.* Prosecutions for serious crimes before domestic courts, when independently and impartially conducted, can be important for shoring up local confidence in the state's ability and willingness to ensure the rule of law. According to this view, human rights trials can play not only a retributive role but also an expressivist one, namely, to communicate the value of law and justice as social goods.[74] By removing the prospect and consequences of domestic legal punishment, amnesties are portrayed as detrimental to this goal. The assumption is that they lead to public cynicism and disillusionment about the rule of law at a time when a society needs to steer itself toward it – especially if the worst crimes and worst offenders go unpunished while lesser crimes and lesser offenders continue to be punished.[75] However, the public may be able to understand amnesty as an extraordinary, onetime measure rather than a habitual one. That is, the public may be intelligent enough to appreciate that an amnesty's purpose may be precisely to help create the conditions necessary to restore the rule of law.[76] This especially holds true where the government in question is viewed as a decent one that is oriented toward the public interest. The issue becomes more complicated, however, when a state introduces amnesties habitually rather than exceptionally.[77]

- *Dignity of victims.* In moral terms, any amnesty – even one that requires the beneficiary to satisfy demanding preconditions – is likely to offend the direct victims of the crimes because it extinguishes the domestic penal liability of the presumed perpetrators. In some cases, an amnesty could even contribute to a feeling of revictimization and prolong or reinforce an existing sense of social isolation and public disbelief about what actually took place. Although claims about the restorative impact of trials on victims are open to question, punishment of the perpetrators is properly presumed to help restore some part of their lost dignity.[78] At the same time, the dignity of victims risks suffering when a guilty party is judged innocent at the end of a fair trial, a risk that is always present. Such a result is not necessarily less painful in the eyes of the victim on account of the trial's fairness.

In summary, there are many reasons why amnesty is viewed as detrimental to domestic criminal prosecutions and, by corollary, to transitional justice. However, we have also observed that the level of harm an amnesty may cause to the attainment of the goals of criminal justice varies according to the nature of the amnesty, and in any event, is often less than what is feared.

3.2. The lesser-evil argument and the limits of trial impact

As is the case for other legal measures or principles that limit the scope for criminal prosecution, a cogent rationale for amnesties may be adduced on a wide range of legitimate policy grounds.[79] Of particular interest here is the assertion that conceding a general amnesty sometimes may be necessary to begin to wind down a period of massive and entrenched terror. It is quite easy to criticize this sort of choice as an outsider who has never known, or who does not directly face, such terror. Yet for persons who suffer under it daily, the immorality of amnesty choices is not as easy to judge. Indeed, such persons may be prepared to tolerate sacrifices to justice that in any other context would seem unthinkable to them.[80] Faced with a choice between survival and justice, we should not be surprised if justice ranks as a low priority in relative terms.[81] In a lose-lose situation an amnesty simply may represent the least worst option – and hence the best option – at a particular point in time.[82]

This lesser-evil argument is more than mere philosophy. One can measure it in real lives and in pain. Even a temporary lull in the fighting can be characterized legitimately, and experienced directly, as a huge gain. The grim reality of many pretransitional justice settings, such as modern-day Somalia and Burma, is that there are no good options to choose from, only bad and worse ones. Such options are mostly a function of the reigning balance of power at a particular period in time.[83] Where that balance of power is particularly unfavorable to the cause of justice, arguments focused only on the legality of a proposed amnesty can seem remote, even indifferent to human suffering. It is not surprising, therefore, for societies in such circumstances to "act on a prudent logic of consequences rather than a narrow logic of legal appropriateness."[84] As Max Pensky writes, in these contexts legal and moral arguments against broad amnesties do not hold up well against consequentialist arguments if "defended by a deontological argument alone: in this case, on the retributivist claim that deserved punishment of perpetrators is such a powerful intrinsic good that it is the source of a duty urgent enough to trump other considerations."[85]

In addition, there is sometimes good reason to be skeptical about the value and effects of trials in contexts of mass violence as compared to amnesties. As Helena Cobban argues, "[T]he language of criminalization is most often the language of political exclusion. . . . By deliberately forswearing both the language and practice of political exclusion, amnesties can make a huge contribution to the interests of long-term peace-building."[86] Professors Jack Snyder and Leslie Vinjamuri also make the important observation that "trials work best when they are needed least" – namely when "spoiler groups are weak" and justice institutions are functional, and "where the demonstration effect of trials is least needed."[87] One also should acknowledge that sometimes it is, precisely, trials or the threat of trials that prompt broad amnesties, as occurred in Argentina, El Salvador, and Afghanistan.[88] The threat of trials can also lead to intensive perpetrator efforts to destroy evidence of mass crime, thus significantly endangering truth recovery efforts.[89]

To be sure, none of this is to suggest that trials should not take place. To the contrary, the deontological and legal arguments for holding them are extremely powerful. Yet in the promotion or planning of trials, one also should bear in mind the surrounding realities that can complicate or frustrate attainment of their underlying objectives. In short, like amnesties, trials should be the object of critical scrutiny.

3.3 Evaluating the legitimacy and impact of amnesties

The foregoing discussion highlights another important but frequently overlooked aspect of amnesties, namely that they tend to impose what may be described as negative obligations. Amnesties require the state to refrain from pursuing justice against certain eligible classes of offenders. They do not typically place any affirmative obligation on the state to investigate, prosecute or punish the ineligible classes of offenders. Of course, the obligation to investigate and judge such offenders may already be present based upon other domestic legislation or international treaty commitments. However, usually the most an amnesty will do is preserve the possibility of justice against them. It usually will not create or affirm the obligation to pursue the excluded classes of offenders in national courts.[90]

In this regard, it is important to note the insufficiency of measuring the legitimacy of an amnesty merely based upon whether it excludes the international crimes of genocide, war crimes, and crimes against humanity. Too often, the sole standard of legitimacy of an amnesty today is whether it excludes such crimes: if it does, it is tolerated and may even be lauded; if it does not, it is condemned.[91] While it is certainly preferable for an amnesty to exclude such crimes, their exclusion is an insufficient basis for treating an amnesty as nationally or internationally acceptable. As this book demonstrates, there are dozens of other possible attributes that can and ought to receive consideration for inclusion or exclusion in an amnesty before one can properly characterize it as principled or unprincipled. Thus, just as it is simplistic to structure the amnesty dilemma as a set of false alternatives between granting an amnesty (bad) and resisting an amnesty (good), it is equally simplistic to structure the set of choices as between an amnesty that excludes genocide, war crimes, and crimes against humanity (good) and one that does not (bad). Indeed, it is worth asking whether South Africa's TRC-related conditional amnesty scheme, which was adopted following extensive national debate and which did not exclude international crimes, was more or less principled than the 2002 amnesty adopted in Macedonia, which did exclude international crimes but which otherwise lacked meaningful attributes of individual accountability.[92]

This brings us to the related, but distinct, question of the proper method and criteria for assessing the impact of amnesties – a gauge of legitimacy in its own right.[93] As a first step in the analysis, one must invoke the distinction between correlation and causation. As social scientists commonly point out, proof of correlation is not proof of causation; to suggest otherwise is a logical fallacy, known as attribution error. Thus, for example, if a broad amnesty precedes a sustained improvement in human rights, this would not prove that the amnesty caused the improvement. Likewise, if a national trial of a despotic leader preceded a sustained improvement in human rights, this would not prove that the trial was the cause of the improvement. Scientific investigation would be necessary to establish:

1. Whether the amnesty or the trial, as the case may be, was the main cause of the improvement in human rights, and if so how;
2. Whether the amnesty or the trial was a minor cause of the improvement in human rights, and if so how;
3. Whether the amnesty or the trial lacked a measurable impact on the improvement in human rights;
4. Whether the improvement in human rights occurred despite the amnesty or trial.[94]

In brief, when it comes to amnesty, the proof of its beneficial effects, its negative effects or its noneffects, as the case may be, is extremely difficult to demonstrate and requires rigorous analysis. Otherwise, the risk of misattribution of cause and effect can easily occur by, for example, citing amnesty as the cause of a bad situation rather than as merely the reflection of it.[95] Yet one should bear in mind that it is impossible to test a counterfactual scenario and establish with certainty, for example, what effects the nonadoption of an amnesty would have generated in a context in which there was an amnesty. Likewise, it is impossible to determine what effects the conduct of a major human rights trial would have generated in a context in which there was not such a trial. Plausibly defending general and positive claims of causation (e.g., that amnesties foster sustainable peace, or that human rights trials foster democratic consolidation) is therefore difficult.

Disproving causation is, by comparison, a much easier task. For example, if a broad amnesty precedes a sustained improvement in peace and security, one could adduce this as proof that such an amnesty does not necessarily cause a decline in peace and security. Similarly, if national trials of despotic leaders precede a sustained improvement in peace and security, one could adduce this as proof that such trials do not necessarily cause a decline in peace and security. In brief, in the amnesty and accountability arena, a single counterexample is all that is necessary to disprove certain causal claims.

A related causal question is the significance of the fact that a great number of countries have used a combination of broad amnesties and targeted human rights trials. Consider only the case of Latin America – including Chile, Argentina, Uruguay, Guatemala, and El Salvador – where at different times over the past decades there have been both broad amnesties and human rights trials.[96] Professor Kathryn Sikkink and Carrie Booth Walling have observed that trials did not destabilize these countries, as some others have claimed.[97] Yet, as the authors themselves note, the countries examined in their research also adopted broad amnesty laws.[98] This therefore begs the question of the degree to which non-destabilization was the result of the countries' amnesties, which shielded the vast majority of perpetrators from criminal accountability, and the degree to which it was the result of a limited number of trials. Again, as long as the aim is to disprove a general claim of causation (e.g., amnesties necessarily undermine democratization), adducing evidence against the claim is relatively straightforward. However, to prove the positive claim (e.g., that trials enhanced democratization) would require examination of a wide range of other variables, including the amnesties.[99] After all, it may be more than mere coincidence that amnesties have been central features in many of the political transitions of the past half century that are consistently cited as successful in terms of building a democratic and human rights culture, as discussed subsequently.

Selection bias, or sample bias, is another issue when it comes to evaluating the impact of amnesties. As Mark Osiel observes:

> Legal scholarship purporting to show that amnesties fail to advance peace and reconciliation tends to practice the most flagrant selection bias. . . . Countries whose relevant experience of transition does not support the author's favoured position on this question (such as Spain, El Salvador, Brazil, and several others) are simply ignored, like inconvenient cases that an opposing advocate can be expected to call to the court's attention. Such methods should be no more acceptable in serious legal scholarship than in social science, where the main point is precisely to compel our confrontation of "inconvenient facts."[100]

Selection bias is particularly troubling in the context of international law, where customary norms arise in part by reference to state practice. Distorted or biased accounts of that practice, including the common failure to cite more than a small percentage of total state practice, can lead to inaccurate legal conclusions.

Selection bias is also visible when it comes to the reluctance to acknowledge the general internal and external consensus that the broad amnesties adopted in a wide range of countries were positive factors at crucial historical moments. This consensus exists not only in respect of the oft-mentioned cases of Spain[101] and Mozambique,[102] two countries in which extremely broad amnesties were adopted at key political junctures and perceived as beneficial, on balance, to their respective transitions to democracy and peace. The same consensus also appears to exist in countries as different as Nigeria,[103] Uruguay,[104] Cambodia,[105] and Aceh (Indonesia).[106] Similarly positive perceptions of amnesty's role exist in relation to scores of older postconflict and democratic transitions, too, such as post–Civil War United States and post–Second World War France.[107] This is not to suggest that every one of these countries went on to become a paragon of virtue and decency. It is also not to suggest that the amnesties actually have been the positive forces that people perceive them to have been. In fact, the relative success of their transitions toward greater democracy or peace was almost certainly due to myriad factors, of which amnesty may have played only a modest part. However, what is certain is that the broad amnesties adopted in these places did not cause them to redescend into equivalent mass violence. To the contrary, these countries became – by any reasonable standard – better places in the post-amnesty period than in the pre-amnesty period.

Opponents of amnesties may choose to omit mention of these generally positive examples when contesting the validity of amnesties. Such selection bias and spinning of the facts may indeed be effective as a form of advocacy. However, such a tactic is highly problematic when it emanates from individuals (e.g., academics) or institutions (e.g., the United Nations) that one expects to be utterly unbiased. Indeed, it is the responsibility of such individuals and institutions to draw our attention to the omitted or exaggerated claims of advocates and lobbyists and highlight areas of ongoing ambiguity or uncertainty. The fact is that research findings on amnesty or any other social science topic shift significantly by simple changes in data sets, definitions, time frames studied, and methods of analysis. Given the limited empirical work to date attempting to isolate the specific effects of amnesty, as compared to those of trials and truth commissions, it is actually much too early to draw empirical conclusions.[108] Especially in new areas of research like this in which sufficient peer review has yet to occur, initial research findings tend to be unstable and therefore should be regarded with caution.[109]

Yet another kind of bias, known as optimism bias, is present in the amnesty debate. This is the bias whereby the likelihood of positive events is overestimated and the likelihood of negative events is underestimated. Applied to amnesty, the bias takes the form of an overestimation of the vulnerability or future unraveling of amnesties and a corresponding underestimation of the entrenchment of amnesties.

As a first observation, it is undeniable that there is an increased risk of the future undoing of amnesties. As Ron Slye observes, "[T]he emerging trend of amnesties in practice (is usually to) delay, rather than prohibit, accountability."[110] The undoing of amnesties can occur in a wide variety of ways. There can be judicial rulings against the amnesty that overturn or circumvent it in whole or in part; there can be executive or legislative repeals or annulments; and there can be legislative amendments to reduce the law's scope. These are only some examples.[111] To the extent the undoing of amnesties represents a trend in practice, it seems linked in no small measure to the increased effectiveness and sophistication of the international human rights movement, or what Margaret Keck and Kathryn Sikkink term *transnational advocacy networks*.[112] As Michelle Sieff and Leslie Vinjamuri Wright note, "Members of these networks have worked to frame the issue of accountability in such a way that it undermines the traditional realist belief that securing peace requires sacrificing justice and replaces it with the idea that justice, or at a minimum, truth, is essential to creating a lasting peace."[113]

An undoubted additional factor is the proliferation of international dispute resolution bodies, ranging from UN treaty bodies, to regional human rights courts and commissions, to international and mixed criminal courts, which have tended to reject domestic amnesties.[114]

Of course, the future undoing of an amnesty, like the future undoing of any legal measure, is everywhere and always an inherent risk. Leaders and governments constantly change, and there is never any guarantee that political successors will view an amnesty in the same light as those of an earlier era.[115] Persons seeking the cover of a broad amnesty can evidently be presumed to be quite aware of this risk. Yet the undiminished recourse to amnesty suggests that in most cases the architects of mass violence will still prefer to take the amnesty they can get, along with its uncontrollable risks, rather than do without it.[116] This choice may itself reflect a degree of optimism bias (i.e., by overestimating the amnesty's durability), but from a realist perspective, all other alternatives may seem objectively worse.[117] Indeed, like it or not, the amnesty option is still a quite reliable one for perpetrators to pursue, even in an era of increased vulnerability of amnesties.[118] The vast majority of the hundreds of amnesties adopted for human rights crimes in the last fifty years are firmly in place – they have not been annulled, repealed, or overturned.

Admittedly, amnesties remain susceptible to nonrecognition by foreign courts and supranational and hybrid bodies, particularly in Latin America, owing to the pervasive anti-amnesty perspective within and outside the Inter-American human rights system.[119] In addition, the continuing legal force of amnesties does not itself preclude domestic human rights trials, because many amnesty laws contain carve-outs for specific crimes, time frames, and so forth.[120] However, with few exceptions, the reality is that national courts – to the extent that they review the constitutionality of national amnesties at all – overwhelmingly tend to uphold them.[121] As for the specific threat represented by the ICC, it is not a pertinent one to all states because of a combination of the Court's restricted temporal mandate (it has no jurisdiction over crimes committed prior to July 2002) and the nonparticipation in the Rome Statute system of eighty-three of the world's states.[122] Concerning the other international and hybrid courts, the issue of amnesty only has been directly relevant in the cases of Sierra Leone and Cambodia.[123]

In short, it is premature to assert that an amnesty is no longer worth the paper it is written on. As an amnestied perpetrator, it is still a rather safe bet to live in, and travel through, most countries of the world without a credible fear of prosecution. Thus, we should not be surprised if most of today's villains continue to pursue the broadest amnesty possible, plan to live within national borders and travel across unthreatening borders, and hope that any future breakdown of the amnesty at the national level occurs only after they have died or become too old to stand trial.[124] To be sure, most despots and warlords are presumably aware of the long reach of modern international and mixed criminal tribunals, which have led to the indictments, arrests, and trials of major evildoers on every continent from Slobodan Milošević to Charles Taylor and Ieng Sary. They also surely are sensitive to and concerned about the increased recourse to foreign courts, which has resulted in extradition, judicial investigations, or trial proceedings against leaders ranging from Augusto Pinochet to Hissène Habré and Alberto Fujimori. However, it is doubtful that most African, Arab, and Asian mass murderers genuinely expect or fear that what happened in Argentina – namely the eventual circumvention and overturning of national amnesty arrangements – could ever happen in their own countries.

Yet what happens when an amnesty does unravel over time – does that mean the decision was doomed from the start? Some seem to suggest so, but their claims are dubious. An amnesty's subsequent unraveling often tells us nothing, or at least very little, about its utility at the time of enactment and during the years it remained in force.[125] Indeed, the fact that an amnesty falls out of favor years or decades after its adoption does not necessarily constitute evidence that the original decision was unnecessary or unwise at an earlier moment in the transition, and for years or decades thereafter. If today in Mozambique a series of prominent national challenges to the validity of earlier amnesties were to arise, this would not prove that the early policies were failed ones. Any later undoing of an amnesty might actually prove the opposite. The undoing may be a direct positive result of the amnesty's passage to the extent that the amnesty facilitated democratic and social stability, which in turn enabled a strengthened rule of law and human rights culture to take root, which in turn allowed the country to outlive the need for the original amnesty.[126] Granted, it always will be difficult to say whether peace and democracy held in such cases because or in spite of an earlier amnesty. However, at a minimum, it is possible to determine the approximate consensus on the issue by reviewing what most expert and inside observers were saying at the time of its enactment and during the early years of its implementation.[127]

States like Spain and France that relied on broad amnesties in earlier and more fragile times in their histories should of course bear those histories in mind when offering advice to states that remain mired in the abyss. In particular, they might refrain from insisting on standards that, if applied in their own years or decades of transition, would have risked massive political and social destabilization. This does not mean such states – now represented by successor governments – should sit on the sidelines. To the contrary, they ideally should be engaged, not least to draw on the lessons from their own national experiences. Yet one hopes they would share their lessons and advice with a humility that takes into account the reasons why, today, they are able to take a stricter legal view of amnesties. Those reasons may have a lot to do with the passage of earlier amnesties.

Admittedly, it may arise that the past will catch up with any state that has relied on broad amnesties to usher in transitions, rendering the amnesties susceptible to being overturned or undone in one way or another. Yet in a time of sustained crisis and conflict, it is hard to fault the human and political instinct to resort to amnesty as a practical, albeit controversial, starting point for rebuilding a country in which everyone can benefit from even rudimentary forms of development, security, and human rights.

3.4 Conclusion

Amnesty is an issue that will not go away. The question is what one can do about it to limit the concessions to impunity. Unfortunately, many debates on amnesty continue to sidestep the complexity of the issue by treating all amnesties in monolithic and absolutist terms, or by alternatively focusing too narrowly or simplistically on the Latin American experiences or the South African model in which an amnesty process figured in a truth commission's mandate. The reality, in fact, is that an amnesty's legitimacy depends on many elements. There are actually dozens of significant choices in the design and negotiation of an amnesty that can, and should, affect our evaluation of any individual amnesty. Such choices make the difference between what one might characterize as a principled versus an unprincipled amnesty.

At the same time, it is important to recognize that even a principled amnesty cannot guarantee accountability in practice. Amnesties are merely legal instruments, and no more or less likely to be honored in the breach than other laws. It is quite possible, for example, for principled amnesties to coexist with a large impunity gap, as is the case in Guatemala, where a limited amnesty adopted in 1996 has not resulted in trials for the thousands of war criminals and others excluded from the law's benefits. This is not to suggest that it is irrelevant what crimes or persons an amnesty covers – to the contrary, it matters enormously, as amnesties legally entrench a measure of domestic impunity. However, we should judge states not merely by their adoption of good laws but also, and to a much greater extent, by their implementation of both the letter and the spirit of such laws.

With such considerations in mind, Part II of this book proposes a detailed methodology to ensure the best amnesty outcomes possible in challenging circumstances. Before presenting that, however, it is important to examine relevant aspects of international law. An amnesty test would be of limited value if uninformed by an awareness of pertinent international norms and related jurisdictional realities.

4. AMNESTIES AND INTERNATIONAL LAW

The focus of this section is on the subset of public international law that concerns state obligations in the areas of international human rights, humanitarian, and criminal law. Emphasis is placed on the aspects of each of these areas of law that most closely relate to the field of transitional justice, which is the specific prism through which amnesties are examined in this book. Though relevant, it is beyond the purpose and scope of this book to parse the many technical differences between international human rights, humanitarian, and criminal law obligations.[128]

The discussion begins with a review of the principal relevant sources of public international law, including treaty sources explicitly and implicitly related to amnesty, and international jurisprudence explicitly related to amnesty. These sources constitute the most direct evidence of the international legal position on the types of amnesties examined in this book. The second part of the discussion focuses on various countervailing considerations concerning amnesty's status under international law. It begins with an argument about the scope of a state's duty to prevent and suppress grave violations. After that follows an analysis of applicable defenses to state breaches of international law that could justify a broad amnesty, and an examination of the possible relevance of treaty-based limitations and derogations that states are permitted to invoke in the realm of human rights. The section concludes with a proposed formulation for reconciling the varied and competing obligations of international law.

4.1 Treaty sources explicitly related to amnesty

It is apposite to begin with an examination of treaty law, specifically of multilateral treaties adopted at the international and regional levels. In this area, what stands out most is the absence of an explicit prohibition of amnesty in any human rights, humanitarian, or criminal law treaty. There is not a single treaty that, in an explicit way, even discourages any kind of amnesty. What are we to make of this astonishing fact? What is its legal significance, both for treaty law and for customary law? Few have mooted the question seriously.

At a minimum, this remarkable fact about amnesties and international law should cause us to question any thesis about widespread state antagonism to amnesties for human rights crimes. If such antagonism was strongly present among a large number of states, what is preventing an explicit amnesty prohibition – or even a minor but explicit amnesty discouragement – from being codified in treaty form? We also know that the absence of a prohibition or discouragement is not because of unawareness of the salience of the amnesty issue in the context of human rights law. It has been a familiar issue on the international scene for decades, if not centuries. Yet on every occasion where an explicit amnesty prohibition or discouragement has been mooted in the context of a multilateral treaty negotiation, states have demonstrated a resolute unwillingness to agree to even the mildest discouragement.[129] Even in the context of the negotiations over the Rome Statute for the ICC, neither an explicit prohibition nor an explicit discouragement was incorporated into the treaty.[130] In the more recent case of the negotiation of the International Convention for the Protection of All Persons from Enforced Disappearance, the suggestion by a few states to incorporate an explicit amnesty prohibition or discouragement nearly caused the treaty negotiations to break down.[131]

How should these facts affect an analysis concerning the customary status of amnesty? Article 38(1)(b) of the Statute of the International Court of Justice (ICJ), the authoritative statement on sources of international law, requires the existence of two elements for an obligation to reach the status of international custom.[132] First, there must be widespread and consistent state practice, often called general practice. Second, such practice must be accompanied by *opinio juris*, meaning the belief that the practice is required as a matter of international law.[133] Truth be told, this is very murky legal terrain, with little agreement on which state obligations have customary status and which do not. Yet under any approach it is hard to reconcile states' refusal to codify an explicit prohibition or discouragement of amnesties in the context of multilateral treaty negotiations with the purported existence of a custom-based amnesty prohibition.[134]

To be sure, the absence of a treaty prohibition hardly is dispositive of the matter, since there are many factors one would have to examine before making any reliable determination about the customary status of amnesties. However, as part of the analysis, one must actually take note of the fact that there is no explicit treaty prohibition or discouragement of amnesty. This is not a fact that a legal scholar or court can simply ignore, as is so often the case.

The next logical question is whether multilateral treaties have *anything* to say about amnesties. Here we come to a second astonishing fact, which further complicates any custom-based claims of an amnesty prohibition: the only explicit mention of amnesty in a multilateral human rights-related treaty is one of encouragement.[135] Article 6(5) of Protocol II to the Geneva Conventions, which deals with noninternational armed conflicts, provides as follows: "At the end of hostilities, the authorities in power shall endeavour to grant the broadest possible amnesty to persons who have participated in the armed conflict, or those deprived of their liberty for reasons related to the armed conflict, whether they are interned or detained."[136] The final text of Article 6(5) received thirty-seven votes in favor and fifteen against, with thirty-one abstentions.[137]

The International Committee of the Red Cross (ICRC) commentary to Article 6(5) states the following at paragraphs 4617 and 4618:

> Amnesty is a matter within the competence of the authorities. It is an act by the legislative power which eliminates the consequences of certain punishable offenses, stops prosecutions and quashes convictions. Legally, a distinction is made between amnesty and a free pardon. The latter is granted by the Head of State and puts an end to the execution of the penalty, though in other respects the effects of the conviction remain in being. This paragraph deals only with amnesty, though this does not mean that free pardon is deliberately excluded. The draft adopted in Committee provided, on the one hand, that anyone convicted should have the right to seek a free pardon or commutation of sentence, and on the other hand, that amnesty, pardon or reprieve of a death sentence may be granted in all cases. That paragraph was not adopted in the end, in order to keep the text simple. Some delegations considered that it was unnecessary to include it because national legislation in all countries provides for the possibility of a free pardon.
>
> The object of this sub-paragraph is to encourage gestures of reconciliation which can contribute to re-establishing normal relations in the life of a nation which has been divided.

Like Article 6(5) itself, the commentary omits to address the question of which crimes could be covered by an amnesty at the end of a noninternational conflict.[138]

The majority of national courts that have applied Article 6(5) have used it as a legal basis to validate or uphold amnesties covering serious crimes, including war crimes that would violate Protocol II to the Geneva Conventions.[139] Perhaps the most well-known analysis to date is the judgment of the South African Constitutional Court in the *AZAPO* case, in which it was held that the amnesty provisions of the 1995 Promotion of Unity and Reconciliation Act (which established the country's TRC) were consistent with both the national constitution and international law.[140] Though its analysis of Article 6(5) is made *in obiter* (i.e., as a judicial aside), the Court offers a compelling explanation of why the article appears specifically in Protocol II and not in humanitarian law treaties that concern international armed conflicts:

> It is one thing to allow the officers of a hostile power which has invaded a foreign state to remain unpunished for gross violations of human rights perpetrated against others during the course of such conflict. It is another thing to compel such punishment in circumstances where such violations have substantially occurred in consequence of conflict between different formations within the same state in respect of the permissible political direction which that state should take with regard to the structures of the state and the parameters of its political policies and where it becomes necessary after the cessation of such conflict for the society traumatised by such a conflict to reconstruct itself. The erstwhile adversaries of such a conflict inhabit the same sovereign territory. They have to live with each other and work with each other and the state concerned is best equipped to determine what measures may be most conducive for the facilitation of such reconciliation and reconstruction. That is a difficult exercise which the nation within such a state has to perform by having regard to its own peculiar history, its complexities, even its contradictions and its emotional and institutional traditions. What role punishment should play in respect of erstwhile acts of criminality in such a situation is part of the complexity.[141]

As is frequently noted, since the end of the Second World War, there have been far more internal conflicts than international ones.[142] In that context, the court's observation's helpfully underscore the differential utility of amnesty in fostering closure of internal conflicts, as opposed to international ones. In many cases, the crimes committed by perpetrators in internal conflicts have not been interethnic only but rather, or additionally, intraethnic, making the pursuit of postconflict reconciliation both more urgent and more complex.[143] As Louise Mallinder explains, this shift in the nature of warfare "has perhaps created a desire for amnesties to enable all the parties to a civil conflict to live together within the state, rather than the belligerent parties to an international war simply retreating behind their respective borders."[144] In this respect, Article 6(5) may be only another example of Professor Stephen Neff's observation that, "over the course of history, war has moulded law at least as surely as law has moulded war."[145]

Yet according to a recent reinterpretation of Article 6(5) by the ICRC, the provision is more limited than its plain wording suggests. In particular, the ICRC has begun to assert that Article 6(5) was aimed to encourage amnesty only for wartime crimes of hostility that are consistent with international humanitarian law obligations (e.g., rebellion, sedition, treason, and other "acts of mere hostility") and not wartime crimes that would violate them.[146] The Inter-American Commission on Human Rights and the UN Human Rights Committee have endorsed this interpretation.[147] A difficulty with the new interpretation, however, is its apparent contradiction with the dominant usage and understanding of the provision by states.[148] In addition, the ICRC study purporting to justify the new position on Article 6(5) examined only a limited number of amnesties.[149] Yet even if this were not the case, the fact remains that the provision does not prohibit or discourage any kind of amnesty. The most one can argue is that it may not encourage certain kinds of amnesties.

In light of the foregoing facts, those who wish to rely on multilateral treaties as a basis to oppose the legality of amnesties for human rights crimes need to develop arguments based on non-amnesty-specific treaty obligations. As it turns out, there are various provisions of relevance, the principal ones of which are reviewed hereafter. The reader should constantly bear in mind, however, that the precise obligations of any state will vary in accordance with its own specific treaty commitments and with any related and valid reservations or declarations made at the time of accession.[150]

4.2 Treaty sources implicitly related to amnesty

This section will analyze five types of non-amnesty-specific treaty obligations and prohibitions that are commonly invoked to justify opposition to the legality of certain amnesties: (1) prosecution obligations, (2) right-to-remedy obligations, (3) investigation obligations, (4) statutory limitation prohibitions, and (5) restrictions on the derogation of certain human rights.

The **first** and perhaps most frequent argument against amnesties centers on the significant number of multilateral treaties that explicitly require criminal prosecution of individuals responsible for specific crimes.[151] The precise nature and scope of the obligation varies from one treaty to the next, but the general obligation to ensure individual criminal accountability is clear.[152] Examples include the following:

> *Genocide*: Article I of the Genocide Convention provides, "The Contracting Parties confirm that genocide, whether committed in time of peace or in time of war, is a crime under international law which they undertake to prevent and to punish."[153] Article IV provides, "Persons committing genocide or any of the other acts enumerated in article III shall be punished, whether they are constitutionally responsible rulers, public

officials or private individuals." The ICJ held that "the principles underlying the Convention are principles recognized by the civilized nations as binding on states, even without any conventional obligations."[154]

Grave breaches of the Geneva Conventions and Protocol I: All states are parties to the four Geneva Conventions.[155] Each convention creates state duties concerning "grave breaches," which include willful killing, torture or inhuman treatment, willfully causing great suffering or serious injury to body or health, and unlawful confinement of civilians committed in the context of international, but not internal, armed conflicts. Among other things, states parties are obligated to search for, prosecute, and punish perpetrators of grave breaches, unless they extradite them for purposes of trial by another state party.[156] Protocol I to the Geneva Conventions, to which 138 states are party, extends the same punishment ("repression") obligations found in the four Geneva Conventions to the breaches and grave breaches declared in the Protocol and adds several other acts as constituting grave breaches.[157] It has been asserted that the official commentary to the Geneva Conventions indicates that the obligation to prosecute grave breaches is absolute.[158] This implies that an amnesty or any similar impediment to prosecution of grave breaches would violate a state's obligations under the treaty. Professor René Provost notes, however, that the duty to prosecute is not only on the particular state party but on every state party.[159] In principle, a state could pass a broad and unconditional national amnesty and seek to extradite rather than prosecute an individual suspected of having committed grave breaches.[160]

Torture: Article 7 of the UN Convention against Torture and Other Cruel, Inhuman or Degrading Treatment or Punishment (CAT) declares an obligation on the part of states parties to prosecute or extradite persons alleged to have committed torture.[161] Yet the precise wording implies something less than an absolute obligation.[162] As Louise Mallinder notes:

> The convention requires any state party, in which an alleged torturer is present, to investigate the facts, and if appropriate, 'submit the case to its competent authorities for the purpose of prosecution' or extradite the suspect. This wording is more ambiguous than the explicit obligations outlined in the Genocide Convention, and consequently has caused many commentators to argue that there is a degree of permissiveness regarding the manner in which a state must carry out its duties under the [CAT].... It seems, instead, to leave the decision on whether

to prosecute alleged torturers to the prosecutorial authorities. The prosecutors may, after considering the case, decide not to proceed for a number of reasons such as a lack of evidence, or because they believe that the prosecution would not be in the public interest, perhaps because it would risk instigating further violence. The scope for prosecutorial determinations on whether to proceed indicates that the duty to prosecute torture, although explicit, is not mandatory.[163]

The definition of torture in Article 1 of the CAT, which is similar to that of the Inter-American Convention to Prevent and Punish Torture,[164] is only applicable to acts committed or authorized by public officials. There is no treaty provision on torture that applies to acts committed outside of the state's direction and control.

Enforced disappearance: Although the treaty has not yet entered into force, Article 3 of the International Convention for the Protection of All Persons from Enforced Disappearance requires states parties to bring to justice those responsible for enforced disappearances.[165] In particular, Article 6 of the convention obligates states to hold criminally responsible those who are both directly and indirectly responsible for the commission of enforced disappearance. Article 11(1) provides:

> The State Party in the territory under whose jurisdiction a person alleged to have committed an offence of enforced disappearance is found shall, if it does not extradite that person or surrender him or her to another State in accordance with its international obligations or surrender him or her to an international criminal tribunal whose jurisdiction it has recognized, submit the case to its competent authorities for the purpose of prosecution.

The Inter-American Convention on the Forced Disappearances of Persons uses a similar formulation.[166] However, like the definition of torture, the definition of forced (and enforced) disappearance is applicable only to state actions. There is no treaty-based concept of enforced disappearance applicable to acts committed outside of the state's direction and control.

Terrorism: Many treaties create state obligations to prosecute various acts of terrorism. Some of these, such as the International Convention for the Suppression of Terrorist Bombings and the International Convention against the Taking of Hostages, require extradition or prosecution "without exception whatsoever."[167] Article 7 of the Convention on the

Prevention and Punishment of Crimes against Internationally Protected Persons uses the same language, while Article 11 of the International Convention for the Suppression of Acts of Nuclear Terrorism requires extradition or prosecution "without exception whatsoever and whether or not the offence was committed in its territory."[168]

Forced labor: Article 25 of the 1930 Forced Labour Convention declares, "The illegal exaction of forced or compulsory labour shall be punishable as a penal offence, and it shall be an obligation on any Member ratifying this Convention to ensure that the penalties imposed by law are really adequate and are strictly enforced."[169]

Since at least the early 1990s, various legal scholars have asserted the incompatibility of amnesties with a number of these treaties.[170] This is hardly surprising. Given that the minimal function of any amnesty is to oust the jurisdiction of courts to prosecute certain crimes, amnesties are in direct conflict with treaty-based prosecution obligations.

Beyond the treaties noted previously, a number of others create an obligation to criminalize certain forms of conduct without explicitly requiring states parties to prosecute the crimes when they occur. For example, the Convention on the Elimination of Racial Discrimination (CERD) requires criminalization of certain forms of racial discrimination without creating an express obligation to prosecute.[171] The Supplementary Convention on the Abolition of Slavery, the Slave Trade, and Institutions and Practices Similar to Slavery, the International Convention on the Suppression and Punishment of the Crime of Apartheid, and the Convention on the Rights of Persons with Disabilities create similarly relevant but limited prosecutorial obligations.[172] Even the Rome Statute of the ICC does not create an explicit duty to prosecute, though the duty is implicit in the principle of complementarity. Specifically, Article 17 of the Rome Statute gives the ICC authority to act in a matter where national authorities are either unwilling or unable to genuinely investigate or prosecute the crimes under its jurisdiction. Those crimes include not only genocide and grave breaches but also: crimes against humanity; "non-grave-breach" war crimes committed in international conflicts; war crimes committed in non-international conflicts; and, potentially, crimes of aggression, also known as crimes against peace.[173]

A **second** treaty-based justification used to oppose the legality of certain amnesties concerns the right-to-remedy provisions established in various human rights treaties. The obligation to ensure an effective remedy in the event of a human rights violation appeared as early as the adoption of the Universal Declaration on Human Rights.[174] Other prominent examples include Article 2(3) of the International Covenant on Civil and Political Rights (ICCPR) and Article 6 of the CERD.[175] Right-to-remedy provisions are also declared in various regional treaties, including the European Convention on Human Rights (ECHR), the American Convention on Human Rights (ACHR), and the African Charter on Human and Peoples' Rights (AfrCHPR).[176]

Broadly understood, the right-to-remedy obligation encompasses, inter alia, state responsibility and authority ensuring the punishment of human rights violators. In that respect, it appears to be in direct conflict with the primary function of amnesties, namely to remove the prospect and consequences of domestic criminal judgment. Yet the right to an effective remedy is not as broad as it may appear. For example, it does not provide private persons with a right to force the state to prosecute a specific person.[177] The decision to prosecute an individual – or alternatively to decline to do so – is for the state to make. In addition, the right to remedy merely places an obligation on the state to make a good faith effort to conduct "a thorough and effective investigation capable of leading to the identification and punishment of those responsible, including effective access for the complainant to the investigatory procedure."[178]

The primary function of right-to-remedy provisions actually is to ensure the right of victims of human rights violations to compensation through a judicial, or possibly nonjudicial, proceeding. In that respect, an amnesty that explicitly removed the right to go to court to obtain civil relief for human rights violations would directly contradict the right to remedy, absent a replacement nonjudicial mechanism to ensure the fulfillment of the right. Even an amnesty that preserved the ability of victims to go to court for civil relief could nevertheless disturb the right to remedy if the availability of such relief was actually contingent on a prior criminal conviction, as is generally the case in civil law systems. Such an amnesty would conflict with the right to remedy in the sense that the derivative consequence of nonprosecution – namely inability to obtain effective civil recovery – would produce the breach.

It also should be noted that, beyond the general right to compensation implied by right-to-remedy provisions, certain human rights treaties also create a right to compensation for the violation of specific rights, such as unlawful detention.[179] To the extent that an amnesty precludes compensation by cutting off access to courts for violations of such rights, the amnesty would likewise conflict with the state's treaty obligations. The same conflict would exist with respect to the more general right-to-compensation provisions found in certain treaties, such as under Article 14 of the CAT.

A **third** treaty-based justification advanced for opposing the legality of certain amnesties is based on provisions declaring an explicit state obligation to investigate certain crimes or violations. Investigation obligations, as one might expect, typically appear in human-rights-related treaties alongside prosecution obligations.[180] To the extent that an amnesty precludes judicial investigations, it would facially breach such treaty provisions. The case would differ, however, in relation to nonjudicial investigations such as those conducted by a truth commission, a national human rights commission, or a public coroner. Amnesties rarely preclude nonjudicial investigations. This partly explains why many national truth commissions have been created despite the existence of broad national amnesties.[181]

A **fourth** treaty-based justification advanced for opposing the legality of certain amnesties is related to prohibitions on statutory limitations for certain international crimes. The Convention on the Non-applicability of Statutory Limitations to War Crimes and Crimes against Humanity is the best-known treaty on the subject.[182] Article 1 of the convention provides that no statutory limitations shall apply to war crimes and crimes against humanity. Article 4 provides that states parties to the convention must ensure that statutory "or other limitations" shall not apply to the prosecution and punishment of war crimes and crimes against humanity, and "shall be abolished."

Article 29 of the Rome Statute similarly provides that genocide, crimes against humanity, and war crimes "shall not be subject to any statute of limitations." Article 7 of the Inter-American Convention on Forced Disappearance of Persons declares, "Criminal prosecution for the forced disappearance of persons and the penalty judicially imposed on its perpetrator shall not be subject to statutes of limitations." The International Convention for the Protection of All Persons from Enforced Disappearance is, however, slightly different. Article 8(1) of the treaty provides:

> Without prejudice to article 5, a State Party which applies a statute of limitations in respect of enforced disappearance shall take the necessary measures to ensure that the term of limitation for criminal proceedings: (a) Is of long duration and is proportionate to the extreme seriousness of this offence; (b) Commences from the moment when the offence of enforced disappearance ceases, taking into account its continuous nature.

The statutory-limitations-based argument against amnesties is straightforward. The claim is that by putting an immediate end to prosecutions for specific crimes, an amnesty effectively erases the protection afforded by statutes of limitation, whose primary function is to preserve the possibility of prosecutions during a designated time frame. The argument, in short, is that it would be logically inconsistent to forbid statutory limitations for specific crimes yet allow amnesties for the same crimes.

This argument is initially appealing but ultimately unconvincing. We already have observed that amnesties and statutes of limitations are different types of legal measures. The main purpose of treaty provisions prohibiting statutory limitations for specific crimes is to prevent states from creating a general or standing law that would restrict, ad infinitum, the timing for prosecution of certain international crimes. The main purpose of an amnesty, by contrast, is to put an immediate end to prosecutions and punishment for specific crimes, not as a general rule, but as an ad hoc, extraordinary legal measure.[183] In other words, the effect of an amnesty would not be to undermine the benefit of the statutory limitation prohibition in any general and prospective sense. It would apply once, and not generally, and would have effect retrospectively, not prospectively.[184]

Another significant weakness in the statutory-limitations–based argument against amnesties is that there is no evidence that states view or treat such prohibitions as per se limits on their discretion to promulgate amnesties. This fact was underscored most recently in the context of the negotiations of the Rome Statute, where the discussions of statutory limitations, and those on amnesties, were conducted and concluded separately. There is no evidence that any government viewed Rome Statute Article 29, which prohibits statutory limitations for ICC crimes, as having legal consequences for the issue of amnesty.

A **fifth** treaty-based justification advanced for opposing the legality of certain amnesties concerns the nonderogability of certain state obligations in the realm of human rights. In times of genuine public emergency threatening the life of a state, governments may temporarily suspend or derogate from certain rights pursuant to certain treaties that contain explicit derogation clauses.[185] However, most derogation clauses provide that certain core rights – including the right to life and the prohibitions against torture and slavery – cannot be the subject of derogation.[186] On this basis, it has been asserted, for example, that an amnesty that includes torture would, ipso facto, violate international law.[187]

However, the argument is mistaken. The fact that the freedoms from state-sponsored torture, murder, or slavery are nonderogable state obligations only establishes that there is a hierarchy of violations. That is to say, it establishes only that certain duties are nonderogable (e.g., ensuring the right not to be tortured) whereas others are not (e.g., ensuring the right of peaceful assembly). Yet nowhere does it state, for example, that the duty to investigate and punish torture or slavery is paramount to the duty to halt or prevent their commission. Instead, there is simply the right to be free from such acts. Indeed, in considering the relevant articles of the ICCPR in this context, they provide only that humans shall not be subjected to state-sponsored torture or slavery.[188]

It is also noteworthy that the obligation to provide an effective remedy is itself a derogable obligation under the terms of the ICCPR – although the Human Rights Committee, responsible for monitoring the treaty's application, has suggested that the obligation may be understood as nonderogable.[189] As with the ICCPR, the relevant provisions to provide an effective remedy for human rights violations are explicitly derogable under the terms of the European Convention on Human Rights.[190] The case of the American Convention on Human Rights is, however, somewhat different. Article 27(2) of the convention provides that the treaty's allowance for derogation

> does not authorize any suspension of the following articles: Article 3 (Right to Juridical Personality), Article 4 (Right to Life), Article 5 (Right to Humane Treatment), Article 6 (Freedom from Slavery), Article 9 (Freedom from Ex Post Facto Laws), Article 12 (Freedom of Conscience and Religion), Article 17 (Rights of the Family), Article 18 (Right to a Name), Article 19 (Rights of the Child), Article 20 (Right to Nationality), and Article 23 (Right to Participate in Government), *or of the judicial guarantees essential for the protection of such rights.* (Emphasis added.)

At first glance, it might seem that the last part of Article 27(2) refers to the notion of effective remedy as expressed in ACHR Article 25. However, a closer reading demonstrates that the reference is instead to Article 8's fair trial guarantees (*garantías judiciales*, in Spanish), thus making explicitly nonderogable only the due process obligations related to judicial proceedings, as and when such proceedings occur during periods of national emergency.[191] Unlike Article 8, however, the Article 25 obligation to ensure the right to a remedy is not explicitly nonderogable in such periods.[192]

In short, it is the negative duty to refrain from the carrying out of violations such as torture or slavery, and not the positive duty to ensure remedies for such violations, which is explicitly nonderogable during a national emergency. As with all acts of derogation under international law, however, one should recall that the suspension of the obligation in question is a temporary one. The underlying right, in this case the right to a remedy, does not disappear.

4.3 Nontreaty sources explicitly related to amnesty

There are some significant international nontreaty sources explicitly dealing with the question of amnesties for grave violations.[193] As a rule, these sources are critical of such amnesties. Although none of them has binding force as a matter of international law – they are all soft law – several of them are important to note.[194]

In the Opening Considerations to this book, there was reference to the first UN report on the topic of amnesties, prepared by Louis Joinet.[195] Although a watershed report, it was prepared only as a study and not as a declaration or set of principles. For that reason, it generally omitted definitive pronouncements on the subject of amnesty.

Another early source on the topic of amnesty is the 1989 UN Principles on the Effective Prevention and Investigation of Extra-legal, Arbitrary and Summary Executions.[196] Article 19 of the Principles provides, "In no circumstances, including a state of war, siege or other public emergency, shall blanket immunity from prosecution be granted to any person allegedly involved in extra-legal, arbitrary or summary executions."

In 1992, in its General Comment 20 on Article 7 of the ICCPR (prohibiting torture), the UN Human Rights Committee made a somewhat more cautious observation: "Amnesties are generally incompatible with the duty of States to investigate such acts (of torture); to guarantee freedom from such acts within their jurisdiction; and to ensure that they do not occur in the future."[197]

The 1993 UN Declaration on the Protection of All Persons from Enforced Disappearances also touches on the subject of amnesty.[198] Article 18(1) of the declaration states, "Persons who have or are alleged to have committed [disappearances] . . . shall not benefit from any special amnesty law or similar measures that might have the effect of exempting them from any criminal proceedings or sanction."[199]

In 1997, Louis Joinet was serving as the UN special rapporteur on "the question of impunity of perpetrators of human rights violations (civil and political)." In that capacity, he formulated the "Set of Principles for the Protection and Promotion of Human Rights through Action to Combat Impunity."[200] Principle 25 deals directly with amnesty and provides:

> Even when intended to establish conditions conducive to a peace agreement or to foster national reconciliation, amnesty and other measures of clemency shall be kept within the following bounds:
> (a) The perpetrators of serious crimes under international law may not benefit from such measures until such time as the State has met the obligations to which Principle 18 refers;[201]
> (b) They shall be without effect with respect to the victims' right to reparation, as referred to in Principles 33 to 36.[202]

In the afterword of the full report, Joinet added the following important caveats:

> 49. To those who might be tempted to regard the set of principles proposed here as an obstacle to national reconciliation, I would answer

this: these principles are not legal standards in the strict sense, but guiding principles intended not to thwart reconciliation but to avoid distortions in policies so that, once beyond the first stage, which is more "conciliation" than reconciliation, the foundations of a "just and lasting reconciliation" may be laid.

50. Before turning over a new leaf one must have read the old one. But the campaign against impunity is not just a legal and political issue: its ethical dimension is all too often forgotten.

51. "From the origins of mankind until the present day, the history of impunity is one of perpetual conflict and strange paradox: conflict between the oppressed and the oppressor, civil society and the State, the human conscience and barbarism; the paradox of the oppressed who, released from their shackles, in turn take over the responsibility of the State and find themselves caught in the mechanism of national reconciliation, which moderates their initial commitment against impunity." This sentiment, which opened the preliminary report submitted to the Sub-Commission in 1993 (E/CN.4/Sub.2/1993/6), is still valid, and makes an appropriate afterword.

In 2004, six years after the adoption of the Rome Statute of the ICC, the subject of amnesty was back on the agenda. During that year, two important UN reports appeared in which amnesty figured explicitly. The first was a follow-up to Joinet's 1997 report, by his appointed successor, Professor Diane Orentlicher.[203] The report was limited to studying best practices, and it provided an extensive survey of such practices in the amnesty realm, with a notable emphasis on the experiences of the Southern Cone of Latin America. A study that examined general practices rather than best practices would have been very different.[204]

The other major amnesty-related report in 2004 was the report of the UN Secretary-General "The Rule of Law and Transitional Justice in Conflict and Post-Conflict Societies."[205] For the purposes of this book, the most significant part of the report is the undertaking by the UN Secretariat to ensure that peace agreements and Security Council resolutions and mandates reject "any endorsement of amnesty for genocide, war crimes, or crimes against humanity, including those relating to ethnic, gender and sexually based international crimes, [and] ensure that no such amnesty previously granted is a bar to prosecution before any United Nations-created or assisted court."[206] An earlier report from 2000 by the Secretary-General had declared this to be a position "consistently maintained" by the United Nations, but the claim strains credulity.[207]

Following on Joinet's 1997 Set of Principles, and drawing on her own 2004 study of best practices in the fight against impunity, Orentlicher presented in 2005 the "Updated Set of Principles for the Protection and Promotion of Human Rights Through Action to Combat Impunity."[208] Concerning amnesties for serious human rights crimes, Principle 24 of the Updated Set of Principles makes the following changes to Principle 28 of Joinet's 1997 Set of Principles:

> Even when intended to establish conditions conducive to a peace agreement or to foster national reconciliation, amnesty and other measures of clemency shall be kept within the following bounds:
> (a) The perpetrators of serious crimes under international law[209] may not benefit from such measures until such time as the State has met the obligations to which Principle 19[210] refers *or the perpetrators have been prosecuted before a court with jurisdiction – whether international, internationalized or national – outside the State in question;* [new language in italics]
> (b) Amnesties and other measures of clemency shall be without effect with respect to the victims' right to reparation, to which Principles 31 through 34 refer, *and shall not prejudice the right to know;* [new language in italics]

An explanatory report followed the publication of the Updated Set of Principles.[211] That report describes the impetus for various changes to Joinet's original Set of Principles, which included "to reflect recent developments in international law and practice, including international jurisprudence and state practice."[212] Yet the report continues to cite only perceived best practices in the area of amnesty and omits contradictory state practice. One must, therefore, read the important assertions it makes about state practice and legal developments in that light.

Other UN organs and mechanisms, with the exception of certain UN human rights bodies, mostly have abstained from general pronouncements on amnesties. For example, the UN Security Council has issued some general resolutions in which it has emphasized the need to fight impunity for international crimes.[213] However, it has yet to issue a general pronouncement on amnesties – although in two interrelated resolutions on women and peace, it stressed the need to exclude, inter alia, gender-based international crimes from amnesty provisions.[214]

In regional multilateral human rights systems, none of the Organization of American States (OAS), the Council of Europe, or the African Union appears to have issued a general resolution or declaration dealing explicitly with the topic of amnesties.

4.4 International jurisprudence explicitly related to amnesties

There is a growing body of international jurisprudence explicitly addressing the question of amnesty for serious international crimes. Sometimes that jurisprudence takes the form of *obiter* comments on the general issue. More often it takes the form of conclusions in relation to the specific amnesty at issue in the case.

As with nontreaty sources, the international jurisprudence on amnesties is mostly condemnatory. However, as Louise Mallinder notes:

> [I]nternational courts have only faced blanket amnesties until now.... [I]t is likely that as states become more innovative in their approaches to transitional justice, the international courts will no longer be able to make sweeping statements condemning amnesty laws, but rather will have to rule on specific provisions within the amnesties themselves, many of which will involve political decisions.[215]

Without wishing to downplay the value of judicial and quasi-judicial decisions on amnesties, it is important to recall that international law precludes relying on such decisions as a primary or exclusive basis for drawing conclusions about the state of the law. Judicial decisions, like the reports issued by UN experts, are merely "subsidiary sources" of international law.[216] This means they can play the secondary role of helping to identify rules of international law, but are not primary sources of law in their own right, as are treaties, custom, and general principles of law.[217] This rule is particularly apposite when it comes to judicial decisions rendered by supranational bodies because their advisory opinions are not binding on any party, and their contentious decisions are binding only on the parties involved in the case.[218] In this respect, their decisions at most provide an indication of what a court might say in future when confronted with the same issue – but no more than that because each case naturally involves its own set of facts.

The value of judicial decisions in relation to proof of the existence of customary norms is similarly limited. We already have observed that custom arises by proof of two things: state practice and *opinio juris.* Thus, while courts can offer observations on perceived trends in customary law or on its perceived content, they cannot "make" customary law. In that respect, any trend in amnesty jurisprudence, as such, bears no direct relation to the formation of custom. State practice and international jurisprudence can even move in contrary directions. Unfortunately, however, this fact is obscured in the international jurisprudence concerning the customary status of amnesties, since supranational courts have not been thorough in their investigation of the amnesty practices of states.[219] Instead, they have tended to cite to rely on the pleadings before them, or on the conclusions of prior cases, no matter how perfunctory or insufficient in their assessment of state practice and irrespective of whether made only *in obiter*.[220]

With these caveats in mind, we now briefly look at general trends in the international jurisprudence on amnesties, in particular that of supranational bodies. While UN treaty bodies and regional human rights commissions are not courts, and thus do not render binding judicial decisions in the international legal sense, they are included here because they have dealt with a large number of cases involving amnesties for gross human rights violations. Concerning the two permanent international courts – the ICJ and the ICC – neither has issued a ruling on a specific amnesty and thus neither features in this section. As for the amnesty jurisprudence of national courts, their decisions are, of course, important in their own right, as well as important in the subsidiary international legal sense. Their decisions sometimes also express far better the ethical anguish and legal complexity of amnesty dilemmas.[221] Yet on questions of international law, national judgments are generally treated as second in rank. Whether this makes sense in the context of amnesty jurisprudence is not a question addressed in this book, but it is perhaps a proper question to consider in the future.[222]

4.4.1 UN treaty bodies

The Human Rights Committee is the authoritative organ of interpretation in relation to the ICCPR. It has issued views (i.e., nonbinding judgments) in several cases arising under the ICCPR's individual petition procedures and involving specific amnesty laws. Invariably it has criticized or disregarded the amnesties.[223]

Although not a jurisprudence per se, the committee's Concluding Observations on states parties' ICCPR compliance reports also have been consistently critical of amnesties.[224] The same holds true for the Concluding Observations of the Committee against Torture in relation to CAT states parties.[225]

4.4.2 Regional human rights courts and commissions

With the exception of the Inter-American human rights system, there is little regional jurisprudence directly dealing with amnesties for grave human rights violations. The European Court of Human Rights, for example, has a substantial jurisprudence – mostly concerning cases of torture in Turkey – that affirms state obligations to prevent, investigate, prosecute, and provide reparation for grave violations.[226] However, it never has issued a judgment in a case involving the types of amnesty that constitute the focus of this book.[227] The African Commission on Human and Peoples' Rights, for its part, has dealt with only two cases involving amnesty laws, and in both instances has been critical of them.[228]

By contrast, the Inter-American human rights complaints system has been the epicenter of amnesty cases for the past two decades. Particularly at the regional level, the amnesty jurisprudence of both the Inter-American Commission and Court has had a very strong influence on the states subject to their jurisdiction. Globally, too, their influence has begun to grow, because no other multilateral human rights system has dealt with the issue in as many cases and in as much detail.

In the early period of the commission's confrontation with amnesties, when the Southern Cone was still in a fragile period of democratic restoration, its approach was tentative. For example, in its 1985–1986 annual report, the commission observed:

> A difficult problem that recent democracies have had to face has been the investigation of human rights violations under previous governments and the possibility of sanctions against those responsible for such violations. The Commission recognizes that this is a sensitive and extremely delicate issue where the contribution it – or any other international body for that matter – can make is minimal. The response, therefore, must come from the national sectors which are themselves affected, and the urgent need for national reconciliation and social pacification must be reconciled with the ineluctable exigencies of an understanding of the truth and of justice.[229]

As democracy gradually consolidated across the region, the commission – and later the court – took a much more activist and condemnatory role on the issue.

In the past two decades, the commission, in particular, has repeatedly declared blanket amnesties – a term it uses to refer to unconditional self-amnesty laws that cover crimes against humanity – as contrary to international law.[230] The Inter-American Court later came to adopt much the same views as the commission. In its most recent judgment on the subject, the *Case of Almonacid-Arellano et al. v. Chile*, the court found the 1978 Chilean self-amnesty decree to be in violation of ACHR Articles 1(1) (obligation to respect rights), 2 (obligation to adopt legal remedies), 8(1) (right to a fair trial), and 25 (right to judicial protection), and thus to be without legal effects.[231] This conformed to its earlier decision in *Case of Barrios Altos v. Peru*, cited at length in the *Almonacid* judgment.[232] Yet it is worth noting that in both of these cases the governments of the states concerned (i.e., Peru and Chile) spurned the amnesty laws in question, which were blatant self-amnesties of the worst variety passed by predecessor regimes. Therefore, these cases were not contentious in the full sense: the laws in question were objectively indefensible and the governments in question did not dispute that the amnesties violated the ACHR.[233] Such cases contrast with those involving other OAS member states such as El Salvador and Uruguay, which to varying degrees and at different times have rejected the commission's views on the legality of their amnesty laws.[234]

4.4.3 International and hybrid criminal courts

International and hybrid criminal courts rarely have had occasion to deal directly with amnesties. The only exceptions are the International Criminal Tribunal for the Former Yugoslavia (ICTY) and the Special Court for Sierra Leone. As of this writing, Ieng Sary, a former Khmer Rouge leader currently in detention and awaiting trial before the Extraordinary Chambers in the Courts of Cambodia, is planning to assert that an earlier amnesty and royal pardon should shield him from prosecution.[235]

Like any criminal court, the ICTY's jurisdiction does not encompass either the authority to nullify or amend an amnesty law, or the competence to assess its constitutionality under national law. Its mandate is limited to making decisions on the criminal responsibility of specific individuals. In that respect, the Court can only disregard an amnesty law or issue nonbinding comments about it. In the one ICTY case explicitly commenting on amnesties, the Court opined *in obiter* on the theoretical prospect of an amnesty purporting to cover acts of torture. The Court observed as follows:

> The fact that torture is prohibited by a peremptory norm of international law has other effects at the inter-state and individual levels. At the inter-state level, it serves to internationally de-legitimise any legislative, administrative or judicial act authorising torture. It would be senseless to argue, on the one hand, that on account of the *jus cogens* value of the prohibition against torture,[236] treaties or customary rules providing for torture would be null and void *ab initio*, and then be unmindful of a State say, taking national measures authorising or condoning torture or absolving its perpetrators through an amnesty law. If such a situation

were to arise, the national measures, violating the general principle and any relevant treaty provision, would produce the legal effects discussed above and in addition would not be accorded international legal recognition. Proceedings could be initiated by potential victims if they had *locus standi* before a competent international or national judicial body with a view to asking it to hold the national measure to be internationally unlawful; or the victim could bring a civil suit for damage in a foreign court, which would therefore be asked inter alia to disregard the legal value of the national authorising act. What is even more important is that perpetrators of torture acting upon or benefiting from those national measures may nevertheless be held criminally responsible for torture, whether in a foreign State, or in their own State under a subsequent regime. In short, in spite of possible national authorisation by legislative or judicial bodies to violate the principle banning torture, individuals remain bound to comply with that principle.[237]

The ICTY had no specific cause, material to the determination of the case, to offer this comment. It is essentially a judicial editorial on the question of amnesty. Nevertheless, many commentators cite it as proof of the state of international law in relation to amnesties. The Court's logic, however, is seriously open to question. To the extent that the torture prohibition may be considered a *jus cogens* norm, this fact would establish only that states are precluded from engaging in torture. To determine whether, when, or how acts of torture may be the subject of an amnesty involves more legal analysis than the Court provides. The Court did not even undertake the prior step of adducing existence of widespread state practice or *opinio juris* in support of its legal assertion concerning amnesty, without which it does not attain customary status, let alone the supercustomary status of *jus cogens*.

As of this writing, the only other internationalized criminal court to have dealt with the question of amnesty is the Special Court for Sierra Leone. In contrast to the ICTY, the cases before the Special Court involved a specific national amnesty and not a theoretical proposition. The first of these cases, *Prosecutor v. Kallon and Kamara*,[238] involved an existential challenge to the jurisdiction of the Court based on a national amnesty previously agreed to by the government of Sierra Leone. Ultimately, the appeals chamber held that the amnesty did not bar the prosecution from proceeding before the Court. This result was hardly a surprise, given the Court's self-interest in finding that it had a right and purpose to exist. The result also was foreseeable for another reason: Article 10 of the Court's own statute expressly provides, "An amnesty granted to any person falling within the jurisdiction of the Special Court in respect of the crimes referred to in articles 2 to 4 of the present Statute shall not be a bar to prosecution."[239]

In its judgment in the case, the appeals chamber offered its views on the general state of international law regarding amnesties. Among other things, it found that the principle of universal jurisdiction excluded the use of amnesty for crimes covered by that principle,[240] and that it was able to "attribute little or no weight to the grant of such amnesty which is contrary to the direction in which customary international law is developing and the obligations in certain treaties and conventions the purpose of which is to protect humanity."[241] The chamber also agreed with the prosecution's arguments about the existence of a "crystallising international norm that a government cannot grant amnesties for serious violations of crimes under international law."[242] It did not accept the assertion of the amici curiae, Diane Orentlicher and the Redress Trust, that such a norm had crystallized.[243] However, the Court did not conduct its own independent analysis of global amnesty practice. Instead, in finding a "crystallising international norm," it appears to have relied entirely on the limited examples presented by the litigants and the amici curiae.[244]

In three subsequent cases – *Prosecutor v. Kondewa*,[245] *Prosecutor v. Gbao*,[246] and *Prosecutor v. Fofana*[247] – the appeals chamber of the Court unanimously upheld its findings from *Kallon and Kamara* on the effects of the Lomé Accord amnesty. However, in *Kondewa*, Justice Robertson delivered a separate opinion with his own detailed views on amnesty. He found that "the degree to which international criminal law forbids or nullifies amnesties must be open to some question."[248] However, like in the *Kallon and Kamara* decision, his conclusions about the state of custom were based on a limited number of amnesty models and experiences. This regrettably distorts the legal findings and affects their reliability.

The Court's judgments, particularly in *Kallon and Kamara*, rightly have been criticized on a number of grounds. These include the latter's confusing claim to be a court possessing universal jurisdiction instead of transferred territorial jurisdiction, the failure to classify the Lomé amnesty according to the specific terms and circumstances of its adoption, and the cursory analysis of the link between an obligation to prosecute and the validity of an amnesty.[249] The Court's approach and conclusions are especially unconvincing when put side by side with the research and findings of amnesty experts such as Louise Mallinder whose comprehensive amnesty research, covering more than five hundred amnesties, reveals the following:

> Only 19 per cent of the amnesties included in the database have explicitly included protection for some or all of the international crimes, although, for many amnesties the crimes occurring, although serious,

did not reach the threshold of crimes under international law. This means that, of the amnesties where crimes under international law were a factor, the proportion granting amnesty for crimes under international law would be higher.[250]

Perhaps the most significant period in the relationship between international crimes and amnesties is after the UN changed its approach to amnesty laws with the signing of the Lomé Accord on 7 July 1999. Between this date and the end of December 2007, 34 amnesty laws have excluded some form of crimes under international law, which has inspired human rights activists to point to a growing trend to prohibit impunity for these crimes. This research has found, however, that during the same period, 28 amnesty laws have granted immunity to perpetrators of crimes under international law, and that consequently, it is too early to suggest that an international custom has emerged.[251]

Based on the available data, the distribution of the attitudes of the international community towards amnesty laws . . . illustrates that the international community is much more likely to support amnesty laws than to criticise them publicly. For example, over five times more amnesty processes received diplomatic support than condemnation. If this pattern is then considered in conjunction with which international actors decline to comment publicly on amnesty laws, whether in support or condemnation, it appears that it is an aberration in the practice of the international community to intervene in the affairs of another state to criticize an amnesty.[252]

Had the Court attempted to follow a similarly rigorous and fact-based approach in its assessment of state practice, a different conclusion about the situation under customary law would have been necessary.

Admittedly, the determination of the existence and content of any customary norm is always a complicated and controversial undertaking. When it comes to amnesty, in particular, two persons looking at the same facts can even come to opposite conclusions. For example, one person may view the widespread resistance to a purported anti-amnesty norm as evidence of an absence of *opinio juris* on the subject, whereas another person may view such resistance as an implicit recognition of the existence of the norm. Although the latter account is more circular in its reasoning, as it means that resistance or endorsement of the norm constitutes evidence of its existence, both views have merit.[253] Yet there should be little tolerance when there is a failure to examine actual amnesty practice, including what amnesty laws actually say, how the enacting parties actually explain and defend them, and how the external community of states actually reacts.[254] On the latter aspect, a review of the outcomes of the UN Human Rights Council's Universal Periodic Review process is telling for its near-total lack of criticism of states that recently adopted amnesties covering human rights crimes, such as Algeria and Afghanistan.[255] For all of these reasons, the legal conclusions of the Special Court and those of the other supranational bodies that have made claims about amnesty's customary basis on the same incomplete assessment of state practice are difficult to accept.

One should note, however, that some legal scholars take the view that customary international law is forming in such a way that *opinio juris* is ahead of state practice in its development. Applied to amnesty, the argument is that despite the inconvenient realities of amnesty practice (i.e., amnesties are still extensively used, accepted, and unlike the practice of torture, openly defended by practicing states), one could still assert the existence of an emerging customary norm on the basis that states increasingly believe themselves forbidden from amnestying certain international crimes. If this were the case, such state beliefs could indeed constitute evidence of an embryonic customary norm. However, a bolder claim would be untenable in light of contradictory state practice and the absence of discouraging or prohibitive wording about amnesties in treaty law.

In conclusion, even based on a selective and partial account of amnesty practice, the most that one can proclaim is the existence of an emerging customary norm against amnesties that purport to cover international crimes. Whether such a norm ultimately emerges, or whether a reinterpretation arises on the basis of a more complete consideration of amnesty practice, is a matter of speculation for the time being.[256]

Having conducted an initial examination of the principal relevant international sources and jurisprudence on amnesty, we now engage in a reassessment by exploring three sets of countervailing considerations on amnesty's status under international law, and then examining the potential applicability of defenses to state breaches of international law and of treaty-based limitations and derogations.

4.5 Other legal rights and obligations

This section explores arguments on amnesty's status under international law that have been examined only rarely or, in some cases, not at all. The point of the exercise is to deepen the legal analysis of amnesties and raise certain considerations for future supranational jurisprudence and soft law sources on amnesty.

Assume for a moment that an unconditional amnesty has been proposed or adopted in a particular state that would violate an explicit international legal obligation to prosecute certain international crimes. For some, the analysis would begin and end there. However, it does not and cannot. Such a conclusion can be reached only after fully examining (i) the facts of the specific case and the full details of the amnesty law in question, (ii) any applicable and countervailing treaty or customary rights and obligations of that state, and (iii) any applicable legal defenses under general principles of international law or the Vienna Convention on the Law of Treaties.[257] In short, there are many analytical legal steps one must take between recognizing a duty to prosecute international crimes and asserting a duty to refrain from amnestying such crimes. If law functioned as simplistically as some suggest – for example, by treating the propositions "state x has a duty to prosecute crime type y" and "state x has a duty to refrain from amnestying crime type y" as synonymous rather than merely interrelated – it would eliminate the essence of what judges must do, namely draw legal conclusions based on analysis of all applicable law and facts. To impose legal conclusions merely on the basis of facial breaches would be to treat courts and treaty bodies as slaves to (frequently nonbinding) general doctrines articulated in cases dealing with entirely different sets of facts and strictly binding only on the parties to those specific cases.

With this general observation in mind, this section examines three arguments concerning the legal evaluation of amnesties under international law.

4.5.1 Whether the right to amnesty is untouched by explicit prosecution commitments

It is not clear that states, in acceding to treaties requiring them to prosecute, do so on the understanding that by such accession they are undoing a presumed prerogative to amnesty the treaty's proscribed crimes on an exceptional and urgent basis. If the issue of amnesty never arose in the context of a treaty's negotiation, one could plausibly argue that an amnesty prohibition was implicit in the prosecutorial obligation. However, the negotiations relating to several multilateral treaties involving prosecutorial obligations did involve open discussion, and ultimate rejection, of the possibility of curbs on amnesty usage.[258] In those cases, a reasonable implication is that the prerogative of amnesty persists in some form in relation to the treaty's crimes notwithstanding any explicit prosecution obligations established in the treaty, and that it would therefore be illogical to equate an obligation to prosecute a certain crime with an obligation to refrain from amnestying the same crime.

Another reason it would be improper to take the specific duty to prosecute a certain crime and conclude that it automatically bars an amnesty for the same crime is because states treat one as an obligation and the other as a right. States understand that they have an obligation to prosecute certain crimes, but they also clearly appear to consider it their right to grant amnesty for the crimes. This simple fact may help explain why many states appear to view their obligation to prosecute and their right to amnesty as essentially compatible.[259]

Granted, in principle, the scope of a state's obligation to prosecute should limit the scope of the right to amnesty. However, judging by state practice, many states appear to treat their right to grant amnesty as outside the purview of international law altogether. They seem, by their actions, to regard it as an implicitly UN Charter–sanctioned component of state sovereignty that remains untouched and untouchable without explicit state transfer or disavowal. Such sovereignty-based reasoning actually has arisen in some amnesty-related cases decided before national courts.[260] It is also consistent with the trite rule of public international law, according to which, that which is not prohibited is permitted.[261]

While it is true that Article 6(5) of Protocol II to the Geneva Conventions constitutes evidence of state willingness to allow some international lawmaking on amnesty,[262] the more salient observation is that the article places no explicit limits on the right to amnesty but instead encourages one form of its usage. Ultimately, the prosecution-based case against amnesty is, on its own, less than convincing in the face of states' intransigence to explicitly limit their sovereign prerogative to amnesty.

4.5.2 Whether there are countervailing obligations with respect to the same violations

We have observed that, with respect to particularly grave violations of international law, states have an obligation to investigate those presumed responsible and to ensure justice against them through prosecution or extradition. For the purposes of this section, I do not wish to contest this general claim, which arguably is beyond dispute at a minimum for the crimes of grave breaches of the Geneva Conventions, genocide, and torture. As previously mentioned, for many lawyers and human rights institutions, an amnesty that failed to exclude these crimes (and possibly others) would produce an irredeemable breach of a state's international legal obligations no matter what the surrounding facts and circumstances were.

Such an assertion, however, begs questioning. While it may constitute a reasonable legal inference, it does not constitute a necessary or automatic legal conclusion. That is because, in addition to the obligations to investigate and impose sanctions on those responsible for such international crimes, states also have obligations of suppression and prevention in respect of those same crimes. This is not only a matter of logic. It is also a matter of law.

Various treaty norms offer support for the existence of the obligation to halt and prevent grave violations from taking place.[263] As the International Court of Justice (ICJ) recently noted in the *Bosnia Genocide* case:

> [T]he Genocide Convention is not the only international instrument providing for an obligation on the States parties to it to take certain steps to prevent the acts it seeks to prohibit. Many other instruments include a similar obligation, in various forms: see, for example, the Convention against Torture and Other Cruel, Inhuman or Degrading Treatment or Punishment of 10 December 1984 (Art. 2); the Convention on the Prevention and Punishment of Crimes against Internationally Protected Persons, Including Diplomatic Agents, of 14 December 1973 (Art. 4); the Convention on the Safety of United Nations and Associated Personnel of 9 December 1994 (Art. 11); the International Convention on the Suppression of Terrorist Bombings of 15 December 1997 (Art. 15).[264]

Appropriately, though, the Court goes on to note, "The content of the duty to prevent varies from one instrument to another, according to the wording of the relevant provisions, and depending on the nature of the acts to be prevented."[265]

The obligations to prevent and suppress violations are not always explicit. Sometimes they are implied as, for example, in treaty references to the obligations to prohibit certain kinds of actions (e.g., torture) or to respect and ensure human rights in a more general manner.[266] In any case, it is extremely rare today for a state to deny having obligations of suppression and prevention with respect to grave human rights violations. At most, they deny having committed the violations, thus implying recognition of those obligations.[267] Concerning their customary status, it is noteworthy that on the rare occasions where the ICJ has chosen to declare a human-rights–related norm as constituting *jus cogens*, it has been in support of suppression and prevention obligations.[268]

Granted, one cannot be certain of the existence of a "general obligation on states to prevent the commission by other persons or entities of acts contrary to certain norms of general international law."[269] At the same time, it is difficult to think of the legal argument against some form of obligation to suppress and prevent when the act in question is a serious international violation. Of course, there are times when it would be unfair to castigate a state for failing to prevent grave violations. For example, it would be unfair to do so in the case of a state that, despite its best efforts, lacks effective control over public officials in large parts of its territory. In this respect, it is important to recognize that the prevention obligation is one of conduct (i.e., best efforts) and not of result.[270] By contrast, it would be fair to rebuke a state for failing to suppress or prevent an international crime when it has the capacity but lacks the willingness to do so. Indeed, as the ICJ has observed, a state obligation to prevent creates a "corresponding duty to act."[271]

In the context of a book on amnesties, the relevance of these obligations should be obvious: a state could arguably seek to give effect to its obligation to prevent by resorting to an amnesty. We are not talking here of prevention in the sense of long-term strategies to help create an improved human rights culture (though amnesty could be invoked potentially in that sense). Primarily we are talking about prevention in the sense of deterring a real and immediate threat. The possibility of invoking an amnesty in this way would not be simple. It would need to involve a complex and multilayered analysis involving questions of evidence, and the balancing of different obligations. That is because in many contexts in which an amnesty is under consideration, the obligations of investigation and redress for the victims of the past, on the one hand, and the obligations of intervention and prevention for the victims of today and tomorrow, on the other hand, can become morally, legally, and politically contradictory. For example, should a fragile but democratic government, backed into a corner by a violent insurrection and unable to assert itself against a powerful military, prioritize redress obligations and thus insist that any future transition pact exclude amnesty for human rights crimes? This position could have real-life consequences for the people still alive in the country, whether for those toiling in slavery today, sure to suffer abduction tomorrow, or about to be raped and tortured. In contexts of mass violence, one cannot reasonably characterize such dire consequences as speculative.

This argument can be framed in an even stronger form. One could fairly ask whether there is anything more central to a state's minimal duties than to ensure that its residents are protected and afforded basic human security. If a state is willing but unable to protect its residents, and the international community is unwilling or unable to intervene supportively, then does the protection of any other public good really matter to any comparable degree? If a general and unconditional amnesty could help facilitate the halt of an emerging or ongoing genocide, or of an intractable decades-old conflict such as that in the Middle East, who would not take it? If the threat of prosecution against a handful of leaders is objectively in the way of peace in the context of a horrendous civil war, who could not countenance a resort to amnesty if it could prevent the murder and maiming of potentially hundreds or thousands of people? In short, if an amnesty could arrest or prevent a social cataclysm, could its opposition be defended – legally or otherwise – merely on the basis of a prior legal obligation to prosecute? The argument in favor of amnesty would seem particularly strong in such cases, especially if it could facilitate an eventual return of the rule of law and a gradual end to the horrors faced not only by today's child soldiers, sex slaves, tortured prisoners, and internally displaced persons, but also by those sure to be in the same position tomorrow.

The point is that if one treats victims' rights seriously and comprehensively, then one must recognize the importance of both punishment and prevention – and in some exceptional cases, of amnesty. This is not only a moral and political argument; it is also a legal one. The submission of this book is that the state obligations of suppression, prevention, investigation, and redress regarding human rights crimes are all important and must be balanced against one another and not assessed in a vacuum. In this regard, it is relevant to recall that, in international law, there is no explicit hierarchy of state obligations among prevention, intervention, investigation, and redress of human rights crimes.[272] Instead, there is only the challenge of reconciling these obligations in some way while respecting general principles of international legal interpretation – such as, for example, the principles that the specific trumps the general, and that the more recent trumps the less recent.[273] Ultimately, in the extraordinary and violent contexts in which amnesties often arise, there are only difficult choices to be made. Sometimes the situation requires one to place more weight on the suppression and prevention obligations, and other times, on the justice obligation.

None of the preceding analysis is meant to suggest that punishment is not an implied obligation or necessary condition of prevention. It is not being asserted, for example, that one ought to lightly forgo the obligation to prosecute domestically by conceding a general amnesty and expect that it will have no effect on the society's values, the rule of law, or the ability of the state to deter future abuses. Quite the contrary: domestic prosecutions may be very important to advance general and specific deterrence, and to help strengthen and rebuild both the administration of justice and the confidence of citizens therein. As the Inter-American Court of Human Rights noted in its seminal 1988 judgment in *Velásquez Rodríguez*:

> [The] duty to prevent includes all those means of a legal, political, administrative and cultural nature that promote the protection of human rights and ensure that any violations are considered and treated

as illegal acts, which, as such, may lead to the punishment of those responsible and the obligation to indemnify the victims for damages. It is not possible to make a detailed list of all such measures, since they vary with the law and the conditions of each State Party. Of course, while the State is obligated to prevent human rights abuses, the existence of a particular violation does not, in itself, prove the failure to take preventive measures. On the other hand, subjecting a person to official, repressive bodies that practice torture and assassination with impunity is itself a breach of the duty to prevent violations of the rights to life and physical integrity of the person, even if that particular person is not tortured or assassinated, or if those facts cannot be proven in a concrete case.[274]

Yet it would be counterproductive and even unfair to insist on a punishment obligation in a setting in which the government in question has no reasonable option to criminally sanction those responsible for human rights crimes. If one is a booster of the prosecution of human rights crimes, in some contexts this may entail tolerance of a broad amnesty. Whether or not we like it, amnesty is sometimes the necessary price for ending a civil war that is precluding the capacity to effectively investigate and prosecute in the first place. Likewise, it is sometimes the necessary price for installing a new government that will have the will to investigate and prosecute new crimes – and perhaps, some day, the opportunity to revisit old crimes as well in the event that the original amnesty is repealed or annulled, as occurred in Argentina.

Granted, amnesty is never the only option. International pressure – for example, in the form of sanctions or in the form of an intervention based on the principle of the responsibility to protect – could potentially help end the circumstances that enable repressive leaders and warlords to blackmail populations into accepting amnesties in the first place.[275] However, the reality is that many rogue state and non-state actors that could be the subject of such international pressure tactics and interventions are not, whereas others that are seldom seem to feel sufficiently pressured to cede power without first seeking and obtaining an amnesty.

Some may nevertheless object to the notion that the duty to punish and the duty to prevent are divisible. Theoretically, they should not be – human rights ought to be considered indivisible.[276] In practice, however, it quickly becomes artificial to treat the duties as legally or factually indivisible, as the preceding scenarios illustrate. Granted, the interdependence of prevention and punishment obligations is clear in treaty and in nontreaty sources alike; yet so, too, is their divisibility. Consider in this context the "Basic Principles and Guidelines on the Right to a Remedy and Reparation for Victims of Gross Violations of International Human Rights Law and Serious Violations of International Humanitarian Law," which the UN General Assembly adopted in 2005 and that provides as follows:

> The obligation to respect, ensure respect for and implement international human rights law and international humanitarian law as provided for under the respective bodies of law, includes, inter alia, the duty to:
> (a) Take appropriate legislative and administrative and other appropriate measures to prevent violations;
> (b) Investigate violations effectively, promptly, thoroughly and impartially and, where appropriate, take action against those allegedly responsible in accordance with domestic and international law;
> (c) Provide those who claim to be victims of a human rights or humanitarian law violation with equal and effective access to justice, as described below, irrespective of who may ultimately be the bearer of responsibility for the violation; and
> (d) Provide effective remedies to victims, including reparation, as described below.[277]

In difficult amnesty contexts, to treat these obligations as indivisible – in time or space – would be to ignore their situational contradiction merely to preserve a theoretical claim of indivisibility. Indeed, it is a reality, and only common sense, that the feasibility of meaningfully upholding all of these obligations simultaneously is not a possibility in some contexts at some times.

Admittedly, there is a risk that, in acknowledging the reality of divisibility in amnesty contexts, cynical governments will begin to treat the different obligations as a menu of discretionary options, rather than a set of unified obligations. Yet such a risk exists in respect of any set of principles, and in the present case can be mitigated by the use of a good-faith metric, which would require the presence of bona fide intentions in conceding or adopting an amnesty. Such a metric should, indeed, form part of any comprehensive legal assessment of the validity of an amnesty justified as necessary to uphold a state's prevention obligation.

Some may still object that certain prosecution obligations are absolute and that the crimes to which they relate (e.g., torture, genocide, and grave breaches of the Geneva Conventions) are non-amnestiable irrespective of the circumstances. However, if the prosecution obligations for such crimes are absolute, how could the suppression and prevention obligations not also be so characterized? If crimes like these are of concern to all humanity and thus demanding of prosecution, then surely for that same reason we have an equal, if not greater, collective international interest in their prevention and suppression.[278] If that is the case, we are back where we began with the same amnesty dilemma in which the various obligations become facially incompatible. If that is not the case (i.e., if the exclusion of such crimes from amnesties is an absolute), we are still not very far ahead in practical terms. Amnesty practice suggests that the exclusion of torture is extremely difficult to achieve given the high number of persons implicated, and the exclusion of grave breaches and genocide would achieve just as little given the relative rarity of international armed conflict and genocide, respectively. In any event, most states clearly see themselves as having the discretion to adopt amnesties that derogate from even the most absolute prosecution obligations in extraordinary circumstances, such as when under threat of military coup or when facing the reality of ongoing mass violence. That is likely because amnesties are, by their very nature, exceptions to the obligation to prosecute that states would feel bound to uphold and vindicate but for the extraordinary circumstance.

To be clear, the suggestion here is not that states will be, or should be, found to bear international responsibility for failing or refusing to concede or adopt an amnesty to fulfill their suppression and prevention obligations. Indeed, it is unimaginable that any judicial body would reach such a conclusion. Instead, the suggestion is that a state might reasonably seek to justify its decision to adopt or concede an amnesty on such a legal basis. The fact is that human rights law contains the elements of a possible legal justification for amnesties of the broadest nature, such that the amnesty would not constitute an internationally wrongful act. Such a justification will be especially compelling, in policy if not always in legal terms, when but for the failure of the community of states to effectively assist the state to prevent the inhuman circumstances that led to the need for an amnesty, the amnesty could have been avoided altogether. In such circumstances, it is fair to ask where the international responsibility should primarily lie. Should it lie with the embattled state that has the will but lacks the ability to stop the atrocities? Alternatively, should it lie with third-party states that have the capacity but lack the will to effectively assist in the suppression and prevention of the atrocities (or that, worse, knowingly contribute to the inhuman circumstances by selling arms or providing financing to those primarily responsible for carrying out the atrocities)?[279] Again, this is not merely a policy question. It is also a question of the boundaries of legal responsibility. As the International Law Commission (ILC) has proclaimed: "A State which aids or assists another State in the commission of an internationally wrongful act by the latter is internationally responsible for doing so if: (a) that

State does so with knowledge of the circumstances of the internationally wrongful act; and (b) the act would be internationally wrongful if committed by that State."[280]

In summary, amnesty contexts usually highlight the inherent dilemma presented by the competing state obligations in the realm of transitional justice. The choices are unfortunately, and inevitably, painful. Indeed, when the concession of an amnesty risks breaching some of the transitional justice obligations (e.g., by undermining the prosecution obligation), and the nonconcession of it risks the same (e.g., by undermining the prevention obligation), there truly are no satisfying choices available.

4.5.3 Whether there are conflicting state obligations between different human rights

In addition to provoking the need to assess and balance competing types of obligations in respect of particular crimes or violations (e.g., prevention and punishment in respect of torture), amnesty situations also create the need to assess and balance competing obligations to ensure different rights.[281] To be precise, although an amnesty may result in violation of certain rights, it may simultaneously be necessary to ensure other ones.

Let us first consider the indisputably paramount human right: the right to life. This right appears in every general human rights treaty. Without it, all other rights truly cease to have meaning. If ending the threat of prosecution through amnesty can potentially enable a state to ensure this right on a wide scale, on what legal and moral grounds can one insist on the maintenance of the threat? Indeed, if the right to life is the ultimate human right, is it even reasonable to argue that the right to justice should prevail? How persuasive is the argument, in the end, that it is so important to prosecute a small number of war criminals that potentially thousands of lives must be lost to preserve the exercise of domestic criminal prosecution? Understandably, no one wishes to talk about the issue in this way. We all prefer to avoid trade-offs of fundamental human rights. However, it is ostrich-like to pretend the dilemma is not present and that the right to life, or simply the right to physical security, is undisturbed when the threat of prosecution is what stands between its fulfilment and its nonfulfilment.[282]

Consider as another example the tension that can exist between state obligations to ensure justice and democracy, as expressed in various human rights treaties.[283] In no treaty does it say that the obligation to prosecute grave violations is superior to the various obligations related to ensuring democratic governance and principles. In human rights, we always insist on the equality of different human rights and the need to guarantee all of them. However, this notion of equality is at odds with the principle of rational sequencing and planning whereby a state – through laws, policies, and finances – prioritizes different rights in different degrees at different times. Taking that into account, is there not a sound legal and policy argument for prioritizing, in some circumstances, the importance of restoring or preserving democracy, if necessary through an amnesty?[284]

If the threat of prosecution is mainly what stands between democracy's restoration and its despoliation, prosecution's defenders bear a heavy burden of justification for their position, particularly when but for the threat of domestic prosecution there would be the possibility of a democratic transition.[285] Indeed, it is hard to fault the choices made in places such as Spain, Uruguay, and South Africa, where amnesties for serious human rights crimes were conceded to secure the return of democracy.[286] Would today's Burmese democratic opposition movement be wrong to make the same choice? Granted, the breach of any democracy-related obligations in such a situation would be presumptively attributable to the outgoing unconstitutional government and not to the blackmailed democratic opposition. Yet the Inter-American Court of Human Rights' jurisprudence clearly states that the democratic successors of such regimes, to the extent the particular amnesty remains in force, will be liable internationally for violating the right to ensure and respect human rights.[287] Does this make sense when it was precisely the original breach of the punishment obligation, through amnesty, that facilitated a successor government's capacity to subsequently respect and ensure a broader set of human rights? Indeed, when democracy is restored, is that not – in relative terms – the best long-term guarantor of the fulfillment of most of the full panoply of human rights? Empirical research on the theory of democratic peace – which holds that liberal, democratic states never go to war with one another – seems clearly to affirm so.[288]

This brings us to yet another tension, namely that between the obligation to mete out justice and the obligation to create the conditions for ensuring such justice can occur. An amnesty may be necessary, in legal and other terms, precisely to have the capacity to enable the transfer of power or the restoration of a modicum of peace that will in turn allow the judicial and other reforms essential for the state to give meaning to the right to an effective remedy. Stated otherwise, an amnesty could actually serve as the first in a progression of legal measures by a state to implement the obligation to respect and ensure human rights within its jurisdiction, including the right to an effective remedy. Granted, a broad and general amnesty ordinarily would prevent a reformed judiciary from dealing with the crimes of the past. However, there are countries – especially, but not only, in Latin America – in which future generations of judges, prosecutors, and lawyers operating in more democratic and physically secure environments have been able and willing to find ways around earlier amnesties so that domestic justice for the past crimes is only delayed but not denied.[289] In this respect, it is important to heed Voltaire's admonition against making the perfect the enemy of the good – in this case, by insisting on a domestic justice that cannot arise because of an absence of the necessary preconditions.[290]

The fact is that sometimes amnesty can serve as the enabler of a better future in which the nonfulfillment of domestic prosecutorial obligations, occasioned by an earlier amnesty, is only temporary.[291] Amnesties, in short, occasionally may be the necessary price for reaching the human rights starting line. It is also worth recalling that the damage of an amnesty to victims' rights, while significant, is only partial. That is because truth commissions, victim compensation programs, official apologies, victim rehabilitation programs, institutional reforms, legal reforms, and criminal and civil trials by international, mixed, or foreign courts can always accompany an amnesty.

4.6 Legal defenses

Whatever one's initial treaty or custom-based conclusions on the legality of a particular amnesty, the legal analysis must advance further. One must consider whether there are legal defenses, also known as "circumstances precluding wrongfulness,"[292] that could serve to excuse on an exceptional basis that which would otherwise constitute a breach of a state's international obligations. The eligible defenses derive from general principles of international law and appear in detail in the Draft Articles on the Responsibility of States for Internationally Wrongful Acts.

Unlike the countervailing considerations on amnesty's international legal position (presented earlier), legal defenses only may be invoked in the event of breach of an international law obligation. In other words, they assume that a breach has occurred as opposed to examining whether or not one has occurred.

No defense described here, if applicable, would relieve a state from meeting its obligations once the "circumstance precluding wrongfulness" ceased to exist.[293] In an amnesty context, this means that when circumstances allow an amnesty for human rights crimes to be revised, repealed, or annulled, the expectation is that this should be done.[294] The obligation to take such measures would be required, however, only "to the extent that the circumstance precluding wrongfulness no longer exists."[295]

A further point is that none of the defenses can justify the violation of a "peremptory norm of general law."[296] As already explained, however, there is no peremptory norm against amnesties for international crimes.

A final general remark is that the threshold of application for the defenses is very high. Accordingly, they should not be invoked lightly. However, there are occasions when the defenses may legitimately apply.[297] Such occasions logically would include the violent and chaotic situations in which amnesty issues arise, and in which the tensions between competing international law obligations are near their highest. Indeed, if such defenses are inappropriate in such situations, then it is open to question to whom they ever could apply.

A first legal defense is that of force majeure. Article 23 of the Draft Articles provides: "The wrongfulness of an act of a State not in conformity with an international obligation of that State is precluded if the act is due to *force majeure*, that is the occurrence of an irresistible force or of an unforeseen event, beyond the control of the State, making it materially impossible in the circumstances to perform the obligation."[298] This principle does not apply when "(*a*) the situation of *force majeure* is due, either alone or in combination with other factors, to the conduct of the state invoking it; or (*b*) the state has assumed the risk of that situation occurring." The International Law Commission's commentary on Article 23 notes that force majeure

> may be due to a natural or physical event (e.g. stress of weather which may divert State aircraft into the territory of another State, earthquakes, floods or drought) or to human intervention (e.g. loss of control over a portion of the State's territory as a result of an insurrection or devastation of an area by military operations carried out by a third State), or some combination of the two. Certain situations of duress or coercion involving force imposed on the State may also amount to *force majeure* if they meet the various requirements of Article 23. In particular, the situation must be irresistible, so that the State concerned has no real possibility of escaping its effects.

However, the loss of control has to be akin to impossibility and not constitute a mere increase in the difficulty of performance. In addition, it cannot be caused by the "neglect or default" of the state.[299]

It is not difficult to conjure relevant examples of force majeure situations. These arise most typically, but not exclusively, in situations of internal armed conflict. Without wishing to enumerate all of the possible force majeure scenarios, it would seem legally feasible to invoke the defense for an amnesty adopted in the context of a civil war or insurgency, where territory is seized by rebel forces from an extremely weak but well-intentioned state, and where the return of the territory and the end of the rebels' reign of terror is conditioned on a grant of amnesty for all crimes.[300] Usually, a state in such a circumstance has contributed to the situation's existence in the first place. However, the commentaries to the article provide the following:

> For paragraph 2 (*a*) to apply it is not enough that the State invoking *force majeure* has contributed to the situation of material impossibility; the situation of *force majeure* must be "due" to the conduct of the State invoking it. This allows for *force majeure* to be invoked in situations in which a State may have unwittingly contributed to the occurrence of material impossibility by something which, in hindsight, might have been done differently but which was done in good faith and did not itself make the event any less unforeseen. Paragraph 2 (*a*) requires that the State's role in the occurrence of *force majeure* must be substantial.

Nevertheless, for the principle of force majeure to apply, the situation must be one of true impossibility, with no other reasonable option.[301]

Article 24 of the Draft Articles establishes the principle of distress, which is a similar defense to force majeure. It provides as follows:

1. The wrongfulness of an act of a State not in conformity with an international obligation of that State is precluded if the author of the act in question has no other reasonable way, in a situation of distress, of saving the author's life or the lives of other persons entrusted to the author's care.
2. Paragraph 1 does not apply if: (*a*) the situation of distress is due, either alone or in combination with other factors, to the conduct of the State invoking it; or (*b*) the act in question is likely to create a comparable or greater peril." Hence, distress may be invoked in a situation of "relative impossibility.

The defense approximates, but falls short of, the force majeure standard of complete impossibility.[302]

It is important to recognize that, historically, the principle of distress has arisen primarily in cases involving aircraft and ships. In that regard, it is not of obvious relevance to the scenarios under consideration in this book. At the same time, there is no inherent reason why it could not apply in a contextually comparable amnesty situation, as, for example, when a head of state concedes an amnesty as the only reasonable way of saving the lives of large numbers of citizens at a particular point in time.

The final international legal defense of note is that of necessity. Article 25 of the Draft Articles defines it as follows:

1.   Necessity may not be invoked by a State as a ground for precluding the wrongfulness of an act not in conformity with an international obligation of that State unless the act: (*a*) is the only way for the State to safeguard an essential interest against a grave and imminent peril; and (*b*) does not seriously impair an essential interest of the State or States towards which the obligation exists, or of the international community as a whole.

2.   In any case, necessity may not be invoked by a State as a ground for precluding wrongfulness if: (*a*) the international obligation in question excludes the possibility of invoking necessity; or (*b*) the State has contributed to the situation of necessity.[303]

Necessity is a defense described as involving a choice "between compliance with international law and other legitimate interests of the State."[304] Appropriately, it is subject to "strict limitations to safeguard against possible abuse."[305] This is clear from the wording of the article, which refers to an act that represents the only way to safeguard the essential interest, and from the fact that the article uses a negative formulation. Concerning the issue of whether a state has contributed to the situation of necessity, the commentary clarifies that "the contribution to the situation of necessity must be sufficiently substantial and not merely incidental or peripheral."[306]

Reading through the cases cited in the commentaries to Article 25, it is surprising to discover the relatively minor perils that led to court-approved invocations of necessity, at least as compared to the perils that circumscribe so many amnesty situations.[307] It is also striking that necessity is one of the few defenses recognized in the legal literature on amnesty, which is otherwise overwhelmingly inimical to recognition of amnesties for serious international crimes.[308] However, even in a situation in which necessity is invoked properly as a legal defense, the actual content of the amnesty may surpass what is demanded by the situation. It might "seriously impair an essential interest of the State or States towards which the obligation exists, or of the international community as a whole," and thus exceed the permissible scope of the defense. Therefore, one must decide each case on its own merits.

4.7 The question of limitations and derogations

The relevance of limitation and derogation clauses found in various human rights treaties often is invoked in the context of attacks and defenses of amnesties and therefore merits comment here.

Limitation clauses are of two main varieties. Some apply only to specific rights, such as those setting out the limitations on holding in camera trials.[309] Others are of a more general nature. For example, Article 30 of the ACHR provides: "The restrictions that, pursuant to this Convention, may be placed on the enjoyment or exercise of the rights or freedoms recognized herein may not be applied except in accordance with laws enacted for reasons of general interest and in accordance with the purpose for which such restrictions have been established."[310] Some states have adopted national equivalents of such clauses in their constitutions.[311]

In general, the invocation of general limitations, such as those found in the ACHR and other treaties, must respond to a "pressing public or social need," pursue a legitimate and authorized purpose, be proportionate to that purpose, and be applied in a nondiscriminatory manner.[312] The question, therefore, arises as to whether such limitation clauses as exist can serve as a basis for justifying broad amnesties. In principle, the answer could be yes. However, such clauses do not exist in many of the treaties of greatest relevance for the amnesties examined in this book, such as the ICCPR, the CAT, the Genocide Convention, and the Geneva Conventions and their Protocols. Consequently, the practical significance of general limitation clauses for purposes of this book's inquiry is low.

In addition to permitted limitations on human rights, some of the core treaties permit derogations from, or suspensions of, some of the human rights they proclaim, including the ICCPR, the ACHR, and the ECHR.[313] However, unlike limitations, derogations are not permitted at all times but only in periods of national emergency, and they may remain in place only temporarily.[314] In addition, derogations are generally permitted only to the extent strictly required in the situation, and only when the derogation is nondiscriminatory as well as consistent with a state's other international legal obligations.[315] Also, as previously noted, derogations are possible only with respect to a limited set of human rights.[316]

Concerning amnesties, the question again arises as to whether the derogation provisions of relevant treaties could serve to justify their adoption. The answer to the question is probably negative. As is the case for limitation clauses, derogation clauses do not exist in many of the treaties of greatest relevance for the amnesties under consideration in this book, with the notable exception of the ICCPR. Moreover, derogations must be temporary, whereas amnesties are customarily intended as permanent measures. Following the arguments previously made in the legal defenses section, a state could conceivably proclaim that its amnesty will be revisited if and when the conditions requiring the original derogation "gradually lessen and allow for partial performance of the obligation."[317] However, in practice a state would be unlikely openly to describe an amnesty as a temporary measure in this way because of the dangerous reaction it could provoke from the amnesty's beneficiaries.

4.8 Reconciling international legal norms

Taking account of the discussion in the preceding sections, the challenge remains of how to reconcile the diverse and competing legal questions concerning amnesties. Putting aside the issue of whether states retain an untouched amnesty-granting power, as well as the issue of whether there is a salient legal defense or applicable limitation or derogation clause, this section will focus on the issue of how to reconcile the inherent tensions between the transitional justice obligations of prevention and redress.

A first observation is that there are no well-settled answers as to precisely how to implement each of these obligations. For example, what are the essential laws and practices necessary to effectively end torture or prevent crimes against humanity? What is the permissible scope of a prosecutor's discretion to make plea bargains or indict for lesser offenses in respect of serious international crimes? How many presumed perpetrators of serious international crimes must a government actually investigate or prosecute when their number rises into the tens of thousands? When will selective prosecutions of those bearing greatest responsibility constitute fulfillment of the obligation to provide redress?[318] As a matter of international law, the answer to such questions is far from certain. Consequently, a "margin of appreciation" arguably is required in assessing the extent to which any state is satisfying, or conversely breaching, its respective transitional justice obligations.[319]

A second general consideration is that the legality of any amnesty is, by necessity, state-specific.[320] The ILC describes this as the principle of independent responsibility. This principle holds that "each State has its own range of international obligations and its own correlative responsibilities."[321] Any proper legal analysis of an amnesty's legality thus requires examination of the relevant state's treaty commitments (including any valid reservations or interpretive declarations it may have made), as well as any binding rules of custom and general principles of law. Ultimately, "there is the possibility that the same conduct may be internationally wrongful so far as one State is concerned but not for another State having regard to its own international obligations."[322]

A third general point concerns whether there is a way to establish a coherent *lex specialis* rule to deal with amnesties. The principle of *lex specialis derogat legi generali* is "a generally accepted technique of interpretation and conflict resolution in international law. It suggests that whenever two or more norms deal with the same subject matter, priority should be given to the norm that is more specific."[323] The need for *lex specialis* arises when there is a treaty that provides for a specific rule but does not state what that rule's relationship is with other rules external to the treaty. In such circumstances, the question arises as to "whether the specific provision is to coexist with or exclude the general rule that would otherwise apply."[324] Usually in that case, the specific rule supersedes the general rule. However, "this is only one of a number of possible approaches towards determining which of several rules potentially applicable is to prevail or whether the rules simply coexist."[325] For example, another principle, known as *lex posterior derogat legi priori*, provides that the later supersedes the earlier.[326]

In practice, the establishment of a *lex specialis* rule tends to proceed by reference to treaties. However, we have observed that when it comes to amnesty, there is no treaty-based prohibition or discouragement of any kind. In addition we have noted that, within and across treaties, and in relation to the same sets of violations, there are specific references to both prosecution obligations and prevention and suppression obligations. As a result, even the supplemental interpretive principle of *lex posterior derogat legi priori* is of little assistance in relation to amnesty. A more pertinent interpretive principle is the one of harmonization, which provides that in cases of conflicts or overlaps between treaty obligations, states should seek to implement them "as far as possible with the view of mutual accommodation."[327] In particular, "when several norms bear on a single issue they should, to the extent possible, be interpreted so as giving rise to a single set of compatible obligations."[328]

In light of the foregoing, what this book proposes is a simple and general test for assessing the merit of any amnesty for human rights crimes, while balancing international law's varied dimensions. In brief, it is proposed that *an amnesty generally deserves to be respected or supported if it is crafted in good faith and in a manner that promises to fulfill a state's transitional justice obligations to the greatest extent possible in the particular context while impairing them as little as possible.*[329] Such a test – which could be used by governments, multilateral institutions, nongovernmental organizations, or courts – would help take us away from a mechanical analysis of the international legality of amnesties. That approach is inappropriate for "a problem as complex and varying as this at the interface of international and national politics."[330] This book's proposed test would instead bring us toward a broader human rights approach in the assessment of amnesties, according to which the focus is on "the restoration and maintenance of public order and the ways in which aggregate human rights may be enhanced."[331]

It is acknowledged that, under international law, the breach of one obligation does not nullify or mitigate the breach of another. However, the proposed test does not contradict that. Rather, it recognizes the near inevitability of multiple breaches in contexts where some kind of amnesty is unavoidable and simply recommends weighing the relative quality and quantity of the various breaches to assess the amnesty's merit.[332] In this respect, as previously noted, one should refute arguments against amnesties that simplistically identify the violation of a prosecution obligation and stop there. Such argumentation ignores the likely existence of multiple breaches of international law. The reality and the paradox of amnesty is that it can, simultaneously, advance some rights and undermine others.

Inevitably, it would be a complex task to measure adherence to this test, but that is precisely as it should be. Complex and multifaceted problems like amnesty require complex and multifaceted analysis and responses. Some understandably would prefer to keep the metric for valid amnesties as simple as possible and oppose multifaceted balancing tests. However, on the issue of amnesty, there are arguably more benefits than costs to a balancing test. As Charles Trumbull observes:

> The principal cost of the balancing test is that it creates uncertainty for both peace negotiators and the parties who would potentially be covered under the amnesty. Rebel leaders may be less likely to agree to an amnesty, and thus stop the hostilities, if they are not certain that the UN, the ICC, or other states will recognize the offered amnesty deal. The most obvious benefit of adopting a balancing test is that it provides flexibility to the United Nations and state leaders. We cannot foresee all the circumstances of the future, and adopting a per se rule might bind the United Nations' hands when the benefits of approving an amnesty overwhelm the costs, as most people agree occurred in South Africa.[333]

The key to effectively operationalizing a balancing test is to ensure that there is enough specificity, in its metrics, for legitimate amnesties to receive the imprimatur of national and international recognition that they deserve and illegitimate ones the rejection that they deserve.

All that said, no test would be of practical value or interest if not applied with a full awareness of the new international framework that affects amnesty decisions. This framework includes, most importantly, the creation of the permanent International Criminal Court and the adoption by the UN Secretariat of a formal amnesty position. The remainder of Part I examines both of these important factors.

5. AMNESTIES AND THE INTERNATIONAL CRIMINAL COURT

Reference already has been made to the ICC in the earlier discussions on the fight against impunity and on the parameters of international law. In this section, the full spotlight is placed on the ICC, the mere existence of which may come to have an unparalleled effect on amnesty outcomes.

The section begins with some basic background about the Court. Thereafter, it proceeds to examine the practical relevance of amnesty to the Rome Statute framework as a whole, including an analysis of the distinct roles of the Prosecutor and the Court's judges. The section then focuses on specific provisions of the Rome Statute that pertain to the issue of amnesty. This is followed by an analysis of ICC practice through the specific lens of the Ugandan situation. The section ends with some final general observations about amnesties and the ICC.

5.1 Background on the ICC

The establishment of the ICC represents both a paradigm shift and the culmination of a recent trend toward accountability for international crimes. It is the world's first and only permanent international criminal tribunal. It was established through the Rome Statute of the ICC, a multilateral treaty to which just over half of the world's states now adhere.[334]

A summary follows of some of the treaty's main features of relevance for this book. These will be familiar to some but not all readers and hence bear mention. A number of them receive more detailed attention in Section 5.3.

- The Court's subject matter jurisdiction encompasses three types of international crime: genocide (Article 6), crimes against humanity (Article 7), and war crimes (Article 8). The Court also may have jurisdiction over the crime of aggression (Article 5(1)(d)), but only after a provision is adopted defining the crime and setting out the conditions under which the Court may exercise jurisdiction with respect to it (Article 5(2)).[335]
- Rome Statute crimes are subject neither to limitation periods (Article 29) nor to state immunities (Article 27(2)).
- The Court lacks retroactive jurisdiction, and thus it is unable to try crimes committed before July 1, 2002, when the Rome Statute came into force.[336] For a state that ratifies the Rome Statute after July 1, 2002, the date of ratification will be the earliest date for jurisdiction by the Court unless the state makes a specific declaration permitting the Court to deal with a Rome Statute crime committed as early as July 1, 2002.[337]

- Article 12 of the Rome Statute provides that the Court can exercise jurisdiction only over individuals who are nationals of a state party or who committed enumerated crimes on the territory of a state party. However, a non-state party may authorize the Court to act in a specific case by making a declaration under Article 12(3) of the Rome Statute. Moreover, under Article 13 of the Statute, the Security Council may refer a country situation to the Court under Chapter VII of the UN Charter, irrespective of whether the state in question is a state party.
- States parties must cooperate with the Court with regard to arrests, sharing of evidence and other matters pursuant to properly executed Court requests, but there are exceptions to the general obligation to cooperate and limited powers of enforcement in cases of noncooperation.[338]
- The Rome Statute operates according to the principle of complementarity, according to which the ICC will act only when states are unable or unwilling genuinely to investigate or prosecute cases at the domestic level (Article 17(1)). The Rome Statute sets out specific factors to determine unwillingness and inability in any particular case (Articles 17(2) and (3)). Rome Statute Article 20(3) reinforces these provisions by creating an exception to the principle of *ne bis in idem* (double jeopardy), giving the Court jurisdiction to hear cases previously tried at the domestic level if such cases were a sham.
- Article 53 gives the Prosecutor discretion to initiate an investigation if, among other things, a case is or would be admissible under Article 17 and would likely serve the "interests of justice." In the event of a decision not to investigate or prosecute, the Court's pretrial chamber may review the Prosecutor's exercise of discretion (Article 53(3)). Furthermore, pursuant to a resolution under Chapter VII of the UN Charter, the Security Council can request a deferral of investigation or prosecution for a renewable period of up to twelve months (Article 16).

For the ICC and many of its supporters, the adoption of the Rome Statute constitutes a watershed in the international approach to dealing with mass atrocities. At the 2007 Nuremberg Conference on Peace and Justice, a senior representative of the ICC Office of the Prosecutor (OTP) put it thus:

- "104 States have voluntarily bound themselves to a Statute that says three key things: impunity is over; national jurisdictions will deal with those responsible through their criminal law; if they cannot or will not, the ICC will step in.
- "The question that should be asked by negotiators is how to make it clear to the parties concerned that the options have changed and that

impunity is no longer available. Any other message is misleading and potentially damaging. What everyone should understand is that the Rome Statute does not make peace deals impossible: it makes impunity for war crimes, crimes against humanity and genocide an unacceptable condition for peace.

- "What was once accepted as an acceptable price to pay for peace is no longer a legal possibility. This is the decision of the States who created the Rome Statute. This is the legal reality.
- "Negotiators can of course still offer amnesties; States can decide for themselves which kinds of amnesties they are prepared to concede and how these square with their international obligations, but the ICC will not be bound by any such amnesty or amnesty-type arrangements. The protection afforded by such deals therefore becomes considerably less attractive."[339]

These assertions present the case very strongly.[340] However, as discussed here, they mask as much as they reveal.

5.2 General considerations about amnesties and the ICC

As a first observation, it is important to recall that neither the Rome Statute nor its Rules of Procedure and Evidence refers to amnesties. Indeed, the Rome Statute does not prohibit, discourage, or encourage amnesties. Reference to them is simply absent.

Second, as is well known, at the ICC Preparatory Commission that preceded the adoption of the Rome Statute, a number of delegations took up the issue of amnesty. The discussion was sparked by a U.S. nonpaper on the subject in which concern was expressed that the Court could end up preventing amnesties essential to restore peace and halt human rights violations.[341] The nonpaper asserted "that a responsible decision by a democratic regime to allow an amnesty was relevant in judging the admissibility of a case."[342] The example was not an abstract one. The Preparatory Commission took place during the time of the South African TRC process, whose truth-for-amnesty model had captivated world attention and received plaudits as a legitimate choice in facing the past and consolidating peace and democracy. Ultimately, however, the issue of amnesty was left unresolved in Rome despite intense debates.

Philippe Kirsch, the chair of the Preparatory Commission who went on to become the ICC's first president, is reported to have said that the Rome Statute deliberately reflects a "creative ambiguity" giving the Court some discretion in dealing with amnesties.[343] As Professor Carsten Stahn further observes, "The Statute does not strictly proscribe a zero tolerance policy towards amnesties for the core crimes. It leaves both the Prosecutor and the Judges of the Court some leeway to strike a balance between the needs of a society in transition and the requirements under . . . international law."[344] This creative leeway or ambiguity is most evident in the complementarity provisions of the Rome Statute. As Anja Seibert-Fohr explains, "The drafters of the Rome Statute . . . wanted the complementarity regime to take account of national reconciliation initiatives entailing legitimate offers of amnesty or internationally structured peace."[345] She notes that Article 17 in particular "reflects the intent of many drafting delegations to accept good faith amnesties granted in the context of a truth commission like the one in South Africa while rejecting bad faith amnesties as the ones granted by South American dictators."[346]

Another part of the Rome Statute's ambiguity on amnesty relates to the question of whether the treaty creates an obligation on states parties to prosecute the crimes falling under its jurisdiction. There is no explicit *aut dedere aut judicare* requirement in the treaty, only a reference in the preamble to the duty of each state party to "exercise its criminal jurisdiction over those responsible for international crimes."[347] That said, a logical reading of the statute seems to imply such a requirement inasmuch as, by design, if a state party does not prosecute acts constituting genocide, crimes against humanity or war crimes, the ICC has authority to do so. However, the ICC Prosecutor will not prosecute all Rome Statute crimes, but only those that pass a specific "gravity threshold."[348] Accordingly, one could reasonably argue that the ICC Prosecutor's policy limits the obligation imposed on states parties as well, which would imply the possibility of amnesty for Rome Statute crimes that do not meet that threshold.

While for some, the Rome Statute's silence or ambiguity on amnesty is a virtue, for others, it creates a problem of legal uncertainty. For example, Professor John Dugard observes, "The silence of the Rome Statute on this subject is both unhelpful and dangerous."[349] In his book on amnesties, Andreas O'Shea goes as far as to present a draft Protocol to the Rome Statute, setting out a proposed procedure and set of criteria that would allow a state party exceptionally to offer amnesty for Rome Statute crimes.[350] Such an approach, however, seemingly lacks support among states parties. The issue of amnesty was unaddressed at the first Assembly of States Parties, which was held during the height of the peace-versus-justice debates surrounding the ICC's arrest warrants against Ugandan rebel leaders. It seems, therefore, that states parties prefer to see how the issue plays out in practice during a number of years before they consider anything as significant as an amnesty protocol.[351]

In the meantime, it would seem prudent for any state party to the Rome Statute to presume that a national amnesty encompassing any of the treaty's crimes will attract the critical scrutiny of the ICC Prosecutor. As Carsten Stahn observes:

The decision to join the ICC system marks a special commitment to accountability.... It implies that the Statute sets the general parameters for the accountability architecture in that domestic society in relation to the crimes over which the Court has jurisdiction. Furthermore, ratification of the Statute grants the ICC an independent right of assessment (*droit de regard*) over the situation and the choices of transitional justice adopted in the domestic context.[352]

In this context, the adoption of a national amnesty creates what Max Pensky usefully describes as a "signalling function," both to the ICC and to the broader international community. He argues:

If amnesties provide impunity, and impunity is equated to criminal injustice, this doesn't mean that amnesties are illegal any more than the failure to punish a crime is itself criminal. What it does mean, however, is that domestic amnesties for international crimes cannot remain a matter of indifference to the international legal community. The amnestying state, in effect, has by its act signalled to the international criminal law community its intention to fail in its international obligations. This signal may in some instances be interpreted as a cry for help; in others as an act of defiance.[353]

The Court and the OTP may, however, interpret this signal in different ways. The OTP's institutional raison d'être is to investigate and prosecute crime, and thus it always will be functionally oriented against amnesty. After all, the OTP is composed of independent prosecutors, not acquiescent diplomats, and as such it would be unwise for any government lawyer to expect that the OTP will consider ICC crimes as potentially amnestiable by a state party. Appropriately, the OTP's official policy at the time of writing is that its job is to prosecute, and that the only way to interpret and apply its treaty mandate effectively is to focus on evidence-driven prosecutions against those most responsible for Rome Statute crimes, and to leave aside political considerations.[354] It argues that any other approach would be self-defeating, because only by prosecuting can the ICC ever hope to deter future international crimes. If the ICC Prosecutor appears as a mere saber rattler, the argument is that his ability to contribute to either peace or justice will evaporate.

Not everyone, however, agrees with this line of thinking. As Max Pensky observes:

The ICC's insistence that it is a legal body, intent only on enforcing the law and not interfering in domestic politics, is ultimately not credible.

For better and for worse, its capacity to influence and in many cases even alter state parties' behaviour makes it an international agent. Its decisions, specifically the measures it is willing to take to enforce conformity with a putatively purely legal norm such as the opposition to domestic amnesties, are also political ones. This point is nearly trivially true. What is less clear is what the ICC will do, and what it ought to do, if (as has happened in it its very first referral) the political and legal strands of a situation are so entangled as to force the ICC to depart from its own self-understanding as a law body, and to make decisions that manifestly straddle the border between law and politics.[355]

Pensky's observations suggest that it is illusory for a body such as the OTP to purport to separate law and politics – as for example when a request for an arrest warrant is issued against the losing presidential candidate in a recent national election,[356] or against a sitting head of state in a case referred to it by the hyperpolitical Security Council,[357] or when a government engaged in armed conflict makes a self-referral to the OTP that results only in charges against the opposing non-state armed actors in the country.[358] The same difficulty in separating law and politics would arise if the OTP launched an investigation against a retired but still-powerful dictator who received amnesty as a condition of the gradual restoration of democratic rule.[359] It may be unfair, but it is difficult to see how the Prosecutor could avoid the "political" label in such cases.[360]

In contrasting the role of the Prosecutor with that of the Court, a crucial, if obvious, distinction is that the job of the Court's judges is to apply the statute impartially in individual cases, not to prosecute. At this stage, it remains premature to assume their views on the significance of the Rome Statute's ambiguous silence on amnesty or on any national amnesty adopted by a state party. It is also important to recall that it is outside the purview of the Court's jurisdiction to decide on an amnesty's legality, as its remit is criminal, not constitutional or supervisory. Hence, the Court's judges could at most disregard a national amnesty, such that it would be inapplicable at the international level but continue to be applicable at the national level. In any case, in the event of amnesty arising in a concrete case, the Court hopefully will treat the issue with the legal and policy complexity it deserves, and thus avoid a mechanical conflation of amnesty with impunity.[361] As Mahnoush Arsanjani comments: "Possible conflicts between national amnesty laws and the jurisdiction of the [ICC] are not theoretical but real, and may prove to be difficult for the Court to resolve. Such a conflict cannot be readily addressed by reference to black-letter law techniques of legal analysis because it involves fundamental questions of policy with far-reaching implications."[362]

A particularly challenging issue for the Court will be how to handle an amnesty adopted by a non-state party. In most cases, the Rome system will be largely irrelevant. Indeed, it is worth recalling a fundamental rule of international treaty law declared in Article 34 of the Vienna Convention on the Law of Treaties: "A treaty does not create either obligations or rights for a third State without its consent." This principle notwithstanding, it is recalled that the Rome Statute enables the ICC to act against the national of a non-state party involved in a war on the territory of a state party. The OTP can also make public the fact that it has placed a situation involving a non-state party under analysis, which can potentially help deter violations and encourage national prosecution of the treaty's crimes in the country in question when such crimes are suspected to have occurred or be occurring.[363] In addition, the Security Council already has referred the situation of one non-state party (Sudan) to the Court pursuant to Article 13 of the Rome Statute. However, in light of the fact that a Chapter VII authorization is required to make such a referral, and because three of the Council's five permanent members are non-states parties, this type of action rarely will occur.[364]

The question of amnesty in the context of non-states parties is also relevant in a different sense. Many of the world's most populous, and in some cases most economically and militarily powerful, states have not ratified the treaty. These include the United States, China, Russia – all permanent members of the Security Council – as well as India, Indonesia, and Brazil. In total, there are eighty-three states still not participating in the Rome system. Their populations represent more than two-thirds of humanity, and the overwhelming majority of them are located in Asia, the Middle East, and North Africa, where amnesties remain in common use. Most of the non-states parties did not even sign the treaty when it was adopted in Rome in 1998, including Burma, China, El Salvador, Guatemala, India, Indonesia, Iraq, Lebanon, Nepal, Nicaragua, Pakistan, Rwanda, Sri Lanka, Tunisia, and Turkey, to name only some of the states of relevance to the issue of amnesty. There are also two states, the United States and Israel, which signed the treaty in Rome but later "unsigned" it. Concerning those that have signed but not ratified the treaty, the list includes many amnesty-relevant states such as Algeria, Angola, Armenia, Bangladesh, Cameroon, Cape Verde, Egypt, Eritrea, Guinea-Bissau, Haiti, Iran, Ivory Coast, Mozambique, Philippines, Russia, Thailand, and Zimbabwe.[365]

Beyond the question of nonratification, there is also the possibility that some current states parties will one day withdraw from the Rome system, as a number of countries have done or have threatened to do in the case of the

ICJ.[366] As of this writing, such a prospect regarding the ICC has become more real given the perception that the Court is too focused on African states, and given the issuance of an arrest warrant against the president of Sudan, which has frightened many other acting heads of state.[367] Furthermore, it is possible that, like Colombia, other states that become parties in future will place an interpretive declaration to the effect that the Rome Statute does not preclude them from passing amnesties.[368] The likelihood of their doing so – despite the Rome Statute's ban on placing reservations – is greater than it was for current states parties. In brief, it is in non-states parties where one can expect the large majority of future amnesty dilemmas to arise. This is a fact we should bear in mind when discussing the present reach and application of the Rome Statute framework.

Concerning current states parties to the Rome Statute, the picture is not altogether encouraging either. Among other things, there is reason to doubt the depth of commitment of some states parties to fighting impunity and the underlying motivation behind their decision to join the Rome system in the first place.[369] Many have terrible human rights records and politicized justice systems, and they may have joined the Rome system because of external political pressure or, alternatively, a perceived opportunity to outsource the burden of prosecution.[370] A significant number of them also signed bilateral "Article 98 agreements" with the United States, which further call into question their adherence to the Rome Statute. These agreements preclude the surrender or transfer to the ICC of a national of either signatory.[371] However, none of this should obscure the fact that there are currently 110 states parties to the Rome Statute, a remarkable achievement by any measure. This level of participation ordinarily should make the ICC secure and sustainable as a permanent institution, even if the uncertainties associated with the issue of amnesty in the Rome Statute will remain.

5.3 Specific Rome Statute provisions related to amnesty

In most of the legal literature on amnesties and the ICC, Articles 16, 17, and 53 of the Rome Statute receive the most attention. Each of these briefly is analyzed here.

1. Article 16 of the Rome Statute deals with deferral of an ICC investigation or prosecution when there is a threat to international peace and security. Pursuant to this article, the Security Council theoretically could be asked to evaluate an amnesty. The article provides as follows:

> No investigation or prosecution may be commenced or proceeded with under this Statute for a period of 12 months after the Security Council,

in a resolution adopted under Chapter VII of the Charter of the United Nations, has requested the Court to that effect; that request may be renewed by the Council under the same conditions.

Most have concluded, correctly in my view, that Article 16 will not prove relevant in practice to the issue of amnesties. As Jessica Gavron explains, amnesties usually are intended to be permanent, whereas Article 16 can function as a "delaying mechanism only, to prevent the Court intervening in the resolution of an ongoing conflict by the Security Council. It would be an unwieldy provision to invoke to achieve permanent respect for an amnesty law."[372] Moreover, the Security Council may end up resisting this limitation on its power in amnesty situations. As Professor Ruth Wedgwood notes, "It is open to question whether the Rome treaty can constitutionally limit the [Security] Council's powers, including the Council's right to set the temporal duration of its own mandates. Article 103 of the UN Charter gives primacy to the Charter over any other treaty obligations."[373] In any case, to date, Article 16 has not been applied in situations involving amnesties. It has been applied only for the awkward purpose of deferring potential ICC investigations or prosecutions against UN peacekeepers who are nationals of non-states parties.[374]

2. Article 17 of the Rome Statute deals with issues of case admissibility before the ICC. Pursuant to this article, and the related procedures contained in Articles 18 and 19,[375] the judges of the ICC can be requested to evaluate an amnesty. Article 17 provides as follows:

(1) Having regard to paragraph 10 of the Preamble and article 1, the Court shall determine that a case is inadmissible where: (a) The case is being investigated or prosecuted by a State which has jurisdiction over it, unless the State is unwilling or unable genuinely to carry out the investigation or prosecution; (b) The case has been investigated by a State which has jurisdiction over it and the State has decided not to prosecute the person concerned, unless the decision resulted from the unwillingness or inability of the State genuinely to prosecute; (c) The person concerned has already been tried for conduct which is the subject of the complaint, and a trial by the Court is not permitted under article 20, paragraph 3;[376] (d) The case is not of sufficient gravity to justify further action by the Court.

(2) In order to determine unwillingness in a particular case, the Court shall consider, having regard to the principles of due process recognized by international law, whether one or more of the following exist, as applicable: (a) The proceedings were or are being

undertaken or the national decision was made for the purpose of shielding the person concerned from criminal responsibility for crimes within the jurisdiction of the Court referred to in article 5; (b) There has been an unjustified delay in the proceedings which in the circumstances is inconsistent with an intent to bring the person concerned to justice; (c) The proceedings were not or are not being conducted independently or impartially, and they were or are being conducted in a manner which, in the circumstances, is inconsistent with an intent to bring the person concerned to justice.

(3)   In order to determine inability in a particular case, the Court shall consider whether, due to a total or substantial collapse or unavailability of its national judicial system, the State is unable to obtain the accused or the necessary evidence and testimony or otherwise unable to carry out its proceedings.

Thus, the Court has the discretion to call off a prosecution if the case would be inadmissible under Article 17. This could arguably include a situation in which a state party adopts an amnesty covering ICC crimes.

Most have concluded, correctly in my view, that Article 17 is the provision of the Rome Statute that offers the most plausible basis to potentially allow for the types of amnesties under examination in this book. For example, it is an open question "whether intense military pressure not to prosecute falls within the category of inability or whether an unwillingness to jeopardise a democratic transition constitutes unwillingness within the terms of the Statute."[377] Be that as it may, the ICC is independent. Thus, even where an amnesty has been adopted in good faith under extreme exigency, the Court's judges might decide to ignore the amnesty and proceed with the case based on a strict interpretation of unwillingness or inability. For now, one can only speculate.

3. The principal relevant parts of Article 53 of the Rome Statute are highlighted here. They deal with the initiation of an investigation at the stage prior to a judicial confirmation of charges. Pursuant to Article 53, the ICC Prosecutor and the Court's judges can be put in the position of having to evaluate an amnesty. Article 53(1) and (2) provides as follows:

(1)   The Prosecutor shall, having evaluated the information made available to him or her, initiate an investigation unless he or she determines that there is no reasonable basis to proceed under this Statute. In deciding whether to initiate an investigation, the

Prosecutor shall consider whether: (a) The information available to the Prosecutor provides a reasonable basis to believe that a crime within the jurisdiction of the Court has been or is being committed; (b) The case is or would be admissible under article 17; and (c) Taking into account the gravity of the crime and the interests of victims, there are nonetheless substantial reasons to believe that an investigation would not serve the interests of justice.

(2) If, upon investigation, the Prosecutor concludes that there is not a sufficient basis for a prosecution because: (a) There is not a sufficient legal or factual basis to seek a warrant or summons under article 58; (b) The case is inadmissible under article 17; or (c) A prosecution is not in the interests of justice, taking into account all the circumstances, including the gravity of the crime, the interests of victims and the age or infirmity of the alleged perpetrator, and his or her role in the alleged crime; the Prosecutor shall inform the Pre-Trial Chamber and the State making a referral under article 14 or the Security Council in a case under article 13, paragraph (b), of his or her conclusion and the reasons for the conclusion.

The interests-of-justice test has been at the heart of the Article 53 debate, and of the global debate on amnesty as such. At first glance, it would seem inapposite to argue that an amnesty can ever be in the interests of justice, because its primary function is to remove the prospect and consequences of domestic criminal justice. However, a central purpose of Article 53 is to authorize the ICC Prosecutor to justify a decision to refrain from a criminal investigation, and therefore the meaning of the term *justice* in the phrase "interests of justice" would seem to extend beyond criminal justice.

In a 2003 draft regulation on the interests of justice, the OTP noted that it might decline to investigate when the start of an investigation would exacerbate a conflict situation or jeopardize completion of a reconciliation or peace process. As Jessica Gavron notes, such an argument "has the unattractive corollary of turning the deterrence argument on its head."[378] However, that corollary is one of design, not inadvertence. On a plain reading of the text, the interests-of-justice test reads like an escape clause for the OTP. It is a guarantee of prosecutorial diplomacy, built into the Rome Statute.

In 2007, the OTP issued a follow-up report on the Article 53 reference to the interests of justice. Among other things, the report stated, "The concept of the interests of justice established in the Statute, while necessarily broader than criminal justice in a narrow sense, must be interpreted in accordance with the objects and purposes of the Statute. Hence, it should not be conceived of so broadly as to embrace all issues related to peace and security."[379] The report further provided, "The best guidance on the Office's approach to these issues can be gathered from the way it has dealt with real situations. The Office will not speculate on abstract scenarios."[380] In that respect, it is salient that in Uganda the OTP has not criticized a long-standing, general, and unconditional amnesty that removes the jurisdiction of national courts over persons responsible for any conflict-related crime, regardless of its severity.[381] The law's only exception is for specific individuals that the Minister of Internal Affairs declares ineligible – in this case, the few individuals who are already objects of ICC arrest warrants. It seems, therefore, that the OTP will oppose an amnesty only to the extent it covers persons against whom the Court has actually issued arrest warrants. It likely will not oppose an amnesty that covers ICC crimes "in general."[382]

As mentioned earlier, a decision by the OTP to refrain or desist from a criminal investigation is reviewable by the Court's judges. At this stage, we only know the OTP's views on the meaning of "interests of justice." We cannot assume its understanding is, or will be, shared by the Court's judges. That said, judicial review may well suit the OTP. As Louise Mallinder observes, "there are clearly risks inherent in permitting the prosecutor to determine when political factors should be considered, 'as it may lead to a judgment on whether a government has acted responsibly by adopting amnesty laws.' In addition, it may cause accusations of impartiality or of politically-motivated prosecutions."[383] The Prosecutor may, therefore, prefer to seek a ruling from the Court on admissibility, thereby "putting the onus of a politically-charged decision on the validity of the Court," and enabling victims to express their views on the purpose and scope of the amnesty to the Court.[384]

5.4 The ICC in Uganda

Until now, all of the OTP's investigations have been initiated through referral, either by states (i.e., Uganda, Democratic Republic of Congo, Central African Republic) or by the Security Council (i.e., Darfur, Sudan). None has arisen through the Rome Statute's *proprio motu* (prosecutor-initiated) mechanism.[385]

Of the different country situations on the ICC's docket, Uganda is the one that has proved the most relevant to this book. The situation of the ICC in Uganda has been the subject of extensive and polarizing debate in recent years, and the question of amnesty has figured centrally throughout. As the ICC's first case, it was bound to be complicated and full of lessons – some specific to Uganda and others of a more general application.

The Court's website contains the following summary background about the situation in Uganda as of 2004:

> The current conflict has persisted for seventeen years, during which time civilians in northern Uganda have been subjected to regular attacks. Tensions began soon after the President Yoweri Museveni took power in 1986. Not long thereafter, a rebel group, the Lord's Resistance Army (LRA), formed from several splinter groups originating from the former Ugandan People's Democratic Army. According to different reports given to the Office of the Prosecutor, the situation has resulted in a pattern of serious human rights abuses against civilians in the region, including summary executions, torture and mutilation, recruitment of child soldiers, child sexual abuse, rape, forcible displacement, and looting and destruction of civilian property.[386]

The ICC accepted the Ugandan referral because of a purported inability, rather than an unwillingness, of Ugandan authorities to capture and arrest the LRA commanders.[387] They are considered primarily responsible for mass atrocities in northern Uganda, although in recent years have shifted their main operations to Congo, Sudan, and the Central African Republic.[388] In hindsight, it appears that the ICC opened the case in northern Uganda on grounds for which it was not, at the time, adequately equipped to respond.[389]

Pursuant to the OTP's investigations, the Court issued arrest warrants against the five top leaders of the LRA in October 2005. This decision is widely credited as a major factor in convincing the LRA to enter a cease-fire agreement and engage in peace talks with the government. As the International Crisis Group's Uganda analyst asserted in 2007, the effects of the arrest warrants belied the claim that the ICC was spoiling peace prospects:

> We are in the midst of the most promising peace initiative in the last 20 years, one which has dramatically improved the security and humanitarian situation in northern Uganda.... Rather than driving the LRA back into the bush, the LRA have been drawn into negotiations. Rather than making civilians more vulnerable, northern Uganda is currently witnessing unprecedented security.[390]

Though compelling, this view was not shared by all close observers. Ugandan analyst Moses Okello, for example, asserted that "it may be the case that the carrot-and-stick threat of indictments led the LRA to the negotiating table, but this is merely speculation informed by opportunism."[391] Whatever the case, the fact is that the arrest warrants coincided with the beginning of peace talks.

Yet if the arrest warrants led to the holding of peace talks, paradoxically they also constituted a principal blockage at those talks. They impeded the prospect of a comprehensive peace agreement to end the conflict and, with it, an end to the appalling situation of child soldiers, bush wives, civilian hostages, and internally displaced persons (IDPs). The LRA leadership, in fact, never ceased to call for the withdrawal of the warrants.[392] The Ugandan government frequently and publicly echoed this wish and at various times openly offered a broad and general amnesty to the LRA, notwithstanding its having called on the ICC to become involved in the first instance. The problem, however, was that the decision about the withdrawal or retention of the warrants was not and is not one for the Ugandan government to make.[393] It also was, and continues to be, impossible for the government to guarantee that the ICC would respect any amnesty it wishes to offer to the LRA.[394] For its part, the OTP remained unconvinced that the withdrawal of the arrest warrants would bring peace, and understandably did not wish to lend credence to the claim that it was the spoiler.[395] As for the Security Council, it preferred not to intervene in the case pursuant to Article 16 of the Rome Statute, and in any event it is doubtful that the LRA leadership would be ready to trust that the Security Council would renew an Article 16 resolution in its favor every twelve months, as would be required by the treaty. In short, the situation was thoroughly blocked.

This "no justice, no peace" situation continued in Uganda for quite some time. Eventually, in February 2008, the government and the LRA appeared to reach a final agreement, inter alia, on the questions of accountability and reconciliation.[396] However, the OTP continued to refuse to withdraw the arrest warrants, the deal remained unsigned, and the LRA has since fully returned to the battlefield. Naturally, some now question whether the entire senior LRA leadership ever genuinely was committed to the peace process.[397] Others question whether the Ugandan government merely used the ICC arrest warrants as bargaining chips to gain leverage at the peace talks. Whatever the case, no one credibly could claim to have been unaware of the LRA's implacable opposition to criminal accountability, even if the unsigned agreement (illusorily) suggested otherwise. In the result, the retention of the ICC arrest warrants – and, by corollary, the prevention of any reliable amnesty arrangement – appear to be direct contributors to the situation of ongoing human misery and suffering in areas of LRA operations.[398] This is not an outcome that simply can be blamed on the Court. Due to the failure by ICC states parties to take adequate measures to execute the arrest warrants against the LRA leaders, justice lacked a real chance. Instead, the peace talks constituted the primary focus of the international community's attention and resources.

Despite the failure of the peace talks and the return to military hostilities, some see value in the quality of the debates the ICC arrest warrants triggered. At international and national levels, the debates touched on crucial questions about balancing the interests of peace and justice, and about the strengths and weaknesses of the Rome Statute in that context.[399] In addition, the debates encouraged a greater understanding of national transitional justice options, as evidenced in groundbreaking victim survey work conducted during the years of the peace process.[400] Ultimately, however, there was nothing – not amnesty, not trials – that the Ugandan government or the peace mediators were in a position to guarantee to the Ugandan public, the perpetrators, or the direct victims and survivors.[401] Once the ICC is operating in a country – whether through state referral, Security Council referral, or some other means – control over the solutions necessarily becomes a shared burden, and all concerned parties enter a realm of uncertainty in which politics inevitably compete with law.[402]

5.5 Conclusion

Hard cases like the Ugandan one, with their inevitable amnesty dilemmas, will continue to be the rule, not the exception, for the ICC. That is because the Court will be involved only in crisis countries during its initial years of operation – given, among other things, its specific temporal mandate.[403] This likely will complicate the development of the Court's jurisprudence, especially in relation to Articles 17 and 53. As the saying goes, "Hard cases make bad law," and the Court will face only hard cases.

The complexity of the ICC's caseload also may push it to redefine its mission. Rather than framing the Court's role as a provider of individual accountability, the focus may turn to the direct and indirect benefits of the Rome Statute framework as a whole in the realm of international justice. Signs of this rebranding already are apparent to some degree. The ICC is increasingly emphasizing, for example, how the threat of ICC prosecution can lead to more principled peace deals,[404] increase the international criminal law component of military training,[405] and encourage changes in domestic legislation and practice through what the OTP terms *positive complementarity*.[406] These signs reflect awareness that in the "court of public opinion," the ICC will lose if it is primarily perceived as a court, whereas it will win if it is perceived primarily as a lynchpin in a new global system of justice. As the OTP emphasized from an early stage, a lack of ICC trials would constitute the best evidence of an effective ICC, as that would imply states parties are able and willing to deal with Rome Statute crimes on their own.[407]

Although claims of this sort are rhetorically appealing, ultimately they are of limited persuasiveness. The fact is that the ICC is a court and, as such, will need to hold enough significant trials to underwrite its present and future relevance. In that respect, the Court has institutional self-interests that sometimes will conflict with the principle of complementarity and the idea of being a court of last resort. As Phil Clark observes, the ICC has "the need to produce fast judicial results, runs on the board, as a new institution."[408] But even this will be difficult. The Court will remain reliant on the cooperation of states parties to effectively carry out its mandate, especially in the execution of arrest warrants.[409] Regrettably, the absence from the Rome Statute of immediate penalties for a failure to cooperate has facilitated a general lack of effective cooperation.[410] If the trend of inadequate cooperation persists or worsens, the risk is that the targets of ICC trials will cease to fear the Court, and it will come to resemble a paper tiger. This would be unfortunate, because sometimes the threat of ICC prosecution will constitute one of the few available levers to mitigate or end amnesty blackmail by perpetrators of mass violence.

Yet even an effective ICC, benefiting from state cooperation, will tend to raise complications for peace and justice by adding one more tension and complication into already fraught and violent country situations. In addition, of the remaining non-states parties to the Rome Statute – in which amnesty dilemmas will be most prevalent – few seem likely to join in the coming years and none may be the object of a future Security Council referral. Yet even if the ICC ultimately accomplishes less than we hope it likely will fail less than we fear. On balance, there is good reason to believe that the world is better off with the ICC than without it, no matter one's position on the issue of amnesty.

6. THE EVOLVING UN POSITION ON AMNESTIES

This final section of Part I discusses the UN approach to amnesties that evolved out of the establishment of the ICC.[411] In September 1998, only weeks after the adoption of the Rome Statute, UN Secretary-General Kofi Annan paid an official visit to South Africa. The country's TRC had gripped the international community's attention in the preceding years, with its compelling images of confrontation between victims and the perpetrators who had applied for amnesty before the TRC's Amnesty Committee. Although fervently supportive of the ICC, the Secretary-General made the following remark about the TRC in a public speech during his visit: "It is inconceivable that, in such a case, the [ICC] would seek to substitute its judgment for that of a whole nation which is seeking the best way to put a traumatic past behind it and build a better future."[412]

Subsequently, in mid-1999, the Office of the UN Secretary-General issued a confidential cable to all UN representatives around the world. Attached to the cable were "Guidelines for United Nations Representatives on Certain Aspects of Negotiations for Conflict Resolution." The guidelines stated that the United Nations could not condone amnesty for war crimes, crimes against humanity, or genocide – the three main crimes enumerated in the Rome Statute.[413] Concerning their confidential nature, Christine Bell observes, "The rationale for privacy can be mooted to lie in the wish to keep the guidelines as an internal almost bureaucratic matter so as not to reveal the mediator's hand."[414]

Remarkably, within months of the distribution of the guidelines, they were put to direct use, albeit sloppily and tardily. This occurred in the context of a classical amnesty situation in Sierra Leone, a failing state mired in a civil war that had produced mass atrocities of a conscience-shocking nature. At that time, the United Nations was participating in peace talks between the government and the Revolutionary United Front (RUF). The peace talks consummated in a final agreement known as the Lomé Peace Agreement, named after the city in which the negotiations took place.

Among other things, the agreement contained a general and unconditional amnesty, which nearly all key stakeholders appear to have considered a necessity to halt the war.[415] As the official copies of the agreement circulated for signature, Francis Okello, the Special Representative of the UN Secretary-General, inserted a written disclaimer into the agreement. The disclaimer stated, "The UN holds the understanding that the amnesty provisions of the Agreement shall not apply to the international crimes of genocide, crimes against humanity, war crimes and other serious violations of international humanitarian law."[416] A case study by Priscilla Hayner on the Lomé talks reveals the following astonishing facts:

> [T]he "disclaimer" about the amnesty inserted by the UN Special Representative was written on only one copy of the accord. However, the text specifically notes that each of the 12 original texts is "equally authentic." Furthermore, this disclaimer was reportedly written onto that one copy after some others had already signed the document, but without any announcement, clarification or discussion.[417]

Over the coming years, Okello's disclaimer revealed itself as a watershed for the UN Secretariat's position on amnesties and ultimately mutated into the public baseline of the United Nations' position.[418] The position received formal expression, inter alia, in the report of the UN Secretary-General entitled "The Rule of Law and Transitional Justice in Conflict and Post-Conflict Societies."[419] Paragraph 64(c) of the report urges that peace agreements and Security Council resolutions and mandates "reject any endorsement of amnesty for genocide, war crimes, or crimes against humanity, including those relating to ethnic, gender and sexually based international crimes, and ensure that no such amnesty previously granted is a bar to prosecution before any United Nations-created or assisted court." However, as Professor Michael Scharf observes:

> Commentators may point to the Secretary General's August 2004 Report to the Security Council on the Rule of Law and Transitional Justice as an indication that the United Nations has recently altered its position on the acceptability of amnesty/exile for peace deals. . . . It is more significant, however, that in the Security Council's debate on the Secretary-General's Report, there was no consensus on this particularly controversial recommendation (only two of the fifteen members of the Council – Brazil and Costa Rica – spoke in favour of it while several opposed it), and the statement approved by the Council at the end of the debate made no reference to the issue of amnesty.[420]

Very shortly after the issuance of the Secretary-General's 2004 report, the UN position, almost furtively, underwent a normative expansion. First, the UN Updated Principles to Combat Impunity redefined the phrase "serious crimes under international law" to encompass "gross human rights violations."[421] Next, Principle 24 of the Updated Set of Principles declared that the perpetrators of serious crimes under international law could not benefit from amnesty measures. This then became, and as of this writing remains, the newer UN position.[422]

In one of the most prominent applications of the revised position, the United Nations boycotted the Commission on Truth and Friendship set up jointly by Indonesia and Timor-Leste. It did so because the mandate authorized the commission to recommend amnesty for persons who provided full confessions of human rights violations.[423] The UN Secretary-General's spokesperson stated that UN policy "is that the Organization cannot endorse or condone amnesties for genocide, crimes against humanity, war crimes or gross violations of human rights, nor should it do anything that might foster them." The spokesperson added that it was "the firm intention of the Secretary-General to uphold this position of principle."[424] This position was encouraged by, and now receives support from, a growing movement of human rights organizations and activist magistrates. Their ongoing external support has created the impression that the United Nations' amnesty position is now a settled global rule.[425]

Whatever its merits, the current formulation of the UN position stands in stark relief with the organization's own previous and longstanding practice.[426] It also marks a major rupture with previously prevalent opinions about the issue in general.[427] In brief, we have gone from a time when amnesties were treated above all as a political issue, fully within the exclusive and sovereign domain of states, to a time when they are treated above all as a legal issue that extends beyond the prerogative of any one state. The new reality of amnesty negotiations for states faced with the issue is that they need to factor in not only a different jurisdictional reality – namely the uncontrollable risk of sealed and public arrest warrants and prosecutions by international, hybrid, and foreign courts – but also the risk of potentially offending the UN Secretariat's position. Offending the position potentially could engender serious consequences including preenactment opposition by the United Nations (with or without an accompanying threat), refusal to witness an agreement containing an amnesty, witnessing the agreement but adding a Lomé-like disclaimer, open rebuke over the amnesty, refusal to participate in the implementation of any amnesty-related process, and discouragement of donor engagement in the implementation of a broader peace-building program.[428]

These potential threats notwithstanding, the new UN position has not closed the debate on amnesty. To the contrary, policy makers inside and outside of the United Nations continue to confront and debate the issue on a regular basis, because circumstances leading to its invocation still abound across the globe. With each new invocation of amnesty, disagreements naturally arise about the relative merits of the new UN position. The substance of such debates, examined here, is highly salient for the design and operation of transitional justice programs and peace-building policies generally. It is also legally salient, as the UN position is a reasonable legal proposition but not a compulsory legal conclusion. It is therefore surprising to see the United Nations become increasingly strident in its anti-amnesty stance.

With this by way of background on the UN position, we now return briefly to the topic of the South African TRC's amnesty scheme and its postapartheid transition more generally. The TRC began operations several years before the United Nations adopted its new amnesty position. As is well known, the international community gave massive support to what was happening in South Africa, providing financial, political, and technical backing throughout. Yet today the United Nations, following its position strictly, would be compelled to boycott the TRC because its amnesty mandate contained a broad definition of "gross violations of human rights" that could easily encompass international crimes and comparably serious human rights violations.[429] Indeed, the TRC's amnesty process involved assessing applications and granting amnesties for precisely such acts. By contrast, the Commission on Truth and Friendship, mentioned earlier, merely had a mandate to recommend amnesty for such violations and yet was the object of a very public UN boycott during its period of operation from 2006–2008.

The implication of the foregoing is clear: adherence to the current UN position would effectively prevent states from adopting the South African model or any comparable variant thereof. In other words, the model that rightly or wrongly inspired so many around the world – not least, as of 1998, the UN Secretary-General himself – is in direct violation of the UN position.[430] Does this make sense? Should it not cause us to question the content of the UN position, the manner of its application, or both? Has the United Nations possibly gone too far, to the point of pushing well-intentioned governments to make potentially hazardous choices in fragile circumstances, else risking pariah status among the international donor community? Alternatively, is the United Nations' new intolerance for amnesties a healthy check on the habitual government instinct to sacrifice victims' rights in favor of a purported collective good? These and related questions are examined in the ensuing discussion.

6.1 Legal questions about the UN position

In the most aggressive application of its position, the United Nations will declare certain amnesties as inconsistent or incompatible with international law. In a less aggressive application of its position, the United Nations will merely indicate that it is unable or unwilling to endorse a particular amnesty because of the failure to exclude international crimes or gross human rights violations. In both cases, though, the implication is that the amnesty is contrary to international law. That is because the opposition emanates from the United Nations itself. This subtle conflation is reinforced when the United Nations describes international law as the basis for its position.[431] As a result – and notwithstanding the fact that the UN Secretariat cannot make law – the UN position tends to be treated as synonymous with the legal position.

Most of the international law claims implied in the UN position already have been discussed and contested. In particular, we noted the fact of state unwillingness to prohibit or discourage amnesty in any multilateral treaty, the reality of mixed state practice, and the improper conflation of prosecution obligations with anti-amnesty obligations. We also noted the importance of balancing states' prevention, suppression, and punishment obligations under international law.

Beyond these previous discussions about the legal merits of anti-amnesty positions, there are additional ones specific to the UN position that bear mention. First, it is not clear whether the UN position would accommodate a temporary or provisional amnesty covering international crimes. As Ron Slye notes, amnesties "are not meant to be temporary."[432] However, there are examples of such amnesties, including the Burundian Law No. 1/004 of May 8, 2003, which grants provisional immunity from prosecution for perpetrators of international crimes until an international judicial commission of inquiry – foreseen in an earlier peace accord – shall have issued findings on the matter.[433] Such amnesties, in theory, can allow a state the possibility of deferring prosecutions when delay may be necessary.[434]

A second area of ambiguity in the UN position concerns children, whom it may make sense to explicitly include in the benefit of an amnesty. By not being explicitly limited to adults, the UN position can create problems for the operation of DDR programs involving child combatants, who are viewed primarily as victims and only secondarily as perpetrators. It can do so by creating a perception of vulnerability to prosecution that does not likely exist in reality.[435] After all, even in ordinary times, children often are immune from criminal responsibility, and adolescents from full criminal punishment. Some may reasonably counter that an anti-amnesty rule explicitly limited to adults would lead to more forced recruitment of child soldiers, forcing them to commit ever more heinous acts. Yet such a concern will remain immaterial as long as the recruitment of child soldiers constitutes an international crime that is the subject of prosecutorial priority.

One final point is that the UN position is not specifically limited in application to "those bearing greatest responsibility" or some similar formulation.[436] Such a specification would seem to be in keeping with the actual practice and prioritization of international and hybrid criminal tribunals. It also would be in keeping with the reality that, in contexts of mass abuse, no combination of national and international justice efforts could ensure fair trials within a reasonable delay against more than a small percentage of those responsible for grave violations.[437]

6.2 Policy questions about the UN position

Beyond questions about the legal basis of the UN position, there is a broad range of policy questions that bears scrutiny. Indeed, amnesty is at least as much a policy question as a legal question.

First, it is beyond dispute that the UN position is neither an absolute good nor an absolute bad. The same was true of its previous positions on amnesty, and the same will be true of any future positions it adopts. Thus, a proper assessment of the current UN position requires us to assess its potential or actual benefits against its potential or actual costs – because it carries both.[438] Analysis of this sort would be required even if the UN position accurately reflected the state of international law, because whatever else it may be, the UN amnesty position is also a policy position. It involves choices, including about having a position in the first place, about the manner of expressing the position, and about the means of applying it. In this respect, the United Nations and its supporters should be confident that (1) having a position is better than having none at all, (2) the current formulation of the position is better than any alternative formulation, and (3) the manner of application of the position is better than any alternative application.

Yet even if the UN Secretariat satisfied itself on each of these points, it would remain important for skeptics to raise questions about the actual impact of the position in the external world, and in particular its impact in securing more peace, democracy, and human rights. After all, the purpose of having the position is, in part, to positively contribute to these global public goods. If such an impact is not evident, the United Nations and its supporters should be seriously concerned. We should be even more concerned if the position, or its manner of application, breaches the do-no-harm principle. This is the minimum form of responsibility for any public-interest institution.[439]

With these initial thoughts in mind, we now examine the principal arguments for and against the UN Secretariat's current amnesty position. For the sake of clarity, two disclaimers are in order. First, nothing expressed here should be understood as opposition or skepticism concerning the value of prosecution of individuals responsible for international crimes and gross human rights violations. To the contrary, the discussion implicitly recognizes that such persons, as a rule, should be prosecuted. The issue is whether and when, extraordinarily, that priority should give way to other more compelling priorities. Second, nothing here is meant to imply that those responsible for the development and application of the United Nations' amnesty position are unmindful of many of the risks and limitations of the position. At the same time, there is no indication of any formal or ongoing internal evaluation, or lessons learned process, concerning the positive and negative impacts of the UN position thus far. The same is true in terms of external evaluations. In that respect, a goal of this discussion is to raise questions and draw attention to possible unintended side effects of the UN position that we ought to debate more openly and broadly than has been the case to date.

6.2.1 The mediation influence argument

Defenders of the UN position assert that it will force UN mediators, and encourage non-UN mediators, to think about justice and international law questions more seriously and deeply than they have in the past and in so doing encourage them to "safeguard a space for justice."[440] By reputation, mediators generally are reluctant to prioritize justice issues in the context of peace negotiations and, in any case, may lack detailed knowledge about the constraints of international law.[441] In some cases, it is the mediators themselves who lead the parties toward amnesty.[442]

Skeptics query whether the UN's position could instead result in UN mediators losing a place at the negotiation table, thus leaving mediation to parties with less commitment to accountability. As Kristina Thorne of the Center for Humanitarian Dialogue observes:

> Every peace process involves negotiation, where insisting on the unconditional nature of specific provisions is likely to be difficult. Usually, provisions also cannot simply be imposed. Many mediators will also be wary of attempting to push for specific solutions, for the pragmatic reason that doing so may mean that they will no longer be welcome at the talks. There are also examples of mediators who have been so successful in pushing for demands – also on justice – in a previous process that their presence will not be welcomed by other conflict parties.[443]

Professor Christine Bell similarly notes that the new UN amnesty position could result in "normative-mediator dodging parties," and that it risks the United Nations ruling itself "out of the mediation business." Although ultimately such a risk is low for the United Nations, because it is usually present at peace talks in one way or another, Bell notes that "it would be clearly undesirable if all those who took their normative commitments seriously were ruled out of business."[444] It also would seem undesirable for UN representatives to become merely participants at mediation processes, not mediators themselves.[445] Apparently, the UN Secretariat was aware of this risk at the time of adopting its amnesty position.[446] However, it may have underestimated the scope of the risk for itself and overestimated the benefits for others.[447]

In addition, because international crimes are the crimes that international, hybrid, and foreign courts are most likely to reject from inclusion in an amnesty, the effect of the new UN position is to force its mediators to negotiate hardest on the elements of an amnesty that will present the least impediments to justice in practice. Such crimes are the most likely ones to be challenged domestically and to be rejected internationally. By contrast, a position that focused on other ways to limit an amnesty's scope – such as making the retention of an amnesty's benefits explicitly conditional on nonrecidivism – could make a significant difference at the domestic level in an area that we have more reason to fear will not be covered through the international jurisprudence on amnesties.[448]

6.2.2 The burden-of-persuasion argument

Defenders of the new UN position assert that it usefully places a burden on those seeking the restoration of peace or democracy to justify forgoing criminal accountability rather than placing a burden on those seeking criminal accountability to demonstrate why prosecutions would not endanger peace or democracy.

Skeptics, however, might question whether this placing of the burden can have the result of putting international justice interests ahead of valid but competing local peace and democracy interests.[449] The burden may seem particularly misplaced when a national government's decision to grant amnesty clearly reflects an overwhelming public sentiment.[450] As Steven Ratner and Jason Abrams argue:

> Although [international] crimes concern all mankind, it is ultimately the people of a state – past, present, and future – who remain most affected. If they have a democratically elected government, it must be their primary voice on this question. If that government rejects accountability in favour of a compromise with former abusers, amnesty, or other forms of impunity, or seeks to use accountability as a weapon against political enemies, almost any effort at accountability seems crippled, if not still-born. Although international law imposes some duties on states to refrain from such policies, proponents of accountability may end up bearing the burden of persuading a government to foreswear impunity.[451]

Professor Dwight Newman similarly comments:

> [W]e can question the too-rapid connection between a claim that international crimes constitute attacks on universal values and a conclusion that states thus must not be permitted to dispose of international crimes except in a manner dictated by the international community. In particular, the real difficulty is that international crimes are simultaneously local crimes, with local effects and with local costs in whatever course of action a state may undertake in response.[452]

It may be countered that pleading public support as a justification for amnesty can be tantamount to pleading internal law as a justification for breach of an international rule, which international law disallows.[453] States cannot, according to this argument, commit themselves to the terms of a treaty and then subsequently plead a democratic exception to their application. Yet such an argument fails to take account of international lawmaking's own democratic deficit. International lawmaking tends to be much less public and participatory than domestic lawmaking.[454] In that respect, insistence on upholding the UN position could lead to the United Nations, and by association, international law, appearing as interfering agents in the eyes of the local population – especially if the UN position contradicts an overwhelming and legitimate local prioritization of peace and security through amnesty.[455] In the end, the government and citizens of such a country may be content to ignore the purported exigencies of international law or simply to live with the consequences of the international legal breach.[456]

A related, and crucial, question is whether the UN position imposes an unfair distribution of the burden of compliance on weak states for what is, in fact, a global public good. As Charles Trumbull observes: "[R]efusing to recognize amnesties places the cost of justice (a good for the entire international community) on conflict-ridden states. People living in states in which the crimes occur may have to bear extended hostilities in order for the international community to receive the benefit of bringing perpetrators to justice."[457] Granted, states bear a heavy burden to justify forgoing their prosecution obligations in respect of applicable international crimes.[458] However, as Mahnoush Arsanjani notes, amnesty may be viewed as a reasonable cost for removing tyrants "in the face of the unwillingness of the international community to pay the price necessary for stopping serious domestic violence."[459] Indeed, it is questionable for the international community to insist on extreme risk taking in support of a rule for which it will bear little of the human costs. Yet the net effect of the UN position, in some cases, is to vilify the weak and embattled state rather than the strong but unwilling international community. The sad reality is that too often it continues to be easier for the international community to mobilize around a court to vindicate the dead, than an army to save the living.

Yet another questionable aspect of the burden-of-persuasion argument is the fact that the UN position does not apply to amnesties adopted in states prior to the United Nations' adoption of the position. This is problematic because the position purports to be universal in application but fails to be so in at least two senses. First, with few exceptions, the most powerful democratic states of the West no longer have any foreseeable need to adopt transitional amnesties in their own domestic contexts.[460] Consequently, the UN position presents no direct threat to them, as it does to other states. Instead, it constitutes an opportunity to advance a new public good for others under the United Nations' banner of universal values. Second, the nonapplication of the UN position to pre–Rome Statute amnesties creates an undeserved free pass for states that adopted or inherited offensive amnesties before 1998. This free pass is not only undeserved – in legal, political, and ethical terms – but also counterproductive to the underlying objectives of the UN position. For example, broad and unconditional amnesties adopted in the 1960s and 1970s in countries such as Spain, Portugal, and France remain in full force.[461] To the extent that such states support and advocate the substantive content of the UN position, the nonrepeal of their own amnesties provides a convenient political pretext for cynical governments to adopt unprincipled amnesties. Such governments merely need to point a finger at countries like Spain and say, "We are following the Spanish approach, therefore leave us alone."[462]

Having reaped the domestic stabilizing benefits of amnesties over a period of decades, countries such as France, Portugal, and Spain are now in a position to do what less stable and democratic states can ill afford to consider, namely to do away with such amnesties altogether.[463] Doing so not only would have great symbolic importance. It also would contribute to the customary law aspirations of those who support the UN amnesty position.[464] In addition, it would be in line with the amnesty jurisprudence discussed earlier, according to which successor governments and judiciaries inheriting amnesties for human rights crimes are required to do everything within their means to cease to give effect to them.[465]

In that context, it is noteworthy that a number of successor governments in South American states – including Argentina, Chile, Uruguay, and Peru – have started to abrogate the amnesty laws they inherited from predecessor governments. Their actions demonstrate a form of political courage. They also demonstrate that as the capacity to do justice for past atrocities increases, the perceived need and legality of prior amnesties tends to decrease. In this regard, other states in Europe and elsewhere that adopted or inherited pre–Rome Statute amnesties covering human rights crimes and that now enjoy incomparable levels of social and political stability would do well to follow the South American example and begin to reconsider their own domestic amnesties.[466] In doing so, they also may come to recall how such amnesties helped facilitate their own political transitions and why, therefore, they ought to be reasonable in the amnesty bar they purport to impose on the vast and still unstable parts of the world where the luxury of spurning amnesty does not exist. As Professor Dan Markel observes:

> With the relative calm of our own period of post-war revitalization and reconciliation, we [in the West] risk forgetting how precarious the existence of early modern life was and, indeed, how precarious political life still is in many parts of the world today.... For this reason, it is necessary to recall our own cultural history to gain a little more understanding of the efforts towards reconciliation elsewhere in the world.[467]

6.2.3 The practical guidance argument

Defenders of the UN position assert that a simple formula, or red line, is required to guide negotiating and implementing parties in a clear and unequivocal manner on justice issues.[468] They also claim that a simple formula is necessary to help set a clear metric for the international community to use in assessing whether or not an amnesty deserves international support or condemnation.

However, skeptics will note that the simplicity and rigidity of the UN position could result in mediators, as well as human rights advocates, being less thoughtful about issues of impunity and the rule of law, thereby stifling possible solutions rather than encouraging policy creativity. For example, recourse to a formulaic approach on amnesties can result in the underexploration of other crucial limitations and conditions, beyond the exclusion of certain crimes, which also should form part of an amnesty.[469] In this regard, it is worth repeating the question of whether the South African TRC's amnesty regime, which did not exclude international crimes, was more or less principled than the 1996 amnesty in Guatemala or the 2002 amnesty in Macedonia, which did exclude certain international crimes but otherwise lacked attributes of accountability.[470] Must not there be something wrong with a principle that leads to such a result? Yet such a result flows directly out of the binary logic of the UN position, which discourages fine-grained analysis. With the UN position, there is only one relevant question: whether the amnesty excludes certain designated crimes. The answer to that question is a simple yes or no, and the answer in the case of South Africa's TRC would have been a no. This would seem an extraordinary, as well as embarrassing, result, but it is the necessary implication of the UN position as conceived and applied.

In practice, the majority of the United Nations' applications of the amnesty position have been in relation to individualized, conditional amnesties contemplated in truth commission mandates. Specifically, the UN position has been used to prevent the replication of the South African TRC model or any comparable variant.[471] Granted, there may be quite valid reasons for rejecting efforts at a modified South African model, such as the lack of a situation of urgency to justify an amnesty, or the absence of a parallel and credible threat of prosecution to make viable a modified truth-for-amnesty model.[472] Yet there also can be very good reasons for supporting such efforts, especially if amnesty is an objectively necessary part of a political settlement.

Among other things, the South African model still stands for the very important proposition that an applicant who fails to disclose his or her crimes will not receive amnesty and thus will remain liable to prosecution.[473] It also, of course, stands for the proposition that an amnesty process encompassing perpetrator disclosures can play a key role in the recovery of truth about past crimes, thus fulfilling to some degree the role of a criminal trial.[474] Such disclosures can have an unprecedented impact in helping to validate individual victim accounts of abuse and to reduce the public space for myths and historical revisionism about the nature and scale of past violations.[475] However, rather than build up from the South African TRC experience, the UN position involves a direct repudiation of it – all to keep intact what may amount to only a theoretical right to prosecution in the particular context.[476] Worse, though, the apparent effects of the UN position have included delaying or impeding the establishment of truth commissions,[477] limiting the capacity of truth commissions in their fact-finding role in relation to grave crimes,[478] and removing the United Nations from constructive engagement in eventual truth commission operations.[479]

An additional weakness of the UN's practical-guidance argument is that one can endorse the underlying premise of the argument without endorsing the specific content of the new UN position (i.e., a slightly different UN position potentially could be more effective).[480] One could also, or alternatively, propose a simple and general rule but supplement it with more detailed and nuanced metrics to ensure that the simple choice does not become the enemy of the wise choice. Such an approach could be described as a guidelines approach, and it would conform to Joinet's original conception of the Set of Principles on impunity from which the UN Secretariat drew much of its initial inspiration on the question of amnesty.[481] In following such an approach, "legal criteria [would] serve not as mechanical limits, but as explicitly postulated public order goals, reflecting values of human dignity, to guide decision makers."[482]

6.2.4 The counterweight argument

Defenders of the UN position assert that it will strengthen the ability of accountability-amenable states or governments to resist amnesty blackmail by those with the ability to perpetuate renewed or ongoing violence. The idea is that, in difficult negotiations, such states will be able to rely on the UN position to say to their blackmailers, "We are internationally prohibited from giving the amnesty you want," or "Even if we gave the amnesty you want, the international community would disregard it," and therefore, "Let's focus on what is negotiable."[483] It similarly is asserted, mutatis mutandis, that the UN position will help accountability-amenable nongovernmental organizations and lawyers to resist and defeat unprincipled national amnesties.[484] Yet another variation on this argument is that the UN position will force accountability-reluctant states to seek more principled transitional justice policies to appease the international community.

However, skeptics may consider that the UN position can end up removing an essential bargaining tool needed to achieve a peace agreement in the first place, thus contradicting any counterweight benefit.[485] Granted, the counterweight effect can increase if there are international efforts (e.g., sanctions and threats of armed force) to reduce the blackmail at the root of the amnesty dilemma. However, where such efforts are absent or insufficient, the theoretical benefit of the counterweight is actually a burden because it cuts off options precisely when they are most needed. It becomes a dead weight rather than a counterweight, putting a solution further away rather than bringing it closer. In a world in which we have effectively lost the option of exile, built a permanent ICC that creates a continuous and uncontrollable risk of arrest and prosecution, and generated an active European and Latin American practice of holding human rights trials before foreign courts, it is only logical to ask whether we needed to prohibit certain amnesties on top of all of this.[486]

Another weakness of the counterweight argument is that the UN position actually could prompt a negotiator to offer leniency and concessions in potentially riskier areas to compensate for the inability to offer a broad amnesty. For example, it could motivate a decision to offer violators the possibility of retaining more powerful positions in the country's security apparatus than would otherwise have occurred. It also could motivate dangerous offers, or illusory forms, of political power-sharing agreements that otherwise might have been avoided. With such agreements in place, wherein all abusers become party to a government of national unity, the prospect of justice can be even more remote than if a formal and conditional amnesty prevailed. In such contexts, there is no need to provide formal amnesty because the parties' control of the levers of power can help ensure that there will not be high-level prosecutions.[487] In short, the removal of the amnesty option can easily push the relevant stakeholders to pursue indirectly that which they cannot pursue directly. It will not eliminate the need for leniency but will more likely drive it underground, in this case resulting in an increase in dangerous power-sharing concessions or in increased impunity without any overt breaching of the UN position.[488] In brief, it is doubtful that taking away the amnesty option will alter any power balance or lead to better transitional justice outcomes. More likely, it will simply lead to concessions in other areas that are based on the realities of the balance of power at the negotiation table.

A skeptic also could make the related point that the UN position fails to take into account both a state's democratic credentials and its motivations in agreeing to an amnesty. It lumps together well-intentioned leaders – including successor governments, who are amenable to accountability but rely on amnesty because they want peace or democracy – with those who do so primarily to ensure their own impunity. This is notwithstanding the fact that good faith is a core principle of international law.[489] However, the effect of the new UN position is to remove the issue of a government's good faith from our evaluation of whether the specific amnesty is acceptable. As the South African Constitutional Court has rightly noted:

> Decisions of states in transition, taken with a view to assisting such transition, are quite different from acts of a state covering up its own crimes by granting itself immunity. In the former case, it is not a question of the governmental agents responsible for the violations indemnifying themselves, but rather, one of a constitutional compact being entered into by all sides, with former victims being well-represented, as part of an ongoing process to develop constitutional democracy and prevent a repetition of the abuses.[490]

The UN position seems particularly out of place in the era of failed, failing, and fragile states, in which official actors are often the least responsible for atrocities as compared to non-state armed groups. Such states need every possible conflict resolution tool to create the beginnings of a functioning state and of a real future for their citizens. Granted, a state's reasons for adopting an amnesty can vary enormously, and its motivations often are difficult to identify with precision.[491] However, a state's intentions and objectives – even if imperfectly understood – ought to be factors in the fair evaluation of any amnesty, whatever crimes it encompasses or excludes.[492]

This is not to say that the purported counterweight effect of the UN position is a mirage. Indeed, sometimes the position will achieve the desired impact. However, the concern is that it may sometimes have precisely the opposite impact, and this fact should be acknowledged. As Professor William Schabas observes, "[T]hose who argue that peace cannot be bartered in exchange for justice, under any circumstances, must be prepared to justify the likely prolongation of an armed conflict."[493]

6.2.5 The rigid and principled stand argument

Defenders of the UN position assert that ethics, as well as concern for the dignity of victims, require such a position even if it causes practical difficulties in peace processes. The argument is that the United Nations is a unique moral authority in the world and that it is important for it to take a principled stand on the issue, notwithstanding any undesired consequences that may result.

Defenders of the position argue that different actors play different roles in amnesty situations, and that the United Nations should hold to its principles, as others always will be there to argue for "exceptions" to the rules.

In response, a skeptic may reasonably contend that it would be irresponsible to ignore the human costs of the policy, and that if the new position's costs ultimately outweigh its benefits, any victories on principle likely will be Pyrrhic ones in practice. Such costs cannot be measured simply by asking the binary question of whether an amnesty satisfies or contradicts the UN position. That would lead to positive conclusions every time the content of the UN position is facially satisfied, without any analysis of the negative impacts – direct or indirect – that may be caused by or associated with the pursuit of positional compliance. The real question – the one that actually provides the full picture of the position's costs – is what specific effects, positive and negative, are resulting from the pursuit of conformity with the UN position? That question merits an exercise in objective research.

Skeptics also may note that the adoption of a rigid stand goes against the leading theory on negotiation, which emphasizes focusing on interests, not positions – an approach that is especially important when one is not able to impose demands on the other negotiating party.[494] As the authors of the leading text on the subject note, "[W]hile adopting a bottom line may protect you from accepting a very bad agreement, it may keep you both from inventing and agreeing to a solution it would be wise to accept."[495] They conclude: "Even with someone like Hitler or Stalin, we should negotiate if negotiation holds the promise of achieving an outcome that, all things considered, meets our interests better than our BATNA (best alternative to a negotiated agreement)."[496]

Rather than adopt a strict stand, some suggest that a better approach would be for the United Nations to treat the substantive position as the default rule – thus, raising the bar on policy – but be flexible in the application. This alternative approach could be described as principled flexibility – as distinct from the current approach, which could be described as principled inflexibility. Both are principled positions – the disagreement is only one of tactic, not of principle. An advantage of the principled flexibility approach is that it would allow for increased contextual analysis and a greater balancing of competing public interest considerations while still preserving the essential content of the substantive position. It also would eliminate the strategic and reputational risks that are inherent to any simplistic, bottom-line approach.[497] While some persons may view flexibility on this issue as an invitation to cynical exploitation that jeopardizes global accountability efforts, they ought to simultaneously acknowledge the risk, if not the reality, that implacable opposition to certain kinds of amnesties will hinder peace efforts – and thus domestic justice efforts – in complicated and massively violent situations. The true choice is not between human rights and realpolitik; it is between different ways of ensuring human rights.

6.2.6 The deterrence of violence argument

Defenders of the new UN position assert that it can help dissuade warlords and tyrants from launching or continuing campaigns of mass violence. Having a rule against amnesty, they argue, can help to counter the perverse incentive to strategically increase levels of violence as a means to obtain a broad and general amnesty.[498]

However, a skeptic quickly will note that requiring an amnesty to exclude international crimes amounts to requiring a threat of national prosecution to remain, which easily can lead to the entrenchment of tyrants or rebel groups, with all of the terrible human consequences that entails.[499] The hard truth is that, where democratic and peaceful actors are not able to impose the terms of a settlement, the likelihood increases that the threat of trials will undermine prospects of a transitional accord. Indeed, considering that the individuals most likely to engage in campaigns of mass violence are those who are most vulnerable to prosecution, one must ask how realistic it is to expect them to agree to peace or the transfer of power if immediately on signature they and their closest cohorts would face criminal punishment and jail.[500] Such individuals, naturally, become "spoilers."[501]

Of course, the conduct of spoilers – and in particular their amnesty black-mail – needs to be openly condemned. *They* are the problem. However, con-demnation does not actually achieve much. It does not change the fact of blackmail, and it rarely mobilizes states with the ability to effectively prevent or end the blackmail into action. In this context, amnesty remains one of the few available, albeit limited, national options to potentially halt or end the blackmail and facilitate the beginnings of a transitional process that over time may include DDR programs, IDP resettlement, and other peace-building measures.

Unfortunately, an effect of the UN position is to push back the possibilities of conflict resolution. The position sends a signal to the blackmailers that their best option is to increase the violence-driven blackmail until the other side to the negotiation finds an amnesty surrogate, such as an increased share of political and military power, to offer as the price for ending the terror. As Professor Jack Snyder observes:

> Where human rights violators are too weak to derail the strengthening of the rule of law, they can be put on trial. But where they have the ability to lash out in renewed violations to try to reinforce their power,

the international community faces a hard choice: either commit the resources to contain the backlash or offer the potential spoilers a deal that will leave them weak but secure.[502]

Amnesties have traditionally been crucial parts of transitional pacts. If they are now off the table, while terror reigns and the balance of power is unsettled, what is there to replace amnesties if not something equal or worse? Ruthless and megalomaniac leaders may tolerate a loss of power if they can get amnesty or exile, but without either, they and their cronies have that much greater cause to consolidate their control through violence and other similar means.[503] In this sense, taking amnesty off the table risks producing only the most illusory forms of victory for human rights.

To be sure, it is a dissatisfying outcome to concede an amnesty in the name of peace or reconciliation, but at the barrel of a gun. Yet it is at least as dissatisfying to concede, at the barrel of the same gun, an unstable power-sharing arrangement with a pitiless and corrupt tyrant or warlord because one is unable to concede certain kinds of amnesty. Ongoing or increased militarization and armed conflict because of an inability to offer a secure amnesty would hardly be a satisfying outcome either. The point is that, in the absence of an ability and willingness on the part of national or international actors to halt or end the blackmail, we need every option possible. As long as the UN position on amnesties remains unchanged, we have one less solution to try, and terrorized civilian populations have one more reason to fear for the worst.

6.2.7 The ethics and rule of law argument

Defenders of the new UN position assert that some prices are not worth paying because the loss in universal values and norms is too high. The idea is that, for certain kinds of crime, we should not even entertain discussion about amnesty because to do so would irredeemably undermine the rule of law and the public's confidence in it.[504]

Skeptics, however, may respond that if the cost of the position in human lives is significantly greater than the cost in terms of abstract principles, the former should trump. From a human rights perspective, the argument seems almost self-evident. As Max Pensky argues:

> [T]he anti-amnesty norm has been justified predominantly as a component of a battle against impunity, and impunity has been understood virtually entirely in non-consequentialist terms, as a retributive principle of narrowly defined criminal justice according to which the desert of punishment alone grounds a positive duty to prosecute and punish, on deontic grounds. If this positive duty – either alone or in combination

with the rights of victims to legal remedy – is taken as a serious side constraint to any consequentialist evaluation of policy options for overcoming endemic violence, then the anti-amnesty norm seems to me to be fatally weak, intuitively implausible, and very defeasible by the kinds of consequentialist considerations all too vividly on display in the Northern Uganda situation.[505]

A skeptic also may remark that there is no guarantee of preserving the rule of law even in situations in which amnesties are avoided. For example, in contemporary civil wars, the monopoly on violence and crime does not usually rest with one side alone. Multiple actors, including state and parastatal forces, may be guilty of horrendous crimes. If in the aftermath of such wars, one side emerges as a clear victor able to impose its terms on the others, criminal justice might apply one-sidedly or as a form of judicial revenge. Such a development would hardly qualify as a contribution to the consolidation of the rule of law.

Another concern about the UN amnesty position relates, paradoxically, to the cost of its successful application. To the extent that an amnesty conforms to the UN position by excluding international crimes and gross human rights violations, it could have the perverse effect of creating the illusion of a rule of law triumph, thus resulting in a relaxation rather than an invigoration of international pressure on the government in question. As previously noted, amnesties tend to create only a negative obligation to refrain from prosecuting those covered by the law. International attention and pressure usually will be required to ensure respect for the corollary obligation to prosecute those not covered by the amnesty (i.e., those presumed responsible for international crimes and gross human rights violations). In brief, amnesties that exclude such crimes do not amount to victories for domestic criminal accountability, but only the future possibility of such accountability.

6.3 Alternatives to the current UN position

Two main arguments were advanced throughout this section – a legal one, namely that the UN position does not reflect customary international law, and a policy one, namely that the UN position may in reality do more harm than good. We now briefly consider what options may exist for an alternative UN position, bearing in mind the organization's preference for plain formulations. At least six options are apparent, each of which also can be described as a position of principle. These are the following:

- "The United Nations considers that amnesties for (crimes x, y, z) are generally incompatible with international law." This formulation would make clear that the UN presumes such amnesties to be in violation of international law yet still leave room for reasonable exceptions based on countervailing legal and policy considerations. In determining whether a particular amnesty overcomes the presumed incompatibility with international law, there would need to be a careful and detailed examination of multiple factors, such as the context, the parties' intentions, the process, the amnesty's legal content, and the likely external demonstration effect.

- "The United Nations will not condone or endorse amnesties that fail to conform to the international legal obligations of the concerned state." This formulation would constitute recognition of the legal reality of amnesties, for which there is no custom-based prohibition. It would engage the United Nations and others in a serious examination of the concerned state's specific international legal commitments – both treaty and customary – with a view to ensuring that they are upheld in letter and in spirit.

- "The United Nations expects all states to make a good faith effort to prosecute (crimes x, y, z), especially against those bearing greatest responsibility for such crimes." This formulation would focus on the affirmative obligation to prosecute as opposed to the negative obligation to refrain from amnestying such crimes. It incorporates a good-faith metric to ensure a government-specific evaluation. In addition, the formulation includes a greatest-responsibility metric to emphasize where prosecutions will inevitably have to focus, and to facilitate a possible DDR process.

- "The United Nations considers that amnesties for (crimes x, y, z) cannot bind international, mixed, or foreign courts." The mere existence of the independent ICC already makes it more difficult for mediators to consider or guarantee the application of an amnesty, no matter how genuine and compelling the need. The current UN position makes it that much harder, and in an area in which there is comparatively little need in light of the globalization of criminal accountability mechanisms.[506] This alternative formulation of the UN position would make clear the organization's opposition to amnesties for grave crimes while implicitly recognizing that a rule of the UN Secretariat cannot in any case bind states at the domestic level. The formulation would have the additional virtue of allowing flexibility in the conception of the amnesty's content.

- "The United Nations will not condone or endorse an amnesty unless it is explicitly revocable for any individual beneficiary who breaches its material terms or who commits, after the amnesty's entry into force, any of the crimes it covers." By adopting such a position, the United Nations would make clear that conflict resolution and the prevention of new human rights violations are the organization's highest priorities, as implied in the UN Charter. In addition, the position would directly contribute to the criminal law's objective of deterrence, both general and specific. It also would keep fully intact the possibility of justice against individuals in breach of the amnesty's terms, including the possibility of their prosecution for both the new and old crimes.[507]

- "The United Nations will proactively advocate truth, justice, reparation, and reform measures in the context of any national or international negotiations on the restoration of good governance or the end of armed conflict." This formulation would convert the current negatively-worded position (which sets out what the United Nations is against) into a positively-worded position (which expresses what the United Nations is for). Taking the position seriously would imply an opposition to most amnesties and a welcome turn toward what can be gained through transitional justice rather than what can be lost through amnesty. The formulation would have the additional benefit of encouraging a creative and customized exploration of a wide range of accountability mechanisms.

Some naturally may react to the foregoing formulations as dangerous because they could attenuate the strength of the current UN position. The concern is understandable. However, one also reasonably could characterize these formulations as refinements of the current position – refinements that increase the prospect of achieving the best human rights outcome in the context of a delicate negotiation, while better reflecting the true state of ambiguity and flexibility in international law.

We also should recall the uncertainty about whether the current UN position is cumulatively producing more harm than good in actual practice. No one has yet assessed the issue seriously. Consequently, just as there would be risks involved in changing the current UN position, there are also risks in maintaining it. The crucial issue is which policy – the current one or a revised one – would offer the most benefits while carrying the least risks.[508]

7. CONCLUSIONS

This first part of the book has examined a number of different aspects of the amnesty debate, including questions of law, policy, and ethics, at both theoretical and practical levels. The term *amnesty* was defined and compared with analogous legal instruments that confer leniency for criminal conduct. There followed an evaluation of the issue of amnesty in the context of the fight against impunity, which paid particular attention to amnesty's relation to the field of transitional justice and which challenged some of the negative claims made about the impact of amnesties. Thereafter the position of amnesties in international law was assessed, raising new questions about its status and proposing several alternative accounts of its potential legality under international law. The discussion then focused on the relevance of the ICC, and the Rome Statute framework as a whole, on the handling of amnesty issues globally. Finally, there was a critical analysis of the current UN policy on amnesties and exploration of alternative formulations.

By way of conclusion, it seems that a fundamental reframing of the debate on amnesty is warranted. The debate is not, as some suggest, between peace and justice, or even between impunity and justice. It is between competing conceptions of justice. It is a debate between those who privilege the human dignity and interests of victims of past abuse through opposition to amnesties for serious crimes, and those who privilege the human dignity and interests of victims of verifiable current abuse and inevitable future abuse through tolerance of amnesties for serious crimes in exceptional cases. In both cases, the issue is one of justice and human dignity. In that respect, it should not be seen as automatically a contradiction – in human rights terms – to be simultaneously pro-prosecutions and pro-amnesties.[509]

Moving forward, we also must avoid a kind of South African exceptionalism whereby every other society in need of amnesty now must uphold a higher standard of accountability than South Africa. Variations on the dilemma South Africa faced in the early 1990s continue to arise all the time around the globe, with some that are more agonizing and intractable, and others that are less so. Yet not for a moment should we imagine that the choices South Africa faced were so unique and exigent that all other societies – even the most broken and failed ones – must do better than it did in its own moment of truth. Indeed, South Africa is more a symptomatic case than an exceptional one.[510]

With these few considerations in mind, Part II will provide a detailed framework of analysis and design to guide the future amnesty dilemmas that will continue to arise – unless and until we demonstrate more ability and willingness to prevent such dilemmas from arising in the first place.

PART II

The Design of Amnesties

1. INTRODUCTION

Accepting the regrettable fact that new amnesties will continue to arise and tend to remain in force years and decades later, this part of the book presents an original amnesty design methodology to help limit the damage that amnesties exact on the international rule of law and victims' rights. Many of the amnesties referred to here are not ones that ever would be supported as such by right-thinking persons. However, the reason for including unprincipled amnesties is the same as the reason for including more principled amnesties, namely, to glean useful lessons and inventive options for possible application in the negotiation and design of future amnesties.

The amnesty framework presented here neither is the first attempt nor will it be the last to list the elements or conditions for a legitimate amnesty. Yet the framework is original – it incorporates elements proposed by others while also filling some important gaps. In that respect, it might be an advance on the status quo in terms of its structure and content. In addition, the framework may prove useful in the design of leniency measures other than amnesty. For, even if the frequency of the worst forms of amnesty periodically diminishes, the general need of leniency options never will disappear as long as negotiation remains a feature of conflict resolution.

The discussion is divided into three main sections. The first section examines the full implications of the proposition that an amnesty covering human rights crimes should be adopted only as a last recourse. This book proposes the last recourse standard as a minimal, and prior, threshold to considering questions of amnesty design. For an amnesty to constitute a last recourse, at least three criteria must be satisfied: first, there must be a situation urgent and grave enough to merit consideration of a potential amnesty; second, there must be an exhaustion of any options that might be appropriate – up to and including the potential use of armed force – to end the urgent and grave human rights situation that facilitates amnesty blackmail; and third, failing the ability to end the urgent and grave situation, all leniency options, short of amnesty, should be exhausted.

The second section discusses the overarching criteria that should be applied to guide specific design choices for an amnesty that has passed the last recourse threshold. First, the process for adopting the amnesty should be as consultative and democratic as possible. Second, the amnesty should be entrenched as minimally as possible in the legal system. Third, the amnesty should pursue a legitimate end. Fourth, the amnesty should confer the minimum leniency possible on the beneficiaries. Fifth, the amnesty should impose the maximum conditions possible on the beneficiaries. Sixth, the amnesty should be designed in a manner that is maximally viable in practice, not only in the sense of having a well-designed supervisory structure but also in the sense of being accompanied – where possible – by transitional justice mechanisms and a range of other peacebuilding measures.

Using the overarching criteria presented in the second section, and drawing on the amnesty database developed for this book, the third section offers a detailed set of specific design options for constructing the content of an amnesty. For example, in the discussion on the criterion of minimum leniency, five subcategories of amnesty design choices are listed: (1) the crimes or acts that are expressly eligible or ineligible for amnesty; (2) the persons who are expressly eligible or ineligible for amnesty; (3) the express legal consequences of the grant of amnesty for the beneficiary; (4) the geographical scope of application; and (5) the temporal scope of application. Within each of these subcategories, more specific design choices are then presented. For example, in the second subcategory, six specific options are presented, including distinctions according to rank and forms of criminal participation, and express exclusion of beneficiaries of prior amnesties.

There is, of course, no guarantee that the application of the proposed framework will result in an amnesty universally regarded as legitimate or effective. One can be certain that some will disagree that a particular amnesty was strictly necessary in the circumstances, sufficiently circumscribed to exclude the right sets of crimes or persons, or adequately accompanied by parallel gestures aimed at assisting the victims. Yet the use of this framework can help to considerably narrow the odds for regret and error. That is not an insignificant result when one considers all that is at stake for victims and society as a whole in contexts of terror and mass violence.

2. LAST RECOURSE THRESHOLD

In Part I of this book, the legal defenses of necessity, distress, and force majeure were discussed. It was argued that any one of them potentially could apply in the context of an amnesty dilemma. While it is impossible to be certain of their applicability in the abstract, as every amnesty context is factually distinct, each of the three defenses contains within it the idea that the action in question constitutes a "last recourse."[1] The argument of this section is that, because of their extreme interference with the ordinary application of the law and the rights of victims, amnesties for human rights crimes should be adopted only as a last recourse. This does not mean that they must fit into one of the three mentioned defenses, because an amnesty could be justified as a last recourse on other legal grounds, such as the need of the state to ensure the right to life or the prevention of other grave violations, as explained in Part I. However, for the adoption or retention of such an amnesty to even merit consideration as a legitimate exercise of law, it must have been adopted as a last recourse in the sense described subsequently. If one takes victims' rights even moderately seriously, such a procedural threshold is evidently necessary.

The last recourse threshold criteria are divided into three sequential parts: first, the determination of whether an urgent and grave situation exists; second, the exhaustion of appropriate options to overcome the urgent and grave situation, and thus reduce the scope for amnesty blackmail; and third, the exhaustion of leniency options, short of amnesty, to end the blackmail resulting from a failure to end the urgent and grave situation.

2.1 Existence of an urgent and grave situation

The last recourse criterion implies, in the first instance, a hard-nosed assessment of the seriousness of the circumstances prompting the need for an amnesty decision in the first place. The situation must be, objectively speaking, exceptional. However, it must also be clearly dangerous to some fundamental interests, such as public and human security on a mass scale. Stated otherwise, it must arise in "wholly exceptional circumstances in which a supreme public interest arises and in which no other reasonable solution presents itself."[2] The situation cannot, in this respect, be merely one of inconvenience. It needs to be one involving a plausible scenario of contin-ued or renewed violence or instability of a high order and on a large scale.[3] As Louise Mallinder rightly argues, a genuine belief in the need for amnesty to avert mass violence ought to be considered a ground in favor of amnesty reco-gnition.[4]

In and of itself, however, the existence or threat of a grave and violent situation is insufficient to justify the invocation of an amnesty covering human rights crimes. Other procedural criteria need to be exhausted before such an amnesty can be properly described as a last recourse.

2.2 Exhaustion of appropriate options to end the urgent and grave situation

When it comes to questions of accountability for international crimes, nego-tiating leverage is often an essential precondition for avoiding amnesty black-mail, and hence avoiding amnesty itself. Granted, sometimes such leverage is unnecessary – as, for example, a situation in which a "mutually hurting stalemate" has been reached.[5] In such instances, the stalemate itself acts as the leverage on the warring parties, making it difficult or undesirable for any side to conduct blackmail. However, in most cases of amnesty, such a stalemate is not present and there will instead be a strong element of blackmail at play. The blackmailer's spoken or unspoken threat is that, without amnesty, there will be no prospect of negotiated settlement and the abuses or mass violence will continue or possibly worsen.

In this regard, a logical means for seeking to avoid amnesty is to work to end the circumstances that enable amnesty blackmail to take place in the first instance. In other words, if one can adopt measures likely to weaken a party that is a genuine enemy of human rights, it may be possible to achieve the leverage necessary to avoid having to negotiate or accept extreme concessions to the cause of justice. As Thomas Friedman has succinctly observed in another context, "When you have leverage, talk. When you don't have leverage, get some. Then talk."[6]

There is a wide range of political, economic, diplomatic, and legal mea-sures that can be invoked to try to achieve such leverage and thus over-come the urgent and grave conditions leading to amnesty blackmail. For example, individual states and multilateral organizations can employ incen-tives such as debt cancellation, as well as "trade access, development assis-tance, beneficial trade agreements, investment offers, or membership in a regional economic organization."[7] They also can engage in coercive diplomacy. This may encompass threats or decisions to impose economic sanctions, aid conditionalities, cultural and sporting bans, travel restrictions, suspension or expulsion from membership in international organizations, withdrawal of military cooperation, severance of diplomatic relations, arms embargoes, and asset freezes.[8] Measures such as these have experienced a mix of failures and successes, but when they are well conceived and enforced, they can be effective in mitigating the pace and scale of perpetration of mass violence.[9] Establishing an international or hybrid commission of inquiry can also increase leverage by creating the threat of embarrassing revelations and potential prosecutions. This, too, is an approach with a reasonably long pedigree in practice.[10] The establishment of an ad hoc international or hybrid criminal tribunal, when backed up with a credible threat of enforcement of arrest warrants, is another potential means of achieving leverage (even if leverage is not the primary raison d'être of such a tribunal).[11] There is also, of course, the prospect of leverage through actions of the ICC prosecutor, who has the ability – if not the goal – to change the dynamics of a conflict by opening and conducting an investigation,[12] or by requesting an arrest warrant.[13]

Prior to or simultaneous with the exercise of any of the foregoing options, there usually are formal negotiation or mediation efforts, or similar types of preventive diplomacy. In the context of such efforts, it often is taken for granted that one or more of the parties expects to receive amnesty as part of any final settlement. However, Priscilla Hayner judiciously observes that one ought not to make such a presumption. Sometimes the unlikeliest of parties will countenance the absence of an amnesty. There are many possible reasons for such an outcome, but at least one is that an amnesty, by its nature, implies wrongdoing.[14] Certain negotiating parties may believe themselves to have clean hands or may have a strong self-interest in preserving such an image, however different the objective facts may be. By refraining to seek an amnesty, such parties actually help indirectly to prevent the grant of amnesty.[15] Paradoxically, these same parties may even advocate justice measures in a political agreement, notwithstanding the fact that the measures ultimately could expose them to personal criminal accountability. Such a scenario can arise, for example, when one party believes that the exclusive or primary culpability for past abuses lies with the other side, while the other side believes the exact opposite. In other words, both sides may see justice measures simultaneously as a tool to vindicate their own legitimacy and claim to clean hands, and as a weapon to harm the public image of their military and political enemies.[16] Such a belief may amount to wishful thinking, but the result for justice is mostly a positive one. The same outcome also could arise where a party in power omits to oppose amnesty because of a sense of invulnerability before the domestic justice system, which it actively may have corrupted during years in government.

Yet there always will be times when such dynamics do not apply and when negotiations and nonviolent measures such as public condemnation, financial incentives, sanctions, inquiries and the like prove insufficient to prevent or end the circumstances that produce amnesty blackmail. Peace agreements, even when successfully concluded, frequently break down on implementation and therefore even the best mediation also has its limits.[17] In addition, arrest warrants may remain unexecuted for years at a stretch, as international courts lack formal enforcement powers. As a result, sometimes the use of armed force, or alternatively the credible threat of armed force, may become a morally necessary option to consider for purposes of ending the conditions of extreme violence and human suffering that facilitate amnesty blackmail. In some instances the use of armed force can be non-coercive in nature, as in the case of preventive deployments by UN troops in Macedonia in the 1990s and by South African troops in Burundi since 2000.[18] Examples such as this are largely uncontroversial, as are a number of modern coercive peacekeeping missions, which typically possess strong civilian protection components.[19] However, the reality is that there are many instances where only coercive peacemaking force will be effective in potentially ending amnesty blackmail.

Here we come to an issue closely related to this book's prevention-oriented philosophy on amnesty, namely, the concept of the responsibility to protect, often referred to as R2P. This principle, which among other things purports to authorize the use of armed force in specific and extraordinary circumstances, was endorsed formally by UN member states in the Outcome Document of the High-Level Plenary Meeting of the General Assembly in September 2005.[20] The document's relevant parts declare as follows:

138. Each individual State has the responsibility to protect its populations from genocide, war crimes, ethnic cleansing and crimes against humanity. This responsibility entails the prevention of such crimes, including their incitement, through appropriate and necessary means. We accept that responsibility and will act in accordance with it. The international community should, as appropriate, encourage and help States to exercise this responsibility and support the United Nations in establishing an early warning capability.

139. The international community, through the United Nations, also has the responsibility to use appropriate diplomatic, humanitarian and other peaceful means, in accordance with Chapters VI and VIII of the Charter, to help protect populations from genocide, war crimes, ethnic cleansing and crimes against humanity. In this context, we are

prepared to take collective action, in a timely and decisive manner, through the Security Council, in accordance with the Charter, including Chapter VII, on a case-by-case basis and in cooperation with relevant regional organizations as appropriate, should peaceful means be inadequate and national authorities manifestly fail to protect their populations from genocide, war crimes, ethnic cleansing and crimes against humanity. We stress the need for the General Assembly to continue consideration of the responsibility to protect populations from genocide, war crimes, ethnic cleansing and crimes against humanity and its implications, bearing in mind the principles of the Charter and international law. We also intend to commit ourselves, as necessary and appropriate, to helping States build capacity to protect their populations from genocide, war crimes, ethnic cleansing and crimes against humanity and to assisting those which are under stress before crises and conflicts break out.

As laudable as the principle of R2P appears, it is important to bear in mind that its legal status is not settled. There is no R2P treaty, and resolutions of the UN General Assembly are not binding.[21] Although under certain circumstances such resolutions may contribute to the progressive establishment of a customary rule, in the absence of any corresponding state practice, R2P could not be considered a customary norm. Furthermore, the R2P concept does not entail a relaxation of the prohibition on the use of force outside of the system of collective security.[22] The General Assembly specifically calls for action to be taken "through the United Nations" and "through the Security Council." Under the UN Charter, an armed intervention not authorized by the Security Council and not justified on the basis of collective self-defense is illegal.[23] This feature of the Charter naturally produces a blockage for the potential use of armed force under the R2P doctrine. The UN Security Council includes five permanent members with veto powers. A coercive armed intervention that is implacably opposed by a permanent member – whether in a matter directly implicating it or in a matter affecting a close ally or vital interest – can potentially be impeded by veto and thereby rendered legally impermissible. In short, in the absence of Security Council authorization of the use of such force, the appeal to the principle of R2P remains mainly a moral one.[24]

Even in the event of Security Council authorization, it is far from certain that a majority of the world's wealthiest and most powerful states would be willing to risk large numbers of their own soldiers' lives in defense of any R2P-based coercive military intervention in the absence of any clear public support or benefit. Already, in far less dangerous circumstances, governments have – with some notable exceptions[25] – found every possible justification for either not sending troops into dangerous situations or not deploying them in a combat capacity.[26] It is difficult to ignore the unfairness of this failure when it is precisely those states able but unwilling to put an end to atrocities that then insist on the need to bar amnesties for those same atrocities. The unfairness is doubly compounded – and possibly tips into the realm of international illegality – when any such states also sell or provide weapons to the known malefactors in the particular conflict or repressive state structure.[27]

In brief, it seems as an international community we have advanced less on the prevention front as compared to our advances on the punishment and anti-amnesty front. In this respect, we would do well to link the question of amnesty and the question of R2P. For a transitional amnesty to constitute a last recourse – as it must – a readiness needs to exist to end the conditions that cause the amnesty dilemma from arising in the first place. And sometimes, even if it is only in the rarest of cases, that will require a coercive use of force consistent with the R2P principle. Unfortunately, since the General Assembly's endorsement of R2P – itself a principle of last recourse – the coercive dimension of the principle has yet to be applied in a concrete situation. This is so notwithstanding a significant number of appeals to do so in the context of manifest national failures in recent years to protect populations from genocide, war crimes, ethnic cleansing, and crimes against humanity in places such as Burma, Sudan, North Korea, and the Democratic Republic of the Congo.[28] The sad truth is that the international community has yet to demonstrate a depth of commitment to the letter and spirit of the promise of "never again."[29]

In the absence of a full-fledged doctrine of R2P and in the face of frequent paralyses of the system of collective security, it is reasonable to question the fairness of condemning those who may try to use amnesty as a way to avoid or end hell.[30] It is not acceptable to allow atrocities to come to their "natural" conclusion and then be ready to act by building a court of justice to prosecute those whom we enabled to kill when the dead still had lives. Naturally, in some contexts, the risks to human lives caused by the use of military intervention clearly will exceed the risks produced in doing nothing, in which case there would be an unjustifiable mismatch between the end (i.e., preventing conditions of amnesty blackmail) and the means (i.e., engaging in military intervention). In addition, the risk to human lives of an armed intervention always will be difficult to measure with a high level of certainty. Every case is a "tough case," and there is no panacea. However, if R2P is a principle we actually need and want to apply in practice, we should have the courage to make use of it when strictly and urgently necessary – and perhaps, as an indirect result, enable the arrest and prosecution of those who most belong in the dock while avoiding the blemish of one more amnesty achieved through blackmail.

2.3 Exhaustion of leniency options short of amnesty to end the blackmail

When all available and appropriate options to end an urgent and grave situation have been exhausted, and amnesty blackmail persists, there is still another crucial step to meet the last recourse threshold. Consideration needs to be given to other leniency measures, short of amnesty, that may be sufficient to meet the level of leniency objectively required in the situation.[31]

Knowing leniency's boundaries (i.e., whether the restoration of peace and democracy is possible without conceding an amnesty) is more art than science in any specific context. However, a generally reliable practice is to consult leading political analysts and human rights defenders of the country in question. Yet that alone is not enough. One also must be aware of the different technical options that exist on the leniency continuum and that should be exhausted before arriving at amnesty, which lies at its extreme end. If a leniency measure short of amnesty appears capable of achieving the equivalent public interest objectives (e.g., ending violent conflict or restoring democracy), then all else being equal, it is the preferable option.

Five types of leniency options, short of amnesty, are examined here: the omission of criminal accountability, reduced sentence schemes, alternative sentence schemes, use immunity schemes, and third-country asylum.

Omission of criminal accountability. In the context of negotiations aimed at ending conflict or changing a political regime, the question of past crimes is usually present in one form or another – and with it the prospect of criminal prosecutions. If third parties such as the United Nations are part of those negotiations, there is an increasing possibility that a specialized war crimes tribunal will be proposed. However, there is likewise a high probability that some of the stakeholders in the negotiations will promote the idea of the very opposite mechanism, namely amnesty. In the struggle between these opposing views, one form that leniency may take is an omission of both – neither explicit prosecution commitments nor explicit amnesty.[32] This was precisely what occurred, for example, at the 2001 Bonn talks concerning the transition out of Taliban rule in Afghanistan.[33] It appears that something similar happened in southern Sudan in respect of the 2005 Comprehensive Peace Agreement.[34] In both cases, the extant lack of any credible risk of domestic prosecution also may have facilitated the omission of amnesty.[35] Another approach is to contemplate the possibility of amnesties, or the possibility of trials, but without any definitive commitment to ensure either.[36]

This occurred, for example, in Liberia in the context of the 2003 Comprehensive Peace Agreement, which envisages only the possibility of a future amnesty,[37] and in Burundi in the context of the Arusha Accord, which envisages two investigative mechanisms, a possible specialized tribunal, and a possible amnesty.[38]

Reduced sentence schemes. As explained in Part I, reduced sentence measures lower but do not eliminate legal responsibility. They ensure there is a sentence that is served.[39] In addition, reduced sentence measures apply only after judgment, whereas amnesties can apply to persons in both prejudgment and postjudgment situations. Consequently, all else being equal, a reduced sentence scheme is preferable – in justice terms – to an amnesty scheme.[40] Colombia has been the site of perhaps more such schemes than any other country in modern times. At the height of narco-terrorism in Colombia in the late 1980s and early 1990s, a series of decrees was issued that required narco-terrorists to give criminal confessions to national courts in exchange for reduced sentences and immunity from extradition to the more-feared U.S. courts.[41] The scheme generally was perceived as successful in breaking up the main drug cartels.[42] A decade later, the Colombian government began separate negotiations with paramilitary groups that had caused untold suffering in the country and for whom a similar fear existed of extradition to U.S. courts.[43] Though controversial, the final law, titled the Justice and Peace Law[44] – which was approved with important modifications by the Colombian Constitutional Court[45] – marked an improvement on the approach of the narco-terrorism decrees. The final version of the law provides for a reduced sentence (misleadingly described as an "alternative sentence") and the conditional suspension of the remainder of the ordinary sentence "for demobilized members of illegal groups who cooperate fully in clarifying crimes, handing over illegally seized property for the purpose of contributing to reparations policies and clearly contributing to dismantle illegal structures."[46] It should be noted, however, that the bulk of paramilitary ex-combatants have received amnesty plus generous benefits; only the worst perpetrators are processed through the mechanisms established by the Justice and Peace Law.[47] Though based on a traditional and community-based form of justice, the *gacaca* system in Rwanda is another version of a reduced sentence scheme.[48]

Alternative sentence schemes. The first draft of Colombia's Justice and Peace Law, called the (draft) Law on Alternative Punishments, proposed a scheme that involved less accountability than the final law but that still ensured criminal accountability.[49] In essence, it proposed an alternative to prison that involved not a reduced sentence but a suspended sentence involving community service and reparation obligations but no jail time.[50] The truth commission model of Timor-Leste, which imposed community service and other obligations on criminal confessants concerning a limited set of offenses, used a similar legal framework.[51]

Use immunity schemes. As explained in *Black's Law Dictionary*, "Use immunity prohibits witness' compelled testimony and its fruits from being used in any manner in connection with criminal prosecution of the witness; on the other hand, transactional immunity affords immunity to the witness from prosecution for the offense to which his compelled testimony relates."[52] In the context of international criminal law, use immunity does not raise the same concerns as transactional immunity, which amounts to amnesty. Use immunity's function is to allow witnesses who are unwilling to testify voluntarily to be compelled to provide testimony that may be self-incriminating, on the condition that such testimony is barred from use against them in a simultaneous or future prosecution, other than for perjury.[53] Hence, use immunity is a preferable form of leniency to amnesty, all else being equal. Inspired by the South African Truth and Reconciliation Commission (TRC), early drafts of truth commission legislation often envision individualized amnesty schemes as a means to motivate perpetrators to confess, without even considering the less extreme alternative of use immunity. If properly designed in combination with a subpoena power, use immunity potentially could achieve the same objective as amnesty with less damage to victims' rights and no harm to procedural fairness.[54]

Third-country asylum. Unlike amnesties, third-country asylum deals – also known as sanctuary or exile arrangements – are not legal measures undertaken for the benefit of entire classes of persons. Instead, they are political measures undertaken for the benefit of specific individuals. In that respect, if an asylum deal can achieve the same public interest result as an amnesty, then it is a preferable option, all else being equal.

An asylum arrangement amounts to a political promise not to prosecute or extradite a presumed criminal, on the condition or understanding that the concerned individual will refrain from criminal activity or political meddling in his or her home country. In the past, asylum sometimes has functioned quite well. As Professor Michael Scharf observes:

> [E]xile and asylum in a foreign country (which puts the perpetrator out of the jurisdictional reach of domestic prosecution) is often used to induce regime change, with the blessing and involvement of significant states and the United Nations. Peace negotiators call this the 'Napoleonic Option,' in reference to the treatment of French emperor Napoleon Bonaparte who, after his defeat at Waterloo in 1815, was exiled to St. Helena rather than face trial or execution. More recently, a number of dictators have been granted sanctuary abroad in return for relinquishing power. Thus, for example, Ferdinand Marcos fled

the Philippines for Hawaii; Baby Doc Duvalier fled Haiti for France; Mengisthu Haile Miriam fled Ethiopia for Zimbabwe; Idi Amin fled Uganda for Saudi Arabia; General Raoul Cédras fled Haiti for Panama; and Charles Taylor fled Liberia for exile in Nigeria – a deal negotiated by the United States and U.N. envoy Jacques Klein.[55]

In recent years, however, the certainty once afforded by asylum deals has eviscerated significantly. First, as a result of a push for accession to the main human rights and related treaties, many more states have taken on specific obligations to extradite or prosecute persons responsible for international crimes. Second, the 110 states parties to the Rome Statute are less likely to participate as host countries for exile arrangements, inter alia, to avoid embarrassment if an ICC arrest warrant were to be issued against an exiled individual within their borders.[56] A third and even more significant complication for exile arrangements is the precedent established by the case of the former Liberian president Charles Taylor. He received asylum in Nigeria in 2003, an action that at the time helped shift the balance of power in his country and bring an end to its civil war.[57] As Michael Scharf notes, "The exile deal averted the crisis and set the stage for insertion of a U.N. peacekeeping mission that stabilized the country and set it on a path to peace and democracy."[58] However, when the Special Court for Sierra Leone issued an international warrant for Taylor's arrest later that same year – a warrant that ultimately was enforced – a major precedent was set. Human rights defenders broadly viewed the annulment of the asylum arrangement as a victory for justice because it reinforced the principle of no safe haven, whereas conflict resolution specialists broadly viewed it as counterproductive for peacemaking.[59] Although Taylor allegedly had broken the asylum deal by continuing to interfere in Liberian politics from his Nigerian sanctuary, this point seldom was captured in the headlines, with the result that exile arrangements have come to be seen as illusions –as traps for naive and foolish leaders.[60] Indeed, what dictator will really believe in the next asylum deal that is offered?[61] The honest answer is very few.[62] As a consequence, rather than seek tenuous exile in a country not one's own, the more attractive course of action for today's dictators and war criminals is to remain in one's own country and pursue the broadest amnesty possible. In the absence of the asylum option, amnesty increasingly is akin to Churchill's notion of democracy: the worst option, except for all the others.

In summary, then, amnesty should be considered only as a last recourse. It needs to arise in a context of urgency, and all appropriate options to prevent or mitigate amnesty blackmail should be exhausted before agreeing to such a measure. Granted, it always will be difficult to determine whether or when such criteria have been met, as fact patterns in amnesty contexts are invariably complex. Yet in a world in which we owe a duty of care to victims, the last recourse threshold is an essential metric for avoiding precipitous and superfluous concessions to accountability. At the same time, whether we like it or not, sometimes amnesty genuinely is a last recourse – as it appears to have been in places ranging from France in the 1960s to Spain in the 1970s, Argentina in the late 1980s, Haiti, Lebanon, and South Africa in the 1990s, and Angola in the early 2000s.

At the point when a situation objectively has reached this stage in any particular context, questions of amnesty design naturally come to the fore. This is the subject of the remaining sections of this part of the book.

3. OVERARCHING PARAMETERS FOR AMNESTY DESIGN

The content and structure of amnesties are technically complex. Unless the approach is constructed carefully, more leniency may be extended than is required in the situation and less accountability included.[63] Indeed, amnesty practice is not only an exercise in defining what ought to be excluded. It is also one of designing what ought to be included.[64]

Before describing any specific and detailed amnesty design choices, it is important to articulate the overarching considerations that should guide the making of those choices. This section will look at six such considerations, beginning with an analysis of the process for adopting a legitimate amnesty and ending with the question of what accompanying measures can help ensure that an amnesty stands the best chance of being effective in practice.

3.1 A legitimate process

The legitimacy of the amnesty adoption process is an important prior issue to discussing questions of an amnesty's content. Surprisingly, international human rights law has nothing specific to say on the question of public consultation and participation in the context of lawmaking and peacemaking processes, with the exception of some limited and indirect jurisprudence on the right to self-determination.[65] It also has nothing to say on the more particular question of victim consultation and victims' participation in such processes. Yet the lack of international legal guidance on this subject has not deterred the evolution of innovations in practice in transitional contexts.[66] Such practices, especially those encompassing the voices of marginalized victims, are coming to be seen as a sine qua non of the legitimacy of transitional justice policies in general.[67] As Professors Patrick Vinck and Eric Stover explain: "To the extent possible, all sectors of a war-ravaged society – the individual, community, society, and state – should become *engaged participants in* – and not merely *auxiliaries to* – the process of transitional justice and social reconstruction – though, undoubtedly, at different times and in different ways."[68]

If consultation and participation in lawmaking and peacemaking are important for their own sake, they also are important for pragmatic reasons. On few issues is this truer than the issue of amnesty, which tends to involve decisions and processes conducted only at the elite level.[69] Granted, there are times when mediators legitimately will need to conduct talks in secret.[70] However, where possible, soliciting the views and integrating the participation of the most relevant constituencies of an amnesty – including women, victims, combatants, civilian returnees, and conflict-affected communities – can help increase the amnesty's ultimate effectiveness.[71] It can ensure that any eventual legislation or policy maximally reflects the realities on the ground and maximally balances the competing needs, preferences, and expectations of relevant stakeholders. Indeed, the mere act of consultation can promote increased ownership of the ultimate outcome.[72] At the same time, no amount of public and victim consultation can legally salvage an amnesty that is, in its content, contrary to a state's specific international legal obligations. Ultimately, consultation is best understood an indicator of an amnesty's legitimacy but not a determinant of its legality.

In the context of any consultation process, one must be attentive to the possibility that those responsible for the bulk of past violence remain sufficiently powerful to intimidate or threaten individuals and groups seeking a more accountability-oriented amnesty.[73] In such cases, participation by the international community sometimes can be a crucial element in mitigating such a factor and in ensuring that meaningful victim consultation and public debate in fact occur. International involvement also can be crucial when the parties to peace talks or political negotiations have a mutual interest in an unprincipled amnesty, as when serious crimes have been committed on a large scale by all sides. In these cases, the international community can help to ensure representation of the public interest and provide technical assistance on pertinent questions of international law and practice, drawing upon expert individuals and institutions as necessary.

Population surveys and focus group interviews are among the most relevant amnesty-related consultation tools to have emerged in recent years. As Patrick Vinck and Eric Stover note:

> Capturing the opinions and attitudes of survivors can be done fairly rapidly and effectively through the use of a range of research methods, including population-based surveys, key informant interviews, and

focus groups. . . . Survey methods offer a systematic, unbiased way to interview a large number of individuals and can identify broad patterns within a given population, such as the scope of exposure to violence and prevailing opinions. The results can further be compared across subgroups based on socio-economic status, education, gender or ethnicity, among others.[74]

The International Center for Transitional Justice has conducted and collaborated on important survey work in contexts where amnesties are on the public agenda, with special emphasis on capturing the views of victims and conflict-affected communities.[75] By highlighting local views, these surveys ensure that the voices of those who will be most affected by any potential amnesty, and to whom particular deference arguably is owed, are made known. As such, the surveys are merely the logical extension of the European legal principle of subsidiarity, according to which decisions and related consultation procedures should occur as near as possible to the local or individual level.[76]

Though important, surveys and focus group interviews have certain limitations. As Graeme Simpson observes:

> Evidence from the field shows that the aspirations and needs of victim communities most affected by the conflict are subtle, fluid and frequently reflect a complex sequencing of changing needs and expectations, themselves heavily dependent on the state of the peace process and the prospects for justice at any particular time. . . . By treating the views of victims and communities as uniform or unchanging, we risk framing perceptions of the "peace vs. justice" dilemma rather crudely on their behalf. Therefore, it is fundamental that we constantly monitor and test victim and community perspectives, rather than make generalized assumptions about them.[77]

Surveys are also limited in the sense that they may tend to reveal the what of a person's views rather than the why. In this regard, other tools such as ethnographic studies and conflict analyses can help provide a deeper understanding of the viewpoints of those consulted. Issues of timing, and concerns about bias and undue influence, present additional challenges to the work of survey designers and implementers.[78] There is also an inherent political risk in conducting surveys, namely, that they may produce results that complicate opposition to an amnesty.[79]

In addition to open-ended local consultations about how generally to deal with legacies of mass abuse, it is benefical also to seek formal suggestions, ideas, and reactions to specific legal and policy initiatives, such as a draft amnesty law. Public input on official amnesty proposals can serve both to reflect and to reinforce democratic values, especially when it includes legislative hearings, as occurred in South Africa prior to the adoption of the TRC legislation.[80] However, as Priscilla Hayner notes, "There are few transitional countries that are as sophisticated as South Africa, with the know-how, patience, civil society infrastructure, and resources to dedicate a year and a half to culling ideas and reactions from across the country."[81] There is also the risk that government-organized hearings and consultations become a pretext for legislative delay and, ultimately, inaction.[82] Yet it is difficult to think of the justification for not making a good faith effort to seek public input on draft amnesty legislation.

Once all consultations are at an end, there comes the moment when an amnesty is presented or considered for adoption. This can occur in various, non-mutually-exclusive ways – parties to peace talks may sign a final agreement that includes an amnesty, the executive branch may issue an amnesty decree, the legislature may promulgate an amnesty law, and so forth. An amnesty also may need to be reviewed or preapproved by the country's highest constitutional court.[83] Whatever legal procedure is used, though, it is important for the amnesty to bear, to the greatest extent possible in the particular jurisdiction, the hallmarks of democratic adoption.[84]

This brings us to one of the more controversial aspects of amnesty practice, namely, whether a public referendum is an appropriate means to approve an amnesty. Referenda on amnesty have been used in a number of places, including New Caledonia (in 1988),[85] Uruguay (in 1989),[86] Ghana (in 1992),[87] and Algeria (in 1999 and 2005).[88] Amnesty referenda may explicitly and exclusively concern the amnesty (e.g., Uruguay) or be incorporated within a decision on a new constitution (e.g., Ghana) or form part of a broader reconciliation scheme (e.g., Algeria). Amnesties may alternatively be approved in referenda-like circumstances, as when they constitute prominent elements of a successful election campaign.[89] It should be noted, however, that certain legal systems explicitly prohibit the approval of amnesties through public referenda.[90] In short, there are diverse rules and practices on whether or how to conduct referenda on transitional amnesties.

At the international level, the UN Working Group on Enforced and Involuntary Disappearances is opposed to the idea of a referendum on amnesty as anathema to fundamental human rights.[91] Similarly, in the academic literature, some question the basic fairness of deciding a question like amnesty through a majority vote. As Charles Trumbull observes, "One can easily imagine a scenario in which the victims of a country constitute a small minority while the perpetrators of the crimes have the support of the majority. In such cases, the majority might approve an amnesty for the perpetrators because they share the same ideology as the perpetrators, not because they value peace over justice."[92] Yet even if the majority in this scenario did value peace over justice, the same tension between majority rule and human rights would arise.[93] One possible middle approach, therefore, could be to treat amnesty as a quasi-constitutional decision and thus require a supermajority of voters to approve it in any referendum.[94] That would recognize the seriousness of amnesty's impact on victims while simultaneously recognizing that, when the threat of justice constitutes a threat to democracy itself, amnesty becomes both a human rights issue and a democratic one.

In the end, the default rule probably should be against referenda on amnesties, especially when the direct victims of the worst crimes constitute a small percentage of the general population.[95] By corollary, it may be difficult to deny the logic of an amnesty referendum in a context in which the vast majority of the population has been directly and severely affected by mass violence. In such a context, decisions on issues of accountability and leniency may be viewed as suitable, or even necessary, subjects for referenda. In these circumstances, however, the amnesty ideally should be presented as a stand-alone issue in an open referendum and not be buried in a larger legal text.[96] It also should be accompanied by a full and transparent national debate involving a relatively free and independent press. Otherwise, the reliability of the results forever will be open to question.[97]

3.2 Minimum legal entrenchment

In addition to the need to ensure a consultative adoption process, it is important for the ultimate amnesty to be as lightly entrenched as possible in domestic law. Given the gravity of the crimes and the importance of the rights at stake, it is incumbent on those negotiating to limit the degree of the amnesty's permanence. The different ways to ensure that an amnesty is lightly entrenched in law are examined further on.

3.3 Legitimate end

No matter its process of adoption or degree of legal entrenchment, an amnesty needs to be geared toward one or more legitimate ends. Among other things, it should declare explicit public interest objectives, such as reconciliation, conflict prevention, or democratic consolidation. An amnesty that is not explicitly aimed at a legitimate end – whatever else its merits – does not deserve national or international support and will be less likely to receive judicial endorsement. The importance of ensuring a legitimate end is also prudential, because victims and the general public expect a clear justification for a measure as extreme as an amnesty covering human rights crimes. Indeed, all else being equal, one can reasonably expect a population to be more tolerant of a broad amnesty if the justification is compelling and credible, and less likely to be so if it is not.

As explained further on, one way to ensure that the legitimate end is tied to an amnesty's terms is by including the justification in the actual amnesty text. It must be kept in mind, however, that most amnesties – even the least legitimate ones – purport to promote the greater good. It is, therefore, crucial to always and independently assess whether the stated aim of the amnesty genuinely matches the reality on the ground.

3.4 Minimum leniency

The existence of a legitimate end is an important, but insufficient, measure of an amnesty's legitimacy. There also must be proportionality between the means chosen and the end pursued, such that the amnesty provides only as much leniency as necessary to attain its stated end.[98]

This metric is crucial in light of the gravity of the crimes and rights at issue. Granted, in any situation, it will be difficult to prove which leniency concessions were actually necessary and which were not. Indeed, only the most context-sensitive stakeholders can make that judgment – and even then it is not possible for any to have perfect knowledge. However, what accountability-amenable stakeholders need to keep in sight is the fact that even seemingly modest limitations in the scope of leniency can create future possibilities of justice for the victims of the amnestied crimes.

In this respect, it is essential to ascertain – as a form of minimum due diligence preceding any leniency concession – whether there are existing or prior amnesties in place. Such amnesties already may extend leniency for certain categories of offenders in relation to particular crimes covering certain time periods. Accordingly, one should be careful to avoid using up negotiating capital on matters that, in legal terms, may be moot on account of prior amnesties that remain in force. In South Africa, for example, earlier broad and unconditional self-amnesties such as the 1961 and 1977 Indemnity Acts seem not to have been factored into the country's TRC legislation in any significant way.[99] Why would someone already covered by these prior amnesties, which remain in force today, ever have applied for amnesty under the TRC scheme? In other countries, too, new amnesties are negotiated as though everything is at stake when, in fact, there are past amnesties that already confer massive leniency for the same crimes and that, if anything, should be proposed to be nullified as part of the negotiation of a new amnesty. One should at least ensure that there is no double amnesty for the same crimes caused by a failure to review past amnesties in the context of a new amnesty negotiation.[100]

By the same token, in considering a country's prior amnesty history, one should avoid becoming hostage to it. The fact that past amnesties in a country have followed a particular form should not overly influence the form of future amnesties. Consider for example the case of Sierra Leone, as described by Priscilla Hayner:

> The political class in Sierra Leone could not imagine a peace agreement being reached in 1999 that would not include an amnesty for all crimes of the war. This assumption was largely based on the reference point of the previous peace agreement of 1996, which included blanket immunity guarantees. Many said that it would have been unrealistic to think that the rebels would settle for less the second time.[101]

Beyond its relevance to Sierra Leone, this example underscores another broader lesson: the importance of canvassing global amnesty practice, and not only national practice, in the design of future amnesties so as to minimize concessions to justice. As explained in more detail subsequently, and drawing on this book's amnesty database, there are a number of practical means for negotiating parties to ensure that an amnesty confers the minimum leniency possible. Such means include ensuring that the amnesty text is as narrow as possible in terms of the categories of crimes and persons it covers, as well as in terms of the legal consequences for any potential beneficiary.

3.5 Maximum conditions

Minimizing the scope of leniency extended through an amnesty is crucial. Equally crucial, however, is maximizing the conditions attached to amnesty eligibility. Such conditions may be said to constitute, within an amnesty's internal framework, the quid pro quo for receiving leniency in the first place.

In recent years the trend is to impose more, and increasingly varied and exigent, conditions on an amnesty's beneficiaries. This is one of the very positive legacies directly attributable to the South African TRC and its amnesty scheme. A noteworthy aspect of this trend is the degree to which amnesties take on a very different legal, political, and moral complexion as the number and rigor of the conditions rise. In general, we could say that the more demanded of a perpetrator by way of conditions, the less it resembles an amnesty; and by corollary, the less demanded of a perpetrator, the more it resembles an amnesty.

Consider, for example, the immunity scheme encompassed in the Timor-Leste truth commission's mandate. It granted individuals full immunity from criminal and civil proceedings arising from "harmful acts" not constituting "serious criminal offences," which the country's hybrid criminal court was expected to handle. The immunity was conditioned on making a confession and apology for the harmful acts; participating in a "Community Reconciliation Process" leading to a court-registered "Community Reconciliation Agreement" between the individual and a "Community of Reception"; and performing the obligations covered in the agreement, which generally encompassed community service and forms of reparation.[102] Despite the full immunity conferred through this scheme, it is not described as an amnesty, but rather as a sui generis scheme of plea-bargaining. Yet the question naturally arises as to what conditions make it not an amnesty and whether (1) the removal of those conditions would convert it into an amnesty, and (2) the insertion of those conditions into other amnesties would render them nonamnesties. Would the mere insertion of a community service requirement into the constitutional court-approved and judge-administered South African amnesty scheme have converted it out of amnesty status?[103] This is not merely an academic question. It goes to the heart of the determination of what we mean by the term *amnesty* and of what constitutes, in any amnesty context, a permissible degree of leniency or alternatively a sufficient level of justice.

We will turn to the practical aspects of this issue further on, when we explore the various types of conditions that can be explicitly inserted into an amnesty scheme. In particular, we will look at two types of conditions: (1) conditions for an individual to obtain the legal and other benefits an amnesty confers, and (2) conditions for an individual to retain those benefits once conferred.

3.6 Maximum viability

In addition to meeting the above criteria, an amnesty should stand a reasonable likelihood of being effective in achieving its own stated objectives. This is not something that simply can be hoped or assumed. Viability depends on the specific content of the amnesty, and on the amnesty's administrative scheme, as explained further on. It also is contingent on at least three other features: (1) a clear understanding and effective targeting of the amnesty's intended beneficiaries, (2) the adoption of parallel transitional justice policies, and (3) the implementation of additional measures that form part of the broader political settlement. Each of these features is briefly examined here.

3.6.1 Typology of context and amnesty beneficiaries

The effective implementation of an amnesty may depend, in part, on factors in the surrounding environment. In particular, it can depend on an informed understanding of the psychology of the amnesty's target beneficiaries. For example, the Turkish government has offered scores of defection-oriented amnesties to rebel groups such as the *Partiya Karkerên Kurdistan* (PKK). Though intended to be attractive to these groups, the amnesties continue to fail, as rebels choose to stay in the field of battle rather than seek legal immunity and a return to civilian life. It seems that the state consistently underestimates the extent to which the rebels are (1) motivated by ideals and thus averse to breaking rank without some clear evidence that their struggle achieved a significant peace dividend for their supporters, (2) distrustful of the state and thus reluctant to put their faith in any national authority designated to administer the amnesty process, and (3) bound by a tight command-and-control structure and thus unable to successfully escape from the larger group even if some of them chose to put individual interests ahead of organizational objectives.[104] The same types of failures have occurred for apparently similar reasons in many other places, such as Guatemala in the 1980s.[105] The point is that the failed amnesties in these cases may be due, in part, to miscalculations about the target beneficiaries and how the state itself is perceived.

A related point concerns the degree to which an amnesty's target beneficiaries stand to yield political and security benefits, as a group, from the amnesty. For example, there is no point offering amnesty to a group whose leaders and followers will be lynched – and know they will be lynched – the moment they seek to reintegrate into civilian or political life under cover of an amnesty. Such an amnesty is unviable ab initio. In such a circumstance, even a risky asylum deal would seem a better alternative. Similarly, an offer of amnesty to the leader of a political party or rebel group who is not merely ruthless but also a bona fide lunatic – or to a leader who systemically has broken prior promises without justification – would seem futile. Given the unlikelihood of such a leader serving as a reliable partner in any future power-sharing arrangement ushered in by an amnesty, the offer of amnesty is best withheld. Other approaches, including military ones, might be the only suitable means to persuade such parties to cede power or disarm.[106]

Yet another implementation issue concerns the utility of mixing context-specific incentives and threats as a means to deal with the amnesty's target beneficiaries. An approach that is all incentives (or, in this case, all amnesty) and no threats, is one that often will fail at the implementation stage.[107] By corollary, an amnesty accompanied by a threat of some kind will tend to stand a better chance of successful implementation. This could take the hard form of a threat of arrest. It also could take the soft form of a threat of amnesty revocation, in the event of a return to violence by the amnestied party. In addition or in the alternative, it could take the procedural form of a threat of trial against anyone failing to apply for amnesty (where amnesty eligibility is conditional on the individual submission of a formal application). Any of these threats could help generate indirect leverage to ensure the effective ongoing implementation of an amnesty scheme, especially when accompanied by external monitoring by civil society or the international community or both.

A final consideration regarding the typology of the amnesty context and the target beneficiaries concerns the need for tailored publicity. Just as war crimes prosecutions need to encompass information and outreach programs, amnesties also may need to be publicized and explained – to combatants who may stand to benefit from the amnesty and any related DDR program, and to the communities that may be expected to receive and reintegrate them after demobilization. In Sierra Leone, for example, early consultations with combatants helped clarify the fact that only a handful of them actually risked prosecution by the Special Court.[108]

Since most combatants are not legally trained, and may even be unfamiliar with how trials operate, education and outreach efforts like this tend to be essential to clarify whether the threat of prosecution they perceive against themselves is exaggerated or underrated, as the case may be.[109] Outreach efforts also may be important to allay fears of violence they anticipate after demobilization.[110] Indeed, combatants may see amnesty as a guarantee not just against prosecutions but also against future intimidation or harassment by state authorities or future civilian neighbors. No longer bearing weapons, ex-combatants may not only feel more vulnerable; they may actually be more vulnerable.

3.6.2 Transitional justice measures

Any conclusion on whether an amnesty gets a passing or failing grade naturally should be based on more than the content of the legal text and the circumstances of its adoption. It also should be based on an evaluation of other key concessions and gains made in the course of an amnesty negotiation. Such gains may include parallel commitments to adopt transitional justice policies, which can help ensure what Pablo de Greiff describes as "external coherence," meaning coherence in the relationship across different policies (in this case, between an amnesty and other external measures that form part of an overall negotiated settlement).[111] In the aggregate, such policies can help mitigate the violation of victims' right to justice on account of the amnesty, increase the degree of compliance with the state's basic international law obligations, and generally contribute to the greater public interest.

Sometimes the agreement or law providing for an amnesty also encompasses explicit transitional justice commitments. For example, there are some amnesty laws that envisage victim rehabilitation measures, including health, educational, and financial support.[112] There are also many instances of laws that simultaneously promise amnesty to perpetrators and compensation to victims.[113] Preferably such laws do not condition compensation on a perpetrator's decision to apply for amnesty,[114] or on a victim's obligation to refrain from seeking truth or justice.[115] There are also various instances of peace agreements that provide for both an amnesty and a truth commission.[116] As we know from the case of South Africa, sometimes an amnesty is actually integrated within the legal mandate of the transitional justice mechanism.[117]

Direct linkages of these sorts are, of course, facially appealing. By incorporating a transitional justice measure into the law that grants amnesty – or alternatively incorporating amnesty into the law that creates the transitional justice mechanism – a closer legal and political nexus is established between benefits for perpetrators and benefits for victims. Yet such an approach can signal an offensive trade-off. It can imply that the transitional justice measure is able to "compensate" for what is lost on account of the amnesty.[118] Such an implication, however, may be both unintended and unfair. Indeed, there may be additional and important transitional justice laws and policies in place that are external to the law or agreement that includes the amnesty. Nevertheless, the perception of a trade-off sometimes may be too powerful for victims and the public to resist.

Whether an amnesty and a transitional justice measure are encompassed in the same legal instrument, the central point is that transitional justice measures ideally should accompany the amnesty to ensure maximal external coherence.[119] Relevant transitional justice policy commitments might encompass any of the following:

- *The creation of a victim reparation program comprising compensatory, restitutionary, rehabilitative, and symbolic components.*[120] Victim reparation programs are state-sponsored initiatives that aim to contribute to repairing, on a massive scale, the material and moral consequences of past abuse experienced by designated classes of victims. Typically they are established on the recommendation of a truth commission, as in Chile, or at a legislature's initiative, as in Germany. Contemporary reparation programs usually provide compensation payments to victims and their families, together with privileged or dedicated access to certain public or private services, such as rehabilitative health care, pension benefits, and educational services. Modern reparation programs increasingly encompass various symbolic forms of reparation, too, including plans for monuments and memorials to preserve and honor the memory of victims. Gender-sensitive and community-focused reparation measures also are beginning to be recommended and used.[121] In cases of crimes of political repression, reparation programs may encompass the restitution of basic legal rights and freedoms.[122]

- *The establishment of a truth commission or similar investigative body.*[123] Truth commissions are ad hoc commissions of inquiry established in, and authorized by, states for the primary purposes of investigating and reporting on key periods of recent past abuse, and making recommendations to remedy such abuse and prevent its recurrence. Such commissions may be established by various means, including peace agreements, executive decrees, and statutory legislation. Most contemporary truth commissions hold public hearings for victims, as such hearings appear to significantly increase public awareness and debate about past abuse – an essential precondition to any meaningful reconciliation process. Inspired by the South African TRC, as well as by other important truth commissions that followed, most commissions today also employ reasonably transparent and participatory procedures for selecting commissioners. In addition, most seek to actively consult and engage with local nongovernmental organizations and victims, which helps enhance the legitimacy of both the process and the final results.

- *The implementation of various institutional and legal reforms.* Countries emerging from war or tyranny often need to adopt institutional and legal reforms to help the country achieve the long-term social, economic and political objectives essential to preventing civic and democratic collapse in the future.[124] Such reforms generally have as their aim the elimination of the conditions that led to the existence of the period of conflict or repression. The range of possible reforms is extremely broad and includes: creating new institutions to protect human rights,[125] dismantling or restructuring institutions prone to abuse,[126] implementing human rights training and professionalization policies and programs,[127] and introducing legal and constitutional amendments to enhance good governance and better protect human rights.[128] Security system reform is particularly crucial for helping reduce the future likelihood of renewed conflict or abuse. While there is a wide array of different reform measures that may be employed, in practice special emphasis is placed on vetting programs, in particular in the police, army, and judiciary. These are integrity-focused personnel screening procedures that have as their central aim to transform specific public security institutions from instruments of repression and corruption into instruments of public service and integrity.[129] Another tool of security system reform, known as census and identification, is increasingly employed as a first step in establishing good governance. A census and identification program consists of a technical audit of a public institution to verify its current state of membership, often distorted by conflict and mismanagement, and to ultimately close the institution's formal boundaries so that subsequent reform processes are more controlled and effective.[130]

- *Trials for serious crimes not covered by an amnesty.* Criminal prosecutions occupy a privileged place in the fight against impunity, particularly when the violations are of a gross and systemic character. From a transitional justice perspective, prosecutions preferably are carried out at the national level, where they have the greatest potential to contribute to deterrence and to the restoration of public confidence in the rule of law. Though a transitional amnesty often will remove the prospect or consequences of domestic criminal prosecution for a number of serious crimes, it is important to recall that the amnesty also may exclude certain categories of offenders and crimes from eligibility. In addition, it may provide for the revocation of such benefits in the event of a material breach of the law's terms or conditions.[131] Persons who may be responsible for excluded crimes or guilty of material breaches of an amnesty's terms should be investigated actively and, evidence permitting, prosecuted.[132] It bears mention that research on the use of amnesties in nontransitional contexts indicates that an amnesty's effectiveness is in fact strongly and positively affected by "a real or a perceived increase in enforcement."[133] In this respect, it is worth recalling that an amnesty's legitimacy ought to be measured not only by how it is written but also by how it is applied.[134]

The foregoing measures of transitional justice are by no means exhaustive. Civil suits may be just as important as criminal prosecutions in some contexts; investigations conducted by national human rights commissions or international commissions of inquiry may yield results that are just as significant as those of truth commissions; comprehensive official apologies sometimes may have an impact that is, in moral terms, just as profound as material compensation; and curricular reforms may be as essential as judicial reforms to helping reduce and prevent future abuse. For the time being, however, the four previously described measures remain the primary means through which transitional justice is conceived and practiced.

Concerning the appropriate structuring and sequencing of relationships among transitional justice mechanisms, there are a few very basic rules of thumb. First, sequencing is itself a secondary task; the first task is to "gain a comprehensive understanding of the local context" and only thereafter to "ask what, whether, and when transitional justice interventions should be initiated."[135] Second, transitional justice mechanisms should be structured, to the maximum extent possible, in a way that maximizes complementarity and minimizes intermechanism conflict or contradiction. Third, interrelationships among mechanisms should not be too vague or complex, which can have the counterproductive effect of causing public confusion and reducing effective participation. Fourth, the different mechanisms of transitional justice generally ought to be sequenced in a manner that helps preserve and enhance the constituent elements of the transition itself – democracy and peace – without which all transitional justice possibilities diminish in scope and quality.[136] Although there is no road map or standard formula for structuring the interrelationships and sequencing of transitional justice mechanisms, following these basic rules of thumb can help keep the big picture in focus once the detailed planning commences.

As a final remark, it should be emphasized that transitional justice mechanisms are merely structures; they do not possess any inherent virtue. There are commendable truth commissions and lamentable ones; there are munificent reparations programs and parsimonious ones; there are fair trials and unfair ones; and so forth. In other words, the mere creation of a transitional justice mechanism is no guarantee whatsoever of positive results. Similarly, the mere undertaking by a state to establish such mechanisms is no guarantee of their ultimate establishment.[137] In brief, to play any mitigating role in relation to the damage wrought by an amnesty, political and even legal promises in the arena of transitional justice must be translated into political and legal action. When that happens, and when good faith is present, much that is in the public interest can be accomplished.

3.6.3 Features of the broader settlement

Without wishing to minimize the importance of transitional justice interventions, it is important to recognize their boundaries. The realities of transitional contexts are such that even a perfect combination of justice, truth, reparation, and reform measures is insufficient – in theoretical and practical terms – to achieve the larger goals of helping to restore civic trust, the rule of law, and respect for human rights. To attain such objectives – to truly resolve the underlying causes of mass violence – transitional justice efforts must be complemented and calibrated with other longer-term public interest objectives such as, depending on the case, the consolidation of peace and democracy, the revitalization of the economy, the provision of public security, and the advancement of local and national reconciliation.[138]

This point explicitly was recognized as early as 1985 in Louis Joinet's original UN study on amnesties. In the concluding section of the study, he observed:

> [T]he amnesty process can only be effective if it is coupled with social, economic or political measures permitting action to deal with the causes, *viz*.: (a) In the short term, the repeal of emergency laws as a corollary of the amnesty: since like causes produce like effects, the release of political prisoners may come to nothing if the emergency laws which permitted massive arrests in violation of human rights subsist; (b) In the medium term, the holding of elections . . . ; (c) In the long term the implementation of economic and social measures attacking the root causes of national dissension.[139]

This passage underscores the vital, but sometimes overlooked, point that an amnesty's greatest chance at legitimacy lies in its potential to facilitate preconditions for the macro-level deliverables of security, democracy, and development.

For an amnesty to succeed, therefore, a number of parallel state-building and peace-building measures may be important. These can include, inter alia, DDR programs for former combatants,[140] repatriation and reintegration programs for refugees and internally displaced persons,[141] large-scale land-reform programs,[142] and the holding of elections in which former armed groups might participate as newly formed political parties.[143] Such measures can increase the legitimacy of an amnesty to the extent that they are rightfully perceived as having been unachievable without it. As Louise Mallinder observes:

> The relationship between amnesty and other measures within a peace process can be sequenced to permit the amnesty to act as the starting point to enable other aspects of the agreement to occur, such as demobilisation, integration of combatants into the armed forces, or the transformation of insurgent groups into political parties that could perhaps participate in governments of national unity.[144]

With "an effective reformist coalition" in place, an amnesty's contribution is more clearly visible and the overarching aim of sustainable state-building comes within closer reach.[145] By corollary, "when not accompanied by a power transfer to new leaders who are genuinely committed to human rights," the utility of an amnesty is less visible and the overarching transitional objectives less likely to be fulfilled.[146]

Granted, an amnesty's implementation almost always will be untidy and unpredictable given the number of potential spoilers that tend to accompany any negotiated settlement, and given the increasingly regional or transboundary nature of mass violence.[147] Indeed, amnesties – and transition processes more generally – are rarely straightforward in their implementation.[148] They can be affected by a complex and broad array of variables including the nature of the public security situation, the overall balance of power, the general economic situation, the presence of long-standing ethnic or intercommunal tensions, the degree of international engagement and involvement, and so forth. In this respect, the best one can do in most cases is to act with maximum due diligence – keeping a constant eye not only on the amnesty process but also, or even more so, on the macro issues of peace, democracy, development, and the effective sharing of national wealth and power.

In summary, there are a number of overarching considerations that need to guide the design of amnesties. Among other things, there needs to be a legitimate process for the adoption of the amnesty. It is also important for the amnesty to be as lightly entrenched as possible to preserve justice options for the future. In addition, there always should be a legitimate end that motivates the promulgation of any amnesty, and the amnesty should offer as little leniency to perpetrators as required by the situation, while imposing as much accountability on them as feasible. The amnesty also must stand a reasonable chance of being effectively implemented, which implies careful analysis of the nature of the target beneficiaries and recognition of the need for accompanying legal and policy measures. With these considerations in mind, we turn now to the specific design choices that can give meaning to this broader framework of objectives.

4. SPECIFIC AMNESTY DESIGN CHOICES

As noted previously, amnesties cannot always be avoided. Military victory may be impossible. Tools of peacemaking, such as sanctions, may be ineffective or inappropriate. In addition, the threat of prosecutions may undermine rather than facilitate the prospects of peace or democratic restoration, and the procedural options outlined earlier, such as reduced sentence regimes, may be insufficient incentives to convince armed factions to disarm and demobilize. In short, sometimes amnesty truly will be a last option, without which there would be no serious prospect for the end of conflict or tyranny. While well-informed tyrants and warlords may realize that amnesties can be disregarded by foreign and international tribunals, or potentially scaled back by national courts or future national governments, such awareness would rarely make them seek anything less than the broadest amnesty possible in the absence of better options. For these and other reasons, the question of an amnesty's content is one of crucial significance.

In terms of an overall litmus test for evaluating the content of an amnesty, this book argues against using a simple and rigid rule. Instead, it argues for detailed case-by-case analysis involving the harmonizing of different state obligations – precisely as it should be for an issue of this complexity and import. Such an approach also reflects the reality that, in most cases of a negotiated amnesty, the final content will include both elements of accountability and elements of leniency. It is all a question of careful weighting and attention to the specifics of the context and the stakeholders.

Overall, there are dozens of different and significant choices to be made in crafting an amnesty. This presents both a challenge and an opportunity for honorable actors confronted with amnesty dilemmas. As Priscilla Hayner notes:

> It is clear that the lack of strong justice components is sometimes due to the strength of perpetrators at the negotiating table, and their insistence on impunity. But it is rare that the dynamics are so simple, or that there is not some room for maneuver. Opportunities are sometimes missed due to ignorance or misunderstanding of the mechanisms and policies that are available; a lack of time or effort to detail such provisions; a failure of creativity, such as in considering limitations or preconditions to immunity schemes; or basic lack of clarity or information about the international legal standards or obligations that pertain.[149]

The challenge is to go beyond the identification of such an opportunity and to actually find the means to act effectively upon it. To that end, what follows is an analysis of the key individual choices to be made in pursuit of each of the amnesty-related objectives previously described, namely (1) minimum legal entrenchment, (2) a legitimate end, (3) minimum leniency, (4) maximum conditions, and (5) maximum viability.

4.1 Minimum legal entrenchment

This section focuses on the relevance of an amnesty's juridical character. There are a number of different ways that the juridical character of an amnesty can be approached to minimize the degree of its entrenchment in national law. One aspect concerns the nature of the legal instrument in which the amnesty appears. A second concerns whether the amnesty is permanent or temporary in its legal character. A third concerns the explicit relation, if any, between the amnesty and other national laws. Each of these issues implies different potential consequences for the process of adopting the amnesty and for the possibilities of subsequent legal challenge, repeal, or annulment.

4.1.1 Nature of legal instrument

Depending on the context and possible requirements of national law, an amnesty may be prescribed within a wide variety of legal instruments. Taking into consideration the objective of minimum legal entrenchment, it is generally best to avoid constitutionalizing an amnesty, which would render it much more difficult to eventually overcome. Instead, to the extent the rules of national law permit, amnesties preferably are adopted as laws or decrees, making them less invulnerable to future repeal, annulment, or judicial review. As to the choice between a law and a decree, the former generally is preferable because it can help imbue the amnesty with greater democratic legitimacy, especially when accompanied by legislative debate and public consultation, as discussed earlier.

In most cases, the presumed motivation in constitutionalizing an amnesty is to deepen its entrenchment, as rules for amending constitutions entail higher procedural thresholds (e.g., requiring supermajorities instead of plain majorities) than rules for amending ordinary laws. In addition, courts do not normally have the power to annul constitutional provisions – only to interpret them. That is true both for a permanent constitution and for an interim one.[150] Examples of constitutional amnesties include those of *Ghana 1992*,[151] *South Africa 1993*,[152] *Indonesia 2000*,[153] and *Burma 2008*.[154]

Constitutional amnesties are the exception rather than the rule. In most cases, amnesties are prescribed in the form of a parliamentary law or a presidential decree. While laws and decrees are both susceptible to subsequent repeal or annulment, some constitutions may limit the scope of judicial and parliamentary review for decrees of an emergency character or may stipulate which branch of government – the legislative or executive – can adopt the amnesty.[155] Some constitutions also may require certain technical procedures to be followed for the adoption of an amnesty law. For example, Article 79 of the Italian Constitution requires amnesty laws to be adopted by two-thirds of each legislative chamber. Article 47 of the Greek Constitution similarly provides that amnesty may be granted only for political crimes and must be passed by a three-fifths majority of parliament. Article 244 of El Salvador's Constitution makes the power of amnesty an executive rather than legislative privilege but explicitly precludes self-amnesty for constitutional violations "during the presidential period in which they were committed."

As is well known, amnesties also may be adopted through a peace accord, as in the cases of *Sierra Leone 1996*,[156] *Ivory Coast 2003*,[157] and *Aceh (Indonesia) 2004*.[158] A peace accord is akin to a contractual agreement and does not generally have binding legislative force unless and until it has been expressly implemented into law at the national level.[159] This is one reason why amnesties contained in peace accords typically are vague on details.[160]

4.1.2 Whether permanent or temporary in character

Another aspect of an amnesty's legal nature concerns whether it is enacted as a permanent or a temporary measure. While amnesties generally are intended to be permanent, where possible it is desirable to make them expressly temporary. Indeed, the default position of any accountability-amenable party in an amnesty blackmail situation should be to urge an amnesty that is temporary rather than permanent.

While the idea of a temporary amnesty diverges from the original Greek notion of *amnēstia*, which implies a permanent "forgetting" of past crimes, it is more consistent with the modern practice of amnesty, which encompasses a wide range of restricted and conditional amnesties.[161] The idea of a temporary amnesty also is more consistent with the extraordinariness of the moment in a state's life when a measure as extreme as amnesty is adopted. One could logically contend that the terms of an amnesty ought to apply only for the period of time necessary to overcome the urgent situation,[162] or alternatively for the period of time beginning with peace talks and ending with the dissolution of a transitional government of national unity.[163]

Yet another variation on this concept is usefully explored by Ron Slye, who postulates the creation of a formal international legal rule permitting the granting of an amnesty for only five or ten years:

> At the end of that period, an evaluation could be made to determine if the beneficiary of the amnesty is entitled to a permanent amnesty or something less. Such a determination could be based upon the actions of the beneficiary during the "probationary" limited amnesty period. This would create an incentive for beneficiaries (1) to show through their words and deeds that they no longer pose a threat to society; (2) to provide personal reparations not only to their immediate victims but to the larger society; and (3) to model human rights positive behavior to similarly situated individuals who might otherwise commit or sponsor gross violations of human rights. It is important that the

life span of the initial amnesty be at least five years, both to provide a sweet enough "carrot" to induce the recipient to give up power and to provide enough time for the beneficiary to demonstrate more than a superficial commitment to human rights and the rule of law. A permanent amnesty at the end of the probationary period might be rare, and could be conditioned on further demonstrations of support, such as participating in a truth commission, testifying at the trial of others, or otherwise assisting in investigations. If a permanent amnesty is not granted, the insufficient actions during the probationary period could be used in mitigation during any subsequent criminal or civil action.[164]

Whether such an approach would be viable in most amnesty contexts is open to question, as Slye himself acknowledges.[165] That is because those seeking amnesties customarily will seek a permanent, rather than a temporary, amnesty for themselves.[166] In addition, there is the risk that a temporary amnesty triggers a resumption of hostilities after the expiration of the initial period of application.

There are, nevertheless, some examples of explicitly temporary immunities from criminal prosecution. The *South Africa 1990* amnesty extended to the president the power to grant temporary immunity if necessary to facilitate ongoing political negotiations or to improve the administration of justice.[167] Section 4 of the Decommissioning Act 1997 (Northern Ireland), which is titled "Amnesty," is another example of temporary immunity. It was designed to ensure that prosecutions did not undermine the process of decommissioning in Northern Ireland.[168] As previously noted, Burundian *Loi No. 1/004 du 8 Mai 2003* also grants provisional immunity from prosecution for perpetrators of international crimes until such time as an international judicial commission of inquiry (foreseen in an earlier peace accord) shall have issued findings on the occurrence of such crimes.[169]

Consistent with the principle of minimal legal entrenchment, at the conclusion of the period of prescribed immunity under any hypothetical temporary amnesty, the immunity benefit should either come to an end (thus raising the possibility of prosecutions) or be reenacted and extended (thus prolonging the suspension of prosecutions). In either case, the decision should be taken only after the conclusion of a formal review by the president, parliament, appellate courts, or an independent commission – and only in accordance with predefined criteria, which could include the degree of compliance with individual performance-based conditions, such as those described subsequently. Such an approach would, in effect, convert the amnesty into a sunset clause. This is a clause in a law that serves to terminate all or portions of the law after a specific date unless further legislative action is taken to extend its relevant parts. Such clauses are in common use in many jurisdictions, especially in relation to modern counterterrorism legislation,[170] as well as constitutions.[171]

An alternative approach could be to design an amnesty that is based on the concept of a sunrise clause. This is a clause in a law that provides for the coming into force rather than the termination of portions of the law – in this case the amnesty portions – after a specific date in the future and upon the satisfaction of specific conditions. The purpose of a sunrise amnesty would be to reinforce Slye's prudential suggestion to balance the incentive of long-term immunity with the threat of the withholding of such immunity in the event of a failure to meet the law's preconditions.

Whether a temporary amnesty that is based on the concept of a sunrise or sunset clause would contradict the UN amnesty position is unclear. Until now, the situation seldom has arisen because those seeking to be amnestied have naturally tended to insist on a permanent and immediate amnesty, notwithstanding the risk of an amnesty's weakening or undoing with the passage of time.[172] However, there is no cause to presume that a temporary or deferred amnesty would automatically be opposed, and there is no obvious justification for not giving prior consideration to one.

4.1.3 Relation between amnesty and other laws

In seeking to challenge an amnesty that has been adopted, it matters what relation the amnesty has to other domestic laws. If the amnesty is in a constitution, it naturally will be superior to statutes and decrees. However, if it is not, an amnesty's sponsor may consider it desirable to stipulate the amnesty law's relationship to other domestic laws in cases of ambiguity or conflict between them. For example, the *Angola 1994* amnesty explicitly provides for its superiority over any other conflicting national laws.[173] The *Ghana 1992* amnesty – itself constitutional – provides for its superiority over any other conflicting constitutional provisions.[174]

Taking into account the objective of minimal legal entrenchment, however, it is generally preferable to omit any express hierarchy between an amnesty law and any related national laws. Such omission will facilitate the work of future courts needing or wishing to draw on related legislation, including domestic human rights laws that ought to figure in any judicial interpretation of an amnesty. However, it may be important to specify the relationship between a new and principled amnesty and any prior and unprincipled amnesties adopted in the same jurisdiction. In such a situation, consideration could be given to making the new amnesty explicitly superior to prior ones.

Another approach in such circumstances might be to specify that the entry into force of the new amnesty will trigger the automatic repeal of the prior amnesties.

4.2 Legitimate end

One way to understand an amnesty's objectives is through the law's preamble, in particular through the explicit ends it articulates, and through any accompanying references to international law. An amnesty's main objectives, along with an explanation of its historical or contextual background, customarily are placed in the preamble of the particular legal instrument. A standard preamble consists of a number of introductory paragraphs that precede the law's operative provisions. While a preamble does not create law, it is relevant to the proper interpretation of ambiguities within the text.

4.2.1 Explicit objectives mentioned in the preamble

As discussed previously, the possible purposes of an amnesty in contexts characterized by human rights crimes may include the facilitation of a transition to democracy, the consolidation of peace and security, the achievement of national unity and reconciliation, the encouragement of defections by guerillas or dissidents, and the repatriation and return of refugees and displaced persons.[175] Almost every amnesty referred to in this book contains a preamble that touches on one or more of these themes.

In general, it is important to incorporate into the preamble explicit and legitimate objectives that might enable future courts to interpret any ambiguities within the amnesty in a way that ensures an interpretation consistent with those objectives. We know, however, that the preamble's statement of objectives may mask the amnesty sponsor's true political motivation, which may have more to do with self-interest in impunity than with any noble ambition to heal a nation. The preamble may, in addition, exaggerate or misrepresent the facts that purport to justify the amnesty in the first instance. Thus, the objectives set out in an amnesty's preamble – no matter how laudable on paper – should not be taken at face value.

The following are examples of amnesty preambles that contain explicit references to facially legitimate objectives:

- *Haiti 1993*: "to achieve national unity in a climate of social peace and on new grounds that will allow the building of the rule of law and favor economic development, which is indispensable for the happiness of the Haitian people."[176]

- *El Salvador 1993*: "the consolidation of peace requires the creation of confidence amongst our society in order to attain the reconciliation and reunification of the Salvadoran family."[177]
- *South Africa 1995*: "to promote national unity and reconciliation in a spirit of understanding that transcends the conflicts and divisions of the past."[178]
- *Algeria 1999*: "to enable those wishing to cease violent activities an opportunity for reinsertion into civil society, and to help in the re-establishment of civil harmony."[179]
- *Uganda 2000*: "to end armed hostilities, reconcile with perpetrators, rebuild communities, and establish peace, security and tranquility."[180]
- *Angola 2002*: "to achieve national reconciliation and help establish a new order."[181]

4.2.2 References to sources of international law

While it is important to ensure that an amnesty's preamble will be interpreted according to an explicit and legitimate set of objectives, it is equally important to include references to public international law principles and treaties. This is to help prevent references to noble objectives, such as peace and reconciliation, from serving as a pretext for future courts to sidestep the exigencies of international law's provisions on truth, justice, reparation, and reform. Although a state's specific international law obligations are binding on it irrespective of whether they appear in an amnesty's preamble, their explicit inclusion can serve to reinforce or safeguard the need to take international law into account in the law's subsequent interpretation. The inclusion of such references also can directly encourage lawyers to base their pleadings on relevant international law and jurisprudence, if not for its binding effect, then at least for its persuasive value.[182]

Although many amnesty preambles make reference to relevant principles of national constitutional and criminal law, few make reference to relevant treaties or principles of international law. One exception is the *El Salvador 1983* amnesty,[183] which refers to the American Declaration on the Rights and Duties of Man and the American Convention on Human Rights. The preamble to the *Haiti 1994* amnesty refers to the same two treaties, as well as the Universal Declaration of Human Rights.[184]

4.3 Minimum leniency

This section looks at the main different means to ensure that no more leniency than necessary is extended through an amnesty. Such means include limiting the amnesty's scope in respect of the following:

- The crimes or acts that are expressly eligible or ineligible;
- The persons who are expressly eligible or ineligible;
- The express legal consequences of the grant of amnesty for the beneficiary;
- The geographical scope of application; and
- The temporal scope of application.

4.3.1 The crimes or acts that are expressly eligible or ineligible

Unless it is general in scope, an amnesty often will set out specific types of crimes as expressly eligible for amnesty. In many cases, an amnesty also will establish certain crimes as expressly ineligible. Together these constitute the amnesty's *ratione materiae* (subject matter scope).

The main forms of crime that usually are deemed eligible are those considered political or those associated with a particular conflict, as the case may be. By contrast, the main forms of crime that usually are deemed ineligible include one or more of the following: economic crimes, human rights crimes, crimes motivated by malice, and various context-specific crimes of special notoriety in a particular country. Beyond these categories, some amnesties specify eligibility only in relation to fully completed criminal acts, whereas others expand the list of eligible acts to include omissions and attempts. Some amnesties also specify a requirement of proportionality between the act and its objective. All of these options are discussed in more detail here.

4.3.1.1 Political versus ordinary offenses distinction. In a context of mass violence, it is important to avoid amnestying serious offenses that lack a clear nexus with past or ongoing repression or conflict. Indeed, an amnesty established in response to a national conflict or political crisis should not serve as a pretext for extinguishing the prospect or consequence of criminal accountability for persons guilty of ordinary offenses (i.e., nonpolitical and non-conflict-related offenses).[185] Thus, an amnesty ideally should specify that it applies only to acts related to the conflict or crisis and for which there was some kind of directly related motivation.[186] It may, however, be difficult in some cases to distinguish political crimes from common crimes (e.g., theft to raise funds for the purchase of weaponry). It may also sometimes be politically undesirable to attempt to make the distinction between ordinary and political offenses, for fear of enabling a criminal syndicate or terrorist group to be treated or viewed as a political movement. Some exceptions, therefore, may exist.

In drafting terms, there are three non-mutually-exclusive ways to effect the inclusion of political or conflict-related offenses. First, there are some actions that are political by their very nature and definition, such as treason (for non-state actors) or preventive detention (for state agents acting under counterterrorism legislation).[187] An amnesty explicitly limited to such actions would have no need to make clear, directly or indirectly, that only political offenses are eligible for leniency. By corollary, an amnesty that covered actions not already understood and defined as political would need to specify that only political offenses are eligible for leniency, or risk encompassing ordinary offenses.[188]

A second way of limiting an amnesty's coverage to political or conflict-related crimes is by referring to the factual context without referring to specifically prescribed offenses. For example, a *Liberia 1993* amnesty covers "all persons and parties involved in the Liberian civil conflict,"[189] an *Angola 1994* amnesty encompasses "illegal acts committed... in the context of the current conflict,"[190] and an *Albania 1997* amnesty covers "crimes connected to the popular revolt."[191] None of these amnesties refers to a particular type of crime, but the contextual qualification used in each serves to exclude ordinary (i.e., nonpolitical or non-conflict related) offenses from the amnesty's ambit. A related way to achieve the same result in an amnesty is to use contextual qualifiers that are implicit. For example, an amnesty may cover crimes committed during a time frame that clearly refers to, but does not expressly identify, a particular context, event, or conflict. However, this type of drafting technique is less precise and risks including ordinary and political offenses in the absence of additional qualifiers.[192]

The third approach, which is more common and more reliable, involves both referring to a specific context or event and expressly limiting application to particular types of offenses. This twin-requirement approach is used in the majority of amnesties examined in the research for this book, though it is important to note that the way in which political offenses are defined or described in these amnesties varies considerably. For example, in some cases, an exhaustive list of specific crimes of an inherently political nature is stipulated without any reference to a person's motivation. Thus, a *Brazil 1979* amnesty includes military desertion and a series of other inherently political crimes without reference to motivation.[193] In other cases, specific political crimes are listed but in a nonexhaustive fashion. The *France 1962* amnesty covers infractions committed in the context of operations for the maintenance of order and directed against the Algerian insurrection, provided they were committed before March 20, 1962.[194] A *Greece 1974* amnesty covers a variety of specific crimes, such as sedition and treason, which are punishable under the Criminal Code and Military Code, together with "other acts having to do with the situation of 21 April 1967 which were intended to overthrow the status quo."[195] In still other cases, a catch-all political crimes category is employed. For example, the *Burundi 1990* and *Burundi 1993* amnesties simply cover "crimes against public security" committed in the course of conflict.[196] The

Angola 1996 amnesty covers "all crimes against the security of the state and all related crimes committed in the framework of the armed conflict as well as all military crimes committed between May 1991 and May 1996."[197]

In a range of other twin-requirement amnesties, the political nature of the offense is determined on the basis of a political motivation that corresponds to explicit evaluation criteria included in the amnesty. For example, a *Romania 1990* amnesty covers political offenses defined as "deeds that had as their purpose (a) protest against dictatorship, the cult of personality, terror or the abuse of power by the authorities; (b) the respect of fundamental human rights and freedoms, exercising political, economic, social and cultural rights, or abolishing of discriminatory practices; (c) the satisfaction of democratic claims."[198] The *South Africa 1995* amnesty covers acts, omissions, and offenses "associated with political objectives and committed in the course of conflicts in the past," and then it provides a long list of related criteria.[199] That list includes, importantly, a proportionality requirement between the (political) act and the political objective.[200] In other cases, by contrast, the requirement of a political motivation is expressed in simpler terms. For example, the *Guatemala 1996* amnesty simply provides that, for state actors, the crime must have had a political and not a personal motive.[201] The *Philippines 2000* amnesty covers crimes committed "in pursuit of political beliefs," and it expressly excludes crimes committed "for personal ends."[202]

Another permutation of the foregoing approach is to broaden the category of political offenses to explicitly include associated or related common crimes. This is the approach used, for example, in the amnesties of *Spain 1977*,[203] *Colombia 1982*,[204] *Honduras 1991*,[205] and *El Salvador 1992*.[206] There are also amnesties that include common crimes that are unrelated to political offenses, such as those of *Romania 1990*[207] and *Kyrgyzstan 2002*.[208] In some of these cases, the policy rationale may have been to deflect accusations of bias or hypocrisy in amnestying heinous political crimes but not minor ordinary offenses, or to deflect public attention from how many political prisoners are released. However, as a general rule, amnesties ideally should exclude ordinary offenses if they are not directly related to or associated with political or conflict-related offenses for the reasons explained earlier in this section. The *Chad 2002* amnesty is an example of an amnesty with provisions explicitly excluding ordinary (or common) offenses.[209]

On a final note, it bears mention that there are international legal limits to what offenses properly may be described as political. For example, the Convention Relating to the Status of Refugees precludes the treatment of genocide or war crimes as political offenses.[210] Extradition law similarly precludes the treatment of such crimes as political.[211] The latter practice can be traced to Article VII of the Genocide Convention, which declares that acts of genocide "shall not be considered as political crimes for the purpose of extradition."[212]

4.3.1.2 Express exclusion of human rights crimes. In some respects, this may be considered the single most important category of amnesty design. If an amnesty excluded all human rights crimes, the rest of the issues around amnesty design would matter much less – and perhaps, for some, not at all. That is because the exclusion of these crimes from an amnesty's ambit would have the effect of preserving domestic justice options in respect of them and would result in a symbolic denunciation of those responsible.

We have observed that the UN Secretariat recently adopted the position that amnesties "can never be permitted to excuse genocide, war crimes, crimes against humanity or gross violations of human rights."[213] Depending on a state's specific international law commitments, and depending on the nature of the violations perpetrated in the particular context,[214] the exclusion of some or all of these crimes may be obligatory for a particular state. Such an obligation of exclusion also may extend to acts involving the obstruction of justice in relation to those responsible for such crimes.[215]

However, as we have seen, in the complex and violent contexts that constitute the primary focus of this book, the exclusion of human rights crimes from amnesties may be completely infeasible. Often, that is because there is usually at least one group able to insist on a significant measure of impunity for some of the most serious crimes. Nevertheless, it remains important to seek to exclude as many human rights crimes as possible from any amnesty, particularly when the language of the text is otherwise general and all encompassing (e.g., amnesty for "all crimes committed during the past conflict").[216] In seeking such exclusions, however, one must envisage not only the provisions of treaties binding on the particular state but also any corresponding domestic legal provisions. As noted in the UN Office of the High Commissioner for Human Rights "rule-of-law tool" on amnesties:

> [I]t is important to read the text of a proposed amnesty in the light of a country's penal code to ensure that the amnesty provisions do not prevent a State from meeting its international legal obligations. Suppose, for example, that genocide has just occurred in a country and that a proposed amnesty covering the period of the genocide explicitly excludes the crimes of genocide and crimes against humanity. On its face, the proposed amnesty would appear to be consistent with the State's duty to ensure prosecution of these two international crimes. Yet that country's criminal code might not make either genocide or crimes against humanity a crime. Despite its language exempting

crimes against humanity and genocide, the proposed amnesty could have the effect of preventing prosecution of the perpetrators.[217]

As noted in Part I of this volume, there is an embryonic trend in recent years to exclude certain types of human rights crimes from amnesties. In reality, the practice of incorporating such exclusions dates back at least several decades. A few early examples include the 1902 Peace Treaty of Vereeniging,[218] and the amnesties of *Hungary 1955*[219] and *Germany (GDR) 1979*,[220] each of which excluded crimes such as war crimes or crimes against humanity. Other examples of selective exclusion of human rights crimes prior to the adoption of the United Nations' new amnesty position appear in the amnesties of *Iran 1980*,[221] *Uganda 1987*,[222] *Nicaragua 1987*,[223] *Guatemala 1996*,[224] and *Albania 1997*.[225]

Beyond genocide, war crimes, crimes against humanity, and gross violations of human rights, there are several other types of international crime, such as terrorism, that could be excluded on the same basis (i.e., on the basis of a state's specific treaty-based or custom-based obligations). We already have observed that several counterterrorism treaties set out uniquely exigent prosecution obligations on states parties that go beyond what is found in treaties dealing with war crimes, genocide, or crimes against humanity.[226] In practice, many amnesties do explicitly exclude terrorism from their ambit.[227]

4.3.1.3 Express exclusion of crimes motivated by greed. Along with human rights crimes, negotiated amnesties explicitly may exclude a range of serious economic crimes or crimes committed for personal gain. Such crimes already may be implicitly excluded from the amnesty because of their presumed non-political character. However, explicit exclusion makes this even clearer and helps to avoid any unintended overlap between certain economic crimes and certain international crimes (e.g., theft in some contexts could amount to pillage, which is a constitutive element of certain war crimes).[228] In addition, absent their explicit exclusion, serious economic crimes unwittingly could be captured in the terms of an amnesty when it encompasses acts directly associated with political or conflict-related offenses (e.g., drug trafficking by rebel groups or paramilitaries).[229]

The exclusion of economic crimes also has the advantage of creating a parallel legal foundation for seeking accountability against perpetrators of mass violence who would otherwise enjoy impunity because of the political nature of their main offenses. This is a rather significant advantage when one considers that the persons responsible for the worst acts of mass violence are often, simultaneously, those responsible for the worst acts of mass corruption.[230]

Notwithstanding the foregoing considerations, many amnesties do not explicitly exclude economic crimes. Paradoxically, amnesty appears to be more readily applied to acts of extreme violence than to acts of mass corruption. The reasons for this may be explained as follows:

> First, certain human rights violations can be rhetorically defended on the basis that they were necessary as part of a war or in pursuit of a greater cause. There is no similar justification available, however, when it comes to acts of corruption, which are only carried out for purposes of personal enrichment. Second, with crimes of corruption, the public may collectively feel that they are the victims of theft. In contrast, human rights violations generally lack this sense of collective victimization because in most cases the violations have not affected the majority of the public.[231]

There are, however, several examples of amnesties that explicitly exclude serious economic crimes. These include the amnesties of *Argentina 1983*,[232] *Tunisia 1989*,[233] *Burundi 1990*,[234] *Romania 1990*,[235] *El Salvador 1993*,[236] *Jordan 1999*,[237] *Philippines 2000*,[238] and *Zimbabwe 2000*.[239]

4.3.1.4 Express exclusion of crimes motivated by malice. Along with the previously mentioned crimes, some amnesties also explicitly exclude crimes motivated by "malice" or "ill intent."[240] Examples of such amnesties include those of *Colombia 1982*,[241] *Uruguay 1985*,[242] and *South Africa 1995*.[243] In a similar vein, the amnesties of *Zimbabwe 1979* and *1980* provide that certain crimes must have been carried out "in good faith" to be eligible for amnesty.[244]

While in practice malicious intent can be very hard to prove, or disprove, the inclusion of such a qualifier may provide a useful limitation – in conjunction with other mentioned limitations – on an otherwise excessively broad amnesty.

4.3.1.5 Express exclusion of selected context-specific crimes. A further possible category of exclusion concerns crimes that were especially prevalent in a prior period of conflict or repression and which, for that reason – or because of their extreme moral degradation – engender significant social opprobrium from the local population, the international community, or both.[245] Examples of offenses falling into this category include, for example, the assassination of religious leaders and diplomats[246] and the trafficking of drugs, artifacts, or persons.[247] Such crimes may be easier to exclude from an amnesty than more standard categories of offense because the chief perpetrators will not wish to give the impression of seeking impunity for the conflict's most emblematic crimes.

From a transitional justice perspective, the explicit exclusion of context-specific crimes has the benefit of opening up a window for future national prosecution that may otherwise be closed because of the practical difficulty of proving complex offenses like crimes against humanity, which require proof of a crime (e.g., rape) and the existence of a broader context (e.g., "a widespread or systematic attack directed against any civilian population").[248]

Some examples of context-specific exclusions can be found in the amnesties of *France 1951* (deportation to death camps),[249] *Northern Ireland/United Kingdom 1969* (acts of sabotage),[250] *Brazil 1979* (terrorism, assault, kidnapping, and assassinations),[251] *Colombia 1981* (kidnapping, extortion, murder of non-combatants, poisoning of water sources),[252] *Argentina 1986* (kidnapping and hiding of minors, and related illegal changes of civil status),[253] *Burundi 1993* (armed robbery and cattle theft when committed as part of a large group),[254] *Croatia 1996* (violation of envoys, destruction of cultural and historic heritage, and unjustified delay in the repatriation of prisoners of war),[255] and *Algeria 2006* (collective massacres, rape, and the use of explosive devices in public places).[256]

Sometimes the context-specific crime may be hard to classify in legal terms and the state may, quite deliberately, resort to ambiguous language. As Louise Mallinder notes, the state may do this "by using phrases such as 'ferocious and barbarous acts', 'atrocious' acts, or 'blood crimes', but failing to define these terms. This ambiguity contributes to concealing the truth about events and denies acknowledgement to the victims."[257] It is, therefore, advisable to seek to define any context-specific offense directly in the text of an amnesty law, to the extent that it is not already codified in other domestic legislation.

4.3.2 The persons who are expressly eligible or ineligible

Negotiating whom to include or exclude from an amnesty is often central to the prospect of a viable transition to democracy or peace. Unless there has been a complete military or political victory, one is invariably negotiating with a party or parties who wield the ability to continue or renew serious violations and who are themselves the most vulnerable to prosecution. Notwithstanding this dilemma, it is desirable for an amnesty to clearly demarcate an explicit *ratione personae* (i.e., personal scope of application).

Most amnesties will set out the specific categories of persons who are eligible for leniency.[258] In many cases, an amnesty also will specify certain categories of persons as being expressly ineligible, even if such persons committed crimes that are covered under the amnesty. In addition, persons tend to be made eligible or ineligible on the basis of affiliation or rank, or on the basis of the nature of their participation in particular crimes. Some amnesties also expressly exclude specific individuals who may have been responsible or previously convicted for certain crimes, or who may have benefited from previous amnesties. Each of these categories is examined here, providing further demonstration of the variety of ways to minimize the scope of leniency an amnesty provides.

4.3.2.1 Distinctions according to affiliations and subaffiliations. An amnesty can cover persons with a wide range of possible affiliations, whether at the state level (e.g., army, police, intelligence agency), the parastatal level (e.g., militia, self-defense groups, paramilitaries), or the non-state level (e.g., national liberation movements, terrorist groups, private companies, religious institutions). There is also a wide range of possible subaffiliations that may be addressed through an amnesty (e.g., when one or more special units of a security institution are responsible for designated offenses).

Naturally, as a general rule, the text of an amnesty should be as precise as possible about the affiliation requirements needed to benefit from the amnesty – especially when it concerns serious crimes. Language that is too general or ambiguous may risk extending the scope of the amnesty to unintended beneficiaries, thus curtailing future domestic justice options.

Although the precise intentions of a state in granting amnesty often are difficult to discern, much is revealed about its motivations by the choices concerning the law's beneficiaries. At one end of the spectrum are so-called self-amnesties, or amnesties given by a government to itself and its allies for crimes directly attributable to them. Such amnesties contravene the general principle of not being judge in one's own cause and, as such, manifest anything but good faith. Examples of self-amnesties include, for example, those of *Turkey 1961*,[259] *France 1962*,[260] *Peru 1967*,[261] *Philippines 1994*,[262] and *Russia 1999*.[263] One must, nevertheless, be careful in characterizing certain laws as self-amnesties. For example, a civilian government may be pressured by the country's military to pass a broad amnesty law. It may then proceed to do so, not out of conviction or solidarity, but out of fear of a coup d'état.[264] Inasmuch as the government in such a situation is not trying to immunize itself from accountability but to protect constitutional rule, it would be inappropriate to characterize such an amnesty as a self-amnesty.[265]

At the opposite end of the amnesty spectrum are what might be called non-self-amnesties, or amnesties given by a state to benefit only its opponents – whether they be political dissidents or armed rebel movements. Such amnesties may be conferred as an incentive to leave the field of battle or, in other contexts, as a means to correct a past political or judicial wrongdoing.[266] The motivation of a state in adopting such amnesties generally may be presumed to be bona fide, absent any clear evidence to the contrary. However, some caution is in order, as such amnesties may in fact amount to political ploys. For example, a government could choose to adopt a non-self-amnesty as a way to publicly impute the conduct of its political enemies and exonerate itself, as the conferral of amnesty can imply past wrongdoing on the part of the amnesty receiver and clean hands on the part of the amnesty giver.[267] Ironically, though, the result of such a ploy would not be entirely negative, because the absence of amnesty benefits for the amnesty giver means that all future domestic justice options against it would remain open (at least to the extent that such options have not been curtailed by other legislation, such as state of emergency decrees immunizing official conduct in defense of the state).[268]

Examples of non-self-amnesties include, for example, the amnesties of *Cambodia 1994,*[269] *Djibouti 1994,*[270] *Uganda 2000,*[271] and *Bahrain 2001.*[272] In terms of state practice, Louise Mallinder observes that non-self-amnesties appear to be the most common type of amnesty adopted by states.[273] This rather surprising fact suggests that amnesty often is used not for the purpose of entrenching impunity for one's own side but rather as a means to end conflict or violence that is afflicting the country.

Between the extremes of self-amnesty and non-self-amnesty are so-called reciprocal or symmetrical amnesties,[274] which encompass anything from an amnesty negotiated by state and non-state actors in which both sides benefit, to an amnesty adopted unilaterally by a state but that benefits both itself and its opponents. Examples of reciprocal amnesties include, for example, the amnesties of *Spain 1977,*[275] *Honduras 1991,*[276] *Tajikistan 1997,*[277] *Angola 2002,*[278] and *Ivory Coast 2007.*[279]

Reciprocal amnesties require careful scrutiny, especially when adopted unilaterally by the state, because they may be tantamount to self-amnesties (e.g., when the overwhelming majority of offenses are objectively attributable to the state and not to the armed opposition).[280] Where reciprocal amnesties result from negotiation, however, the motivations are less suspicious. Yet even then it is important to closely examine the facts because the amnesty could be equivalent to a collective self-amnesty, as when both sides have committed a comparable and significant number of grave crimes. Reciprocal amnesties adopted by democratically elected governments and bolstered by public debate and consultation, as occurred most famously in South Africa with the 1995 Promotion of National Unity and Reconciliation Act, are the least suspect.[281]

Notwithstanding the above considerations, it should be recalled that there are narrower categories of affiliation and subaffiliation that also can be incorporated in the drafting of, or subsequent amendments to, amnesties. For example, the *Algeria 1999* amnesty applies only to members of a restricted list of terrorist organizations set out in the criminal code, not to terrorist organizations in general.[282] The *Philippines 2000* amnesty applies to the army and police only, not to other state institutions.[283] The *Solomon Islands 2000* amnesty applies only to specific rebel groups and specific security forces within government.[284] Such specificity in the eligible classes of beneficiaries is welcome from the perspective of accountability because it serves to minimize, with greater precision, the scope of leniency conceded through the amnesty.[285]

4.3.2.2 Distinctions according to rank. In addition to specifying affiliation (e.g., amnesty *x* applies only to members of the national police), it may be important for an amnesty to also specify eligibility according to rank (e.g., amnesty *x* applies only to members of the national police below, or alternatively above, the rank of captain). Admittedly, such distinctions in rank can appear unrealistic in some circumstances. For example, in the context of an amnesty negotiation, the exclusion of leaders from the amnesty's scope is ordinarily quite difficult to achieve because they or their proxies are the ones with whom one is negotiating. Such leaders may be able to compromise in some areas and accept certain unfavorable conditions of a transitional settlement, but they are unlikely to sign an agreement that exposes them to full prosecution immediately after signature.

Accountability-oriented parties must nevertheless consider the possible use of rank distinctions, especially if a DDR program is part of the broader settlement. That is because the absence of a rank qualifier in an amnesty (e.g., limiting the amnesty to senior ranks of a rebel or paramilitary group) may dissuade lower ranks from DDR participation. Such individuals are unlikely to be the objects of prosecution, and therefore any theoretical gain in the preservation of justice options often is outweighed by the practical loss in conflict resolution terms.[286] However, this does not mean that individuals of lower rank are more deserving of amnesty than their commanders. As Ron Slye observes, "An amnesty limited to subordinates . . . will also result in those who were most immediately responsible for torture and other atrocities walking free with minimal accountability and no punishment."[287] It is, indeed, not obvious that many victims of torture or similar abuses will feel that justice has been served if their direct torturer goes unpunished while the distant leader ends up behind bars; one cannot stand for the other.

Concerning state practice in this area, there are many examples of amnesties that expressly qualify inclusion or exclusion on the basis of rank within an amnesty-eligible institution. These include the amnesties of *Greece 1974* (excludes those chiefly responsible for political crimes directed against the constitutional order),[288] *Portugal 1976* (excludes military leaders),[289] and

Cambodia 1994 (excludes political leaders).[290] In contemplating exclusions of this sort, it can be beneficial to refer to relevant norms of contemporary international criminal law. These provide useful terminology regarding the principle of command responsibility,[291] as well as the corollary principle of due obedience to superior orders.[292]

A final consideration on making exclusions based on rank is to not lose sight of the possible parallel application of official immunities such as state and head-of-state immunity. These immunities may shield political leaders from criminal prosecution, notwithstanding the deliberate exclusion of the same persons from the terms of an amnesty.[293]

4.3.2.3 Distinctions according to forms of criminal participation. In addition to limitations based on affiliation and rank, amnesty eligibility also can be restricted on the basis of the nature of a person's participation in the crimes in question. Although some amnesties cover persons irrespective of the manner of participation in an eligible crime, others expand or narrow eligibility on the basis of the nature of such participation.

Every legal tradition defines forms of criminal participation somewhat differently but the following categories are in wide and general use: committing or attempting to commit a crime, ordering a crime, aiding or abetting a crime, conspiring with others to commit a crime, inciting commission of a crime, and being an accessory after the fact.[294] Participation qualifiers of this sort can be found, for example, in the amnesties of *Zimbabwe 1980* (includes conspiracy, incitement, and attempt to commit eligible offenses),[295] *Guatemala 1982* (includes authors, accomplices, and those who covered up eligible crimes),[296] *Venezuela 2000* (includes authors, collaborators, accomplices, and adherents),[297] and *Uganda 2000* (applies to actual participants, collaborators, and anyone assisting or aiding in war or armed rebellion against the government).[298]

Consistent with the ideal of excluding those in command positions from eligibility for amnesty, it is desirable to exclude persons who gave orders to commit atrocities. Again, however, one must recognize the reality that such persons, often leaders, are usually unwilling to agree to an amnesty that excludes them from eligibility.

A comparably difficult challenge is whether and how to amnesty criminal collaborators in the aftermath of a long period of nationwide collaboration such as occurred, for example, in the context of Nazi occupations across Europe during the Second World War and Soviet occupations during the Cold War.[299] Given the scale of forced and unforced collaboration in such settings, it is often tempting to extend leniency very far, including to public officials whose ongoing service may be necessary for the state to continue functioning.[300]

4.3.2.4 Express exclusion of beneficiaries of prior amnesties. Some amnesties expressly exclude those who benefited from previous amnesties. Examples include the amnesties of *Portugal 1976*[301] and *Philippines 2000*.[302] In a similar vein, and with like purpose and effect, some amnesties expressly exclude recidivists. Examples of the latter include the amnesties of *Burundi 1990*[303] and *Zimbabwe 2000*.[304]

These exclusions send an important signal about state intolerance for repeat abusers and underscore the crucial message that amnesty beneficiaries should not expect to receive leniency in future should they be foolish enough to commit new crimes. As explained further on, this message can be further reinforced by making the original amnesty revocable in the event that new offenses are committed.[305]

4.3.2.5 Express exclusion of foreign mercenaries. Some amnesties expressly exclude non-nationals or foreign mercenaries from eligibility. Examples include the amnesties of *Angola 2000*[306] and *Ivory Coast 2003*.[307] The likely purpose of such exclusions is dual: to vilify foreigners who may be perceived as having contributed to a country's conflict and to preserve the possibility of domestic criminal trials against them.

Considering modern-day challenges such as foreign terror networks operating in Iraq, Somalia, and Pakistan, the motivation for excluding such persons or groups from any national amnesty would seem compelling. However, the exclusion of non-nationals from a national amnesty may complicate the resolution of conflicts of a transboundary nature.[308] In addition, some armed groups reasonably may be characterized as national liberation movements and, as such, may attract the participation of well-intentioned foreigners who wish to express solidarity with the movement's just cause (e.g., idealists who fought with the African National Congress in South Africa). At the end of a conflict, such persons ideally should receive the same treatment under an amnesty as their national counterparts in the movement.

4.3.2.6 Express exclusion of specific individuals. Perhaps the most precise way to stipulate who qualifies under the terms of an amnesty is to have an appendix to the law that actually names the specific individuals who are excluded. Normally, such a list should consist only of names of persons against whom there is credible evidence of wrongdoing that has been verified by an independent judicial or quasi-judicial authority or by an independent ombudsman or commission of inquiry. The use of such a list also should be accompanied by an appropriate procedure for named persons to challenge their inclusion on the list.[309]

Provided such conditions of procedural fairness are met, this approach may be a useful one because of its exactness and its contribution to the goal of minimum leniency. This list approach was used in the *Uganda 2000* amnesty, as amended, which excludes from the law's benefits only a handful of named individuals (i.e., the Lord's Resistance Army leaders who are subjects of ICC arrest warrants).[310] The *Yemen 1994* amnesty similarly excludes sixteen persons named in an arrest warrant issued by the public prosecutor, which is annexed to the law.[311] The same approach was used, albeit more confusingly, in the case of the *1996 Croatia* amnesty.[312]

4.3.3 Express legal consequences of grant of amnesty for the beneficiary

There are many possible legal consequences of a grant of amnesty for the beneficiary. Beneficiaries may receive immunity from prosecution only, or they may receive immunity from other forms of liability as well. For persons who are the subjects of investigation, subpoenas, warrants, trials, judgments, or sentences, there is a wide range of possible legal consequences that may differ from other beneficiaries who are not the subject of such proceedings. In addition, amnesties sometimes provide for a range of possible consequences with regard to personal records of eligible persons, and for rights of action against third parties. Amnesties also can vary the legal consequences for beneficiaries according to the gravity of the offense committed, including by the insertion of prospective prohibitions. Each of these variables is discussed herein.

4.3.3.1 Immunity of individual from prospective forms of liability. Ideally an amnesty will be expressly limited to immunity from prosecution. In most cases, that is what perpetrators fear most, at least in comparison to civil liability. As Andreas O'Shea observes:

> I am aware of no examples of [amnesty] laws that only cover civil and not criminal liability. This is understandable. Given that the major objectives of an amnesty law are usually to facilitate political transition and the reconciliation of the nation, the principal concern for immunity is in the criminal field. The potential deprivation of liberty and, in those states still employing the death penalty, the potential loss of life of the political offender, are the gravest consequences for – and the immediate concern of – the political offender.[313]

By limiting an amnesty's legal effects to immunity from criminal liability, the possibilities for judicial investigations, truth commissions, civil suits, non-judicial disciplinary actions, and extradition proceedings remain open, thus representing a gain for accountability options.[314] In legal systems in which civil redress is structurally dependent on the availability of criminal redress, however, the gain in limiting the amnesty to immunity from prosecution may be largely illusory.[315] This is especially the case for civil law systems, where civil recovery often is directly contingent on a prior criminal conviction.[316] Yet civil recovery may be illusory for other reasons, too, such as the dysfunction of postconflict justice systems or the insolvency of perpetrators. Nevertheless, as a rule, it is preferable to formally preserve the legal possibility of civil redress by limiting the amnesty's scope to immunity from prosecution.[317]

Examples of amnesties that are limited to immunity from prosecution – and that, in some cases, expressly rule out immunity from civil actions – include those of *Spain 1977*,[318] *Angola 1994*,[319] *Haiti 1994*,[320] *Guatemala 1996*,[321] and the *Democratic Republic of Congo 2009*.[322] The *Algeria 1990* amnesty provides that the expunging of the criminal judgments is without prejudice to the rights of third parties, who can obtain civil relief as though the criminal judgment was still intact.[323]

Not all amnesties are limited to immunity from criminal prosecution. In fact, there are many amnesties that expressly provide for immunity from criminal and civil liability.[324] Examples of such amnesties include those of *Turkey 1982*,[325] *Nicaragua 1990*,[326] and *Solomon Islands 2000*.[327] Although the approach of including civil immunity in an amnesty is inherently problematic, it does not close the door to accountability altogether. Accountability may still be possible through judicial and nonjudicial investigations, disciplinary sanctions, and extradition – unless the amnesty provides otherwise, as some unfortunately do. For example, a *Peru 1995* amnesty extended immunity to investigation,[328] as did the *Mexico 1994* amnesty concerning violence in the state of Chiapas.[329] A *Solomon Islands 2000* amnesty law cancels the effects of any disciplinary proceedings affecting individual beneficiaries.[330] There does not, however, appear to be any amnesty that expressly excludes extradition to a foreign court or to an international criminal tribunal.[331] Yet with the rise of international and mixed criminal tribunals, and the increased recourse to criminal and civil trials before foreign courts, the question of extradition could become a significant issue in future amnesty negotiations.[332]

4.3.3.2 Effect on ongoing investigations, subpoenas, warrants, and trials. Where an amnesty provides immunity from criminal or civil liability, the impact is different on persons who are not the active subjects of investigation, subpoenas, warrants, or trials, than on persons who are. In the former case, there is often no affirmative step that is required of the beneficiary to enjoy such immunity (unless the amnesty is application-based).[333] In the latter case, the person is already the subject of a legal process, and thus, in many cases, he or she may have to take an affirmative step and cancel or bring to an end the particular proceeding to confirm his or her eligibility for amnesty.

From an accountability preservation perspective, it is preferable for an amnesty to specify that it will have no application to ongoing investigations, subpoenas, warrants, or trials. This approach is also more consistent with the principle of separation of powers between legislative, executive, and judicial branches.

State practice in this area varies widely. The *Argentina 1987* amnesty revokes outstanding summonses.[334] The *El Salvador 1993* amnesty calls for immediate cancellation of arrest orders and immediate cancellation of judicial proceedings.[335] The *Zimbabwe 1979* amnesty requires that ongoing trials be discontinued and adds that costs are to be left "in the discretion of the court."[336] The *Honduras 1991* amnesty provides that all ongoing and future cases against persons whose acts were amnestied are to be dismissed.[337] In another variation, the *Chile 1978* amnesty expressly precludes the termination of one particular judicial investigation.[338] The *Colombia 2003* amnesty provides that the legal benefit to the applicant – whether pardon, conditional amnesty, or cancellation of investigation and trial proceedings – is determined according to where the concerned individual stands within the judicial process at the time of his or her application.[339]

4.3.3.3 Effect on prior judgments and sentences. Earlier we examined the question of whether and how an amnesty ensures immunity from prospective forms of legal liability. A related but separate question is whether and how an amnesty applies to prior or existing civil judgments and criminal convictions. Here again the issue touches on the principle of separation of powers and more specifically the principle of *res judicata*, which holds that "a matter once judicially decided is finally decided."[340] This principle is sacrosanct in many legal traditions, although all legal systems allow pardons from criminal judgments and do not treat those as violations of *res judicata*. However, the benefit and justification for breaching the principle of *res judicata* and overturning such judgments are less apparent in the case of amnesties. Whereas with a pardon the underlying judgment normally remains in place, with an amnesty any underlying judgment usually is deemed null and void. All else being equal, therefore, it is preferable for prior civil and criminal judgments to remain undisturbed by an amnesty – unless, of course, the judgments were rendered pursuant to unfair trials.

There is diverse state practice on this issue. For example, the amnesties of *Hungary 1992*[341] and *El Salvador 1993*[342] provide for release from prison and voiding or cancellation of the prison sentence. The amnesties of *Uganda 2000*[343] and *Greece 1974*[344] provide for prison release and judgment cancellation but only after investigation and approval by public prosecutors, who have an affirmative obligation to investigate each case. The *Luxembourg 1955* and *Afghanistan 1991* amnesties provide for cancellation of the sentence, unless the sentence was accompanied by the obligation to pay a fine, in which case the fine would first have to be paid.[345] The *Belgium 1945* amnesty goes one step further: it denies restitution of fines previously paid in connection with the criminal judgment of an amnestied party.[346]

There are also many amnesties that exclude application to prior criminal judgments and sentences. Examples of such exclusions are found in the amnesties of *Guatemala 1986* (excludes those against whom a verdict was issued in relation to an eligible crime),[347] *Romania 1990* (excludes those convicted of a long list of eligible crimes),[348] and *El Salvador 1992* (excludes those convicted of political crimes in jury trials).[349] The *Burundi 1990* amnesty excludes both defendants and convicts of certain crimes.[350]

In still other cases, amnesties have provided for conditional forms of release and suspended sentences for convicts rather than full and unconditional releases. For example, the *Algeria 1999* amnesty envisages temporary release from prison while the amnesty applicant's disclosures are verified. During that time, the applicant must remain on good behavior and fulfill a range of "obligatory compliance measures" imposed by the state.[351] This example invites a more general prescription: if some form of release from prison is deemed necessary for convicts in a particular amnesty context, it ideally should be application-based, require a prior official investigation of the disclosures made in the application, and operate as a conditional release or suspended sentence rather than a full and unconditional release.

Concerning prior civil judgments, most amnesties do not address the question at all and seem on the whole to leave such judgments in place. In some cases, amnesties explicitly have provided for them to remain intact. For example, the *South Africa 1995* amnesty declares the continuation in force of civil judgments issued prior to a final decision on any individual amnesty application.[352] The *Zimbabwe 1979* amnesty, by contrast, provides that if a judgment was not enforced prior to the amnesty's coming into force, it cannot be enforced subsequently.[353]

4.3.3.4 Effect on personal records. As explained in Part I, amnesties and pardons are related but different types of leniency measures. Among the distinguishing features of pardons, one is particularly relevant here: the fact that pardons lead to the release from prison of the convicted person but leave the underlying

judgment and related personal records in place. From an accountability perspective, this is how it should be with amnesties, too, when they affirmatively
provide for the release of individuals who were previously convicted in a fair
trial.[354]

Most amnesties are silent on the question of how to handle existing official
records that relate to a person's alleged or proven responsibility for eligible
crimes. The implication of this silence is that nothing is to be done with the
records following a grant of amnesty. However, there are examples of amnesties
that expressly expunge personal records. Some of these are inspired by a
desire to invalidate unjust prior convictions, such as a *Spain 1977* amnesty.[355]
The *Burkina Faso 1991* and *Djibouti 1993* amnesties preserve the recorded
judgments but prohibit any person from recalling or citing the offenses or the
sentences in future.[356] A different example is the amnesty of *South Africa 1995*,
which provides that records of amnesty applicants are to be deemed expunged
if their application is successful.[357]

4.3.3.5 Effect on third parties. Taking into account the objective of minimum
leniency, an amnesty generally should apply only to the individuals who committed eligible offenses. However, sometimes an amnesty may go further and
offer immunity – criminal, civil, or both – to third parties that might bear legal
responsibility. Such immunity normally is conferred according to the principle of vicarious liability, which provides that the employer, whether state
or non-state, is legally or corporately responsible for the negligent acts and
omissions of subordinate employees.

When it comes to amnesties, vicarious liability normally should remain
undisturbed. However, there may be circumstances where such liability may
be conditionally extinguished in whole or in part. For example, where an
impoverished successor government inherits a legacy of mass abuse that is
not of its own making and it wishes to provide a comprehensive out-of-court
reparations program for the victims of that abuse, it may be reasonable for the
state to conditionally extinguish its vicarious liability through an amnesty or
similar legislation. Providing immunity from vicarious liability also may be
legitimate when criminal disclosures through an amnesty application process
(e.g., as occurred in the case of the South African TRC) potentially could
expose the state to vicarious liability claims on a mass scale.[358]

4.3.3.6 Variation in legal consequences depending on crime or rank. It is implicit
in the foregoing discussion that the consequences of an amnesty for eligible
persons will be uniform as between each person. However, some amnesties
vary legal consequences depending on the particular crime and the nature

of a person's participation in it. For example, an amnesty can provide that persons responsible for violent crimes receive less favorable benefits than those responsible for nonviolent crimes. This type of approach generally is desirable because it permits the use of proportionality in the allocation of positive and negative legal consequences.[359] It is also more consistent with standard criminal sentencing practice, which aims to treat like cases alike and unalike cases unalike in accordance with their differences. Consequently, whenever possible, it is best to avoid a uniform set of consequences for all eligible amnesty beneficiaries in respect of all eligible crimes and instead vary the consequences according to the type and number of crimes committed by the individual in question, his or her form of participation in each, and his or her rank within the eligible institution.

An example of such an amnesty is that of *Burundi 1993*, in which full amnesty was granted for less serious crimes, but only a sentence reduction for more serious crimes.[360] Similarly, the *Algeria 1999* amnesty provides that those who did not murder, permanently disable, rape, commit collective massacres, or use explosives in a public place are eligible to receive immunity from prosecution, whereas those who committed certain of those acts are eligible only for probation, conditional release, reduced sentences, or exemption from the death penalty.[361] Analogous to the truth commission model adopted in Timor-Leste, the legal consequences of amnesty also could be made contingent on the gradual fulfillment of various conditions, such as participation in a DDR process, the revelation of one's crimes, or the performance of community repentance measures. In other words, the degree of immunity for the beneficiary could increase in a sequential manner tied to the individual's step-by-step fulfillment of such conditions.[362]

4.3.4 Geographical scope of application

Most amnesties do not expressly provide a *ratione loci* (i.e., geographical scope of application) for eligibility. They do not state whether the amnesty will apply to crimes committed anywhere in the country, to those committed in selected parts of the country only, or to those committed outside of the country. In such instances, therefore, the implied presumption is that the amnesty applies to crimes committed anywhere in the country.[363]

Yet if crimes were committed exclusively in selected parts of the country, an amnesty ideally should be limited to crimes committed within those specific areas. This would be yet another way to minimize the scope of leniency an amnesty confers. Examples of such subnational amnesties include those of *United States 1902* (which excludes crimes committed in certain parts of country that were under civilian rule),[364] *Philippines 1976* (which is limited to provincial jurisdictions where there was unrest),[365] and *Democratic Republic of Congo 2009* (which is limited to crimes committed in North and South Kivu).[366]

4.3.5 Temporal scope of application

We already have discussed the duration of an amnesty law's application. Later in the discussion, we will examine the question of the timeframe within which an amnesty applicant must come forward. The present section concerns an amnesty's *ratione temporis* (i.e., the time period within which the crimes must have occurred for them to be eligible for leniency under the amnesty).

Taking into consideration the objective of minimum leniency, ideally an amnesty's *ratione temporis* should be as circumscribed as possible, covering only the periods of time when the main violations took place and not extending to related but more peripheral periods. State practice on this issue is, however, rather mixed.

As one might expect, most amnesties specify an explicit period during which the crimes must have been committed. For example, it is common for amnesties to specify that eligible crimes must have been committed both after a specific date (i.e., start date) and before a specific date (i.e., end date). This is the case, for example, with the amnesties of *Chile 1978,*[367] *Brazil 1979,*[368] *Nicaragua 1990,*[369] *Mozambique 1992,*[370] and *Albania 1997.*[371] Sometimes, however, the start and end dates are not expressly stated but rather implied in descriptive phrases such as "during the recent conflict." This is typical of amnesties contained in peace agreements, including those of *Liberia 1993* and *Democratic Republic of the Congo 1999,*[372] possibly because such agreements require the promulgation of more detailed and specific implementing legislation subsequent to the signing of the agreement.

In contrast to this practice, some amnesties reference an end date but no precise start date. Examples of such amnesties include those of *Uruguay 1986,*[373] *El Salvador 1992,*[374] and *Philippines 1994.*[375] Presumably this is done because the start date is irrelevant (i.e., the amnesty deliberately extends backward in time without end) or implied (e.g., a reference to "the period of military rule" might imply a specific start date). In other cases, such as the amnesties of *Guatemala 1983* and *Uganda 2000,*[376] there is reference to a specific start date but no reference to an explicit end date, other than the final date on which an application for amnesty can be submitted or on which the legislation ceases to have effect absent legislative renewal. This practice is risky because it can amount to a license to commit ongoing crimes without the discipline imposed by an immediate end date. The practice is nevertheless common in respect of defection-oriented amnesties that are adopted to encourage political dissidents or rebel soldiers to abandon their struggles.[377]

4.4 Maximum conditions

This section looks at two different ways of ensuring accountability with respect to an amnesty beneficiary. Specifically, it examines (1) conditions for obtaining amnesty and (2) conditions for retaining amnesty.

Unlike the prior sections, which were primarily concerned with how to limit the scope and legal consequences of an amnesty, this section is primarily concerned with the goal of imposing the most demanding conditions possible on any potential or actual amnesty beneficiary. The insertion of such conditions into amnesties increasingly is being practiced by states.[378] It is important, however, to reiterate that the degree to which elements of accountability can be incorporated into an amnesty usually is inversely related to the power of the party seeking the amnesty. The more powerful the party, the fewer and the weaker the elements of accountability normally will be. Conversely, the less powerful the party, the more and the stronger the elements of accountability will be. It is also important to underscore that conditionality of any sort works only when there is a willingness and capacity for enforcement.[379] In such cases, the possible range of useful amnesty conditions is almost limitless and can be combined in a variety of ways, as explained herein.

4.4.1 Conditions for obtaining individual grants of amnesty

A great number of amnesties place preconditions on potential beneficiaries, the nonfulfillment of which results in the denial of amnesty. Here are discussed only the most common and most apt preconditions vis-à-vis amnesties for human rights crimes. Such preconditions help insert an important degree of accountability into the amnesty-granting process, especially when paired with postconferral conditions for retaining the amnesty.

4.4.1.1 Requirement to submit an individual application. Most amnesties do not provide for the administration of individual grants of amnesty. Eligibility is presumed (i.e., automatic) and individuals need not affirmatively apply. There are, however, an increasing number of examples of amnesties that require persons to apply for eligibility,[380] whether formally (e.g., by submitting a written and signed application or request) or informally (e.g., by presenting themselves in person to a designated authority). Examples of application-based amnesties include those of *Colombia 1981*,[381] *El Salvador 1983*,[382] *Philippines 1994*,[383] *South Africa 1995*,[384] *Algeria 1999*,[385] and *Uganda 2000*.[386] The chief advantage of requiring an application is the insertion into the process of a level of both voluntariness and accountability.[387] The burden of proof of eligibility is on the individual, not on the state.[388]

As between a formal and written amnesty application, and an informal and unwritten one, the former is naturally preferable when taking into account the objective of maximum conditionality. In South Africa, amnesty applicants had to complete forms that required detailed information on specific human rights violations, including questions that forced them to give the reason not only for applying for amnesty but also for having originally committed the acts for which amnesty was being sought. In Uganda, amnesty application forms pose a range of questions that are used to facilitate the operation of a related DDR program.[389]

It is important to appreciate, however, that application-based amnesty procedures can be extremely demanding in terms of time and resources. Even the South African TRC's Amnesty Committee – a relatively well-resourced amnesty body – struggled to get through its caseload. The challenge of processing amnesty applications in a timely manner nearly undid the committee until they added more judges – and even then it took years longer than planned.[390] Consequently, when the application caseload is potentially overwhelming in number and complexity, and when a state's financial and technical capacity is relatively low, prudence would dictate that the amnesty law and procedure should be targeted at only the most serious cases. There could still be an application process for the inevitably larger number of "less serious" cases, but it could operate in a simplified manner.[391]

4.4.1.2 Requirement to meet application deadline. For application-based amnesties to work well, there needs to be a short but reasonable application deadline and, ideally, the threat of judicial investigation following expiration of the deadline against those who fail to come forward on time.

Application-based amnesties, including most of those mentioned earlier, tend to provide a deadline to benefit from the amnesty. The period typically ranges from one month to twelve months, often reserving the possibility to extend the end date if necessary. These deadlines are beneficial because they create an extra incentive to come forward and apply, and thus participate in a national reconciliation process. However, it is important to ensure that an application period is neither too short (leaving insufficient time to advertise the option) nor too long (creating the incentive to continue the violence for a longer period, in direct opposition to the amnesty's underlying purpose).[392] With a fixed deadline in place, the incentive for combatants in a civil war to return to civilian life is increased because there is no future guarantee of amnesty, whether through renewal of the original amnesty or enactment of a new one. By corollary, the absence of a fixed deadline or the repeated extension or renewal of the same amnesty can counterproductively deter conflict resolution.[393] Therefore, it is generally advisable to create and publicize the threat of imposing a supplementary legal punishment against those who do not come forward before the deadline and are later captured and tried.

4.4.1.3 Requirement of full and accurate disclosure of crimes. Some application-based amnesties, including the one devised for the TRC in South Africa, obligate applicants to provide a full description of the crimes they committed and for which they claim entitlement to amnesty.[394] Garth Meintjes and Juan Méndez rightly observe that, "to the extent that amnesty applicants are required expressly to acknowledge both the criminality of their actions and their culpability, it should be seen as upholding rather than denying the victims' right to justice."[395]

Beyond the South African case, other examples of amnesties that require disclosure of crimes include those of *Portugal 1976*,[396] *Poland 1984*,[397] and *Algeria 1999 and 2006*.[398] It is noteworthy that many of these same laws also expressly provide for the retraction of amnesty on the discovery of material misrepresentations of fact in the original application that cannot reasonably be excused. The *Algeria 1999* amnesty, for example, envisages the affirmative prosecution of the crimes that formed the subject of the defective or deceptive application.[399] The *Portugal 1976* amnesty goes even further, by providing that the penalty for the original infraction increases as a result of the deception.[400]

Amnesties also may obligate applicants to disclose knowledge or evidence about the crimes of others. Though rarely required of applicants, information about third parties can be especially valuable when a conflict is ongoing. Usually in such circumstances a state is more interested in identifying combatants' whereabouts or the details of their command and control structures than in eliciting information for purposes of criminal prosecution.[401] Such conflict-related intelligence, if used for legitimate purposes, can help to improve the overall national security situation.[402] It also may reveal the whereabouts of missing persons.[403] Such an approach nevertheless risks corrupting the amnesty process, as the amnesty-generated revelations against third parties could be abused or manipulated by the state. In addition, a requirement to disclose the crimes of third parties could hamper a speedy conclusion of the conflict, as those eligible for an amnesty might be dissuaded from coming forward in the first place because of threats against them from those most likely to be adversely implicated.

Whether an applicant is required to disclose his or her own crimes only or those of others as well, he or she should ideally be required to provide a full description of such crimes, including a list of documentary and physical evidence within his or her possession or control. Surprisingly, most amnesties are not explicit about the kind of information and evidence applicants must provide as part of a complete application.[404] In any event, prior to adopting a detailed disclosure requirement, a serious evaluation should be done of the domestic capacity to implement a scheme of such operational complexity.[405] Truth recovery work can easily be impaired or undercut when an implementing body lacks adequate resources to verify the factual claims made.

Even if the capacity exists to implement an application-based amnesty process with robust disclosure requirements, expectations around the results should be kept in check because there are many reasons perpetrators may prefer to remain silent and forgo the possibility of obtaining amnesty. Such reasons may include distrust of the state or the implementation body, risk of family and community humiliation, fear of revenge attacks, concern about breaking rank with former comrades, or continued belief in the legitimacy or noncriminality of the amnesty-eligible actions. A lack of participation by eligible applicants also may occur for want of a credible threat of prosecution.[406] The lack of such a threat will tend to affect participation by more senior offenders in particular.[407] While their nonparticipation in the amnesty process will have the negative effect of reducing the amount of truth that is revealed out of court, it will have the positive effect of preserving the option of truth and justice in court against them. In this regard, it is worth noting that in South Africa the option of prosecution remains legally available against any perpetrator who did not receive immunity from prosecution under the TRC amnesty process or any prior amnesty such as the 1990 or 1992 indemnity schemes.[408] Whether there is the political will to carry forward with such prosecutions is a separate question.[409]

4.4.1.4 Requirement of apology.

It sometimes may be important to condition grants of amnesty on the making of an unqualified public apology, particularly in contexts where apologies are broadly considered as beneficial or necessary to the successful reintegration of ex-combatants or to a process of victim or societal healing.[410] Apology or acknowledgment could alternatively be a precondition of amnesty at the organizational rather than individual level such that a rebel, militia, or paramilitary group could be required to acknowledge its systemic wrongdoing as a first step in a broad amnesty process.

The idea of explicit acknowledgment of wrongdoing may, however, be inappropriate in various circumstances or at certain points in time. For example, if it is a condition of obtaining amnesty, an apology may tend to appear involuntary and insincere, thus eviscerating its potential symbolic and psychological value. In addition, it may be unrealistic or unfair to condition amnesty on an apology when the crimes in question were committed with a strong ideological motivation, such as a struggle for self-determination. At the same time, in the absence of an apology requirement, the significant risk is that amnesty applicants may not apologize at all for their crimes.

4.4.1.5 Requirement of public hearing. If an application-based amnesty process requires the disclosure of crimes, and possibly an apology, it would generally be important for the disclosure and apology to occur via a public hearing, as was the case with many amnesty applicants in South Africa.[411] The requirement of a public hearing is a crucial element of accountability and has the potential to lead to a different, and possibly greater, degree of public interest and truth recovery than a trial. As Ron Slye has observed:

> [I]t seems clear that in South Africa the amnesty hearings have resulted in substantially more participation by the accused than one finds in a typical trial. In a trial setting, the accused may, and often does, participate passively.... Their goal is to escape liability, and thus to raise as much doubt as possible about the claims of the state or the accused's alleged victims.[412]

In principle, the purpose of an amnesty hearing is the exact opposite of this – one must prove one's guilt and therefore convincingly disclose one's criminality.[413]

However, a public hearing may not lead to catharsis for the victim or the society, let alone for the amnesty applicant.[414] The body responsible for organizing the hearing must also be strict in its control of the proceedings and insistent on full cooperation, lest the amnesty applicant abuse the public platform for mischievous purposes, such as to justify or explain away his or her crimes.[415] Nevertheless, taking into consideration the objective of maximum conditionality, it is important to give consideration to a public hearing requirement, provided that there is a discretion on the part of the amnesty body to hold closed hearings. Such hearings may be necessary for reasons of security or privacy. They also may be necessary as an alternative means for truth revelation, as some perpetrators only may be willing to give a full account of their crimes, and the crimes of others, outside of the public spotlight.[416]

4.4.1.6 Requirement to participate in tradition-based justice process. Traditional justice – or what a recent and groundbreaking report usefully terms *tradition-based justice* – is an area that has been receiving increased attention in the fields of transitional justice and conflict resolution.[417] As the report in question notes, "There have been too few systematic attempts to analyze and assess the role and impact of traditional mechanisms in post-conflict settings."[418]

Tradition-based practices that include elements of accountability and social healing can be found on all continents.[419] Especially in Africa they have been linked with questions of amnesty and international justice, including in places such as Rwanda (*gacaca*), Uganda (*mato oput, nyono tong gweno*), Sierra Leone (*Kpaa Mende*), Burundi (*Bashingantahe*), and Mozambique (*magamba*).[420] Because these practices were not originally designed to deal with crimes against humanity, there are naturally limitations on what they can contribute to justice or reconciliation without significant modifications. At the same time, one must appreciate their inherent strengths, including that they tend to be more informal, more accessible, and potentially more locally resonant than Western models of justice and reconciliation. These strengths sometimes can be leveraged to help fill the massive "impunity gap" that ensues from any extended period of violent conflict or repressive rule.[421]

In some contexts, it may be possible to condition the granting of amnesty on participation in a tradition-based justice process. Such a requirement would be functionally akin to the idea of conditioning a grant of amnesty on participation in a truth commission process, as was done in South Africa.[422] However, it would be important to ensure that any conditioning of amnesty on obligatory participation in a tradition-based practice would not be counterproductive, bearing in mind that the reconciliation value of a tradition-based practice may reside in its voluntary character.

4.4.1.7 Requirement of restitution and community service. In addition to or in lieu of a formal apology, financial restitution or community service by the perpetrator could be made an explicit individual condition of eligibility for amnesty (irrespective of the state of the amnestied party's personal finances). Required acts of this sort are habitually integrated into criminal sentencing procedures in common law countries. They are also typical features of tradition-based justice mechanisms.[423] Restitution of illicit economic gains, in particular those made through wartime activity or regime-related corruption, also can help reinforce the link between past crime and the obligation of restitution. Part or all of the recuperated illegal funds potentially can be used for a comprehensive victim reparations program.

The primary purpose of conditioning an amnesty on acts of restitution and community service is to impose an additional and due measure of accountability on the applicant, and to deliver funds and infrastructural support to victims and their communities that might otherwise be unavailable. Although there do not appear to be any amnesties for human rights crimes that have explicitly incorporated such individual conditions, restitution and community service requirements did form part of the leniency schemes adopted in Timor-Leste[424] and in Colombia.[425] Not every state, however, will have the resources and capacity to administer such a scheme in the aftermath of repression or war. An alternative and procedurally simpler approach, therefore, may be to condition amnesty on the payment of a fixed fine to the state, the proceeds of which can be redistributed to victims.[426]

4.4.1.8 Requirement of relocation and supervision. Along with other preconditions of eligibility, the conferral of amnesty may be conditioned on temporary relocation to a part of the country where the risk of violence is significantly lower and where the activities of the amnesty applicant can be more effectively monitored. This would be akin to a release-on-bail scheme and might include regular supervision as well as reporting requirements by the applicant.[427] Such a scheme would partly fulfill criminal law's objective of incapacitation and DDR's objective of enhanced public security.[428]

Yet such a precondition could be applied only if it was clearly presented and accepted by the applicants, considering that it impinges on their human right to freedom of movement.[429] In addition, the supervised relocation could not be permanent but would instead need to be for a limited and fixed duration (which could be predetermined by the amnesty law or decided on by the body responsible for administering the amnesty).[430] Although analogies to this concept can be found in domestic criminal practice and supported within the terms of international law,[431] no precedent for such an amnesty condition was discovered in the course of this research.

Exile is, of course, another form of relocation, except that it involves leaving the country rather than simply relocating within it. Assuming there is a country willing to act as a host, an amnesty could be conditioned on the removal of certain leaders from their official positions and their exile from the country. For example, in the case of the Governor's Island Accord in Haiti, as a precondition for receiving amnesty, General Cédras and his entourage were obligated to resign and take exile in Panama.[432] The American and British governments extended a similar offer to former Iraqi president, Saddam Hussein, prior to invading the country in 2003.[433] If an exile conditionality is employed, it ideally should encompass an ongoing supervision requirement to ensure respect of its terms. As previously observed, however, the option of exile has become significantly less attractive and feasible since the extradition of Charles Taylor from Nigeria.[434]

4.4.1.9 Requirement of DDR participation. Amnesties issued in contexts of armed conflict often make voluntary surrender, or disarmament and demobilization, an explicit condition of a beneficiary's eligibility.[435] Examples include the amnesties of *Mexico 1978*,[436] *Colombia 1981*,[437] *Guatemala 1983*,[438] *Uganda 2000*,[439] and *Solomon Islands 2000*.[440] For such a condition to be effective, it is important that the government and the DDR implementation body enjoy a minimum degree of credibility.[441] Failing that, the incentive of amnesty likely will fail.[442] Cash inducements also may be required to make such an amnesty effective. As Louise Mallinder notes, "In many amnesty processes, insurgents do not simply have to turn themselves in, but are also encouraged or required to surrender their weapons, ammunitions and explosives. Sometimes, cash incentives, known as 'buy back' programmes, are introduced. These offer payments usually on a varying scale depending on the type of weaponry that is surrendered."[443]

Whatever disarmament and demobilization conditions are linked to the amnesty, one must recognize that such conditions are insufficient in and of themselves to ensure the sustainable reintegration of former combatants, which is a longer-term process.[444] Thus, it may be advisable in future to condition the legal benefits of an amnesty on effective participation for an initial trial period in the reintegration phase of a DDR program. Specifically, DDR and amnesty conditions could be linked in such a way that at every turn when an ex-combatant has to perform some amnesty-related act of accountability (e.g., an act of restitution in a community of reception), there is an acknowledgment and a benefit, such as an increase in the economic support package.[445] This approach could apply equally to state and non-state combatants – for example, rebel groups could insist on the disarming of self-defense militia and paramilitaries on the same terms.

4.4.1.10 Requirement of renunciation of violence. There are a number of amnesties that are made conditional on a sworn or written renunciation of violence, or the maintenance of a cease-fire, or both. Examples of such amnesties include those of *Poland 1984*,[446] *Algeria 1999*,[447] *Uganda 2000*,[448] and *Afghanistan 2007*.[449] Provided that such forms of affirmation and renunciation are voluntary, conditions of this sort seem unobjectionable from a normative and legal standpoint and could even have significant symbolic value.

Another approach may be to condition amnesty not only on the applicant's renunciation of violence and pledge to obey the law, but also on related legal and financial pledges by parents, guardians, or community leaders, akin to the procedures for posting bail in a criminal court. For example, to qualify under the *Philippines 1973* amnesty, the beneficiary not only had to disarm and renounce in writing any membership in a subversive group, but also had to "have his parents/guardians, or prominent members of his community pledge in writing that he shall remain peace-loving and law-abiding."[450] In principle, such an approach has the positive effect of making community peace a community responsibility and not only a state one.

4.4.1.11 Requirement of release of hostages and prisoners of war. There is a long-standing practice as part of cease-fire agreements and final peace agreements to include conditions for the exchange and release of prisoners and missing persons in accordance with the requirements of international law.[451] Consistent with that practice, and taking into account the widespread abduction of children and women in modern warfare, amnesties ideally should be conditioned on the release and return of hostages and other prisoners of war. There are numerous precedents of such an amnesty condition. Examples include the amnesties of *Guatemala 1982*,[452] *Mexico 1994*,[453] and *Fiji 2000*.[454]

4.4.1.12 Requirement of cooperation with law enforcement authorities. Some amnesties require, as a condition of eligibility, the cooperation of the applicant with law enforcement authorities. This may include the obligation to fully disclose relevant information about command structures, arms suppliers, and illicit trade routes, to provide assistance in locating bodies of missing persons, or to act as a witness at trial proceedings. Such conditions are typical in defection-oriented amnesties, as for example the *Algeria 1999* amnesty, which is conditional on the applicant's participation in the government's "fight against terrorism," though it does not specify the form of the participation.[455] A *Peru 1992* amnesty is conditional, inter alia, on sharing details about the operations and names of leaders of terrorist groups.[456] By analogy, a subsequent Peruvian law on "effective collaboration" is conditional on providing useful information on organized crime to state law enforcement authorities. It requires the applicant and the state to enter into a contract allowing the state to impose a diverse set of additional and court-validated obligations on the applicant (e.g., reporting obligations in relation to employment and residence, performance of acts of reparation and community service).[457]

4.4.2 Conditions for retaining individual grants of amnesty

The conferral of immunity upon fulfillment of preconditions should not constitute the end of an amnesty process but the beginning of a new one. If there are preconditions only for obtaining amnesty, and no conditions for retaining it, the level of an applicant's good faith and seriousness in seeking to fulfill the preconditions of eligibility may decrease significantly. The absence of conditions of amnesty retention would, in addition, eviscerate the capacity of the state to hold accountable those who abuse the process. Accordingly, conditions of retention are essential to any prudent amnesty scheme.

4.4.2.1 Requirement of nonbreach of amnesty's preconditions. A first and crucial condition for retention of the benefits of an amnesty is linked to the preconditions of eligibility. It could turn out that, after an amnesty's conferral, a prior material misrepresentation of facts by the applicant is discovered. When that is the case, there should be a consequence for the applicant that is foreseen in the amnesty's terms. Specifically, an amnesty should be explicitly revocable when a serious breach of any condition of eligibility is later discovered. In such event, the person ideally should be prosecuted both for the crime of perjury or fraud and for the original crimes, subject to his or her right against self-incrimination. Such a condition is crucial to help ensure a good-faith effort by applicants to fulfill an amnesty's preconditions in the first place.

4.4.2.2 Requirement of nonrecidivism. In addition to being explicitly revocable for any material incompliance with an amnesty's preconditions of eligibility, the benefits of an amnesty should be subject to revocation when any new human rights crime of comparable gravity is committed. Here again, an act of recidivism ideally should result in prosecution both for the crime of perjury or fraud and for the original crimes, subject to the right against self-incrimination. Examples of amnesties that make nonrecidivism an explicit condition of retention include those of *Iran 1980,*[458] *Romania 1990,*[459] *Lebanon 1991,*[460] *Angola 1994,*[461] and *Iraq 2008.*[462]

All else being equal, the general population is probably more likely to accept amnesty for past crimes if nonrecidivism is a condition included within the amnesty. Moreover, the concern about amnesties creating or reinforcing a culture of impunity is diminished significantly when such a condition is explicitly incorporated into an amnesty and subsequently enforced. At the same time, it always should be precisely stated in the amnesty what types of new crimes would be sufficiently serious to occasion the loss of amnesty, what legal consequences could ensue (e.g., merely loss of the amnesty or also punishment for the original crimes), and when those consequences would take effect. In principle, there should be no adverse legal consequences for the amnesty beneficiary until after he or she has been legally convicted in accordance with due process.

4.4.2.3 Requirement of compliance with prospective prohibitions. An additional condition for retaining an amnesty might be the placement of prospective prohibitions on the beneficiaries. Depending on a wide range of possible factors – such as the gravity of the crime committed, the level of remorse expressed, and the likelihood of recidivism – prohibitions might be placed on the beneficiary's ability to occupy certain positions in the security sector or to purchase or carry arms during a prescribed period.[463] Any such post-conferral conditions would, however, need to be expressly stipulated in the amnesty text. If not, their application would need to follow strict procedures to compensate for the lack of prior informed consent on the part of the amnesty beneficiaries. Such conditions also might need to be balanced, in some cases, with the human rights of the beneficiary, especially if the decision is taken by a nonjudicial or quasi-judicial body.[464]

4.4.2.4 Parallel requirement of pledges by the larger group. In addition to any conditions of retention at the individual level, there also could be conditions at the group level to lock in broader guarantees of good conduct in a new era. The *Colombia 1993* and *Colombia 1997* amnesties are examples of this approach.[465] Commenting on the idea of group pledges from a historical perspective, Ruti Teitel has observed that, "after the American Civil War, amnesties were made conditional on the Confederacy's continued loyalty to the Union. . . . This trade-off of the balancing of perpetrators' political rights in exchange for support of the newly constituted union and for the aim of political stability mirrors punishment's more conventional goals of assuring the rule of law."[466] A similar group pledge was also "read in" to the Lomé Peace Agreement by the Special Court for Sierra Leone, which determined that maintenance of a cease-fire was an implied condition of the agreement.[467] The release of political prisoners in Northern Ireland following the 1998 Good Friday Agreement also was linked to a broader organizational commitment to disarm.[468]

A related issue is what should happen to individuals who continue to respect an amnesty's conditions notwithstanding a formal breach by their former affiliated group. Presumably, the principle of individual responsibility should apply such that the cooperating individual will not be prejudiced for actions outside his or her control.

4.5 Maximum viability

This section focuses on the viability of the amnesty's own terms and procedures. While earlier in the discussion we looked at viability in terms of the trustworthiness of the implementing body, here we look at viability in terms of the capacity and fairness of the amnesty's formal administrative scheme.

Many amnesties set out an administrative process for the consideration of individual grants of amnesty, designating a specific body for the task. In addition, a number of amnesties establish important rules about victim participation in amnesty proceedings. Some also envisage the possibility of contestation of amnesties by rejected applicants. Each of these variables is briefly discussed here.

4.5.1 The supervisory body and its mandate

The minority of amnesties explicitly provide for a body or a process to administer individual grants of immunity. Eligibility is presumed, and the presumption engenders no resistance unless or until someone tries to prove ineligibility in a court of law (or conversely, to prove eligibility, as when one is already the object of a criminal proceeding). However, there are examples of amnesties providing for a designated body to administer individual grants of immunity, as described subsequently. It is important for such bodies to bear the hallmarks of independence and impartiality to conduct a procedure that will have the appearance and reality of fairness.[469] The designated body also should wield the requisite technical capacity to carry out its mandate or else risk ineffectiveness.[470] In this respect, it is noteworthy that the *Colombia 1982* amnesty contained a provision requiring one year of restructuring and capacity-building to equip the National Police to carry out its supervisory functions under the law.[471]

As to their terms of reference, it is generally desirable to imbue amnesty bodies with a robust mandate and set of powers akin to a modern truth commission, including the power to grant or recommend amnesty for individual applicants, search premises, seize evidence, subpoena witnesses and documents, and provide effective victim and witness support and protection. The chief advantage of having such powers is an increased ability to assess whether full disclosure has been given by an amnesty applicant, thus increasing his or her incentive to tell the whole truth and provide full cooperation. It is also generally desirable to empower or require an amnesty body to conduct public outreach, take statements from victims, conduct investigations into the facts alleged in amnesty applications, and hold private and public hearings for amnesty applicants.[472]

The preceding powers must, however, be balanced with the rights of the amnesty applicants. An amnesty body endowed with far-reaching powers should observe high standards of procedural fairness and thus include lawyers or judges as members. After all, the rejection of an amnesty application may entail severe legal and other consequences for an applicant.[473]

In terms of specific models for an amnesty body, the main choices are the following: an ad hoc amnesty commission, a truth commission, the courts, a government office, a specially deputized agency, or combinations of one or more of these (e.g., a deputized agency processes applications and a court makes the final decision on whether to extend amnesty).[474]

Concerning ad hoc amnesty commissions, it is very difficult to obtain information about the precise mandates of such commissions and their effectiveness in practice. The least that can be said is that the range of mandates appears to be quite broad. For example:

- Some commissions have a mandate to directly grant or deny amnesty (e.g., *Philippines 1994*),[475] including by virtue of having the authority to determine whether the acts in question in a particular case were politically motivated (e.g., *Rwanda 1963*).[476]
- Some have a mandate to recommend but not directly grant or deny amnesty (e.g., *Algeria 1999*).[477]
- Some have a mandate to administer the reception of amnesty applications without making binding determinations or formal recommendations (e.g., *Chad 1983*).[478]
- Some have a mandate to resolve difficulties of implementation and individual complaints referred by the government (e.g., *Jordan 1973*).[479]
- Some have a mandate to carry out a variety of additional tasks such as overseeing the process of demobilization, reintegration, and resettlement of applicants, and establishing a presence in conflict areas (e.g., *Colombia 1982*).[480]

Regarding the composition of amnesty commissions, the commissioners tend to be political appointees with limited independence from the appointing government.[481] In terms of powers, it is rare for commissions to wield powers of subpoena, search and seizure, or witness protection.[482] As a result, in the absence of special arrangements with other state bodies, ad hoc amnesty commissions are likely incapable of conducting in-depth investigations. With respect to their activities, these commissions do not generally conduct public outreach campaigns – the Ugandan Amnesty Commission being at least one notable exception – nor do they tend to conduct statement taking from victims or present cases at public hearings before the victims and the public.

As noted previously, truth commissions are another type of body that has been used to administer amnesties. The best-known example remains the South African Truth and Reconciliation Commission (TRC).[483] The TRC's commissioners were appointed following a rigorous public nomination and selection process and were selected primarily on the basis of their integrity, not on the basis of political patronage. Through its Amnesty Committee, which comprised judges and lawyers, the TRC had the power to grant or deny full or partial amnesty to applicants on condition of receiving valid criminal confessions. The TRC also had the power to search premises and seize evidence, subpoena witnesses, and operate a witness protection program. In terms of its activities, the TRC conducted extensive public outreach, took thousands of statements from victims, conducted investigations into the facts alleged in amnesty applications, and held thousands of private and public hearings for amnesty applicants. The TRC was obligated to give priority to applications from prisoners, who comprised the vast majority of applicants, and also was empowered to call for suspension of civil and criminal proceedings pending determination of individual applications by the Amnesty Committee. The committee's decisions were reviewable by the TRC itself (as the superior legal entity) and by the courts.[484] Other truth commissions have the power to grant or recommend amnesty (e.g., Kenya),[485] or the power to recommend but not grant amnesty (e.g., Liberia).[486]

Many other countries have considered similar amnesty-recommending or amnesty-granting powers in national truth commission mandates, including Burundi, Nepal, and Fiji.[487] These amnesty-linked truth commission proposals have met strong resistance from many international and national nongovernmental organizations, as well as from some departments of the UN Secretariat, such as the Office for the High Commissioner of Human Rights.[488] The reaction to the terms of reference of the Indonesia/Timor-Leste Commission of Truth and Friendship, which had the power to "recommend amnesty for those involved in human rights who cooperate fully in revealing the truth," is another well-known example that already has been mentioned.[489] It also may be noted that in 2006 a proposed truth commission amnesty-granting power was deemed unconstitutional, along with the entire law, by the Indonesian Constitutional Court.[490]

A third possibility for the administration of amnesties is to simply rely on existing courts to grant or deny amnesty, with the burden of proof of eligibility falling on the amnesty applicant. In one case, a single judge was delegated responsibility for the final stage of a complex amnesty process.[491] More typically, specific chambers are given a role in resolving amnesty cases. This was the approach taken, for example, in the amnesties of *France 1957*,[492] *Guatemala 1996*,[493] and *Iraq 2008*.[494] However, as a general rule, courts should not be relied on for the primary administration of amnesties because of their complex rules of procedure and evidence, and the need to avoid clogging them up with tasks that can be handled fairly by nonjudicial or quasi-judicial bodies. Yet as noted in this book's Final Considerations, courts can play other important roles in relation to amnesties, including the adjudication of constitutional challenges to proposed or existing amnesty legislation and case-specific challenges to individual applications of such legislation.[495]

A fourth administrative option, albeit one that risks politicizing what arguably should be a technical and objective exercise, is to have the government itself administer the amnesty decisions. For example, the *Sudan 1972* amnesty left the decision on individual cases to the president, on recommendation by a special amnesty commission.[496] The *Uruguay 1986* amnesty placed primary decision making about amnesty eligibility in cases of forced disappearance in the hands of the executive branch of government.[497] The *Cambodia 1994* amnesty left decision making on individual applications up to the king acting alone.[498]

A final option for the administration of amnesties is to deputize existing state and non-state agencies to receive but not necessarily decide on individual applications. For example, the *Philippines 1987* amnesty created local centers of reception to receive applications and then forward them to a special amnesty commission.[499] The *Colombia 1981* amnesty designated any national political, judicial, military, or diplomatic authority to receive requests for amnesty and – as a safeguard against abuse – provided for disciplinary sanction in the event that a receiving official failed to comply with the law's requirements.[500] The *Guatemala 1982* amnesty deputized selected government offices, the Red Cross (Guatemala), universities, and churches to serve as surrender points.[501] The *Uganda 2000* amnesty provides that Ugandans living outside the country can report to a Ugandan diplomatic mission, consulate, or "any international organization which has agreed with the Government of Uganda," while Ugandans in the country can present themselves to the nearest army or police unit.[502]

4.5.2 Contestation of individual amnesties by victims

With the notable exception of amnesties administered by truth commissions, victims generally have been excluded as participants in amnesty processes, notwithstanding the impact that individual amnesties may have on their ability to pursue justice before domestic courts.

In the case of the South African TRC, there were several ways that victims were integrated as participants. The TRC actually created and issued detailed procedural rules to ensure that the rights of victims could be protected during the amnesty process. These included the following measures:

1. A senior staff member of the Amnesty Department was appointed as an amnesty victim coordinator with a staff complement.
2. Witness protectors who were experienced members of the security forces were available for the protection of victims.
3. Investigators were required to obtain statements from victims about the incidents in question.
4. The scheduling of hearings had to take into account the location and availability of victims and their legal representatives, so that they could attend the hearing. Victims had to be notified of the date and venue

of the hearing at least fourteen days before the hearing. As far as was practical and reasonable, the committee was responsible for providing transport and accommodation for victims.

5. The hearing documentation containing the amnesty application and relevant documentation were made available to victims and their legal representatives.

6. The committee had to arrange for the services of a legal representative for victims who were not legally represented.

7. Logistics staff had to take care of travel, accommodation, and catering arrangements for victims.

8. "Briefers," who were qualified mental health workers, were responsible for attending to the emotional well-being of victims for the duration of hearings. Briefers played an invaluable role in assisting grief-stricken victims and relatives.

9. Victims or the relatives of the victims and any witnesses they wished to call were permitted to give evidence at hearings. Victims who were unable to contribute toward the merits were allowed to make a statement rather than testify if they so preferred. These statements normally dealt with contextual or background factors and subjective views and experiences, often critical to issues of reconciliation and closure for victims.[503]

In short, victims had a reasonable opportunity to contest the conferral of an amnesty before it was granted.[504] This approach was not only appropriate, considering what was at stake for the victims, it was also prudential. In judicial and quasi-judicial proceedings, the process matters as much or more as the results – as the literature on procedural justice indicates.[505]

While participation by victims is inherently desirable, with it comes responsibility. The *Cambodia 1994* amnesty, for example, provided that anyone who testified falsely against an applicant could be punished by a sentence of between two to five years (and the victim of the false testimony could acquire a right to damages).[506] This highlights that victims' participation rights should not be unlimited but instead calibrated with the interests of parties that stand to be adversely affected by an amnesty procedure.

4.5.3 Contestation of individual amnesties by rejected applicants

As noted earlier, some amnesties are administered by nonjudicial bodies that have the power to deny immunity to individual applicants. When this occurs, it is appropriate to permit judicial review of the decision on the same grounds that such review is allowed in respect of other decisions taken by administrative or quasi-judicial bodies.[507] Examples of amnesties that explicitly provide for some form of judicial review include those of *Yugoslavia 1973*,[508] *Russia 1992*,[509] and *Philippines 1994*.[510]

A related question is what effect a denial of amnesty should have in any future judicial proceeding involving the refused applicant. The *South Africa 1995* amnesty states that no court can draw an adverse inference against an individual who is denied amnesty.[511] The *Philippines 1946* amnesty takes this one step further by expressly allowing amnesty to be used as a defense in a future prosecution, even if the administrative body expressly rejected the amnesty application.[512]

As a general rule, fairness would seem to dictate that courts be expressly precluded from drawing adverse inferences in respect of any refused applicant. Moreover, to the extent that a person is compelled to testify against himself or herself in the course of an amnesty application process, use immunity should apply in order to prevent self-incriminating information disclosed by the person from being used against him or her in any contemporaneous or subsequent criminal, civil, or administrative proceedings (except in prosecutions for perjury or for the giving of contradictory evidence).[513]

5. CONCLUSIONS

This part of the book aimed to provide a comprehensive methodology for improving the design of amnesties that are required in extreme circumstances. This involved three sequential stages of analysis: first, an account of why an amnesty covering human rights crimes should be adopted only as a last recourse; second, a discussion of several overarching criteria that should guide specific design choices for an amnesty that meets the last recourse threshold – namely a legitimate process, a legitimate end, minimum legal entrenchment, minimum leniency, maximum conditionality, and maximum viability; and third, an examination of the specific design options for constructing the content of such an amnesty.

While the discussion focused on the design of amnesties, it is important to reiterate that much of what has been said can be applied equally to other forms of legal leniency. Indeed, there is a broad spectrum of legal measures that exists between, at one extreme, total amnesty, and at the other, total accountability. The key is to do everything possible, through debate and design, to preserve options for accountability for the sake of both victims and the society's future legal, political, and moral foundations. In that regard, this discussion has attempted to provide a theoretical and practical framework for limiting rather than encouraging amnesties while also trying to avoid the quixotic view that broad amnesties are somehow unnecessary or fading from use. Today, perhaps more than ever, we need to be extremely sophisticated in our handling of the amnesty question, in the same way and to the same degree that we need to be sophisticated about other democracy-building and peace-building tools.

In the end, the view expressed here is that even a broad and unconditional amnesty may deserve our support when, but for its adoption, there would be social cataclysm. After all, states should be expected to fulfill their international obligations to the maximum extent possible but not to the point of self-destruction. It is also worth recalling that amnesty is typically only one issue within a much larger negotiation process in which other important bargains on democracy, peace, and justice are being struck. Accordingly, an amnesty's validity should not be evaluated in isolation from other key concessions and gains made in the course of such a negotiation. It should be viewed in the context of the whole package of settled terms regarding questions of justice, broadly understood.[514] In the context of a contentious negotiation, the price for these and other justice gains might involve concessions on the question of amnesty that, only when viewed in isolation, appear indefensible.

In conclusion, when it comes to amnesty, a broad human rights paradigm and not a narrow anti-impunity paradigm is required, because more than the fight against impunity is at stake. The issue of amnesty cuts to the very core dilemmas of human rights prevention and protection and should not be reduced to a mere question of accountability for past abuses. Ending impunity, however vital as an objective, is only part of what is required to "respect and ensure" human rights in a sustained and meaningful form. Besides, as many legal scholars note, there is an emerging rule against impunity but not necessarily one against amnesty.[515] That is partly because amnesty can be accompanied, inter alia, by criminal trials before international, mixed, or foreign courts and civil trials before domestic and supranational courts. These may collectively constitute "sufficient" justice in some contexts and thus satisfy any emerging rule against impunity. In this respect, a rule or norm against impunity does not automatically or necessarily imply a rule against amnesty – the concepts are merely related, not synonymous.

The reassuring fact is that a society can still face its past in innumerable important ways notwithstanding the adoption of a broad and unconditional amnesty. In most cases, amnesties only preclude domestic prosecutions while leaving every other transitional justice option available, including truth commissions, victim reparation programs, and institutional reform measures. We would all do well to recall this in future debates on the subject.

As argued in this book's Final Considerations, we also should recall that an amnesty's adoption does not represent the definitive end even of domestic prosecution possibilities. It may mark instead the beginning of a long period of amnesty contestation through national courts and legislatures.

Final Considerations: On the Perennial Contestation of Amnesties

The focus of this book has been on the broad legal and policy debates about amnesties as a tool of transition, and on the effective design of amnesties to limit the damage to justice options and to maximize accountability.

In the book's Opening Considerations, we examined the many reasons why amnesty is of perpetual relevance in global affairs. There was a brief analysis of the changed context in which amnesty dilemmas unfold, including a tracing of the ideological move away from leniency and toward accountability. In addition, questions were raised concerning the wisdom and pace of this shift, and a more open and interdisciplinary debate was urged.

In Part I (The Debate on Amnesties), the term *amnesty* was defined and contrasted with other legal measures that also have the effect of restricting the criminal jurisdiction of national courts. This was followed by an evaluation of the issue of amnesty in the context of transitional justice and the global and local fight against impunity. Thereafter, the discussion focused on the place of amnesties within public international law, providing an analysis of amnesties and the core obligations of states regarding human rights crimes. A number of questions were posed about the popular legal view of amnesties, and several alternative understandings were put forward, such as the need to consider a balancing of the duty of punishment with the duty of prevention of violations. There followed from this an evaluation of the relevance of the International Criminal Court and the Rome Statute framework as a whole on the resolution of amnesty dilemmas, as well as a critical examination of the evolving UN position on amnesties. Both of these developments have elevated but also complicated the achievement of peace and human security. Part I then concluded by observing that the debate on amnesty is a crucial one for the fields of human rights and conflict resolution alike, and that it is a debate in need of less posturing and more critical thinking.

In Part II (The Design of Amnesties), an original methodology was presented for the design of amnesties to help to better contain their ill effects on the international rule of law and victims' rights. The discussion began by exploring how and why an amnesty covering human rights crimes should be adopted only as a last recourse. This was followed by a presentation of the overarching criteria that should be applied to guide specific design choices for an amnesty that has passed the last-recourse threshold. The remainder of Part II laid out a comprehensive set of design options for constructing the content of an amnesty with a view to ensuring, inter alia, that the amnesty pursues a legitimate end, is lightly entrenched in the domestic legal system, confers the minimum amount of leniency on the beneficiaries, imposes the maximum conditions, and offers the greatest likelihood of being effectively administered and implemented.

As we have noted throughout, transitional amnesties are generally intended to be permanent. That is precisely why they need to be rigorously debated and carefully crafted. Yet we also know that history is full of struggles against injustice and for the preservation of memory. Time and again, the forgotten victims and survivors – even if few in number – remain steadfast in their determination to see justice done in their own individual cases and in the countries in which the atrocities were actually committed.

An important question therefore arises: what can be done about an existing amnesty that is illegitimate and unwanted? That is a subject we briefly explore in this concluding section. After all, the passage of an amnesty need not constitute the end of domestic criminal justice efforts against the perpetrators of past crimes. It could instead mark the start of a new struggle to challenge, limit, or remove the amnesty.[1] It could, indeed, have the counterintuitive effect of mobilizing victims and civil society into campaigning on the issue of justice.

The subject of challenging amnesties is not only relevant for victims and families but also for successor governments that may face the question of what to do about an amnesty that they inherit. A classic example is Chile, where a self-amnesty adopted by the Augusto Pinochet regime in 1978 remains in place despite twenty successive years of democratic governance.[2] In Chile, the amnesty issue is not about a de novo amnesty negotiated by a democratically elected government but about the degree to which such a government is unable or unwilling to disturb a past amnesty. The reality anywhere is that a future government may or may not feel bound to honor the decisions of its political predecessors.

The usual route for contesting an amnesty is through the domestic courts, as national amnesties bind only national courts. Such contestation may take several forms. The classic approach is to bring a case seeking a declaration of unconstitutionality.[3] This has successfully occurred in only a few jurisdictions, including Argentina[4] and Indonesia.[5] In other jurisdictions – such as Honduras[6] and El Salvador[7] – the scope of amnesty laws has been narrowed through judicial decisions to remove their unconstitutional parts. In several other cases, national amnesty laws such as those in Sierra Leone,[8] Algeria[9] and Fiji,[10] have been or remain the subject of ongoing constitutional challenges.

In addition to challenges concerning an amnesty's constitutionality, case-specific challenges to the application of an amnesty can also be brought. As Naomi Roht-Arriaza and Lauren Gibson explain:

> [C]ourts may decide that in order to determine whether or not an amnesty law applies in a specific case of murder or disappearance, they must investigate – including calling witnesses and taking testimony – until they can assure themselves that the case comes within the bounds of the amnesty. Here again, at the end of the day the most likely result is a finding that the amnesty applies, yet the court insists on proceeding through an investigatory phase. One explanation is that these results allow judges to assert their proper power and role in a more modest, and therefore tenable, fashion. Another is that judges, especially lower court judges who disagree with the decision to uphold the legality of an amnesty, may look to these mechanisms as a way of discomfiting the alleged perpetrators, who are forced to respond to requests for testimony. They may also be seen as providing at least some closure, or solace, for the families of victims.[11]

Reflecting on the situation in the 1990s, the authors concluded that "facial challenges to amnesty laws have generally fared badly, while limited, case-specific and as-applied challenges have done better. Courts are not in a position, especially in emerging or fragile democracies, to buck an elite consensus or negotiated settlement that includes an amnesty."[12] More recently, amnesty expert Louise Mallinder drew the same general conclusion, noting that the comparative inclination to disapply an amnesty in individual cases while upholding it in facial challenges may be due to fear of conflict with those in government.[13]

This raises the related question of the timing for bringing court challenges against illegitimate amnesties. In most cases, it will take years, if not decades, before the conservative judges who once served an authoritarian or corrupt regime can be replaced by a new generation of more liberal and human rights–sensitive judges.[14] Such gradual reform may be necessary across an entire judicial sector, but it will tend to have greatest importance at the appellate level where final decisions on constitutionality are rendered. With this consideration in mind, bringing a legal challenge too early may risk having the counterproductive effect of entrenching rather than undermining the amnesty's constitutionality and legitimacy through judicial affirmation.

The argument here is not that court challenges should necessarily or always be delayed. For example, a challenge may be brought with full anticipation of its rejection but with the advance intention of exhausting domestic remedies. That would make the case eligible for consideration by a UN treaty body or a regional human rights court or commission.[15] Such an approach may be especially appropriate for a state in the jurisdiction of the Inter-American or European human rights courts, because their judgments have a binding character at the national level.[16]

The place of international law within a national legal system, an area known as reception law, is another pertinent topic when it comes to court challenges against amnesties.[17] In most countries, it is insufficient simply to invoke a state's treaty and customary international law commitments before a domestic court. One must also demonstrate the reception or incorporation of those commitments into the domestic law, according to the relevant rules of reception in the particular jurisdiction. As explained in Part II, international law that has been received into domestic law can be of assistance in contesting an amnesty, whether in a constitutional challenge or in a case-specific one.[18]

If the necessary political will exists, an alternative to using the courts is to seek to have the amnesty nullified or repealed by the legislature. This has occurred in two countries: Argentina[19] and Bangladesh.[20] However, there are many reasons why such an approach may be infeasible or undesirable, including fear that domestic courts will become flooded with cases following the amnesty's repeal, or lack of sufficient votes across party lines, as in Chile.

It is also worth noting that, in some jurisdictions, the legal distinction between nullification and repeal is significant. An act of nullification creates the legal fiction that the law in question was never adopted in the first place – it is treated as null *ab initio*. By contrast, an act of repeal creates no such legal fiction.[21] As a result, in some jurisdictions, an act of repeal may be in tension with the international human right to receive the benefit of the lighter penalty concerning acts that, at the time of their commission, were not criminal "according to the general principles of law recognized by the community of nations."[22] Whether an amnesty is repealed or nullified, one must also consider whether the prescription period for the amnestied crimes lapsed during the period in which the amnesty was in force, in case the act of repeal or nullification needs to expressly address the issue.

Another option for contestation in the political arena is to seek an interpretive law or declaration requiring the courts to interpret an amnesty in a new way. This has been attempted on many different occasions in Chile, where the sheer diversity of legislative efforts is instructive in and of itself. As the Inter-American Court of Human Rights noted in *Almonacid-Arellano v. Chile*:

> To the date of this judgment, six bills of law aimed at amending Decree Law No. 2.191 were submitted. Two of these bills proposed an interpretation of the aforementioned decree law through another law, and set forth that the decree should not be enforced regarding crimes against humanity given the impossibility to declare them extinguished and susceptible of amnesty. The third bill was aimed at extending the period covered by the Decree Law until March 11, 1990. The fourth bill sought to prevent the commencement of proceedings to impose liability upon those individuals mentioned as perpetrators, accomplices or accessories after the fact, "rendering any criminal or civil action related thereto extinguished" and suggested that any pending lawsuits should be definitely dismissed "without further proceedings." The fifth bill was intended to regulate the application of the Decree Law and to establish that, in the case of detained-disappeared persons, the judge should continue investigating "with the sole aim of discovering the location of the victims or their remains." None of the five bills was passed. The sixth bill was recently submitted and its purpose is to declare Decree Law No. 2.191 invalid under public law.[23]

Opting for an interpretive law or declaration is, of course, less powerful in symbolic terms than a formal act of repeal or nullification. However, it may be a useful approach in the absence of sufficient political will to do more.

A final approach to domestic contestation of an illegitimate amnesty is the use of a referendum. A number of countries around the world permit referenda on a wide range of issues, contingent on the prior collection of a sufficiently large number of signatures from the general public. In Uruguay, there is a movement to hold a second referendum on a 1986 amnesty that was initially adopted through a referendum.[24] The Ghanaian truth commission also recommended a referendum on the transitional provisions of the national constitution, which contain a sweeping amnesty that likewise was adopted through an earlier referendum.[25]

Despite the many different options for contestation, the chances of ultimately overturning an unprincipled amnesty are regrettably very low, taking into consideration state practice to date. It is possible that, over time, the circumstances leading to the invocation of new amnesties will diminish, thus avoiding the need for contestation strategies. After all, there is evidence that the number of armed conflicts and coups d'état are globally decreasing,[26] and that nearly two-thirds of the world's states have become electoral democracies.[27] Yet judging by the increasing quantity and range of amnesties adopted since the end of the Cold War,[28] and taking into consideration that civilians rather than combatants constitute the overwhelming targets and victims of armed conflict,[29] a more realistic forecast is that the need for amnesties will persist, and with it the need for contestation strategies.

This underscores the importance of becoming more proactive as an international community in helping states to overcome unprincipled amnesties. A proactive effort could, for example, encompass targeted actions to increase the technical capacity of domestic courts, especially at the appellate level, in countries where amnesties were reluctantly adopted. It also could encompass greater action to empower the local nongovernmental organizations, victims' associations, and lawyers who inevitably will bring the legal and political challenges against any amnesty in the ensuing years.

Even with this support, in most cases it will likely take a whole generation before an amnesty is fully undone – if it happens at all. However, in the meantime, the call for justice will strengthen and bring along with it important public debates about how to deal with a legacy of abuse. That is at least one potential consolation concerning this otherwise bleak subject.

Summary Guidelines
for Effective Amnesty Design

OVERALL TEST

- Is the amnesty crafted in good faith and in a manner that promises to fulfill a state's transitional justice obligations to the greatest extent possible in the particular context while impairing them as little as possible?

THRESHOLD ISSUES

Last-recourse threshold

- Existence of an urgent and grave situation
- Exhaustion of appropriate options to end the urgent and grave situation
- Exhaustion of leniency options short of amnesty to end the blackmail
  - Omission of criminal accountability
  - Reduced sentence schemes
  - Alternative sentence schemes
  - Use immunity schemes
  - Third-country asylum

Overarching parameters for amnesty design

- A legitimate process
- Minimum legal entrenchment
- A legitimate end
- Minimum leniency
- Maximum conditions
- Maximum viability
  - Typology of context and amnesty beneficiaries
  - Transitional justice measures
  - Features of the broader settlement

SPECIFIC DESIGN CHOICES

1. Minimum legal entrenchment

- Nature of legal instrument
- Whether permanent or temporary in character
- Relation between amnesty and other laws

2. Legitimate end

- Explicit objectives mentioned in the preamble
- References to sources of international law

3. Minimum leniency

- The crimes or acts that are expressly eligible or ineligible for amnesty:
  - Distinction between political and ordinary offenses
  - Express exclusion of human rights crimes
  - Express exclusion of crimes motivated by greed
  - Express exclusion of crimes motivated by malice
  - Express exclusion of selected context-specific crimes
- The persons who are expressly eligible or ineligible for amnesty:
  - Distinctions according to affiliations and subaffiliations
  - Distinctions according to rank
  - Distinctions according to forms of criminal participation
  - Express exclusion of beneficiaries of prior amnesties
  - Express exclusion of foreign mercenaries
  - Express exclusion of specific individuals

- The express legal consequences of the grant of amnesty for the beneficiary:
  - Immunity of individual from prospective forms of liability
  - Effect on ongoing investigations, subpoenas, warrants, and trials
  - Effect on prior judgments and sentences
  - Effect on personal records
  - Effect on third parties
  - Variation in legal consequences depending on crime or rank
- Geographical scope of application
- Temporal scope of application

4. Maximum conditions

- Conditions for obtaining amnesty
  - Requirement to submit an individual application
  - Requirement to meet application deadline
  - Requirement of full and accurate disclosure of crimes
  - Requirement of apology
  - Requirement of public hearing
  - Requirement to participate in tradition-based justice process
  - Requirement of restitution and community service
  - Requirement of relocation and supervision
  - Requirement of participation in disarmament, demobilization, and reintegration program
  - Requirement of renunciation of violence
  - Requirement of release of hostages and prisoners of war
  - Requirement of cooperation with law enforcement authorities
- Conditions for retaining amnesty
  - Requirement of nonbreach of amnesty's preconditions
  - Requirement of compliance with prospective prohibitions
  - Requirement of nonrecidivism
  - Parallel requirement of pledges by the larger group

5. Maximum viability

- The supervisory body and its mandate
- Contestation of amnesty decisions by victims
- Contestation of amnesty decisions by rejected applicants

APPENDIX 2

Selected Excerpts from International Legal Instruments

TREATY SOURCES

1977 – Protocol II to the Geneva Conventions, Article 6.5

At the end of hostilities, the authorities in power shall endeavour to grant the broadest possible amnesty to persons who have participated in the armed conflict, or those deprived of their liberty for reasons related to the armed conflict, whether they are interned or detained.

NONTREATY SOURCES

1989 – UN Principles on the Effective Prevention and Investigation of Extra-legal, Arbitrary, and Summary Executions, Article 19

In no circumstances, including a state of war, siege or other public emergency, shall blanket immunity from prosecution be granted to any person allegedly involved in extra-legal, arbitrary or summary executions.

1993 – UN Declaration on the Protection of All Persons from Enforced Disappearances, Article 18(1)

Persons who have or are alleged to have committed offences referred to in Article 4, paragraph 1, above, shall not benefit from any special amnesty law or similar measures that might have the effect of exempting them from any criminal proceedings or sanction.

2004 – Report of the Secretary-General on the Rule of Law and Transitional Justice in Conflict and Post-Conflict Societies, UN Doc. S/2004/616, Paragraphs 10, 32, and 64

Section IV. Basing assistance on international norms and standards

10. United Nations norms and standards have been developed and adopted by countries across the globe and have been accommodated by the full range of legal systems of Member States, whether based in common law, civil law, Islamic law, or other legal traditions. As such, these norms and standards bring a legitimacy that cannot be said to attach to exported national models which, all too often, reflect more the individual interests or experience of donors and assistance providers than they do the best interests or legal development needs of host countries. These standards also set the normative boundaries of United Nations engagement, such that, for example, United Nations tribunals can never allow for capital punishment, United Nations–endorsed peace agreements can never promise amnesties for genocide, war crimes, crimes against humanity or gross violations of human rights, and, where we are mandated to undertake executive or judicial functions, United Nations–operated facilities must scrupulously comply with international standards for human rights in the administration of justice.

X. Filling a rule of law vacuum

32. Additionally, strategies for expediting a return to the rule of law must be integrated with plans to reintegrate both displaced civilians and former fighters. Disarmament, demobilization and reintegration processes are one of the keys to a transition out of conflict and back to normalcy. For populations traumatized by war, those processes are among the most visible signs of the gradual return of peace and security. Similarly, displaced persons must be the subject of dedicated programmes to facilitate return. Carefully crafted amnesties can help in the return and reintegration of both groups and should be encouraged, although, as noted above, these can never be permitted to excuse genocide, war crimes, crimes against humanity or gross violations of human rights.

XIX. Moving forward: conclusions and recommendations

64. Ensure that peace agreements and Security Council resolutions and mandates:

(a) Give priority attention to the restoration of and respect for the rule of law, explicitly mandating support for the rule of law and for transitional justice, particularly where United Nations support for judicial and prosecutorial processes is required;

(b) Respect, incorporate by reference and apply international standards for fairness, due process and human rights in the administration of justice;

(c) Reject any endorsement of amnesty for genocide, war crimes, or crimes against humanity, including those relating to ethnic, gender and sexually based international crimes, ensure that no such amnesty previously granted is a bar to prosecution before any United Nations–created or assisted court; . . .

2005 – Report of Diane Orentlicher, independent expert to update the Set of Principles to combat impunity, UN Doc. E/CN.4/2005/102/Add.1, Principles 19 and 28

19. States shall undertake prompt, thorough, independent and impartial investigations of violations of human rights and international humanitarian law and take appropriate measures in respect of the perpetrators, particularly in the area of criminal justice, by ensuring that those responsible for serious crimes under international law are prosecuted, tried and duly punished. Although the decision to prosecute lies primarily within the competence of the State, victims, their families and heirs should be able to institute proceedings, on either an individual or a collective basis, particularly as *parties civiles* or as persons conducting private prosecutions in States whose law of criminal procedure recognizes these procedures. States should guarantee broad legal standing in the judicial process to any wronged party and to any person or non-governmental organization having a legitimate interest therein.

28. Even when intended to establish conditions conducive to a peace agreement or to foster national reconciliation, amnesty and other measures of clemency shall be kept within the following bounds:

(a) The perpetrators of serious crimes under international law may not benefit from such measures until such time as the State has met the obligations to which principle 19 refers or the perpetrators have been prosecuted before a court with jurisdiction – whether international, internationalized or national – outside the State in question; (new language in italics)

(b) Amnesties and other measures of clemency shall be without effect with respect to the victims' right to reparation, to which principles 31 through 34 refer, and shall not prejudice the right to know[.]

APPENDIX 3

Selected Excerpts from Jurisprudence on Amnesties

1. *Case of Almonacid-Arellano et al. v. Chile*, Inter-American Court of Human Rights, Judgment of September 26, 2006 (Preliminary Objections, Merits, Reparations and Costs), paras. 105–29.
2. *Prosecutor v. Allieu Kondewa* (Decision on Lack of Jurisdiction/Abuses of Process: Amnesty Provided by the Lome Accord), Special Court for Sierra Leone, Appeals Chamber, Case No. SCSL-2004–14-AR72(E), May 25, 2004, paras. 30–57 (Separate Opinion of Justice Robertson).
3. *Azanian Peoples Organization (AZAPO) and Others v. President of the Republic of South Africa and Others*, Constitutional Court of South Africa, Case No. CCT17/96 (July 25, 1996), Judgment of Mahomed DP.

1. *Case of Almonacid-Arellano et al. v. Chile*, Inter-American Court of Human Rights, Judgment of September 26, 2006 (Preliminary Objections, Merits, Reparations and Costs), paras. 105–129

b) Impossibility to grant an amnesty for crimes against humanity

105. According to the International Law *corpus iuris,* a crime against humanity is in itself a serious violation of human rights and affects mankind as a whole. In the *Case of Prosecutor v. Erdemovic,* the International Tribunal for the Former Yugoslavia stated that:

Crimes against humanity are serious acts of violence which harm human beings by striking what is most essential to them: their life, liberty, physical welfare, health, and or dignity. They are inhumane acts that by their extent and gravity go beyond the limits tolerable to the international community, which must perforce demand their punishment. But crimes against humanity also transcend the individual because when the individual is assaulted, humanity comes under attack and is negated. It is therefore the concept of humanity as victim which essentially characterises crimes against humanity.[127]

106. Since the individual and the whole mankind are the victims of all crimes against humanity, the General Assembly of the United Nations has held since 1946[128] that those responsible for the commission of such crimes must be punished. In that respect, they point out Resolutions 2583 (XXIV) of 1969 and 3074 (XXVIII) of 1973. In the former, the General Assembly held that the "thorough investigation" of war crimes and crimes against humanity, as

127 Cf. International Criminal Tribunal for the Former Yugoslavia, *Prosecutor v. Erdemovic*, Case No. IT-96–22-T, Sentencing Judgment, November 29, 1996, at para. 28.

> Crimes against humanity are serious acts of violence which harm human beings by striking what is most essential to them: their life, liberty, physical welfare, health, and or dignity. They are inhumane acts that by their extent and gravity go beyond the limits tolerable to the international community, which must perforce demand their punishment. But crimes against humanity also transcend the individual because when the individual is assaulted, humanity comes under attack and is negated. It is therefore the concept of humanity as victim which essentially characterises crimes against humanity.

128 Cf. UN, Extradition and punishment of war criminals, adopted by the General Assembly of the United Nations in Resolution 3 (I) of February 13, 1946; Confirmation of the Principles of International Law recognized by the Charter of the Nuremberg Tribunal, adopted by the General Assembly of the United Nations in Resolution 95 (I) of December 11, 1946; Extradition of war criminals and traitors, adopted by the General Assembly of the United Nations in Resolution 170 (II) of October 31, 1947; Question of the punishment of war criminals and of persons who have committed crimes against humanity, adopted by the General Assembly of the United Nations in Resolution 2338 (XXII) of December 18, 1967; Convention on the Non-Applicability of Statutory Limitations to War Crimes and Crimes against Humanity, adopted by the General Assembly of the United Nations in Resolution 2391 (XXIII) of November 25, 1968; Question of the punishment of war criminals and of persons who have committed crimes against humanity adopted by the General Assembly of the United Nations in Resolution 2712 (XXV) of December 14, 1970; Question of the punishment of war criminals and of persons who have committed crimes against humanity adopted by the General Assembly of the United Nations in Resolution 2840 (XXVI) of December 18, 1971, and Crime Prevention and Control, adopted by the General Assembly of the United Nations in Resolution 3021 (XXVII) of December 18, 1972.

well as the punishment of those responsible for them "constitute an important element in the prevention of such crimes, the protection of human rights and fundamental freedoms, the encouragement of confidence, the furtherance of cooperation among peoples and the promotion of international peace and security."[129] In the latter, the General Assembly stated the following:

> War crimes and crimes against humanity, wherever they are committed, shall be subject to investigation and the persons against whom there is evidence that they have committed such crimes shall be subject to tracing, arrest, trial and, if found guilty, to punishment. . . .
>
> States shall not take any legislative or other measures which may be prejudicial to the international obligations they have assumed in regard to the detection, arrest, extradition and punishment of persons guilty of war crimes and crimes against humanity.[130]

107. Likewise, Resolutions 827 and 955 of the Security Council of the United Nations,[131] together with the Charters of the Tribunals for the Former Yugoslavia (Article 29) and Rwanda (Article 28), impose on all Member States of the United Nations the obligation to fully cooperate with the Tribunals for the investigation and punishment of those persons accused of having committed serious International Law violations, including crimes against humanity. Likewise, the Secretary General of the United Nations has pointed out that in view of the rules and principles of the United Nations, all peace agreements approved by the United Nations can never promise amnesty for crimes against humanity.[132]

108. The adoption and enforcement of laws that grant amnesty for crimes against humanity prevents the compliance of the obligations stated above. The

---

129 Cf. UN, Question of the punishment of war criminals and of persons who have committed crimes against humanity, adopted by the General Assembly of the United Nations in Resolution 2583 (XXIV) of December 15, 1969.

130 Cf. UN, Principles of International Cooperation in the Detection, Arrest, Extradition and Punishment of Persons Guilty of War Crimes and Crimes against Humanity, adopted by the General Assembly of the United Nations in Resolution 3074 (XXVIII) of December 3, 1973.

131 Cf. UN Resolution of the Security Council S/RES/827 for the establishment of the International Criminal Tribunal for the Former Yugoslavia of March 25, 1993; and Resolution of the Security Council S/RES/955 for the establishment of an International Criminal Case for Rwanda of November 8, 1994.

132 Cf. UN Report of the Secretary-General S/2004/616 on the Rule of Law and Transitional Justice in Conflict and Post-Conflict Societies of August 3, 2004, para. 10.

Secretary General of the United Nations, in his report about the establishment
of the Special Tribunal for Sierra Leone stated the following:

> While recognizing that amnesty is an accepted legal concept and a
> gesture of peace and reconciliation at the end of a civil war or an internal
> armed conflict, the UN has consistently maintained the position that
> amnesty cannot be granted in respect of international crimes such
> as genocide, crimes against humanity, or violations of international
> humanitarian law.[133]

109. The Secretary General also informed that the legal effects of the amnesty
granted in Sierra Leone had not been taken into account "given their illegality
pursuant to international law."[134] Indeed, the Charter for the Special Tribunal
for Sierra Leone stated that the amnesty granted to persons accused of crimes
against humanity, which are violations of Article 3 of the Geneva Conventions
and Additional Protocol II,[135] as well as of other serious violations of international humanitarian law, "shall not be an impediment to subject [them] to
trial."

110. The obligation that arises pursuant to international law to try, and, if
found guilty, to punish the perpetrators of certain international crimes, among
which are crimes against humanity, is derived from the duty of protection
embodied in Article 1(1) of the American Convention. This obligation implies
the duty of the States Parties to organize the entire government system, and
in general, all agencies through which the public power is exercised, in such
manner as to legally protect the free and full exercise of human rights. As
a consequence of this obligation, the States must prevent, investigate, and
punish all violations of the rights recognized by the Convention and, at the
same time, guarantee the reinstatement, if possible, of the violated rights, and
as the case may be, the reparation of the damage caused due to the violation
of human rights. If the State agencies act in a manner that such violation goes
unpunished, and prevents the reinstatement, as soon as possible, of such rights
to the victim of such violation, it can be concluded that such State has not

133 Cf. UN Report of the Secretary-General S/2000/915 on the Establishment of a Tribunal for
Sierra Leone, of October 4, 2000, para. 22.
134 Cf. UN Report of the Secretary-General S/2000/915 on the Establishment of a Tribunal for
Sierra Leone, of October 4, 2000, para. 24.
135 Cf. UN Additional Protocol to the Geneva Conventions of August 12, 1949, regarding the
Protection of Victims of Non-international Armed Conflicts (Protocol II).

complied with its duty to guarantee the free and full exercise of those rights to the individuals who are subject to its jurisdiction.[136]

111. Crimes against humanity give rise to the violation of a series of undeniable rights that are recognized by the American Convention, which violation cannot remain unpunished. The Court has stated on several occasions that the State has the duty to prevent and combat impunity, which the Court has defined as "the lack of investigation, prosecution, arrest, trial, and conviction of those responsible for the violation of the rights protected by the American Convention."[137] Likewise, the Court has determined that the investigation must be conducted resorting to all legal means available and must be focused on the determination of the truth and the investigation, prosecution, arrest, trial, and conviction of those persons that are responsible for the facts, both as perpetrators and instigators, especially when State agents are or may be involved in such events.[138] In that respect, the Court has pointed out that those resources which, in view of the general conditions of the country or due to the circumstances of the case, turn to be deceptive, cannot be taken into account.[139]

112. In the *Case of Barrios Altos* the Court has already stated that:

> all amnesty provisions, provisions on prescription and the establishment of measures designed to eliminate responsibility are inadmissible, because they are intended to prevent the investigation and punishment of those responsible for serious human rights violations such as torture, extra-legal, summary or arbitrary execution and forced disappearance, all of them prohibited because they violate non-derogable rights recognized by international human rights law.[140]

---

136 Cf. Case of Velásquez-Rodríguez. Judgment of July 29, 1988. Series C, no. 4, para. 166, and Case of Godínez-Cruz. Judgment of January 20, 1989. Series C, no. 5, para. 175.

137 Cf. Case of the Ituango Massacres, supra note 14, para. 299; Case of the "Mapiripán Massacre," Judgment of September 15, 2005. Series C, No. 134, para. 237; Case of the Moiwana Community, Judgment of September 15, 2005. Series C, No. 134, para. 203.

138 Cf. Case of Ximenes-Lopes, supra note 14, para. 148; Case of Baldeón-García, supra note 14, para. 94; and Case of the Pueblo Bello Massacre, Judgment of January 31, 2006. Series C, no. 140, para. 143.

139 Cf. Case of Baldeón-García, supra note 14, para. 144; Case of the 19 Merchants, Judgment of July 5, 2004. Series C, no. 109, para. 192; and Case of Baena Ricardo et al. Jurisdiction. Judgment of November 28, 2003. Series C, No. 104, para. 77.

140 Cf. Case of Barrios Altos. Judgment of March 14, 2001. Series C, No. 75, para. 41.

113. It is worth mentioning that the State itself recognized in the instant case that "amnesty or self-amnesty laws are, in principle, contrary to the rules of international human rights law."[141]

114. In view of the above considerations, the Court determines that the States cannot neglect their duty to investigate, identify, and punish those persons responsible for crimes against humanity by enforcing amnesty laws or any other similar domestic provisions. Consequently, crimes against humanity are crimes which cannot be susceptible of amnesty.

c) Enforcement of Decree Law No. 2.191 from August 21, 1990

115. Since it has already been established that the crime against Mr. Almonacid-Arellano is a crime against humanity, and that crimes against humanity cannot be susceptible of amnesty, the Court must now determine if under Decree Law No. 2.191 amnesty is granted for such crime, and if such were the case, the Court must further determine whether the State has breached its obligation arising from Article 2 of the Convention upon keeping such law in force.

116. Article 1 of Decree Law No. 2.191 (*supra* para. 82(10)) grants a general amnesty to all those responsible for "criminal acts" that were committed from September 11, 1973 to March 10, 1978. Furthermore, Article 3 of such Decree Law excludes a series of crimes from such amnesty.[142] The Court notes that murder, being a crime against humanity, is not included on the list provided in Article 3 of the said Decree Law. This was also the determination made by the Chilean courts that heard the instant case upon its application (*supra* paras. 82(20) and 82(21)). Likewise, this Court, though not requested to decide on other crimes against humanity in the instant case, draws the attention to the fact that other crimes against humanity such as forced disappearance, torture, and genocide, among others, are not excluded from such amnesty.

---

141 Cf. Final written arguments of the State (record on the Merits of the Case, Volume III, folio 723.)

142 Pursuant to Article 3 of Decree Law No. 2.191 amnesty shall not be granted to "those persons against whom criminal actions are pending for the crimes of parricide, infanticide, robbery aggravated by violence or intimidation, drug production or dealing, abduction of minors, corruption of minors, arson and other damage to property; rape, statutory rape, incest, driving under the influence of alcohol, embezzlement, swindling and illegal exaction, fraudulent practices and deceit, indecent assault, crimes included in Decree Law No. 280 of 1974 as amended; bribery, fraud, smuggling and crimes included in the Tax Code."

117. The Court has confirmed on several occasions that:

> Under the law of nations, a customary law prescribes that a State that has signed an international agreement must introduce into its domestic laws whatever changes are needed to ensure execution of the obligations it has undertaken. This principle is universally valid and has been characterized in case law as an evident principle (*"principe allant de soi"*; *Exchange of Greek and Turkish populations,* avis consultatif, 1925, C.P.J.I., Series B, No. 10, p. 20). Accordingly, the American Convention stipulates that every State Party is to adapt its domestic laws to the provisions of that Convention, so as to guarantee the rights embodied therein.[143]

118. Pursuant to Article 2 of the Convention, such adaptation implies the adoption of measures following two main guidelines, to wit: i) the annulment of laws and practices of any kind whatsoever that may imply the violation of the rights protected by the Convention, and ii) the passing of laws and the development of practices tending to achieve an effective observance of such guarantees.[144] It is necessary to reaffirm that the duty stated in i) is only complied when such reform is effectively made.[145]

119. Amnesty laws with the characteristics as those described above (*supra* para. 116) leave victims defenseless and perpetuate impunity for crimes against humanity. Therefore, they are overtly incompatible with the wording and the spirit of the American Convention, and undoubtedly affect rights embodied in such Convention. This constitutes in and of itself a violation of the Convention and generates international liability for the State.[146] Consequently, given its nature, Decree Law No. 2.191 does not have any legal effects and cannot remain as an obstacle for the investigation of the facts inherent to the instant case, or

143 Cf. Case of Garrido and Baigorria. Reparations (art. 63(1) of the American Convention on Human Rights). Judgment of August 27, 1998. Series C, No. 39, para. 68; Case of Baena Ricardo et al. Judgment of February 2, 2001. Series C, No. 72, para. 179.

144 Cf. Case of Ximenes-Lopes, supra note 14, para. 83; Case of Gómez-Palomino. Judgment of November 22, 2005. Series C, No. 136, para. 91; and Case of the "Mapiripán Massacre," supra note 137, para. 109.

145 Cf. Case of Raxcacó-Reyes. Judgment of September 15, 2005. Series C, No. 133. para. 87; Case of the Indigenous Yakye Axa Community, supra note 5, para. 100; and Case of Caesar. Judgment of March 11, 2005. Series C, No. 123, paras. 91 and 93.

146 Cf. Case of Barrios Altos. Interpretation of the Judgment on the Merits (art. 67 of the American Convention on Human Rights). Judgment of September 3, 2001. Series C, No. 83, para. 18.

for the identification and punishment of those responsible therefor. Neither can it have a like or similar impact regarding other cases of violations of rights protected by the American Convention which occurred in Chile.[147]

120. On the other hand, even though the Court notes that Decree Law No. 2.191 basically grants a self-amnesty, since it was issued by the military regime to avoid judicial prosecution of its own crimes, it points out that a State violates the American Convention when issuing provisions which do not conform to the obligations contemplated in said Convention. The fact that such provisions have been adopted pursuant to the domestic legislation or against it "is irrelevant for this purpose."[148] To conclude, the Court, rather than the process of adoption and the authority issuing Decree Law No. 2.191, addresses the *ratio legis*: granting an amnesty for the serious criminal acts contrary to international law that were committed by the military regime.

121. Since it ratified the American Convention on August 21, 1990, the State has kept Decree Law No. 2.191 in force for sixteen years, overtly violating the obligations set forth in said Convention. The fact that such Decree Law has not been applied by the Chilean courts in several cases since 1998 is a significant advance, and the Court appreciates it, but it does not suffice to meet the requirements of Article 2 of the Convention in the instant case. Firstly because, as it has been stated in the preceding paragraphs, Article 2 imposes the legislative obligation to annul all legislation which is in violation of the Convention, and secondly, because the criterion of the domestic courts may change, and they may decide to reinstate the application of a provision which remains in force under the domestic legislation.

122. For such reasons, the Court determines that by formally keeping within its legislative *corpus* a Decree Law which is contrary to the wording and the spirit of the Convention, the State has not complied with the obligations imposed by Article 2 thereof.

d) Enforcement of Decree Law No. 2.191

123. The above mentioned legislative obligation established by Article 2 of the Convention is also aimed at facilitating the work of the Judiciary so that

---

147 Cf. Case of Barrios Altos, supra note 140, para. 44.
148 Cf. Certain Powers of the Inter-American Commission of Human Rights (arts. 41, 42, 44, 46, 47, 50, and 51 of the American Convention on Human Rights). Advisory Opinion OC-13/93 of July 16, 1993. Series A, No. 13, para. 26.

the law enforcement authority may have a clear option in order to solve a particular case. However, when the Legislative Power fails to set aside and/or adopts laws which are contrary to the American Convention, the Judiciary is bound to honor the obligation to respect rights as stated in Article 1(1) of the said Convention, and consequently, it must refrain from enforcing any laws contrary to such Convention. The observance by State agents or officials of a law which violates the Convention gives rise to the international liability of such State, as contemplated in International Human Rights Law, in the sense that every State is internationally responsible for the acts or omissions of any of its powers or bodies for the violation of internationally protected rights, pursuant to Article 1(1) of the American Convention.[149]

124. The Court is aware that domestic judges and courts are bound to respect the rule of law, and therefore, they are bound to apply the provisions in force within the legal system. But when a State has ratified an international treaty such as the American Convention, its judges, as part of the State, are also bound by such Convention. This forces them to see that all the effects of the provisions embodied in the Convention are not adversely affected by the enforcement of laws which are contrary to its purpose and that have not had any legal effects since their inception. In other words, the Judiciary must exercise a sort of "conventionality control" between the domestic legal provisions which are applied to specific cases and the American Convention on Human Rights. To perform this task, the Judiciary has to take into account not only the treaty, but also the interpretation thereof made by the Inter-American Court, which is the ultimate interpreter of the American Convention.

125. By the same token, the Court has established that "according to international law, the obligations that it imposes must be honored in good faith and domestic laws cannot be invoked to justify their violation."[150] This provision is embodied in Article 27 of the Vienna Convention on the Law of Treaties, 1969.

126. In the instant case, the Judiciary applied Decree Law No. 2.191 (*supra* paras. 82(20) and 82(21)), which had the immediate effect to discontinue the investigation and close the case file, thus granting impunity to those

---

149 Cf. Case of Ximenes-Lopes, supra note 14, para. 172; and Case of Baldeón-García, supra note 14, para. 140.
150 Cf. International Responsibility for the Issuance and Application of Laws in Violation of the Convention (Arts. 1 and 2 of the American Convention on Human Rights), Advisory Opinion OC-14/94 of December 9, 1994, Series A, No. 14, para. 35.

responsible for the death of Mr. Almonacid-Arellano. Pursuant to the afore-said, his next of kin were prevented from exercising their right to a hearing by a competent, independent, and impartial court, and likewise, they were prevented from resorting to an effective and adequate remedy to redress the violations committed in detriment of their relative and to know the truth.

127. Pursuant to the case law of this Court:

> in the light of the general obligations established in Articles 1(1) and 2 of the American Convention, the States Parties are obliged to take all measures to ensure that no one is deprived of judicial protection and the exercise of the right to a simple and effective recourse, in the terms of Articles 8 and 25 of the Convention. Consequently, States Parties to the Convention which adopt laws that have the opposite effect, such as self-amnesty laws, violate Articles 8 and 25 in relation to Articles 1(1) and 2 of the Convention. Self-amnesty laws lead to the defenselessness of victims and perpetuate impunity; therefore, they are manifestly incompatible with the aims and spirit of the Convention. This type of law precludes the identification of the individuals who are responsible for human rights violations, because it obstructs the investigation and access to justice and prevents the victims and their next of kin from knowing the truth and receiving the corresponding reparation.[151]

128. Therefore, the Court considers that the application of Decree Law No. 2.191 was contrary to the obligations embodied in Article 1(1) of the American Convention in violation of the rights of Elvira del Rosario Gómez-Olivares and of Alfredo, Alexis, and José Luis Almonacid-Gómez, embodied in Articles 8(1) and 25 of the Convention, for all of which the Chilean State is internationally responsible.

129. As a conclusion of all questions addressed in this section the Court A), considers that the murder of Mr. Almonacid-Arellano was part of a State policy to repress certain sectors of the civilian population, and that it constitutes an example of a number of other similar illegal acts that took place during that period. The crime committed against Mr. Almonacid-Arellano cannot be susceptible of amnesty pursuant to the basic rules of international law since it constitutes a crime against humanity. The State has violated its obligation to

---

151   Cf. Case of Barrios Altos, supra note 140, para. 43.

modify its domestic legislation in order to guarantee the rights embodied in the American Convention because it has enforced and still keeps in force Decree Law No. 2.191, which does not exclude crimes against humanity from the general amnesty it grants. Finally, the State has violated the right to a fair trial and the right to judicial protection and has not complied with its obligation to respect guarantees in detriment of the next of kin of Mr. Almonacid-Arellano, given the fact that it applied Decree Law No. 2.191 to the instant case.

2. *Prosecutor v. Allieu Kondewa* (Decision on Lack of Jurisdiction/Abuses of Process: Amnesty Provided by the Lome Accord), Special Court for Sierra Leone, Appeals Chamber, Case No. SCSL-2004-14-AR72(E), May 25, 2004, paras. 30–57 (Separate Opinion of Justice Robertson)

30. The United Nations and the Government of Sierra Leone agreed to a clause in the Court's Statute which directed that an amnesty (i.e. the Lomé Amnesty) "shall not be a bar to prosecution" for the international crimes referred to in Articles 2-4 of the Statute. Their apparent concern was that the Lomé Amnesty might have some legal life left in it, and the avowed intention was to invalidate it "to the extent of its illegality under international law".[18] No doubt the Secretary-General thought that in international law, no amnesty could bar prosecution for "the international crime of genocide, crimes against humanity, war crimes and other serious violations of international humanitarian law" – an understanding spelled out by his representative Ambassador Okelo, at the end of the Lomé negotiations.[19] I must therefore consider whether that understanding represents international law, or wishful thinking. Since international law draws upon state practice and as recently as 2003, a few days before the invasion of Iraq, an amnesty offer was made by the US and UK to Saddam Hussein – a man widely accused of 'genocide, crimes against humanity, war crimes and other serious violations of international law' – the degree to which international criminal law forbids or nullifies amnesties must be open to some question.

31. Amnesty is an almost totemic absolution of rank and file combatants at the end of a civil war. One recent example is found in the peace agreement reached in Liberia in August 2003, with UN support, which requires the

---

18   Report of the Secretary-General, para. 24.
19   See S. E. Rowe, "Sierra Leone – The Search for Peace, Justice and Reconciliation", in Canadian Council on International law (Ed.) *Globalisation, People, Profit and Progress*, (Kluwer, 2002), p. 46.

transitional government to consider a "general amnesty".[20] Those who claim that international law invalidates all amnesties for all combatants for all crimes face not only the reality of state practice, where amnesties in peace agreements are common, but also Article 6(5) in the 1977 Protocol II to the Geneva Conventions:[21]

> At the end of hostilities, the authorities in power shall endeavour to grant the broadest possible amnesty to persons who have participated in the armed conflict, or those deprived of their liberty for reasons related to the armed conflict, whether they are interned or detained.

32. Protocol II has not been ratified by some important states and Article 6(5) is in any event a "best endeavours" provision. Although "broadest possible amnesty" would seem to apply to all crimes, it is plain from the context (Section 6 of Protocol II provides minimum standards for war crimes prosecutions) that it is not intended to encourage amnesties which would infringe international law, such as unilateral pardons for crimes (e.g., genocide) which the state is under a compelling duty to prosecute. The drafting history of the sub-section shows that it contemplates a Lincoln-style amnesty ("to restore the tranquility of the commonwealth") for rank and file combatants who have fought on opposite sides according to the laws of war, especially for [soldiers] on the losing side who have been detained by the end of the conflict. This is the basis on which some commentators have re-interpreted 'broadest possible amnesty' to exclude violations of international law, for which an amnesty is unavailable.[22] This point was not specifically considered by the South African Constitutional Court in the AZAPO case[23] which approved an amnesty which was not "blanket" because each person had to be considered in the circumstances of individual cases by a Truth and Reconciliation Commission. The Court drew support from Article 6(5), but did not consider whether "broadest

---

20 *Comprehensive Peace Agreement Between the Government of Liberia and the Liberians United for Reconciliation and Democracy (LURD) and the Movement for Democracy in Liberia (MODEL) and Political Parties* LURD, MODEL 18, Accra, August 2003, Article 34.

21 Protocol additional to the Geneva Conventions of 12 August 1949 and relating to the protection of victims of noninternational armed conflicts (Protocol II), 8 June 1977, in force 7 December 1978.

22 See Inter-Am Comm HR Case 10.480 (El Salvador), Report No. 1/99, para. 116 (1999), stating: "The preparatory work for Article 6(5) indicates that the purpose of this precept is to encourage amnesty, . . . as a type of liberation at the end of hostilities for those who were detained or punished merely for having participated in the hostilities. It does not seek to be an amnesty for these who have violated international humanitarian law."

23 *Azanian Peoples Organisation* (AZAPO)*and others* v. *President of* the *Republic of South Africa,* 1996 (4) SA 671 (CC), 691.

possible amnesty" would exclude persons for international crimes. But it obviously encourages *domestic* amnesties, to restore tranquility to states that have been at war with themselves, by pardoning "persons who have participated in the armed conflict". Sensibly, it would apply to rank and file participants, but not to the authors of such conflicts. Thus, tranquility might well be assisted by pardoning the mass of soldiers in rival armies – the purpose of Article 6(5) – but whether it is assisted by pardoning leaders who gave orders for mass murder of civilians is quite another matter. In South Africa, the Truth and Reconciliation Commission itself used pardon as a plea bargaining device, requiring those who wished to obtain an amnesty to tell, in public, the whole truth and to give evidence against accomplices in the event that any were put on trial.

33. One of the difficulties about invalidating peace settlement amnesties which apply to armies numbering tens of thousands is the practical impossibility of holding effective trials for all accused of war crimes. Another is in distinguishing between the "ordinary" crimes, for which the defendant is immune to prosecution, and the international crimes for which he is not, although both kinds of charges will be based upon the same events. One feature that gives an international crime its special gravity is the fact that it is commonly conceived and directed by state or group leaders, as part of a widespread and systematic persecution. But even within these horrific categories of mass murder and mass torture, there are obvious distinctions in moral culpability between foot-soldiers, accomplices, military authorities and national leaders. The "authors" of international crimes are those with the imagination or the authority – the power to conceive or to implement, or the power to stop. The sea change in the international community's approach to amnesty, from regarding it as the blessing of forgiveness to reproaching it as the curse of impunity, has turned on the dawning realisation of the unacceptability of amnesties for the "authors" of crimes against humanity, i.e. those who bear the greatest responsibility. It seems to me that international criminal law has developed at least so far as to make this same distinction, namely that amnesties cannot absolve the political and military leaders who bear greatest responsibility for genocide, torture, crimes against humanity and grave breaches of international and humanitarian law. This development has come, somewhat ironically, by way of reaction to the very power that political and military leaders have exploited, especially in Latin America, to pardon themselves or to manipulate or pressure new governments to bestow pardons upon them.

34. Although amnesty did not feature in the main trial at Nuremberg, the allies were aware of some local immunity statutes passed by quislings in areas of Nazi occupation. Thus the definition of crimes against humanity in Article 6(c) of

the Charter 24 was expressed to apply *"whether* or *not (the crime was) in violation of the domestic law of the country where perpetrated".* This is the basis for the imposition of criminal responsibility in international law on individuals in relation to crimes against humanity even if they are not crimes in domestic law (and even if they are, if domestic law bars prosecution for them). Hence the International Law Commission summary of "Principles of international law recognised in the Charter of the Nuremberg Tribunal and in the Judgment of the Tribunal"[24] includes as principle 2:

> The fact that internal law does not impose a penalty for an act which constitutes a crime under international law does not relieve the person who committed the act from responsibility under international law.

35. This would logically include the situation where a domestic amnesty purports to immunise a person or a class of persons from prosecution for acts which collectively can be characterised as an international law crime. It was to prevent quisling leaders from claiming any benefits from their own amnesty statutes that Allied Control Council Law No. 10[25] provided that no Nazi-era law could bar military tribunal trials or punishment for crimes against peace, war crimes or crimes against humanity.[26]

36. In the 1980s the Inter-American Commission took its stand on this principle to invalidate self-amnesty laws passed under pressure from military leaders who were involved in approving torture and "disappearances" that were common policy in, for example, Chile, Argentina, Guatemala and El Salvador in the preceding decade. Many of these amnesties were upheld by local courts, in defiance of the Commission, and despite the fact that its rulings were consistent applications of the principles in the Inter-American Convention on Human Rights. Even an amnesty approved by a plebiscite was condemned by the Commission: the excuse that it showed "the express will of the Uruguayan people to close a painful chapter in their history" was ruled contrary to the obligation to investigate human rights violations and hence a violation of the rights of relatives of the disappeared.[27]

---

24 Principles of International Law Recognized in the Charter of the Nuremberg Tribunal and in the Judgment of the Tribunal, adopted by the United Nations International Law Commission, 2 August 1950, (1950) *Yearbook of the ILC*, Vol. II, 374.

25 Allied Control Council Law Number 10, adopted at Berlin 20 December 1945, (1946) 3 Official Gazette of the Control Council for Germany, 50–55.

26 See Article II(5).

27 Inter-American Commission on Human Rights, Uruguay Report – Legal Effects of the 1986 amnesty law (confirmed by referendum), incompatible with the ACHR, [1992] 13 HRLJ, No.9-10, 340, Report No. 29/92, 2 October 1992, para. 22; Argentina Report – Amnesty laws

37. An example of a case adjudicated by the Inter-American Court in this period was that relating to the *Los Hojas* massacre. After the El Salvador legislative assembly passed an amnesty decree specifically providing impunity for all army officers who participated, the Inter-American Court ruled that

> the present amnesty law, as applied in these cases, by foreclosing the possibility of judicial relief in cases of murder, inhumane treatment and absence of judicial guarantees, denies the fundamental nature of most basic human rights. It eliminates perhaps the single most effective means of enforcing such rights, the trial and punishment of offenders.[28]

The Court held that the government responsible for the armed forces had, by legislating an amnesty, breached the victim's rights to life (Article 4), personal security and integrity (Article 5), due process (Article 8) and juridical protection (Article 25) and had failed to comply with its Article 1 obligation to guarantee human rights to all its citizens.

38. In 1992, when this decision was delivered, it was treated disrespectfully: the government reacted to the court's ruling by passing an even broader amnesty law. Nonetheless, it marked the beginning of a refusal by international courts and commissions to countenance the spectacle of the state forgiving itself its own wrongs or the increasing phenomena of new governments giving amnesties at the insistence of one continuing branch of the old – the military and the police. These decisions had the result of denying the benefit of amnesties to those who bear greatest responsibility for crimes against humanity – high ranking state officials who could not be pardoned by the state itself and rebel leaders who force a war-weary government to offer them a pardon in exchange for peace.

39. In the same year – 1992 – the Human Rights Committee ruled that the obligation in the International Covenant on Civil and Political Rights ("Civil Covenant") to provide an effective remedy against violation of rights by state officials meant that the amnesties for acts of torture:

> are generally incompatible with the duty of states to investigate such acts; to guarantee prosecution of such acts within their jurisdiction; and

---

and Presidential decree of pardon violate the victims' human rights, ibid., 336-9, Report No. 28/92, 2 October 1992.

28   Inter-American Commission on Human Rights, El Salvador Report – State's responsibility for 1983 Las Hojas massacre, [15'93] 14HRLJ, No. 5-6, 167, Report No. 26/92, 24 September 1992, para. 169.

to ensure that they do not occur in the future. States may not deprive
individuals of the right to an effective remedy, including compensation
and such full rehabilitation as may be possible.[29]

40. All international human rights treaties have rules that require governments
to investigate violations and provide an effective remedy. By Article 2(3) of
the Civil Covenant, for example, state parties undertake to ensure that victims
of rights violations "shall have an effective remedy, notwithstanding that the
violation has been committed by persons acting in an official capacity". In
case of violations as grave as crimes against humanity, it may be that no
remedy short of prosecution could be considered "effective" (see paragraph
53 below). Article 2(3) does not provide individuals with a right to force a
state to prosecute, but does put an obligation on the state to prosecute any
suspects who have been credibly accused as a result of the investigation.[30]

41. Conventions dealing with crimes against humanity and war crimes consistently require legal action to be taken against suspects. Thus, the Torture
Convention requires each state party to ensure prompt and impartial investigation of torture allegations (Article 12).[31] The Genocide Convention[32] imposes
an obligation to punish, irrespective of whether perpetrators are "constitutionally responsible rulers, public officials or private individuals" (Article 4),
after trial either by "a competent tribunal" of the state where the act occurred
or by an international penal tribunal (Article 6). The 1949 Geneva Conventions provide that states have an obligation to search for war criminals, and
to bring them (irrespective of their nationality) before their own courts or
else extradite them for trial in another jurisdiction. The Civil Covenant and
the European" and Inter-American Conventions" all require that rights be
respected and protected by law and that victims shall have an effective remedy
in the event of violation. When the right to life is violated, certainly on the
scale of genocide or massacre, only prosecution could be "effective".

42. State practice supportive of the duty to prosecute crimes against humanity
may be found in many UN resolutions. In 1973, the General Assembly adopted
a set of Principles of International Cooperation in the Detection, Arrest, Extradition, and Punishment of Persons Guilty of War Crimes and Crimes against

---

29   Human Rights Committee, General Comment no. 20 (on Article 7), 44'1, session (1992).
30   See *Bautista v. Colombia* (1995), HRC 27, para. 8.6.17.
31   *Convention Against Torture And Other Cruel, Inhuman Or Degrading Treatment Or Punish-
      ment*, 4 February 1985.
32   Convention on the Prevention and Punishment of the Crime of Genocide, adopted by UN
      General Assembly on 9 December 1948, 78 UNTS 277.

Humanity.[33] Principle I provides that suspects shall be subject to tracing, arrest, trial and, if found guilty, to punishment. The 1993 Vienna Declaration is to similar effect.[34] Although there have been many such publicized failures to prosecute, these have been *realpolitik* failures, in some cases explained by the practical impossibility of financing and organizing proper trials for thousands of perpetrators (although Rwanda, notably, has attempted this task). This justification for inaction from lack of resources cannot be advanced as an excuse for failure to prosecute the handful of persons who bear the greatest responsibility for international crimes.

43. In 1988 came the ground-breaking decision of the Inter-American Court in the *Velasquez Rodriguez Case*,[35] concerning a student who "disappeared" at the hands of the Honduran military, which then denied its responsibility for his murder. The Court held the Honduran Government liable under the Inter-American Convention:

> the state must prevent, investigate and punish any violation of the rights recognised by the Convention . . . The state has a legal duty to take reasonable steps to prevent human rights violations and to use the means at its disposal to carry out a serious investigation of violations committed within its jurisdiction, to identify those responsible, impose the appropriate punishment and ensure the victim adequate compensation . . . [36]

44. I conclude this brief survey of current attitudes by international legal bodies towards the impermissibility of amnesty statutes at least in relation to perpetrators alleged to bear command responsibility for massacres, by citing recent decisions of two courts of high persuasive authority. In its judgment in the *Barrios Altos Case,* which concerned the responsibility of senior government officials (including ex-President Fujimori) for authorizing a mass killing of fifteen students, the Inter-American Court held in terms that blanket amnesties were incompatible with the duties of state parties to the Inter-American Convention:

> This Court considers that all amnesty provisions, provisions on prescription and the establishment of measures designed to eliminate

---

33   GA resolution 3074(XXVIII), 3 December 1973.
34   A/CONF.157/23, 12 July 1993.
35   Inter-Am Ct HR (Ser. C) No.4 (judgment) (1988).
36   Ibid., paras. 166, 174, and 176.

responsibility are impermissible, because they are intended to prevent the investigation and punishment of those responsible for serious
human rights violations such as torture, extra-judicial summary or
arbitrary execution and forced disappearance, all of them prohibited
because they violate non-derogable rights recognised by international
human rights law.[37]

45. An ICTY Trial Chamber has ruled that a domestic amnesty covering crimes
the prohibition of which has the status of a *jus cogens* norm "would not be
accorded international legal recognition". In *Prosecutor v Anto Furundzija* the
Court noted:

> It would be senseless to argue, on the one hand, that on account of
> the *jus* cogens value of the prohibition against torture, treaties or cus-
> tomary rules providing for torture would be null and void *ab initio,*
> and then be unmindful of a state say, taking national measures autho-
> rising or condoning torture or resolving its perpetrators through an
> amnesty law. If such a situation were to arise, the national measures,
> violating the general principle and any relevant treaty provision, would
> produce the legal effects discussed above and would not be accorded
> international legal recognition . . . What is even more important is that
> perpetrators of torture acting upon or benefiting from these national
> measures may nevertheless be held criminally responsible for torture,
> whether in a foreign state, or in their own state under a subsequent
> regime.[38]

46. The African Commission on Human Rights has adopted the same approach
in condemning an amnesty law in Mauritania,[39] in promulgating the "Robben
Island guidelines for the prohibition and prevention of torture" and in condemning various states for failing to conduct investigations and failing to prosecute senior officials of security forces and governments involved in human
rights violations.[40]

47. There is a substantial body of cases, comments, rulings and remarks
which denies the permissibility of amnesties in international law for crimes

---

37   *Barrios Altos Case (Chumbipuma Aguirre et al. v. Peru),* 75 Inter-Am Ct HR (Ser. C),
     Judgment (2001), para. 41.
38   *Prosecutor v Furundzija,* Case No. IT-95-l7/1, Judgment, 10 December 1998, para. 155.
39   *Mauritania Communications* 54/91 61/91 96/93 98/93 164/97-196/97 2110/98.
40   See decision in *Social and Economic Rights Actions v. Nigeria,* COMM 155/96, para. 44.

against humanity and war crimes. The Human Rights Committee ("HRC"), the Committee against Torture, the Special Rapporteur on Torture, the Inter-American Court and Commission, the ICTY, the African Commission and many renowned jurists speak with one voice in finding that blanket amnesties are impermissible (although the HRC adds "in general"): they produce impunity and violate state duties to investigate and punish perpetrators as well as the victims' rights to justice. But to survey all these statements is necessarily to observe the depressing number of occasions on which they have been provoked by state practice to the contrary. The fact that international legal bodies universally condemn states which grant amnesties for crimes against humanity has not stopped states, including the most powerful (as with the US/UK amnesty offer to Saddam Hussein in 2003[41]) from resorting to them in cases of perceived necessity. The Prosecution argues that a rule prohibiting amnesty has now crystallised as a universal norm of international law, but since that crystallisation process must show support in state practice as well as juristic writing, how can the practice of states to grant amnesties be explained away? To some extent, perhaps, by the fact that state practice looks not only to what states do, but whether they have any qualms about doing it: many states still torture, but they do not admit to doing so and international law finds a consensus in the fact that they all deplore its use. There is, too, a hand-wringing quality about the excuses for amnesty by states which grant them: these can range from Peru's confession (in the *Barrios Altos Case*) that international law was thereby violated, to the reaction of the UK foreign minister when taxed with his offer of impunity to Saddam: "the world is imperfect".[42] States condemned for granting amnesties are beginning to show some embarrassment when called to account by the UN Human Rights Commission for breaching legal obligations. This official response of "confession and avoidance" is taken into account in identifying the crystallization of a rule of customary international law, in the way described by the ICJ in *Nicaragua v US:*

> In order to deduce the existence of customary rules, the court deems it sufficient that the conduct of states should, in general, be consistent with such rules, and that instances of state conduct inconsistent with the given rule should generally have been treated as breaches of that rule, not as indications of the recognition of a new rule. If a state acts in a way *prima facie* incompatible with a recognised rule, but defends its conduct by appealing to exceptions or justifications contained within

---

41   See para. 30 above.
42   Jack Straw, interviewed BBC, 10 January 2003. See Hansard, Vol. 936, 19 March 2003, for the Prime Minister's comments.

the rule itself, then whether or not the state's conduct is in fact justifiable on that basis, the significance of that attitude is to confirm rather than to weaken the rule.[43]

48. It may therefore be said that state practice is changing to conform with the consistent view that blanket amnesties are, at least "in general", impermissible in international law for international crimes. What can also be detected, in what may be the development of an interim position, is a focus on major malefactors, the intellectual or commanding 'authors' of torture and genocide, who will not be permitted to escape through a pardon that exonerates their underlings. The mesh of the international law dragnet may be excessively loose at this rudimentary stage of its development, but it nonetheless serves to entangle the biggest fish – those who can credibly be accused of bearing the greatest responsibility for international crimes.

49. This is not so much a limitation on the rule as an application of it to those whose level of responsibility demands retribution, irrespective of cost or convenience or other apparently counter-veiling public interest. This follows from the fundamental duties and rights outlined above, which have been identified in the Conventions and invoked to demonstrate an obligation to prosecute. That obligation must be more powerful – indeed, overwhelming – when applied to those political and military leaders without whose authorisation or encouragement the crimes against humanity would not have been committed by "small fry" and common soldiers. Such leaders are the real "perpetrators of serious crimes under international law" who cannot benefit from a peace agreement under the simple principle of the Vienna Declaration that "states should abrogate legislation leading to impunity for those responsible for grave violations of human rights such as torture and prosecute such violations, thereby providing a firm basis for the rule of law".[44] There is no doubt that the sea change in international opinion is a reflection of public concern at the spectacle of truculent leaders, credibly accused of the worst human rights violations, living happily ever after an actual or implied amnesty. Removing them from the stage is no longer enough: the clear implication from all human rights treaties is that they must face justice, although their followers may be spared as a reconciliation measure. In my judgement, the rule against impunity which has crystallized in international law is a norm which denies the legal possibility of pardon to those who bear the greatest responsibility for crimes

43   (1996) ICJ reports, para. 186.
44   World Conference on Human Rights, Vienna Declaration and Programme of Action, 25 June 1993, NCONF.157/23, 12 July 1993, para. 60.

against humanity and for widespread and serious war crimes – certainly those which involve "serious violations" of Common Article 3 of the Geneva Conventions. The current state of the rule against impunity is neatly reflected in the Statute of the Special Court for Sierra Leone: Article 1 restricts the Court's jurisdiction to those who bear the greatest responsibility, and Article 10 denies amnesty to those very persons.

50. There are ways other than criminal prosecution to bring war crimes home to war criminals and offer some solatium to victims. Truth and Reconciliation Commissions ("TRC") have been much in vogue in transitional times, sometimes as an easier alternative for governments but increasingly as a genuine forum for truth telling and as a means to map a post-conflict future. But apart from a few well-publicized examples from South Africa, TRC procedures do not usually produce confessions of guilt from political and military leaders or powerful state officials.[45] Those who bear greatest responsibility seem to bear least sense of shame: they have usually defended their actions as having been required by the national interest. The TRC process, involving public confrontation with victims or relatives, may produce a degree of individual reconciliation when policemen and soldiers apologise, but not the sense of closure for grieving relatives which comes after a trial and sentence of major culprits. The message that most helps victims to come to terms with human loss – that their suffering has not been in vain because the perpetrator is locked away and other perpetrators may be deterred – is not available. Truth commissions may reveal truth, in the sense of finding out where bodies are buried and who ordered the disappearance and why: but that sort of truth without a follow-up prosecution, is unlikely to produce much satisfaction. Naming and shaming is no path to reconciliation when those who are named remain unashamed. Financial compensation from a national commission or through civil actions is another alternative. But many such victims feel demeaned by the notion that money can meaningfully compensate for their loss other than as a measure of punishment (the satisfaction of the ex-President Marcos torture victims derived not from the size of their damages award but from the fact it had been extracted from his own secret bank accounts). Once again, these alternatives to criminal trial point to the need to penalize those who bear greatest responsibility – such as rulers, arms dealers, government officials and other mongers of war whose ill-gotten gains may be traceable and confiscatable as part of their sentence after conviction at a criminal trial.

---

45   See *Prosecutor v. Norman*, Case No. SCSL-2003-08, Decision on Appeal by the Truth and Reconciliation Commission for Sierra Leone, 28 November 2003, para. 22.

51. The stage I discern international criminal law to have reached is to have produced a rule that invalidates amnesties offered under any circumstances to persons most responsible for crimes against humanity (genocide and widespread torture) and the worst war crimes (namely those in Common Article 3 of the Geneva Conventions). In the sphere of international law, the acts of these perpetrators (if capable of proof beyond reasonable doubt) must always remain amenable to trial and punishment. That prospect may deter them from accepting a peace settlement and may cause more loss of life in the short run, but less in the long run: we cannot speculate. The rule is one of international law, however, and cannot prevent one state or alliance of states from offering a safe haven to a tyrant. The haven will only be "safe", of course, so long as he remains in it. States which wish to offer effective amnesties to international criminals must be prepared to suffer their continuing presence and to abide the consequences – political, diplomatic and perhaps in time legal – of their actions.

Abuse of Process

52. The consequence of the Court's ruling in its Decision on Challenge to Jurisdiction: Lomé Accord Amnesty is that this amnesty cannot operate in international law to provide immunity from prosecution to those alleged to bear the greatest responsibility for crimes against humanity. Article 10 of the Special Court's Statute cannot be disapplied, because it complies with – indeed it embodies – a rule of customary international law. This applicant, however, has a fall-back position: if the amnesty cannot bar his prosecution, might it nonetheless, on the assumption that he can prove that he personally complied with its terms, be prayed it in aid of an application to stop his trial on the grounds of abuse of process? 1 will answer this question in principle, recognizing the possibility that some commanders guilty of pre-Lomé war crimes may be able to prove that in reliance upon the amnesty they laid down arms and never took them up again, or only took them up out of necessity to defend against unprovoked attacks from enemy forces which were breaching the ceasefire. That fact would provide, in my view, significant justification of sentence were they convicted, but can it serve to bar their trial in the first place?

53. Abuse of process is a common law doctrine by which a national court has an inherent power permanently to stay a properly brought prosecution on two broad grounds: 1) if it concludes that a fair trial is impossible and 2) if, although possible, to conduct such a trial would inevitably undermine the

integrity of the court or of the justice system.[46] The first ground is applicable to international criminal courts – indeed is one of the defining characteristics of the "independence" required of any legal tribunal. The second, however, confronts the logic of the unforgivable crime: how can it ever undermine a court's integrity to conduct a fair trial when the charge is as heinous as a crime against humanity? The cases where national courts have invoked the second head generally concern prosecutions brought in circumstances where the law has not provided an adequate defence (e.g, of entrapment) or where the defendant has been brought into the jurisdiction unlawfully or in breach of extradition requirements.[47] International crimes are so grave that it is difficult to see how inducements to commit them could be relevant other than to mitigation, and the extradition breaches that might stop the trial of a fraudster in a national court can hardly be allowed to abort the prosecution of an Eichmann. A national court may use its inherent power as an expression of its disapproval of police or prosecutorial misconduct, on the principle that the end does not justify the means. *Eichmann* suggests that punishing crimes against humanity is an obligatory end that unlawful means may in some circumstances justify, although certainly not if they themselves amount to international crimes. An international criminal court would undermine its own integrity were it to permit a prosecution to go ahead based on a confession extracted by torture, for example, so the second head of abuse, if it is available to international tribunals, must necessarily be more limited in its application than in domestic courts.

54. That is, perhaps, the lesson of the *Barayagwiza* case[48] where the ICTR Appeals Chamber at first applied the doctrine of abuse of process to release a defendant because of prosecutorial misconduct, then subsequently ordered his re-arrest and trial after hearing fresh evidence that the prosecutor's conduct was not so bad after all. There is no moral or any other equivalence between prosecution "misconduct" – usually the product of ineptitude or over-zealousness – and a defendant's alleged misconduct if it involves giving orders for mass murder. In this situation, it would be inappropriate to discipline the prosecutor by freeing the defendant. Curial strictures, which may lead to the prosecutor's dismissal or demotion or payment of liabilities in costs, are the appropriate remedy in such cases, unless the delay consequent upon the misconduct has caused such prejudice to the defence (e.g. through the death or fading memory of defence witnesses) that a fair trial is no longer possible.

---

46   *R v. Latif* [1996] 1 WLR 104, per Lord Steyn.
47   *R v. Horseferry Road Magistrates' Court Ex parte Bennett* [1994] 1 AC 42.
48   *Barayagwiza v. Prosecutor*, Case No. ICTR-97-19-AR72, Decision, 3 November 1999.

Proof of serious prejudice to the conduct of the defence is the precondition for a successful abuse application on the first ground and will be a matter for the Trial Chamber to assess. I cannot immediately see how reliance on an amnesty could be pleaded as a cause of such serious prejudice to a defendant that a fair trial would be impossible: the evidence in relation to his conduct prior to Lomé will not be affected by his actions afterwards.

55. The second ground, defined as "where in the circumstances of a particular case, proceeding with the trial of the accused would contravene the court's sense of justice due to pre-trial impropriety or misconduct"[49] was relied upon in *Barayagwiza,* which adopted the leading common law authorities on abuse.[50] The court found that the prosecution had been egregiously negligent, and "the only remedy available for such prosecution inaction and the resultant denial of his rights is to release the appellant and dismiss the charges against him".[51] I consider this to be an unsatisfactory approach, for reasons given in the preceding paragraph. It was based on the second head of abuse, as defined above, which focuses too broadly on "pre-trial impropriety or misconduct". If a fair trial is still possible, pre-trial impropriety or misconduct will not normally be a reason to stop it. On the other hand, it is possible to envisage situations where even a fair trial, without any prosecution misbehaviour, would be a spectacle destructive of public confidence in the justice system, as in the case of an obviously deranged or dying defendant in the dock.

56. There can be no question of prosecutorial misconduct by proceeding in the face of the Lomé Amnesty, given that Article 10 of the Statute expressly provides that an amnesty shall not bar a prosecution. That does not dispose of an argument based on the second head of abuse under which it may be open to a defendant to claim that his trial, however fair, would nonetheless be destructive of public confidence in the court or the system of international justice it dispenses. But the performance of a condition in order to obtain an amnesty does not obliterate the guilt irrevocably attached to the commission of a crime against humanity for which the amnesty is given. There can be no basis for the abuse argument, (namely that an international criminal court would confound its own mission by denying a defendant, accused of bearing greatest responsibility for inhuman crimes, the benefit of an invalid amnesty promise on which he relied) when international law denies such persons the benefit even of a valid amnesty. Amnesty compliance may, however, be invoked

---

49   Ibid., para. 77.
50   Ibid., paras 74–77.
51   Ibid., para. 106.

in support of the second head of abuse in a situation which is not suggested here, namely when the prosecutor in the course of pre trial proceedings offers a pardon to an indictee – e.g. in return for a guilty plea and "queen's evidence" against accomplices and then reneges on the deal. This is a literal abuse of process which, as national court decisions show, affects the conscience of the court and may well incline it to hold the prosecutor to his word if the defendant has performed his side of the bargain. But the Special Court Prosecutor is in no way concerned with or affected by the Lomé Amnesty, and is obliged by statute to disregard it. That disregard cannot amount to an abuse of process.

Conclusion

57. There is no reason to disapply Article 10 of the Statute: it reflects customary international law which nullifies amnesties given to persons accused of bearing great responsibility for serious breaches of international law. There is no evidence before this court of Prosecution misconduct of a kind that would amount to an abuse of process.

3. *Azanian Peoples Organization (AZAPO) and Others v. President of the Republic of South Africa and Others*, Constitutional Court of South Africa, Case No. CCT17/96 (July 25, 1996), Judgment of Mahomed DP

[1] For decades South African history has been dominated by a deep conflict between a minority which reserved for itself all control over the political instruments of the state and a majority who sought to resist that domination. Fundamental human rights became a major casualty of this conflict as the resistance of those punished by their denial was met by laws designed to counter the effectiveness of such resistance. The conflict deepened with the increased sophistication of the economy, the rapid acceleration of knowledge and education and the ever increasing hostility of an international community steadily outraged by the inconsistency which had become manifest between its own articulated ideals after the Second World War and the official practices which had become institutionalised in South Africa through laws enacted to give them sanction and teeth by a Parliament elected only by a privileged minority. The result was a debilitating war of internal political dissension and confrontation, massive expressions of labour militancy, perennial student unrest, punishing international economic isolation, widespread dislocation in crucial areas of national endeavour, accelerated levels of armed conflict and a dangerous combination of anxiety, frustration and anger among expanding proportions of the populace. The legitimacy of law itself was deeply wounded as the country haemorrhaged dangerously in the face of this tragic conflict which had begun to traumatise the entire nation.

[2] During the eighties it became manifest to all that our country with all its natural wealth, physical beauty and human resources was on a disaster course unless that conflict was reversed. It was this realisation which mercifully rescued us in the early nineties as those who controlled the levers of state power began to negotiate a different future with those who had been imprisoned, silenced, or driven into exile in consequence of their resistance to that control and its consequences. Those negotiations resulted in an interim Constitution[1] committed to a transition towards a more just, defensible and democratic political order based on the protection of fundamental human rights. It was wisely appreciated by those involved in the preceding negotiations that the task of building such a new democratic order was a very difficult task because of the previous history and the deep emotions and indefensible inequities it had generated; and that this could not be achieved without a firm and generous commitment to reconciliation and national unity. It was realised that much of the unjust consequences of the past could not ever be fully reversed. It might be necessary in crucial areas to close the book on that past.

[3] This fundamental philosophy is eloquently expressed in the epilogue to the Constitution which reads as follows:

National Unity and Reconciliation
   This Constitution provides a historic bridge between the past of a deeply divided society characterised by strife, conflict, untold suffering and injustice, and a future founded on the recognition of human rights, democracy and peaceful co-existence and development opportunities for all South Africans, irrespective of colour, race, class, belief or sex.
   The pursuit of national unity, the well-being of all South African citizens and peace require reconciliation between the people of South Africa and the reconstruction of society.
   The adoption of this Constitution lays the secure foundation for the people of South Africa to transcend the divisions and strife of the past, which generated gross violations of human rights, the transgression of humanitarian principles in violent conflicts and a legacy of hatred, fear, guilt and revenge.
   These can now be addressed on the basis that there is a need for understanding but not for vengeance, a need for reparation but not for retaliation, a need for ubuntu but not for victimisation.
   In order to advance such reconciliation and reconstruction, amnesty shall be granted in respect of acts, omissions and offences associated with political objectives and committed in the course of the

---

1   Act 200 of 1993, which is referred to in this judgment as "the Constitution."

conflicts of the past. To this end, Parliament under this Constitution shall adopt a law determining a firm cut-off date, which shall be a date after 8 October 1990 and before 6 December 1993, and providing for the mechanisms, criteria and procedures, including tribunals, if any, through which such amnesty shall be dealt with at any time after the law has been passed.

With this Constitution and these commitments we, the people of South Africa, open a new chapter in the history of our country.

Pursuant to the provisions of the epilogue, Parliament enacted during 1995 what is colloquially referred to as the Truth and Reconciliation Act. Its proper name is the Promotion of National Unity and Reconciliation Act 34 of 1995 ("the Act").

[4] The Act establishes a Truth and Reconciliation Commission. The objectives of that Commission are set out in section 3. Its main objective is to "promote national unity and reconciliation in a spirit of understanding which transcends the conflicts and divisions of the past." It is enjoined to pursue that objective by "establishing as complete a picture as possible of the causes, nature and extent of the gross violations of human rights" committed during the period commencing 1 March 1960 to the "cut-off date."[2] For this purpose the Commission is obliged to have regard to "the perspectives of the victims and the motives and perspectives of the persons responsible for the commission of the violations."[3] It also is required to facilitate

> " ... the granting of amnesty to persons who make full disclosure of all the relevant facts relating to acts associated with a political objective ... "[4]

The Commission is further entrusted with the duty to establish and to make known "the fate or whereabouts of victims" and of "restoring the human and civil dignity of such victims" by affording them an opportunity to relate their own accounts of the violations and by recommending "reparation measures" in respect of such violations[5] and finally to compile a comprehensive report in

---

2   Described in the epilogue to the Constitution as "a date after 8 October 1990 and before 6 December 1993." "Cut-off date" is defined in section 1 of the Act to mean "the latest date allowed as the cut-off date in terms of the Constitution as set out under the heading 'National Unity and Reconciliation'."
3   Section 3(1)(a).
4   Section 3(1)(b).
5   Section 3(1)(c).

respect of its functions, including the recommendation of measures to prevent the violation of human rights.[6]

[5] Three committees are established for the purpose of achieving the objectives of the Commission.[7] The first committee is the Committee on Human Rights Violations which conducts enquiries pertaining to gross violations of human rights during the prescribed period, with extensive powers to gather and receive evidence and information.[8] The second committee is the Committee on Reparation and Rehabilitation which is given similar powers to gather information and receive evidence for the purposes of ultimately recommending to the President suitable reparations for victims of gross violations of human rights.[9] The third and the most directly relevant committee for the purposes of the present dispute is the Committee on Amnesty.[10] This is a committee which must consist of five persons of which the chairperson must be a judge.[11] The Committee on Amnesty is given elaborate powers to consider applications for amnesty.[12] The Committee has the power to grant amnesty in respect of any act, omission or offence to which the particular application for amnesty relates, provided that the applicant concerned has made a full disclosure of all relevant facts and provided further that the relevant act, omission or offence is associated with a political objective committed in the course of the conflicts of the past, in accordance with the provisions of sections 20(2) and 20(3) of the Act.[13] These sub-sections contain very detailed provisions pertaining to what may properly be considered to be acts "associated with a political objective." Sub-section (3) of section 20 provides as follows:

> "Whether a particular act, omission or offence contemplated in subsection (2) is an act associated with a political objective, shall be decided with reference to the following criteria:
> (a) The motive of the person who committed the act, omission or offence;

6   Section 3(1)(d).
7   Section 3(3).
8   Sections 3(3)(a), 12 and 14.
9   Sections 3(3)(c), 23 and 25. The recommendations of the committee are themselves considered by the President who then makes recommendations to Parliament. This is considered by a joint committee of Parliament and the decisions of the joint committee, after approval by Parliament, are implemented by regulations made by the President. Section 27.
10   Section 3(3)(b).
11   Section 17(3). It is common cause that the Committee on Amnesty, in fact appointed by the President, includes three judges of the Supreme Court.
12   Section 19.
13   Section 20(1).

(b) the context in which the act, omission or offence took place, and in particular whether the act, omission or offence was committed in the course of or as part of a political uprising, disturbance or event, or in reaction thereto;

(c) the legal and factual nature of the act, omission or offence, including the gravity of the act, omission or offence;

(d) the object or objective of the act, omission or offence, and in particular whether the act, omission or offence was primarily directed at a political opponent or State property or personnel or against private property or individuals;

(e) whether the act, omission or offence was committed in the execution of an order of, or on behalf of, or with the approval of, the organisation, institution, liberation movement or body of which the person who committed the act was a member, an agent or a supporter; and

(f) the relationship between the act, omission or offence and the political objective pursued, and in particular the directness and proximity of the relationship and the proportionality of the act, omission or offence to the objective pursued, but does not include any act, omission or offence committed by any person referred to in subsection (2) who acted-

   (i) for personal gain: Provided that an act, omission or offence by any person who acted and received money or anything of value as an informer of the State or a former state, political organisation or liberation movement, shall not be excluded only on the grounds of that person having received money or anything of value for his or her information; or

   (ii) out of personal malice, ill-will or spite, directed against the victim of the acts committed."

[6] After making provision for certain ancillary matters, section 20(7) (the constitutionality of which is impugned in these proceedings) provides as follows:

(7) (a) No person who has been granted amnesty in respect of an act, omission or offence shall be criminally or civilly liable in respect of such act, omission or offence and no body or organisation or the State shall be liable, and no person shall be vicariously liable, for any such act, omission or offence.

   (b) Where amnesty is granted to any person in respect of any act, omission or offence, such amnesty shall have no influence upon the criminal liability of any other person contingent upon the liability of the first-mentioned person.

(c) No person, organisation or state shall be civilly or vicariously liable for an act, omission or offence committed between 1 March 1960 and the cut-off date by a person who is deceased, unless amnesty could not have been granted in terms of this Act in respect of such an act, omission or offence.

Section 20(7) is followed by sections 20(8), 20(9) and 20(10) which deal expressly with both the formal and procedural consequences of an amnesty in the following terms:

(8) If any person–
    (a)   has been charged with and is standing trial in respect of an offence constituted by the act or omission in respect of which amnesty is granted in terms of this section; or
    (b)   has been convicted of, and is awaiting the passing of sentence in respect of, or is in custody for the purpose of serving a sentence imposed in respect of, an offence constituted by the act or omission in respect of which amnesty is so granted, the criminal proceedings shall forthwith upon publication of the proclamation referred to in subsection (6) become void or the sentence so imposed shall upon such publication lapse and the person so in custody shall forthwith be released.

(9) If any person has been granted amnesty in respect of any act or omission which formed the ground of a civil judgment which was delivered at any time before the granting of the amnesty, the publication of the proclamation in terms of subsection (6) shall not affect the operation of the judgment in so far as it applies to that person.

(10) Where any person has been convicted of any offence constituted by an act or omission associated with a political objective in respect of which amnesty has been granted in terms of this Act, any entry or record of the conviction shall be deemed to be expunged from all official documents or records and the conviction shall for all purposes, including the application of any Act of Parliament or any other law, be deemed not to have taken place: Provided that the Committee may recommend to the authority concerned the taking of such measures as it may deem necessary for the protection of the safety of the public."[14]

14   Subsection 6 which is referred to in sub-sections 8 and 9 simply provides that the Committee must by proclamation in the Gazette make known the full names of any person to whom

[7] What is clear from section 20(7), read with sections 20(8), (9) and (10), is that once a person has been granted amnesty in respect of an act, omission or offence

(a) the offender can no longer be held "criminally liable" for such offence and no prosecution in respect thereof can be maintained against him or her;

(b) such an offender can also no longer be held civilly liable personally for any damages sustained by the victim and no such civil proceedings can successfully be pursued against him or her;

(c) if the wrongdoer is an employee of the state, the state is equally discharged from any civil liability in respect of any act or omission of such an employee, even if the relevant act or omission was effected during the course and within the scope of his or her employment; and

(d) other bodies, organisations or persons are also exempt from any liability for any of the acts or omissions of a wrongdoer which would ordinarily have arisen in consequence of their vicarious liability for such acts or omissions.

[8] The applicants sought in this court to attack the constitutionality of section 20(7) on the grounds that its consequences are not authorised by the Constitution. They aver that various agents of the state, acting within the scope and in the course of their employment, have unlawfully murdered and maimed leading activists during the conflict against the racial policies of the previous administration and that the applicants have a clear right to insist that such wrongdoers should properly be prosecuted and punished, that they should be ordered by the ordinary courts of the land to pay adequate civil compensation to the victims or dependants of the victims and further to require the state to make good to such victims or dependants the serious losses which they have suffered in consequence of the criminal and delictual acts of the employees of the state. In support of that attack Mr Soggot SC, who appeared for the applicants together with Mr Khoza, contended that section 20(7) was inconsistent with section 22 of the Constitution which provides that

[e]very person shall have the right to have justiciable disputes settled by a court of law or, where appropriate, another independent or impartial forum.

_____

amnesty has been granted, together with sufficient information to identify the act, omission or offence in respect of which such amnesty has been granted.

He submitted that the Amnesty Committee was neither "a court of law" nor an "independent or impartial forum" and that in any event the Committee was not authorised to settle "justiciable disputes." All it was simply required to decide was whether *amnesty* should be granted in respect of a particular act, omission or offence.

[9] The effect of an amnesty undoubtedly impacts upon very fundamental rights. All persons are entitled to the protection of the law against unlawful invasions of their right to life, their right to respect for and protection of dignity and their right not to be subject to torture of any kind. When those rights are invaded those aggrieved by such invasion have the right to obtain redress in the ordinary courts of law and those guilty of perpetrating such violations are answerable before such courts, both civilly and criminally. An amnesty to the wrongdoer effectively obliterates such rights.

[10] There would therefore be very considerable force in the submission that section 20(7) of the Act constitutes a violation of section 22 of the Constitution, if there was nothing in the Constitution itself which permitted or authorised such violation. The crucial issue, therefore, which needs to be determined, is whether the Constitution, indeed, permits such a course. Section 33(2) of the Constitution provides that

> "[s]ave as provided for in subsection (1) or any other provision of this Constitution, no law, whether a rule of common law, customary law or legislation, shall limit any right entrenched in this Chapter."
>
> Two questions arise from the provisions of this sub-section. The first question is whether there is "any other provision in this Constitution" which permits a limitation of the right in section 22 and secondly if there is not, whether any violation of section 22 is a limitation which can be justified in terms of section 33(1) of the Constitution which reads as follows:
> "The rights entrenched in this Chapter may be limited by law of general application, provided that such limitation–
> (a) shall be permissible only to the extent that it is–
>   (i) reasonable; and
>   (ii) justifiable in an open and democratic society based on freedom and equality; and shall not negate the essential content of the right in question, and provided further that any limitation to–
> (aa) a right entrenched in section 10, 11, 12, 14(1), 21, 25 or 30(1)(d) or (e) or (2); or

(bb) a right entrenched in section 15, 16, 17, 18, 23 or 24, in so far as such right relates to free and fair political activity, shall, in addition to being reasonable as required in paragraph (a)(i), also be necessary."

[11] Mr. Marcus, who together with Mr. D Leibowitz appeared for the Respondents, contended that the epilogue, which I have previously quoted, is indeed a "provision of this Constitution" within the meaning of section 33(2). He argued that any law conferring amnesty on a wrongdoer in respect of acts, omissions and offences associated with political objectives and committed during the prescribed period, is therefore a law properly authorised by the Constitution.

[12] It is therefore necessary to deal, in the first place, with the constitutional status of the epilogue. In the founding affidavit in support of the application for direct access to this court made by the deputy president of the first applicant, reliance was placed on the Constitutional Principles contained in schedule 4 to the Constitution and it was submitted that

"[the] Constitutional Principles in Schedule 4 enjoy a higher status to that of other sections of the Constitution, in that, in terms of Section 74(1) of the Constitution, it is not permissible to amend the Constitutional Principles and they shall be included in the final Constitution. To the extent that, therefore, the post-end clause is in conflict with Constitutional Principle VI, the latter should prevail."

Constitutional Principle VI provides that "[t]here shall be a separation of powers between the legislature, executive and the judiciary, with appropriate checks and balances to ensure accountability, responsiveness and openness."

[13] During oral argument before us this submission was wisely not pressed by counsel for the applicants. Even assuming in favour of the applicants that there is some potential tension between the language of section 20(7) of the Act and Constitutional Principle VI, it can be of no assistance to the applicants in their attack on the status of the epilogue. The purpose of schedule 4 to the Constitution is to define the principles with which a new constitutional text adopted by the Constitutional Assembly must comply.[15] The new constitutional text

---

15   Section 71(1) of the Constitution. Executive Council, *Western Cape Legislature, and Others v. President of the Republic of South Africa and Others* 1995 (4) SA 877 (CC); 1995 (10) BCLR 1289 (CC) at para. 41; *Premier, KwaZulu-Natal, and Others v. President of the Republic of*

has no force and effect unless the Constitutional Court has certified that the provisions of the text comply with these Constitutional Principles.[16]

[14] The Constitutional Principles have no effect on the <u>status</u> of the epilogue. That status is determined by section 232(4) of the Constitution which provides as follows:

> "In interpreting this Constitution a provision in any Schedule, includ-ing the provision under the heading '*National Unity and Reconciliation*', to this Constitution shall not by reason only of the fact that it is con-tained in a Schedule, have a lesser status than any other provision of this Constitution which is not contained in a Schedule, and such provision shall for all purposes be deemed to form part of the substance of this Constitution."

The epilogue, therefore, has no lesser status than any other part of the Con-stitution. As far as section 22 is concerned it therefore would have the same effect as a provision within section 22 itself which enacted that:

> Nothing contained in this sub-section shall preclude Parliament from adopting a law providing for amnesty to be granted in respect of acts, omissions and offences associated with political objectives committed during a defined period and providing for the mechanisms, criteria and procedures, including tribunals, if any, through which such amnesty shall be dealt with at any time after the law has been passed.

What is clear is that Parliament not only has the authority in terms of the epilogue to make a law providing for amnesty to be granted in respect of the acts, omissions and offences falling within the category defined therein but that it is in fact obliged to do so. This follows from the wording in the material part of the epilogue which is that "Parliament under this Constitution *shall* adopt a law" providing, inter alia, for the "mechanisms, criteria and procedures... through which... amnesty shall be dealt with."

[15] It was contended that even if this is the proper interpretation of the status of the epilogue and even if the principle of "amnesty" is authorised

---

South Africa and Others 1996 (1) SA 769 (CC); 1996 (12) BCLR 1561 (CC) at para. 12; *The Azanian Peoples Organisation and Others v. The Truth and Reconciliation Commission and Others* (CPD) Case No 4895/96, 9 May 1996, not yet reported, at 20-1 ("the AZAPO case").

16   Section 71(2) of the Constitution.

by the Constitution, it does not authorise, in particular, the far-reaching amnesty which section 20(7) allows. In his heads of argument on behalf of the applicants, Mr. Soggot conceded that the wording of the epilogue provides

> . . . a clear indication that the Constitution contemplates the grant of amnesty in respect of offences associated with political objectives and committed in the course of the conflicts of the past, including offences involving gross violations of human rights.

At the commencement of oral argument Mr. Soggot informed us, however, that he had been instructed by his clients to withdraw this concession and he therefore did not abandon the submission that section 20(7) was unconstitutional in all respects and that Parliament had no constitutional power to authorise the Amnesty Committee to indemnify any wrongdoer either against criminal or civil liability arising from the perpetration of acts falling within the categories described in the legislation.

Amnesty in respect of criminal liability

[16] I understand perfectly why the applicants would want to insist that those wrongdoers who abused their authority and wrongfully murdered, maimed or tortured very much loved members of their families who had, in their view, been engaged in a noble struggle to confront the inhumanity of apartheid, should vigorously be prosecuted and effectively be punished for their callous and inhuman conduct in violation of the criminal law. I can therefore also understand why they are emotionally unable to identify themselves with the consequences of the legal concession made by Mr. Soggot and if that concession was wrong in law I would have no hesitation whatsoever in rejecting it.

[17] Every decent human being must feel grave discomfort in living with a consequence which might allow the perpetrators of evil acts to walk the streets of this land with impunity, protected in their freedom by an amnesty immune from constitutional attack, but the circumstances in support of this course require carefully to be appreciated. Most of the acts of brutality and torture which have taken place have occurred during an era in which neither the laws which permitted the incarceration of persons or the investigation of crimes, nor the methods and the culture which informed such investigations, were easily open to public investigation, verification and correction. Much of what transpired in this shameful period is shrouded in secrecy and not easily capable of objective demonstration and proof. Loved ones have disappeared, sometimes mysteriously and most of them no longer survive to tell their

tales. Others have had their freedom invaded, their dignity assaulted or their reputations tarnished by grossly unfair imputations hurled in the fire and the cross-fire of a deep and wounding conflict. The wicked and the innocent have often both been victims. Secrecy and authoritarianism have concealed the truth in little crevices of obscurity in our history. Records are not easily accessible, witnesses are often unknown, dead, unavailable or unwilling. All that often effectively remains is the truth of wounded memories of loved ones sharing instinctive suspicions, deep and traumatising to the survivors but otherwise incapable of translating themselves into objective and corroborative evidence which could survive the rigours of the law. The Act seeks to address this massive problem by encouraging these survivors and the dependants of the tortured and the wounded, the maimed and the dead to unburden their grief publicly, to receive the collective recognition of a new nation that they were wronged, and crucially, to help them to discover what did in truth happen to their loved ones, where and under what circumstances it did happen, and who was responsible. That truth, which the victims of repression seek so desperately to know is, in the circumstances, much more likely to be forthcoming if those responsible for such monstrous misdeeds are encouraged to disclose the whole truth with the incentive that they will not receive the punishment which they undoubtedly deserve if they do. Without that incentive there is nothing to encourage such persons to make the disclosures and to reveal the truth which persons in the positions of the applicants so desperately desire. With that incentive, what might unfold are objectives fundamental to the ethos of a new constitutional order. The families of those unlawfully tortured, maimed or traumatised become more empowered to discover the truth, the perpetrators become exposed to opportunities to obtain relief from the burden of a guilt or an anxiety they might be living with for many long years, the country begins the long and necessary process of healing the wounds of the past, transforming anger and grief into a mature understanding and creating the emotional and structural climate essential for the "reconciliation and reconstruction" which informs the very difficult and sometimes painful objectives of the amnesty articulated in the epilogue.

[18] The alternative to the grant of immunity from criminal prosecution of offenders is to keep intact the abstract right to such a prosecution for particular persons without the evidence to sustain the prosecution successfully, to continue to keep the dependants of such victims in many cases substantially ignorant about what precisely happened to their loved ones, to leave their yearning for the truth effectively unassuaged, to perpetuate their legitimate sense of resentment and grief and correspondingly to allow the culprits of such deeds to remain perhaps physically free but inhibited in their capacity

to become active, full and creative members of the new order by a menacing combination of confused fear, guilt, uncertainty and sometimes even trepidation. Both the victims and the culprits who walk on the "historic bridge" described by the epilogue will hobble more than walk to the future with heavy and dragged steps delaying and impeding a rapid and enthusiastic transition to the new society at the end of the bridge, which is the vision which informs the epilogue.

[19] Even more crucially, but for a mechanism providing for amnesty, the "historic bridge" itself might never have been erected. For a successfully negotiated transition, the terms of the transition required not only the agreement of those victimized by abuse but also those threatened by the transition to a "democratic society based on freedom and equality."[17] If the Constitution kept alive the prospect of continuous retaliation and revenge, the agreement of those threatened by its implementation might never have been forthcoming, and if it had, the bridge itself would have remained wobbly and insecure, threatened by fear from some and anger from others. It was for this reason that those who negotiated the Constitution made a deliberate choice, preferring understanding over vengeance, reparation over retaliation, ubuntu[18] over victimisation.[19]

[20] Is section 20(7), to the extent to which it immunizes wrongdoers from criminal prosecution, nevertheless objectionable on the grounds that amnesty might be provided in circumstances where the victims, or the dependants of the victims, have not had the compensatory benefit of discovering the truth at last or in circumstances where those whose misdeeds are so obscenely excessive as to justify punishment, even if they were perpetrated with a political objective during the course of conflict in the past? Some answers to such difficulties are provided in the sub-sections of section 20. The Amnesty Committee may grant amnesty in respect of the relevant offence only if the perpetrator of the misdeed makes a full disclosure of all relevant facts. If the offender does not, and in consequence thereof the victim or his or her family is not able to discover the truth, the application for amnesty will fail. Moreover, it will not suffice for the offender merely to say that his or her act was associated with a political objective. That issue must independently be determined by the Amnesty Committee pursuant to the criteria set out in section 20(3),

---

17   Sections 33(1)(a)(ii) and 35(1) of the Constitution.
18   The meaning of that concept is discussed in *S v. Makwanyane and Another* 1995 (3) SA 391 (CC); 1995 (6) BCLR 665 (CC) at paras. 224–7; 241–51; 263 and 307–13.
19   See the 4th paragraph of the epilogue to the Constitution.

including the relationship between the offence committed and the political objective pursued and the directness and proximity of the relationship and the proportionality of the offence to the objective pursued.

[21] The result, at all levels, is a difficult, sensitive, perhaps even agonising, balancing act between the need for justice to victims of past abuse and the need for reconciliation and rapid transition to a new future; between encouragement to wrongdoers to help in the discovery of the truth and the need for reparations for the victims of that truth; between a correction in the old and the creation of the new. It is an exercise of immense difficulty interacting in a vast network of political, emotional, ethical and logistical considerations. It is an act calling for a judgment falling substantially within the domain of those entrusted with lawmaking in the era preceding and during the transition period. The results may well often be imperfect and the pursuit of the act might inherently support the message of Kant that "out of the crooked timber of humanity no straight thing was ever made."[20] There can be legitimate debate about the methods and the mechanisms chosen by the lawmaker to give effect to the difficult duty entrusted upon it in terms of the epilogue. We are not concerned with that debate or the wisdom of its choice of mechanisms but only with its constitutionality. That, for us, is the only relevant standard. Applying that standard, I am not satisfied that in providing for amnesty for those guilty of serious offences associated with political objectives and in defining the mechanisms through which and the manner in which such amnesty may be secured by such offenders, the lawmaker, in section 20(7), has offended any of the express or implied limitations on its powers in terms of the Constitution.

[22] South Africa is not alone in being confronted with a historical situation which required amnesty for criminal acts to be accorded for the purposes of facilitating the transition to, and consolidation of, an overtaking democratic order. Chile, Argentina and El Salvador are among the countries which have in modern times been confronted with a similar need. Although the mechanisms adopted to facilitate that process have differed from country to country and from time to time, the principle that amnesty should, in appropriate circumstances, be accorded to violators of human rights in order to facilitate the consolidation of new democracies was accepted in all these countries and truth commissions were also established in such countries.

---

20   Immanuel Kant paraphrased in Isaiah Berlin's essay on "Two concepts of Liberty" in *Four Essays on Liberty* (Oxford University Press, Oxford 1969), at 170. See also Ackermann J in *Ferreira v. Levin NO and Others; Vryenhoek and Others v. Powell NO and Others* 1996 (1) SA 984 (CC); 1996 (1) BCLR 1 (CC) at para. 53.

[23] The Argentinean truth commission was created by Executive Decree 187 of 15 December 1983. It disclosed to the government the names of over one thousand alleged offenders gathered during the investigations.[21] The Chilean Commission on Truth and Reconciliation was established on 25 April 1990. It came to be known as the Rettig Commission after its chairman, Raul Rettig. Its report was published in 1991 and consisted of 850 pages pursuant to its mandate to clarify "the truth about the most serious human right violations . . . in order to bring about the reconciliation of all Chileans."[22] The Commission on the Truth for El Salvador was established with similar objectives in 1992 to investigate "serious acts of violence that have occurred since 1980 and whose impact on society urgently demands that the public should know the truth."[23] In many cases amnesties followed in all these countries.[24]

[24] What emerges from the experience of these and other countries that have ended periods of authoritarian and abusive rule, is that there is no single or uniform international practice in relation to amnesty. Decisions of states in transition, taken with a view to assisting such transition, are quite different from acts of a state covering up its own crimes by granting itself immunity. In the former case, it is not a question of the governmental agents responsible for the violations indemnifying themselves, but rather, one of a constitutional compact being entered into by all sides, with former victims being well-represented, as part of an ongoing process to develop constitutional democracy and prevent a repetition of the abuses.

[25] Mr. Soggot contended on behalf of the applicants that the state was obliged by international law to prosecute those responsible for gross human rights violations and that the provisions of section 20(7) which authorised amnesty for such offenders constituted a breach of international law. We were referred in this regard to the provisions of article 49 of the first Geneva Convention for the Amelioration of the Condition of the Wounded and Sick in Armed Forces in the Field, article 50 of the second Geneva Convention for the Amelioration of the Condition of Wounded, Sick and Shipwrecked Members of Armed Forces at Sea, article 129 of the third Geneva Convention relative

---

21   Pasqualucci "The Whole Truth and Nothing But the Truth: Truth Commissions, Impunity and the Inter-American Human Rights System," 12 *Boston University International Law Journal* 321 (1994) at 337–8.

22   Id. at 338, quoting the National Commission on Truth and Reconciliation "Report of the Chilean Commission on Truth and Reconciliation" Berryman (trans.) (1993).

23   Id. at 339, quoting the Report of the Commission on the Truth for El Salvador "From Madness to Hope: The 12-Year War in El Salvador" United Nations s/25500 (1993).

24   Id. at 343.

to the Treatment of Prisoners of War and article 146 of the fourth Geneva Convention relative to the Protection of Civilian Persons in Time of War. The wording of all these articles is exactly the same and provides as follows:

> The High Contracting Parties undertake to enact any legislation necessary to provide effective penal sanctions for persons committing, or ordering to be committed, any of the grave breaches...

defined in the instruments so as to include, inter alia, wilful killing, torture or inhuman treatment and wilfully causing great suffering or serious injury to body or health.[25] They add that each High Contracting Party shall be under an obligation to search for persons alleged to have committed such grave breaches and shall bring such persons, regardless of their nationality, before its own courts.[26]

[26] The issue which falls to be determined in this Court is whether section 20(7) of the Act is inconsistent with the Constitution. If it is, the enquiry as to whether or not international law prescribes a different duty is irrelevant to that determination. International law and the contents of international treaties to which South Africa might or might not be a party at any particular time are, in my view, relevant only in the interpretation of the Constitution itself, on the grounds that the lawmakers of the Constitution should not lightly be presumed to authorise any law which might constitute a breach of the obligations of the state in terms of international law. International conventions and treaties do not become part of the municipal law of our country, enforceable at the instance of private individuals in our courts, until and unless they are incorporated into the municipal law by legislative enactment.[27]

[27] These observations are supported by the direct provisions of the Constitution itself referring to international law and international agreements.

---

25 Article 50 of the first Geneva Convention; art. 51 of the second Geneva Convention; art. 130 of the third Geneva Convention and art. 147 of the fourth Geneva Convention.

26 Article 49 of the first Geneva Convention; art. 50 of the second Geneva Convention; art. 129 of the third Geneva Convention and art. 146 of the fourth Geneva Convention.

27 *R v. Secretary of State for the Home Department*, Ex parte Brind and Others [1991] 1 AC 696 (HL) at 761G–762D; *Pan American World Airways Incorporated v. S.A. Fire and Accident Insurance Co. Ltd.* 1965 (3) SA 150 (A) at 161C; *Maluleke v. Minister of Internal Affairs* 1981 (1) SA 707 (B) at 712G–H; *Binga v. Cabinet for South West Africa and Others* 1988 (3) SA 155 (A) at 184H–185D; *S v. Petane* 1988 (3) SA 51 (C) at 56F–G; Hahlo and Kahn, *The South African Legal System and Its Background* (Juta & Co Ltd, Kenwyn 1968) at 114; Dugard, *International Law: A South African Perspective* (Juta & Co Ltd, Kenwyn 1994) at 339–46.

Section 231(3) of the Constitution makes it clear that when Parliament agrees to the ratification of or accession to an international agreement such agreement becomes part of the law of the country only if Parliament expressly so provides and the agreement is not inconsistent with the Constitution. Section 231(1) provides in express terms that

> [a]ll rights and obligations under international agreements which immediately before the commencement of this Constitution were vested in or binding on the Republic within the meaning of the previous Constitution, shall be vested in or binding on the Republic under this Constitution, unless provided otherwise by an Act of Parliament.

It is clear from this section that an Act of Parliament can override any contrary rights or obligations under international agreements entered into before the commencement of the Constitution. The same temper is evident in section 231(4) of the Constitution which provides that

> [t]he rules of customary international law binding on the Republic, shall unless inconsistent with this Constitution or an Act of Parliament, form part of the law of the Republic.

Section 35(1) of the Constitution is also perfectly consistent with these conclusions. It reads as follows:

> In interpreting the provisions of this Chapter a court of law shall promote the values which underlie an open and democratic society based on freedom and equality and shall, where applicable, have regard to public international law applicable to the protection of the rights entrenched in this Chapter, and may have regard to comparable foreign case law.

The court is directed only to "have regard" to public international law if it is applicable to the protection of the rights entrenched in the chapter.

[28] The exact terms of the relevant rules of public international law contained in the Geneva Conventions relied upon on behalf of the applicants would therefore be irrelevant if, on a proper interpretation of the Constitution, section 20(7) of the Act is indeed authorised by the Constitution, but the content of these Conventions in any event do not assist the case of the applicants.

[29] In the first place it is doubtful whether the Geneva Conventions of 1949 read with the relevant Protocols thereto apply at all to the situation in which

this country found itself during the years of the conflict to which I have referred.[28]

[30] Secondly, whatever be the proper ambit and technical meaning of these Conventions and Protocols, the international literature[29] in any event clearly appreciates the distinction between the position of perpetrators of acts of violence in the course of war (or other conflicts between states or armed conflicts between liberation movements seeking self-determination against colonial and alien domination of their countries), on the one hand, and their position in respect of violent acts perpetrated during other conflicts which take place within the territory of a sovereign state in consequence of a struggle between the armed forces of that state and other dissident armed forces operating under responsible command, within such a state on the other. In respect of the latter category, there is no obligation on the part of a contracting state to ensure the prosecution of those who might have performed acts of violence or other acts which would ordinarily be characterised as serious invasions of human rights. On the contrary, article 6(5) of Protocol II to the Geneva Conventions of 1949 provides that

> [a]t the end of hostilities, the authorities in power shall endeavour to grant the broadest possible amnesty to persons who participated in the armed conflict, or those deprived of their liberty for reasons related to the armed conflict, whether they are interned or detained.

28   The Geneva Conventions of 1949 apply only to cases of "declared war or of any armed conflict which may arise between two or more of the High Contracting Parties." (No High Contracting Parties were involved in the South African conflict.) The Conventions were extended by article 1(4) of Protocol Additional to the Geneva Conventions of 12 August 1949, and relating to the Protection of Victims of International Armed Conflicts (Protocol I) (adopted on 8 June 1977) to "armed conflicts in which peoples are fighting against colonial domination and alien occupation and against regimes in the exercise of their rights of self-determination." Even if the conflict in South Africa could be said to fall within this extension (this was not accepted by the Cape Supreme Court in the *AZAPO* case referred to in footnote 15 supra), Protocol I could only become binding after a declaration of intent to abide thereby had been deposited with the Swiss Federal Council in terms of article 95 as read with article 96 of this Protocol. This Protocol was never signed or ratified by South Africa during the conflict and no such "declaration" was deposited with *that* Council by any of the parties to the conflict. As far as Protocol Additional to the Geneva Conventions of 12 August 1949, and relating to the Protection of Victims of Non-International Armed Conflicts (Protocol II) (also adopted on 8 June 1977) is concerned, it equally cannot assist the case of the applicants because it is doubtful whether it applies at all (see article 1(1) to Protocol II) but if it does, it actually requires the authorities in power, after the end of hostilities, to grant amnesty to those previously engaged in the conflict.

29   See, for example, Dugard, supra note 28 at 333; and see further the references contained in footnotes 31, 32, and 33, infra.

[31] The need for this distinction is obvious. It is one thing to allow the officers of a hostile power which has invaded a foreign state to remain unpunished for gross violations of human rights perpetrated against others during the course of such conflict. It is another thing to compel such punishment in circumstances where such violations have substantially occurred in consequence of conflict between different formations within the same state in respect of the permissible political direction which that state should take with regard to the structures of the state and the parameters of its political policies and where it becomes necessary after the cessation of such conflict for the society traumatised by such a conflict to reconstruct itself. The erstwhile adversaries of such a conflict inhabit the same sovereign territory. They have to live with each other and work with each other and the state concerned is best equipped to determine what measures may be most conducive for the facilitation of such reconciliation and reconstruction. That is a difficult exercise which the nation within such a state has to perform by having regard to its own peculiar history, its complexities, even its contradictions and its emotional and institutional traditions. What role punishment should play in respect of erstwhile acts of criminality in such a situation is part of the complexity. Some aspects of this difficulty are covered by Judge Marvin Frankel in a book he authored with Ellen Saideman.[30]

"The call to punish human rights criminals can present complex and agonising problems that have no single or simple solution. While the debate over the Nuremberg trials still goes on, that episode – trials of war criminals of a defeated nation – was simplicity itself as compared to the subtle and dangerous issues that can divide a country when it undertakes to punish its own violators. A nation divided during a repressive regime does not emerge suddenly united when the time of repression has passed. The human rights criminals are fellow citizens, living alongside everyone else, and they may be very powerful and dangerous. If the army and the police have been the agencies of terror, the soldiers and the cops aren't going to turn overnight into paragons of respect for human rights. Their numbers and their expert management of deadly weapons remain significant facts of life. . . . The soldiers and police may be biding their time, waiting and conspiring to return to power. They may be seeking to keep or win sympathisers in the population at large. If they are treated too harshly – or if the net of punishment is cast too widely – there may be a backlash that plays into their hands. But their victims cannot simply forgive and forget.

---

30   Frankel *Out of the Shadows of the Night: The Struggle for International Human Rights* (Delacorte Press, New York 1989) at 103–4.

These problems are not abstract generalities. They describe tough realities in more than a dozen countries. If, as we hope, more nations are freed from regimes of terror, similar problems will continue to arise. Since the situations vary, the nature of the problems varies from place to place."

The agonies of a nation seeking to reconcile the tensions between justice for those wronged during conflict, on the one hand, and the consolidation of the transition to a nascent democracy, on the other, has also been appreciated by other international commentators.[31] It is substantially for these reasons that amnesty clauses are not infrequent in international agreements concluded even after a war between different states.

> Amnesty clauses are frequently found in peace treaties and signify the will of the parties to apply the principle of *tabula rasa* to past offences, generally political delicts such as treason, sedition and rebellion, but also to war crimes. As a sovereign act of oblivion, amnesty may be granted to all persons guilty of such offences or only to certain categories of offenders.[32]

[32] Considered in this context, I am not persuaded that there is anything in the Act and more particularly in the impugned section 20(7) thereof, which can properly be said to be a breach of the obligations of this country in terms of the instruments of public international law relied on by Mr. Soggot. The amnesty contemplated is not a blanket amnesty against criminal prosecution for all and sundry, granted automatically as a uniform act of compulsory statutory amnesia. It is specifically authorised for the purposes of effecting a constructive transition towards a democratic order. It is available only where there is a full disclosure of all facts to the Amnesty Committee and where it is clear that the particular transgression was perpetrated during the prescribed period and with a political objective committed in the course of the conflicts of the past. That objective has to be evaluated having regard to the careful criteria listed in section 20(3) of the Act, including the very important relationship which the act perpetrated bears in proportion to the object pursued.

31 See Orentlicher "Settling Accounts: The Duty To Prosecute Human Rights Violations of a Prior Regime," 100 *Yale LJ* 2537 (1991) at 2544 and by the same author "A reply to Professor Nino" 100 *Yale LJ* 2641 (1991). See also a recent interview with the same author commenting on the South African Truth Commission in *Issues of Democracy*, published by the United States Information Services, Johannesburg, Vol. 1, No 3, May 1996 at 33.

32 Bernhardt (ed) *Encyclopedia of Public International Law*, (North-Holland, Amsterdam, London, New York, Tokyo 1992) Vol. I at 148 and Bernhardt (ed) *Encyclopedia of Public International Law*, (North-Holland, Amsterdam, New York, Oxford 1982) Vol. 3, "Use of Force, War and Neutrality, Peace Treaties (A-M)" at 14–15.

Amnesty in respect of the civil liability of individual wrongdoers

[33] Mr. Soggot submitted that chapter 3 of the Constitution, and more particularly section 22, conferred on every person the right to pursue, in the ordinary courts of the land or before independent tribunals, any claim which such person might have in civil law for the recovery of damages sustained by such a person in consequence of the unlawful delicts perpetrated by a wrongdoer. He contended that the Constitution did not authorise Parliament to make any law which would have the result of indemnifying (or otherwise rendering immune from liability) the perpetrator of any such delict against any claims made for damages suffered by the victim of such a delict. In support of that argument he suggested that the concept of "amnesty," referred to in the epilogue to the Constitution, was, at worst for the applicants, inherently limited to immunity from criminal prosecutions. He contended that even if a wrongdoer who has received amnesty could plead such amnesty as a defence to a criminal prosecution, such amnesty could not be used as a shield to protect him or her from claims for delictual damages suffered by any person in consequence of the act or omission of the wrongdoer.

[34] There can be no doubt that in some contexts the word "amnesty" does bear the limited meaning contended for by counsel. Thus one of the meanings of amnesty referred to in The Oxford English Dictionary is " . . . a general overlooking or pardon of past offences, by the ruling authority"[33] and in similar vein, Webster's Dictionary gives as the second meaning of amnesty "a deliberate overlooking, as of an offense."[34] Wharton's Law Lexicon also refers to amnesty in the context "by which crimes against the Government up to a certain date are so obliterated that they can never be brought into charge.[35]

[35] I cannot, however, agree that the concept of amnesty is inherently to be limited to the absolution from criminal liability alone, regardless of the context and regardless of the circumstances. The word has no inherently fixed technical meaning. Its origin is to be found from the Greek concept of "amnestia" and it indicates what is described by Webster's Dictionary[36] as "an act of oblivion." The degree of oblivion or obliteration must depend on the circumstances. It can, in certain circumstances, be confined to immunity from criminal prosecutions and in other circumstances be extended also to

33   *The Oxford English Dictionary*, 2nd ed., Vol. I at 406.
34   *Webster's New Twentieth Century Dictionary*, 2nd ed. at 59.
35   *Wharton's Law Lexicon*, 14th ed. at 59.
36   Supra note 35.

civil liability. Describing the effects of amnesty in treaties concluded between belligerent parties, a distinguished writer states:

> An amnesty is a complete forgetfulness of the past; and as the treaty of peace is meant to put an end to every subject of discord, the amnesty should constitute its first article. Accordingly, such is the common practice at the present day. But though the treaty should make no mention of it, the amnesty is necessarily included in it, from the very nature of the agreement. Since each of the belligerents claims to have justice on his side, and since there is no one to decide between them (Book III, 188), the condition in which affairs stand at the time of the treaty must be regarded as their lawful status, and if the parties wish to make any change in it the treaty must contain an express stipulation to that effect. Consequently all matters not mentioned in the treaty are to continue as they happen to be at the time the treaty is concluded. This is also a result of the promised amnesty. *All the injuries caused by the war are likewise forgotten; and no action can lie on account of those for which the treaty does not stipulate that satisfaction shall be made; they are considered as never having happened.* But the effect of the settlement or amnesty can not be extended to things which bear no relation to war terminated by the treaty. Thus, claims based upon a debt contracted, or an injury received, prior to the war, but which formed no part of the motives for undertaking the war, remain as they were, and are not annulled by the treaty, unless the treaty has been made to embrace the relinquishment of all claims whatsoever. The same rule holds for debts contracted during the war, but with respect to objects which have no relation to it, and for injuries received during the war, but not as a result of it. [My emphasis][37]

[36] What are the material circumstances of the present case? As I have previously said, what the epilogue to the Constitution seeks to achieve by providing for amnesty is the facilitation of "reconciliation and reconstruction" by the creation of mechanisms and procedures which make it possible for the truth of our past to be uncovered. Central to the justification of amnesty in respect of the criminal prosecution for offences committed during the prescribed period with political objectives, is the appreciation that the truth will not effectively

---

37   De Vattel *The Law of Nations or the Principles of Natural Law Applied to the Conduct and to the Affairs of Nations and of Sovereigns* trans. by Fenwick (Carnegie Institute of Washington, Washington 1916) at 351, paras. 20–2, quoted by Friedman JP and Farlam J in the *AZAPO* case, supra note 15 at 24.

be revealed by the wrongdoers if they are to be prosecuted for such acts. That justification must necessarily and unavoidably apply to the need to indemnify such wrongdoers against civil claims for payment of damages. Without that incentive the wrongdoer cannot be encouraged to reveal the whole truth which might inherently be against his or her material or proprietary interests. There is nothing in the language of the epilogue which persuades me that what the makers of the Constitution intended to do was to encourage wrongdoers to reveal the truth by providing for amnesty against criminal prosecution in respect of their acts but simultaneously to discourage them from revealing that truth by keeping intact the threat that such revelations might be visited with what might in many cases be very substantial claims for civil damages. It appears to me to be more reasonable to infer that the legislation contemplated in the epilogue would, in the circumstances defined, be wide enough to allow for an amnesty which would protect a wrongdoer who told the truth, from both the criminal and the civil consequences of his or her admissions.

[37] This conclusion appears to be fortified by the fact that what the epilogue directs is that

> amnesty shall be granted in respect of acts, omissions and offences. . . .

If the purpose was simply to provide mechanisms in terms of which wrongdoers could be protected from criminal prosecution in respect of offences committed by them, why would there be any need to refer also to "acts and omissions" in addition to offences? The word "offences" would have covered both acts and omissions in any event.

[38] In the result I am satisfied that section 20(7) is not open to constitutional challenge on the ground that it invades the right of a victim or his or her dependant to recover damages from a wrongdoer for unlawful acts perpetrated during the conflicts of the past. If there is any such invasion it is authorised and contemplated by the relevant parts of the epilogue.

The effect of amnesty on any potential civil liability of the state

[39] Mr. Soggot contended forcefully that whatever be the legitimate consequences of the kind of amnesty contemplated by the epilogue for the criminal and civil liability of the wrongdoer, the Constitution could not justifiably authorise any law which has the effect of indemnifying the state itself against civil claims made by those wronged by criminal and delictual acts perpetrated by such wrongdoers in the course and within the scope of their employment

as servants of the state. Section 20(7) of the Act, he argued, had indeed that effect and was therefore unconstitutional to that extent.

[40] This submission has one great force. It is this. If the wrongdoer in the employment of the state is not personally indemnified in the circumstances regulated by the Act, the truth might never unfold. It would remain shrouded in the impenetrable mysteries of the past, leaving the dependants of many victims with a grief unrelieved by any knowledge of the truth. But how, it was argued, would it deter such wrongdoers from revealing the truth if such a revelation held no criminal or civil consequences for them? How could such wrongdoers be discouraged from disclosing the truth if their own liberty and property was not to be threatened by such revelations, but the state itself nevertheless remained liable to compensate the families of victims for such wrongdoings perpetrated by the servants of the state?

[41] This is a serious objection which requires to be considered carefully. I think it must be conceded that in many cases, the wrongdoer would not be discouraged from revealing the whole truth merely because the consequences of such disclosure might be to saddle the state with a potential civil liability for damages arising from the delictual acts or omissions of a wrongdoer (although there may also be many cases in which such a wrongdoer, still in the service of the state, might in some degree be inhibited or even coerced from making disclosures implicating his or her superiors).

[42] The real answer, however, to the problems posed by the questions which I have identified, seems to lie in the more fundamental objectives of the transition sought to be attained by the Constitution and articulated in the epilogue itself. What the Constitution seeks to do is to facilitate the transition to a new democratic order, committed to "reconciliation between the people of South Africa and the reconstruction of society." The question is how this can be done effectively with the limitations of our resources and the legacy of the past.

[43] The families of those whose fundamental human rights were invaded by torture and abuse are not the only victims who have endured "untold suffering and injustice" in consequence of the crass inhumanity of apartheid which so many have had to endure for so long. Generations of children born and yet to be born will suffer the consequences of poverty, of malnutrition, of homelessness, of illiteracy and disempowerment generated and sustained by the institutions of apartheid and its manifest effects on life and living for so many. The country has neither the resources nor the skills to reverse fully these

massive wrongs. It will take many years of strong commitment, sensitivity and labour to "reconstruct our society" so as to fulfill the legitimate dreams of new generations exposed to real opportunities for advancement denied to preceding generations initially by the execution of apartheid itself and for a long time after its formal demise, by its relentless consequences. The resources of the state have to be deployed imaginatively, wisely, efficiently and equitably, to facilitate the reconstruction process in a manner which best brings relief and hope to the widest sections of the community, developing for the benefit of the entire nation the latent human potential and resources of every person who has directly or indirectly been burdened with the heritage of the shame and the pain of our racist past.

[44] Those negotiators of the Constitution and leaders of the nation who were required to address themselves to these agonising problems must have been compelled to make hard choices. They could have chosen to direct that the limited resources of the state be spent by giving preference to the formidable delictual claims of those who had suffered from acts of murder, torture or assault perpetrated by servants of the state, diverting to that extent, desperately needed funds in the crucial areas of education, housing and primary health care. They were entitled to permit a different choice to be made between competing demands inherent in the problem. They could have chosen to direct that the potential liability of the state be limited in respect of any civil claims by differentiating between those against whom prescription could have been pleaded as a defence and those whose claims were of such recent origin that a defence of prescription would have failed. They were entitled to reject such a choice on the grounds that it was irrational. They could have chosen to saddle the state with liability for claims made by insurance companies which had compensated institutions for delictual acts performed by the servants of the state and to that extent again divert funds otherwise desperately needed to provide food for the hungry, roofs for the homeless and black boards and desks for those struggling to obtain admission to desperately overcrowded schools. They were entitled to permit the claims of such school children and the poor and the homeless to be preferred.

[45] The election made by the makers of the Constitution was to permit Parliament to favour "the reconstruction of society" involving in the process a wider concept of "reparation," which would allow the state to take into account the competing claims on its resources but, at the same time, to have regard to the "untold suffering" of individuals and families whose fundamental human rights had been invaded during the conflict of the past. In some cases such a family may best be assisted by a reparation which allows the young in

this family to maximise their potential through bursaries and scholarships; in other cases the most effective reparation might take the form of occupational training and rehabilitation; in still other cases complex surgical interventions and medical help may be facilitated; still others might need subsidies to prevent eviction from homes they can no longer maintain and in suitable cases the deep grief of the traumatised may most effectively be assuaged by facilitating the erection of a tombstone on the grave of a departed one with a public acknowledgement of his or her valour and nobility. There might have to be differentiation between the form and quality of the reparations made to two persons who have suffered exactly the same damage in consequence of the same unlawful act but where one person now enjoys lucrative employment from the state and the other lives in penury.

[46] All these examples illustrate, in my view, that it is much too simplistic to say that the objectives of the Constitution could only properly be achieved by saddling the state with the formal liability to pay, in full, the provable delictual claims of those who have suffered patrimonial loss in consequence of the delicts perpetrated with political objectives by servants of the state during the conflicts of the past. There was a permissible alternative, perhaps even a more imaginative and more fundamental route to the "reconstruction of society," which could legitimately have been followed. This is the route which appears to have been chosen by Parliament through the mechanism of amnesty and nuanced and individualised reparations in the Act. I am quite unpersuaded that this is not a route authorised by the epilogue to the Constitution.

[47] The epilogue required that a law be adopted by Parliament which would provide for "amnesty" and it appreciated the "need for reparation," but it left it to Parliament to decide upon the ambit of the amnesty, the permissible form and extent of such reparations and the procedures to be followed in the determination thereof, by taking into account all the relevant circumstances to which I have made reference. Parliament was therefore entitled to decide that, having regard to the resources of the state, proper reparations for those victimised by the unjust laws and practices of the past justified formulae which did not compel any irrational differentiation between the claims of those who were able to pursue enforceable delictual claims against the state and the claims of those who were not in that position but nevertheless deserved reparations.

[48] It was submitted by Mr. Soggot that the reference to the "need for reparation" in the epilogue is contained only in the fourth paragraph of the epilogue and does not appear in the directive to Parliament to adopt a law "providing for the mechanisms, criteria and procedures, including tribunals, if any,

through which . . . amnesty shall be dealt with . . . ." He argued from this that what the makers of the Constitution must have contemplated was that the ordinary liability of the state, in respect of damages sustained by others in consequence of the acts of the servants of the state, remained intact, and was protected by section 22 of the Constitution. In my view, this is a fragmentary and impermissible approach to the structure of the epilogue. It must be read holistically. It expresses an integrated philosophical and jurisprudential approach. The very first paragraph defines the commitment to the "historic bridge" and the second paragraph expands on the theme of this bridge by elevating "the pursuit of national unity, . . . reconciliation between the people of South Africa and the reconstruction of society." It then goes on in the third paragraph, in very moving and generous language, to "secure" the "foundation" of the nation by transcending "the divisions and strife of the past, which generated gross violations of human rights" and elects, in eloquent terms in the next paragraph, to make the historic choice in favour of understanding above vengeance, *ubuntu* over victimisation and "a need for reparation but not for retaliation." This philosophy then informs the fifth paragraph which directs Parliament to adopt a law providing for amnesty and is introduced by the words "[i]n order to advance such reconciliation and reconstruction, amnesty shall be granted. . . . " The reference to "*such* reconciliation and reconstruction" embraces the continuing radiating influence of the preceding paragraphs including the reference to "the need for reparation." Approached in this way, the reparations authorised in the Act are not alien to the legislation contemplated by the epilogue. Indeed, they are perfectly consistent with, and give expression to, the extraordinarily generous and imaginative commitment of the Constitution to a philosophy which has brought unprecedented international acclaim for the people of our country. It ends with the deep spirituality and dignity of the last line:

"Nkosi sikelel' iAfrika – God sen Suid-Afrika"

The indemnity of organisations and persons in respect of claims based on vicarious liability

[49] It was not contended by Mr. Soggot that even if the state was properly rendered immune against claims for damages in consequence of delicts perpetrated by its servants, acting within the scope and in the course of their employment, individuals and organisations should not enjoy any similar protection in respect of any vicarious liability arising from any unlawful acts committed by their servants or members. He was correct in that attitude.

Apart from the fact that the wrongdoers concerned might be discouraged from revealing the truth which implicated their employers or organisations on whose support they might still directly or indirectly depend, the Constitution itself could not successfully have been transacted if those responsible for the negotiations which preceded it and the political organisations to which they belonged, were going to remain vulnerable to potentially massive claims for damages arising from their vicarious liability in respect of such wrongful acts perpetrated by their agents or members. The erection of the "historic bridge" would never have begun.

Conclusion

[50] In the result, I am satisfied that the epilogue to the Constitution authorised and contemplated an "amnesty" in its most comprehensive and generous meaning so as to enhance and optimise the prospects of facilitating the constitutional journey from the shame of the past to the promise of the future. Parliament was, therefore, entitled to enact the Act in the terms which it did. This involved more choices apart from the choices I have previously identified.[38] They could have chosen to insist that a comprehensive amnesty manifestly involved an inequality of sacrifice between the victims and the perpetrators of invasions into the fundamental rights of such victims and their families, and that, for this reason, the terms of the amnesty should leave intact the claims which some of these victims might have been able to pursue against those responsible for authorising, permitting or colluding in such acts, or they could have decided that this course would impede the pace, effectiveness and objectives of the transition with consequences substantially prejudicial for the people of a country facing, for the first time, the real prospect of enjoying, in the future, some of the human rights so unfairly denied to the generations which preceded them. They were entitled to choose the second course. They could conceivably have chosen to differentiate between the wrongful acts committed in defence of the old order and those committed in the resistance of it, or they could have chosen a comprehensive form of amnesty which did not make this distinction. Again they were entitled to make the latter choice. The choice of alternatives legitimately fell within the judgment of the lawmakers. The exercise of that choice does not, in my view, impact on its constitutionality. It follows from these reasons that section 20(7) of the Act is authorised by the Constitution itself and it is unnecessary to consider the relevance and effect of section 33(1) of the Constitution.

---

38   In paras. 44 and 45 supra.

Order

[51] In the result, the attack on the constitutionality of section 20(7) of the Promotion of National Unity and Reconciliation Act 34 of 1995 must fail. That was the only attack which was pursued on behalf of the applicants in this Court. It accordingly follows that the application must be, and is, refused.

Chaskalson P, Ackermann, Kriegler, Langa, Madala, Mokgoro, O'Regan and Sachs JJ concur in the judgment of Mahomed DP.

Notes

Opening Considerations: On the Perennial Relevance of Amnesties

1. UN Sub-Commission on Prevention of Discrimination and Protection of Minorities, Res. 1983/34.
2. L. Joinet, "Study on Amnesty Laws and Their Role in the Safeguard and Promotion of Human Rights," UN Doc. E/CN.4/Sub.2/1985/16/Rev.1.
3. UN Sub-Commission on Prevention of Discrimination and Protection of Minorities, Res. 1991/110.
4. L. Joinet, "Question of the Impunity of Perpetrators of Human Rights Violations (Civil and Political)," U.N. Doc. E/CN.4/Sub.2/1997/20/Rev1.
5. Ibid., at para. 1.
6. Ibid., at para. 2. It is unclear why the Latin American experience appears to have come to shape the global amnesty debate at a time when similar amnesties were in wide use in other parts of the world. It is also unclear why widespread public resistance to amnesties did not emerge in Latin America until the 1980s, given that countries such as Argentina had a long experience of using amnesties.
7. Ibid., at para. 3.
8. Ibid., at para. 4.
9. See, e.g., Office of the United Nations High Commissioner for Human Rights, *Rule of Law Tools for Post-Conflict States: Amnesties* (Geneva: United Nations, 2009), at 33, which asserts as follows: "While in some instances an individual's full disclosure of the truth about violations may justify a reduction in sentence, measures of transitional justice such as the establishment and operation of truth commissions should not exempt perpetrators from criminal process in exchange for their testimony." At ibid.,

the publication further asserts: "But although South Africa's amnesty was not tested before an international human rights body, it is doubtful whether it would survive scrutiny under the legal standards developed by such bodies as the Human Rights Committee and the Inter-American Commission on and Court of Human Rights."

10. Transitional justice encompasses criminal trials, so there is no actual contradiction between international criminal law and transitional justice. The point is that transitional justice is most closely associated with the South African TRC, and thus with truth commissions and amnesties rather than criminal trials.

11. L. Mallinder, *Amnesty, Human Rights and Political Transitions: Bridging the Peace and Justice Divide* (Oxford: Hart, 2008), at 18–22.

12. F. Fukuyama, *The End of History and the Last Man* (New York: Free Press, 1992). Fukuyama's central thesis of the end of history was the subject of many fierce critiques. See, e.g., J. Derrida, *Specters of Marx: The State of the Debt, the Work of Mourning, and the New International*, trans. Peggy Kamuf (New York: Routledge, 1994).

13. M. Pensky, "Amnesty on Trial: Impunity, Accountability, and the Norms of International Law" (2008) 1 Ethics & Global Politics 1, at 18.

14. R. Slye, "The Legitimacy of Amnesties under International Law and General Principles of Anglo-American Law: Is a Legitimate Amnesty Possible?" (2002) 43 Va. J. Int'l L. 173, at 179.

15. Note that in France there is a centuries-old tradition of using amnesty after great civil crises to unify the country. See, e.g., S. Gacon, *Amnistie: De la Commune à la guerre d'Algérie* (Paris: Seuil, 2002), at 353, 359, 360, and 367.

16. R. Kagan, *Of Power and Paradise* (London: Vintage, 2004), at 37.

17. Cass Sunstein coined the term *norms cascade*, which refers to a sudden and significant shift in the legitimacy of norms and the actions related to them. See C. Sunstein, *Free Markets and Social Justice* (New York: Oxford University Press, 1997), at 32–69.

18. R. Parker, "Fighting the Sirens' Song: The Problem of Amnesty in Historical and Contemporary Perspective" (2001) 42 Hungarian J. Legal Stud. 69, at 88–9. See also L. Vinjamuri and A. Boesenecker, "Religious Actors in Transitional Justice," in T. Banchoff, ed., *The New Religious Pluralism* (Oxford: Oxford University Press, 2008); and J. J. Moore, "Problems with Forgiveness – Granting Amnesty under the Arias Plan in Nicaragua and El Salvador" (1991) 43 Stan. L. Rev. 733, at 736, who speaks of "rescuing amnesty from political exploitation and incorporating it within a philosophy of true forgiveness that is respectful of human rights law."

19. See, e.g., H. Arendt, *Origins of Totalitarianism* (New York: Meridian, 1958), at 241, who famously observed about the impotence of justice in the face of crimes against humanity that "[m]en are unable to forgive what they cannot punish and . . . they are unable to punish what turns out to be unforgivable."

20. Remarks of Alex Boraine, former vice chair of the South African TRC, Heinrich Böll Conference on February 24, 2007 (Istanbul).

21. See, e.g., L. Huyse, "The Process of Reconciliation," in D. Bloomfield, T. Barnes, and L. Huyse, eds., *Reconciliation after Violent Conflict: A Handbook* (Stockholm: International Institute for Democracy and Electoral Assistance, 2003), at 19–21, referring to three stages of reconciliation, the first being the replacement of fear by nonviolent coexistence.

22. See, e.g., P. Ricoeur, *Memory, History, Forgetting* (Chicago: University of Chicago Press, 2004). See also R. Shaw, *Rethinking Truth and Reconciliation Commissions*, U.S. Institute for Peace, February 2005; and R. Shaw, "Memory Frictions: Localizing the Truth and Reconciliation Commission in Sierra Leone" (2007) 1 Int'l J. Transitional Justice 183, at 194–6, discussing the Sierra Leonean expression "cool heart" (kol hart), which refers to a desirable emotional condition in which a person overcomes anger and becomes capable of healthy social relationships.

23. See, e.g., V. Igreja and B. Dias-Lambranca, "Restorative Justice and the Role of *Magamba* Spirits in Post-Civil War Gorongosa, Central Mozambique," in L. Huyse and M. Salter, eds., *Traditional Justice and Reconciliation after Violent Conflict: Learning from African Experiences* (Stockholm: International Institute for Democracy and Electoral Assistance, 2008). See also "Southern African Regional Assessment Mission Reports," International Center for Transitional Justice, October 2007–December 2008, at 11, describing the mission's findings in Angola: "General amnesty was accepted as the only viable option, given the intensity and duration of the conflict, as well as the perception that the majority of Angolans had in some way participated in or supported the war.... Across the spectrum of people interviewed, there was an overwhelming expression of war fatigue; the opposition to any form of truth commission seemed to stem not only from not wanting to talk about the past, but also not wanting to open up old wounds."

24. For a detailed account of the parameters of the debate, see, e.g., D. Orentlicher, "'Settling Accounts' Revisited: Reconciling Global Norms with Local Agency" (2007) 1 Int'l J. Transitional Justice 10, at 14.

25. D. Markel, "The Justice of Amnesty? Towards a Theory of Retributivism in Recovering States" (1999) 49 U. of Toronto. L.J. 389, at 444.

26. That is not actually the point of the exercise. My intention is rather to show the following: (1) the interdependence of the various public goods; (2) how some of them are not only ends (e.g., truth) but also means to help achieve other listed goods (e.g., truth as a means to advance reconciliation); (3) how some of the listed goods are simultaneously a precondition and a consequence of other ones (e.g., institutional reform as a precondition for democracy, and vice versa); and (4) how there is no sensible way to prioritize these in the abstract (i.e., the relative priority of any public good will depend on the specifics of the context).

27. See, generally, J. Galtung and C. Jacobsen, *Searching for Peace: The Road to TRANSCEND* (London: Pluto Press, 2000).

28. Report of UN Secretary-General, "In Larger Freedom," UN Doc. A/59/2005. See also H. Shue, *Basic Rights* (Princeton, NJ: Princeton University Press, 1996). In his book, Shue distinguishes between two basic rights – security and subsistence – and human rights. He argues that the latter have no meaningful application to the sphere of democratization unless and until the former two basic rights are minimally provided. His larger point is that human rights are meaningless without reasonable expectations of enforcement, and that enforcement requires basic security.

29. See, generally, J. Shklar, *Legalism: Law, Morals, and Political Trials* (Cambridge, MA: Harvard University Press, 1964). See also L. Joinet, "Un état des lieux des principes et standards internationaux de la justice transitionnelle," in M. Bleeker, ed., *La justice*

transitionnelle dans le monde francophone (Geneva: Swiss Ministry of Foreign Affairs, 2007), at 15: "Dans ces situations, entre l'idéalement souhaitable et le pratiquement possible, sur le terrain il nous faut choisir, le pire étant l'immobilisme par excès de légalisme."

Part I: The Debate on Amnesties

1. *Oxford English Dictionary*, 2nd ed., 20 vols. (Oxford: Oxford University Press, 1989).
2. B. Garner and H. Black, eds., *Black's Law Dictionary*, 8th ed. (St. Paul, MN: Thomson/ West, 2006).
3. A. O'Shea, *Amnesty for Crime in International Law and Practice* (The Hague: Kluwer Law International, 2002), 1–2.
4. B. Chigara, *Amnesties in International Law: The Legality under International Law of National Amnesty Laws* (London: Longman Group, 2002), 1–2.
5. General Amnesty, 1994 (Morocco).
6. Decree Law 2.191, 1978 (Chile).
7. Law on General Amnesty, 1996 (Croatia).
8. Decree Law 89–83, 1983 (Guatemala).
9. Decree Law 173/74, 1974 (Portugal).
10. Law No. 26479, June 14, 1995 (Peru).
11. Decree No. 03-001, 2003 (Democratic Republic of the Congo).
12. The Amnesty Act, 2000 (Uganda).
13. Law Nullifying the State's Claim to Punish Certain Crimes (Ley de Caducidad), Law No. 15.848, 1986 (Uruguay). The pact was reached in 1984, two years prior to the ultimate promulgation of the amnesty.
14. Promotion of National Unity and Reconciliation Act, 1995 (South Africa).
15. Clemency Order, No. 1, 1988 (Zimbabwe).
16. Peace agreement between the Government of Sierra Leone and the Revolutionary United Front of Sierra Leone 1999 (Sierra Leone). Not every peace agreement is binding internationally; but every agreement is binding contractually and hence still constitutes a "legal measure" that imposes performance obligations on the signatory parties. See, generally, C. Bell, "Peace Agreements: Their Nature and Legal Status" (2006) 100 American J. Int'l L. 373.
17. Decree No. 62-328 of March 22, 1962 (portant amnistie de faits commis dans le cadre des opérations de maintien de l'ordre dirigées contre l'insurrection algérienne) (France).
18. Executive Decree 128/2003 (Colombia)
19. Law of National Reconciliation, Legislative Decree 147, January 23, 1992 (El Salvador).
20. Memorandum of Understanding between the Government of the Republic of Indonesia and the Free Aceh Movement, August 15, 2005.
21. Law No. 4, April 4, 2002 (Angola).
22. Law No. 15/92, 1992 (Mozambique).
23. Law 98-08 on Civil Harmony, 1999 (Algeria).

24. Of course the same is true, mutatis mutandis, of trials: "There are criminal trials and civil trials; group trials and individual trials; full-length trials and summary trials; trials in common law jurisdictions and trials in civil law jurisdictions; trials in person and trials *in absentia;* trials by specialized tribunals and trials by ordinary tribunals; trials in public and trials *in camera*; trials by judge and trials by jury; and so forth." M. Freeman, *Truth Commissions and Procedural Fairness* (New York: Cambridge University Press, 2006), at xv in Preface.

25. Law No. 23521 ("Due Obedience"), June 4, 1987 (Argentina).

26. L. Joinet, "Question of the Impunity of Perpetrators of Human Rights Violations (Civil and Political)," UN Doc. E/CN.4/Sub.2/1997/20/Rev1, para. 36.

27. There are also legal traditions that mix the two concepts. France and some of its former colonies apply the concept of *grâce amnistiante*. See R. Levy, "Pardons and Amnesties as Policy Instruments in Contemporary France" (2007) 36 Crime & Just. 551, at 561 (2007). Certain amnesties also distinguish, within the terms of the laws themselves, the conferral of pardons (for cases in which the judgment has already been issued) and the conferral of amnesties (for those in which it has not). See, e.g., Decree 922 providing for amnesty and pardon, 1953 (Italy).

28. There is some jurisprudence at the national level that deals with limits on executive pardon power, but mostly it serves to confirm the power's largely unrestricted nature. See, e.g., C. Blum, "Policy Brief: Pardons," International Center for Transitional Justice, November 2008. However, in one notable recent case, the Argentine Supreme Court revoked pardons issued by former President Carlos Menem on the grounds that the pardon power could not extend to crimes against humanity. See "Argentine Court Overturns Pardon," BBC News (http://news.bbc.co.uk), July 13, 2007.

29. It should be noted, however, that in some countries amnesties have been adopted with such regularity that they may cease to be considered exceptional. See, e.g., R. Levy, "Pardons and Amnesties as Policy Instruments in Contemporary France," supra note 27, at 553, describing France's practice of issuing annual amnesties on Bastille Day to reduce prison overcrowding.

30. Professor Ronald C. Slye has observed that the subsequent repeal or disregard of an amnesty converts it into a form of reverse statute of limitation. "Amnesties in practice appear to accomplish the opposite of statutes of limitation and laches. The latter provide a window of opportunity for parties to assert their rights, and then foreclose those rights if they are not timely asserted. Amnesties preclude the assertion of rights immediately. While their intention is to forever preclude such an assertion, in practice, many amnesties appear to only postpone the assertion of rights. The Argentinean and Chilean amnesties, for example, which in their immediate aftermath effectively foreclosed any assertion of rights against their beneficiaries, have recently given way to the assertion of such rights. Contrary to the policy rationales supporting statutes of limitation and laches, the rationale supporting these amnesties appears to be that the immediate assertion of rights may be fraught with dangers, which recede with the passage of time. These amnesties thus become the equivalent of reverse statutes of limitation; that is, they delay the right to bring a claim until an appropriate period of time has passed." R. Slye, "The Legitimacy of Amnesties under International Law

and General Principles of Anglo-American Law: Is a Legitimate Amnesty Possible?" (2002) 43 Va. J. Int'l L. 173, at 234.

31. See, generally, J. Barker, *Immunities from Jurisdiction in International Law* (New York: Oxford University Press, 2009). Immunities may protect against more than domestic prosecution; they also may protect against extradition to a third state for purposes of trial.

32. See, generally, E. Chereminsky, "Prosecutorial Immunity" (1999) 15 Touro L. Rev. 1643.

33. L. Mallinder, *Amnesty, Human Rights and Political Transitions: Bridging the Peace and Justice Divide* (Oxford: Hart, 2008), at 14.

34. J. Gavron, "Amnesties in the Light of Developments in International Law and the Establishment of the International Criminal Court" (2002) 51 Int'l & Comp. L.Q. 91, at 115.

35. See, e.g., Office of the United Nations High Commissioner for Human Rights, *Rule of Law Tools for Post-Conflict States: Amnesties* (Geneva: United Nations, 2009), at 5.

36. The Amnesty Act, 2000 (Uganda); Law 98-08 on Civil Harmony, 1999 (Algeria); Executive Decree 128/2003 (Colombia); National Reconciliation Charter, 2007 (Afghanistan).

37. Note, by analogy, the various emergency and counterterrorism laws in force around the world, many of which grant ex ante immunity for a broad range of acts carried out in defense of the state. Such laws purport to legalize actions that would ordinarily be illegal, including arbitrary detention and torture. Depending on the subject matter, such ex ante forms of immunity can be tantamount to a license to commit crime.

38. See Part II, "Maximum conditions," subsection 4.4.4.2, "Requirement of nonrecidivism."

39. See, e.g., L. Joinet, "Question of the Impunity of Perpetrators of Human Rights Violations (Civil and Political)," supra note 26, para. 36; *Prosecutor v. Kondewa*, Decision on Lack of Jurisdiction/Abuse of Process: Amnesty provided by the Lomé Accord (Special Court for Sierra Leone, Appeals Chamber), Case No. SCSL-2004-14-AR72 (E) (May 25, 2004), para. 15.

40. L. Joinet, "Study on Amnesty Laws and Their Role in the Safeguard and Promotion of Human Rights," UN Doc. E/CN.4/Sub.2/1985/16/Rev.1, para. 5. See also R. Teitel, *Transitional Justice* (Oxford: Oxford University Press, 2000), 55.

41. M. Pensky, "Amnesty on Trial: Impunity, Accountability, and the Norms of International Law" (2008) 1 Ethics & Global Politics 1, at 7. At 8: "What remains true, this complex question notwithstanding, is that South Africa's complicated experiment in balancing the needs of democratic peace with criminal justice, whatever else we may make of it, was certainly also a traditional application of the sovereign power of a nation-state, with a new ruling political party eager to establish its sovereignty and legitimacy, to authorize quite dramatic deviations from the ordinary course of the domestic rule of law, in pursuit of some other desired political outcome."

42. There is yet another reason to avoid overstating the political realm's monopoly on deviations from application of the criminal law. Courts can still exercise their prerogative of judicial or constitutional review, which could result in overturning or

upholding an amnesty. In addition, citizens may retain the right to bring prosecutions as private citizens notwithstanding a state's renunciation of its prosecutorial prerogative.

43. See, e.g., "Colombia: Flawed Demobilization Offers De Facto Amnesty," Amnesty International Alert, November 2005.

44. Further confusion on this point is apparently introduced in the *Rule of Law Tools for Post-Conflict States: Amnesties*, supra note 35, at 8-9. The publication creates the redundant term *de jure amnesty*. It then distinguishes the terms *de facto amnesty* and *de jure amnesty*. Finally, it treats "disguised amnesties" – which are *de jure* measures – as a a sub-category of *de facto* amnesties.

45. See, e.g., Law of Civil Harmony, No. 98-08, 1999 (Algeria); Décret loi du 9 septembre 1993 portant amnistie (Burundi); Decreto-Ley 25499, 1992 (Peru).

46. See, generally, Part II, "Minimum leniency," subsection 4.3.3.6, "Variation in legal consequences depending on crime or rank."

47. R. Teitel, *Transitional Justice*, supra note 40, at 58.

48. See, e.g., "What Is Transitional Justice?" http://www.ictj.org.

49. "The etymology of the phrase [transitional justice] is unclear, but it had already become a term by the 1992 publication of the three-part volume *Transitional Justice: How Emerging Democracies Reckon With Former Regimes* edited by Neil Kritz, which brings together the early and significant texts of the field": L. Bickford, *The Encyclopedia of Genocide and Crimes against Humanity*, Vol. 3 (Macmillan Reference USA, 2004), at 1045.

50. See the Opening Considerations to this volume for discussion of the apparent paradigm shift. See also Nuremberg Declaration on Peace and Justice, U.N. Doc. A/62/885, sec. III.1 (annex to the letter dated June 13, 2008, from the permanent representatives of Finland, Germany, and Jordan addressed to the U.N. Secretary-General).

51. See, e.g., *Almonacid-Arellano et al. v. Chile* (Admissibility Petition), Inter-Am. C.H.R, Case No. 12.057, Report No. 44/02 (judgment of October 9, 2002), at para. 150, where the Inter-American Court of Human Rights finds that "the 'historical truth' included in the reports of [Chile's truth commissions] is no substitute for the duty of the State to reach the truth through judicial proceedings."

52. Law No. 15.848, 1986 (Uruguay).

53. See, e.g., the judgment of the Colombian Constitutional Court dealing with the Law on Justice and Peace (Law 975/2005), a statute establishing a reduce sentence scheme to enable the demobilization of Colombian paramilitaries: *Gustavo Gallón y otros* (judgment of May 18, 2006), Sentencia C-370/2006, Expediente D-6032 (Colombian Constitutional Court), paras. 5.1–5.16. In one of the most sophisticated and nuanced legal judgments in the realm of transitional justice, the court emphasized, inter alia, that a limitation on the right to justice can also constitute a means for achieving peace and contributing to victims' rights to truth, reparation, and the nonrecurrence of violations.

54. Consider, for example, the case of Angola: "Over a period of 41 years of permanent fighting, UN-endorsed amnesties were granted in all four peace agreements but these

concessions failed to stop war restarting. The Angolan case study shows that, at least in this case, it was the cessation of armed foreign intervention in the conflict . . . rather than the grant of amnesty . . . that proved the crucial factor for the achievement of a lasting peace." J. Doria, "Angola: A Case Study in the Challenges of Achieving Peace and the Question of Amnesty or Prosecution of War Crimes in Mixed Armed Conflicts" (2002) 5 Y.B. Int'l Humanitarian L. 3, at 7.

55. M. Okello, "The False Polarisation of Peace and Justice in Uganda," at 2 (Paper presented at the Building a Future on Peace and Justice conference, Nuremberg, June 25–27, 2007).

56. See, e.g., C. Bell, *On the Law of Peace: Peace Agreements and the Lex Pacificatoria* (Oxford: Oxford University Press, 2008), at 250, where the author discusses the tension between transitional justice's commitments to accountability on the one hand and to amnesty on the other.

57. See *Prosecutor v. Laurent Semanza*, Case No. ICTR-97-20-T, para. 554 (May 15, 2003).

58. See, e.g., J. Andenaes, *Punishment and Deterrence* (Ann Arbor: University of Michigan Press, 1974); C. L. Ten, *Crime, Guilt and Punishment* (Oxford: Clarendon Press, 1987); E. A. Lind and T. R. Tyler, *The Social Psychology of Procedural Justice* (New York: Plenum Press, 1988); J. Murphy and J. Hampton, *Forgiveness and Mercy* (Cambridge: Cambridge University Press, 1990); C. Nino, *Radical Evil on Trial* (New Haven: Yale University Press, 1996).

59. M. Pensky, "Amnesty on Trial," supra note 41, at 9. At 21: "In fact, what amnesties threaten is not impunity at all, since prior to a due determination of criminal guilt or innocence there simply can be no talk of what sanctions are deserved. Instead, what is lost in the amnesty is a broader normative good, and one that is importantly indeterminate between law and democratic politics: accountability."

60. See Black's Law Dictionary, s.v. "specific deterrence."

61. See, generally, Part II, "Maximum conditions," subsection 4.4.4.2, "Requirement of non-recidivism."

62. M. Drumbl, "Collective Violence and Individual Punishment: The Criminality of Mass Atrocity" (2005) 99 Nw. Univ. L. Rev. 539, at 590. At 591: "For some people the value of killing or dying for a cause actually exceeds the value of living peacefully without the prospect of punishment."

63. C. Trumbull, "Giving Amnesty a Second Chance" (2007) 25 *Berkeley J. Int'l L.* 283, at 309. At 311–12: "Significantly, perpetrators of serious crimes under international law are not common criminals. They are often motivated by an ideology of group superiority, and are therefore less likely to alter their behavior because of the threat of prosecution."

64. See, generally, Part II, "Maximum viability," subsection 3.6.1, "Typology of context and amnesty beneficiaries."

65. See Black's Law Dictionary, s.v. "general deterrence."

66. The large-scale violations committed in Kosovo during the 1999 conflict occurred six years after the establishment of the International Criminal Tribunal for the Former Yugoslavia and days after the unsealing of an indictment against former Serbian President, Slobodan Milošević. See, generally, Independent International Commission

on Kosovo, *Kosovo Report: Conflict, International Response, Lessons Learned* (Oxford: Oxford University Press, 2000). The massive violations committed in Darfur (Sudan) continued even after the issuance of the ICC arrest warrants against the Sudanese minister of the interior, who subsequently was appointed minister of humanitarian affairs. As of this writing, the president of Sudan's reaction to a subsequent ICC arrest warrant issued against him is equally troubling: he ordered all non-Sudanese humanitarian aid agencies to depart the country, leaving Darfur's displaced civilians in peril. See, generally, "Sudan: Justice, Peace and the ICC," International Crisis Group, July 2009.

67. See, e.g., G. Scheers, "Measuring Success in Complex Settings: GPPAC's Experiences with Planning, Monitoring and Evaluation," in *Assessing Progress on the Read to Peace*, www.gppac.net.

68. See, generally, Part II, "Maximum conditions," subsection 4.4.1, "Conditions for obtaining individual grants of amnesty."

69. See discussion in Part II, "Minimum leniency," subsection 4.3.2, "The persons who are expressly eligible or ineligible for amnesty."

70. See, generally, M. Drumbl, *Amnesty, Punishment, and International Law* (New York: Cambridge University Press, 2007), chap. 2 ("Conformity and deviance").

71. See, e.g., A. O'Shea, *Amnesty for Crime in International Law and Practice*, supra note 3, at 77–78: "The theory of reformation is inappropriate for political offences since it is unlikely that punishment would change strongly held political convictions, which may even be reinforced as a result of the actions of the perceived oppressor."

72. See, generally, Part II, "Maximum conditions," subsection 4.4.1, "Conditions for obtaining individual grants of amnesty."

73. See, generally, Part II, "Maximum conditions."

74. See, generally, M. Osiel, *Mass Atrocity: Collective Memory, and the Law* (New Brunswick: Transaction, 1997); M. Drumbl, *Amnesty, Punishment, and International Law*, supra note 70, at 173–9. This does not, however, mean they will result in any kind of social catharsis. See, e.g., M. Pensky, "Amnesty on Trial," supra note 41, at 21: "Trials are institutionalized contests between antagonists, of course, and not collective searches for consensus. The goal of prosecution is the determination of legal guilt or innocence, rather than the formation of some deliberative agreement."

75. In the film "The Dictator Hunter," Reed Brody of Human Rights Watch remarks, "If you kill one person, you go to jail. If you kill 40 people, they put you in an insane asylum. But if you kill 40, 000 people, you get a comfortable exile with a bank account in another country, and that's what we want to change here."

76. A. O'Shea, *Amnesty for Crime in International Law and Practice*, supra note 3, at 84. See also P. Hayner, *Unspeakable Truths: Confronting State Terror and Atrocity* (New York: Routledge, 2001), at 189, where the author quotes Paulo Borges Coelho as having made the following observation about post–civil war Mozambican fears of a return to violence: "'Maybe people are too busy trying to recover, and they know that the price to pay for peace is to forget.'"

77. See, e.g., L. Mallinder, *Amnesty, Human Rights and Political Transitions*, supra note 33, at 68–71, where she discusses state practice concerning "rolling" amnesties.

78. See, e.g., M. Drumbl, *Amnesty, Punishment, and International Law*, supra note 70, at 41–4, 62–3.

79. For example, the double jeopardy rule (i.e., the principle that one cannot be tried twice for the same crime) constitutes a limitation on the scope for criminal prosecution. However, we support the principle – with some exceptions – because its moral and policy benefits outweigh its costs.

80. See, e.g., "When the War Ends: A Population-Based Survey on Attitudes about Peace, Justice and Social Reconstruction in Northern Uganda," International Center for Transitional Justice, the Human Rights Center (University of California, Berkeley), Payson Center for International Development (Tulane University), December 2007, at 3: "The main priorities for respondents (who were allowed to give more than one response to this question) were health care (45%), peace (44%), education for the children (31%), and livelihood concerns (including food, 43%; agricultural land, 37%; money and finances, 35%). These priorities had not changed substantially since 2005, although the emphasis on health care was new. Only 3 percent of respondents mentioned justice as their top priority." See also K. Gallagher, "No Justice, No Peace: The Legalities and Realities of Amnesty in Sierra Leone" (2000) 23 T. Jefferson L. Rev. 149, where the author describes initial overwhelming public support for the Lomé Peace Agreement in Sierra Leone which contained a general amnesty.

81. Support for justice may nevertheless remain strong in absolute terms. See, e.g., P. Vinck and P. Pham, "Ownership and Participation in Transitional Justice Mechanisms: A Sustainable Human Development Perspective from Eastern DRC" (2008) 2 Int'l J. Transitional Justice 398, at 402–3, where the authors summarize results of a survey they organized at a time of renewed fighting in eastern DRC in 2007: "Consistent with findings from our research in Uganda, justice, reintegration and reconciliation issues were not frequent priorities among respondents when peace, security and basic needs were not yet met. Peace (50.5 percent) and security (34.1 percent) were the most frequently stated priorities, followed by livelihood concerns, including financial assistance (26.8 percent), education (26.4 percent) and food and water (25.8 percent). Few respondents identified providing justice (2.3 percent) or arresting those responsible for violence (1.6 percent), punishing those responsible (1.3 percent) and encouraging reconciliation (1.3 percent) as being among their immediate priorities." At 404–5 they further note: "Respondents' priorities reflect Abraham Maslow's hierarchy of needs, identifying means for survival and safety as the basic priorities. . . . As long as basic survival needs are not met and safety is not guaranteed, social reconstruction programs, including transitional justice mechanisms, will not be perceived as a priority and will lack the level of support needed for their success. . . . Although justice, truth seeking and prosecutions were not frequently listed among respondents' priorities, most respondents said that those who committed war crimes should be held accountable (84.6 percent) and that holding them accountable was necessary for peace (81.7 percent). This means that any process that would hinder future public accountability for the crimes that were committed, such as amnesty, is not the preferred option. In

fact, although two-thirds (68.3 percent) of respondents were willing to forgive war criminals if this were the only way to have peace, most respondents favored peace with trials (61.9 percent) over peace with forgiveness (38.1 percent)."

82. See, e.g., the Final Report of the Sierra Leone Truth and Reconciliation Commission, chap. 6, at 4, where the commission declared itself "unable to condemn the resort to amnesty by those who negotiated the Lomé Peace Agreement" as too high a price to pay for peace. See also L. Langer, *Holocaust Testimonies: The Ruins of Memory* (New Haven: Yale University Press, 1993), who uses the term "choiceless choice" to describe the impossibility of making morally significant choices in conditions such as those of German concentration and extermination camps during the Shoah.

83. Michelle Sieff and Leslie Vinjamuri argue "the balance of political forces at the end of a conflict precludes certain institutional options and makes others more likely." M. Sieff and L. Vinjamuri Wright, "Reconciling Order and Justice? New Institutional Solutions in Post-Conflict States" (1999) 52 J. Int'l Affairs 757, at 760. The authors argue, fairly, that the goals of individual political leaders also play a role, as in the case of Nelson Mandela in South Africa.

84. J. Snyder and L. Vinjamuri, "Trials and Errors: Principle and Pragmatism in Strategies of International Justice" (2004) 28 Int'l Security 5, at 40.

85. M. Pensky, "Amnesty on Trial," supra note 41, at 17. By corollary, he notes at ibid.: "Consequentialist arguments can often harbor a tendency to justify unpalatable rights violations once the potential benefits of a given policy rise to a sufficient level."

86. H. Cobban, *Amnesty after Atrocity? Healing Nations after Genocide and War Crimes* (Boulder, CO: Paradigm, 2006), at 208. The stigma of an indictment or arrest warrant can also complicate peace negotiations. See, e.g., "Sudan: Justice, Peace and the ICC," International Crisis Group, supra note 66, at 23, concerning the ICC arrest warrant against Sudan's President: "Many Darfur IDPs and refugees regarded the Bashir arrest warrant as a signal their hardships at the hands of NCP-sponsored militias were being recognised and acted upon. The Darfur rebel groups saw it as further isolating and delegitimising the NCP and a sign of support for the military option and regime change. Their negotiating position may harden in consequence. They continue rearming and mobilising, notably in Um Garas in Chad, and preparing for a possible resurgence of violence similar to what happened in the first years of the Darfur crisis." Viewed differently, however, the same arrest warrant could be characterized as a factor facilitating conflict resolution to the extent it may help to isolate uncooperative actors.

87. J. Snyder and L. Vinjamuri, "Trials and Errors," supra note 84, at 19, 20, and 25.

88. On Argentina, see, generally, C. Nino, "The Duty to Punish Past Abuses of Human Rights Put into Context: The Case of Argentina" (1991) 100 Yale L.J. 2619; on El Salvador, see P. Hayner, *Unspeakable Truths*, supra note 76, at 91–3; on Afghanistan, see, "Afghanistan: President Pressured to Sign Controversial Amnesty Bill," IRIN (UN Office for the Coordination of Humanitarian Affairs), February 26, 2007: "On 31 January, the country's 249-seat lower house initiated the amnesty-for-all bill in defiant reaction to a Human Rights Watch (HRW) report in which Karzai's government was

called upon to prosecute all those accused of mass human rights violations and war crimes in the country."

89. See, e.g., J. Snyder and L. Vinjamuri, "Trials and Errors," supra note 84, at 12, citing T. Garton Ash: "The ICTY's decision to investigate rebel atrocities led the guerrillas to destroy evidence of mass graves, creating a pretext for hard-line Slavic Macedonian nationalists to renew fighting in late November 2001 and to occupy Albanian-held terrain." Similarly, Indonesian soldiers dug up the graves of East Timorese victims and moved the cadavers to West Timor, in Indonesia, to reduce the chances of criminal accountability. Associated Press, "Indonesian Inquiry Recommends Changes against Own Military Leadership over E. Timor," http://www.unb.ca/bruns/9900/issue17/intnews/indonesia.html.

90. Note, however, that amnesties do not always and exclusively take the form of an obligation to refrain. For example, an amnesty may require the state to take affirmative actions to release eligible persons from prison. See discussion in Part II, "Legal consequences."

91. See Section 6 herein, "The Evolving UN Position on Amnesties."

92. See Decree No. 01–1117/1 Proclaiming the Law on Amnesty, 2002 (Macedonia); Promotion of National Unity and Reconciliation Act, 1995 (South Africa).

93. Although an amnesty's impact is not something that one can assess at the time of its enactment, its trajectory of implementation, post-adoption, is at least as relevant a criterion for assessing an amnesty's composite legitimacy as the text of the actual law.

94. Discussing contexts in which armed conflict persists despite the offer of an amnesty, Louise Mallinder observes: "In such cases, the failure of amnesty to end the violence may not be attributable to the amnesty itself, but rather to the wider political context in which it was introduced. For example, offering amnesty during a conflict may cause the state to appear weak. If such weakness is perceived by insurgents, it may encourage them that victory is close and inspire them to continue fighting, rather than surrender." L. Mallinder, *Amnesty, Human Rights and Political Transitions*, supra note 33, at 12.

95. For example, it is frequently claimed or implied that civil war resumed in Sierra Leone shortly after the adoption of the Lomé Peace Agreement as a result of its broad amnesty provision. See, e.g., OHCHR, *Rule of Law Tools for Post-Conflict States: Amnesties*, supra note 35, at 3: "Amnesties that exempt from criminal sanction those responsible for human rights crimes have often failed to achieve their goals and instead seem to have emboldened beneficiaries to commit further crimes. A well-known example is the amnesty provision of the 1999 Lomé Peace Agreement, which not only failed to end armed conflict in Sierra Leone but also did not deter further atrocities." But see P. Hayner, "Negotiating Peace in Sierra Leone: Confronting the Justice Challenge," International Center for Transitional Justice and Center for Humanitarian Dialogue, December 2007, at 23–4.

96. See, e.g., L. Vinjamuri, "Accountability and Peace Agreements: Mapping Trends from 1980 to 2006," Center for Humanitarian Dialogue, September 2007. The combination of broad amnesties and human rights trials is also found outside of Latin America (e.g., Greece, the Philippines, and Sierra Leone).

97. K. Sikkink and C. Walling, "The Impact of Human Rights Trials in Latin America" (2007) 44 J. Peace Research 427, at 442.

98. Ibid., at 435: "Particularly striking is the combination of the use of amnesties and the use of some kind of human rights trials. Amnesties were used in various forms in 16 of the 19 transitional countries in Latin America. Further, many of these countries passed multiple amnesty laws. Of the 16 countries that passed an amnesty law, 15 also had human rights trials."

99. Sikkink and Walling state that they are unable to conduct such an assessment: "Note that, in the Latin American cases, we cannot compare the effectiveness of amnesties to trials because every transitional country in Latin America except Guyana, Grenada, and Paraguay had an amnesty" (ibid., at 436). That such a comparison would be complex, there is no doubt. That it would be impossible is questionable.

100. M. Osiel, "Modes of Participation in Mass Atrocity" (2005) 39 Cornell Int'l L.J. 793, at 811.

101. See, e.g., R. Teitel, *Transitional Justice*, supra note 40, at 53. See also P. Aguilar, "The Timing and the Scope of Reparation, Truth and Justice Measures: A Comparison of the Spanish, Argentinian, and Chilean Cases," in K. Ambos, J. Large, and M. Wierda, eds., *Building a Future on Peace and Justice* (Berlin: Springer, 2009), at 507. The 1977 Spanish amnesty was the first law passed by the new parliament. Aguilar also notes that the early years of the transition were not as peaceful as sometimes suggested, adding to the public fear that facing the past could provoke a new conflict.

102. See, e.g., P. Hayner. *Unspeakable Truths*, supra note 76, at 185, 201; "Southern African Regional Assessment Mission Reports," International Center for Transitional Justice, October 2007–December 2008, at 39.

103. See, e.g., L. Joinet, "Study on Amnesty Laws and Their Role in the Safeguard and Promotion of Human Rights," supra note 40, para. 41, where Joinet cites the 1970 amnesty used to end the Biafran conflict as an effective example of a peace strategy.

104. See, e.g., J. Errandonea, "Droits de l'homme et état de droit: le cas de la loi d'amnistie en Uruguay," in R. Fregosi, ed., *Droits de l'homme et consolidation de la démocratie en Amérique du sud* (Paris: l'Harmattan, forthcoming 2009).

105. See, e.g., R. Slye, "The Cambodian Amnesties: Beneficiaries and the Temporal Reach of Amnesties for Gross Violations of Human Rights" (2004) 22 Wisc. Int'l L.J. 99, at 107; P. Hayner, *Unspeakable Truths*, supra note 76, at 195–200.

106. See, e.g., E. Aspinall, "Peace without Justice? The Helsinki Peace Process in Aceh," Centre for Humanitarian Dialogue, April 2008, at 5 and 17–18.

107. See, e.g., R. Slye, "The Cambodian Amnesties," supra note 105, at 107. See also R. Meister, "Forgiving and Forgetting: Lincoln and the Politics of National Recovery," in C. Hesse and R. Post, eds., *Human Rights in Political Transitions: Gettysburg to Bosnia* (New York: Zone Books, 1999). On France, see, generally, R. Levy, "Pardons and Amnesties as Policy Instruments in Contemporary France" (2007) 36 Crime & Just. 551. France passed a total of ten amnesty laws between 1946 and 1959 "that gradually obliterated the consequences of the French defeat of 1940, the German occupation, and the policy followed by the collaborationist Vichy regime, as well as the liberation and the purge that marked the end of the conflict." Ibid. at 562.

108. See, e.g., O. Thoms, J. Ron, and R. Paris, "The Effects of Transitional Justice," Centre for International Studies (University of Ottawa) working paper, April 2008. The paper critically reviews various studies, including L. Payne, T. Olsen, and A. Reiter, "Does Transitional Justice Work?" (paper presented at the International Studies Association Convention, San Francisco, March 26–29, 2008); and T. Lie, H. Binningsbø, and S. Gates, "Post-Conflict Justice and Sustainable Peace," Post-Conflict Transition Working Paper No. 5, World Bank Policy Research Working Paper 4191 (April 2007).

109. See, e.g., A. Suhrke and I. Samset, "What's in a Figure? Estimating Recurrence of Civil War" (2007) 14 Int'l Peacekeeping, 195, at 201, where the authors caution against the premature adoption of social science results: "[F]indings should be interpreted with great caution in areas where little work has been done, and, as in this case [of research on the cause of civil wars], where one set of authors has dominated the production and distribution of policy-relevant knowledge. Because there is a tendency for different data sets to produce different findings, a great deal of caution should be exercised when drawing conclusions."

110. R. Slye, "The Cambodian Amnesties," supra note 105, at 118.

111. See, generally, the Final Considerations of this volume.

112. See M. Keck and K. Sikkink, *Activists beyond Borders* (Ithaca, NY: Cornell University Press, 1998), chap. 1.

113. M. Sieff and L. Vinjamuri Wright, "Reconciling Order and Justice?," supra note 83, at 761.

114. See Section 4, "Amnesties and International Law."

115. See, e.g., M. Osiel, "Modes of Participation in Mass Atrocity," supra note 100, at 811; R. Slye, "Amnesty, Truth, and Reconciliation: Reflections on the South African Amnesty Process," in R. Rotberg and D. Thompson, eds., *Truth vs. Justice: The Morality of Truth Commissions* (Princeton, NJ: Princeton University Press, 2000), at 172.

116. In M. Osiel, *Making Sense of Mass Atrocity* (New York: Cambridge University Press, 2009), at 232, the author observes, "An effective democratic transition almost necessarily reallocates power in ways likely to call the terms of the initial deal into question later on, when former rulers and their allies no longer occupy prominent positions that enable them to obstruct change. Multinational corporations have long learned to expect their bargains to obsolesce in this way. Departing dictators and their minions accept a similar risk and bargain around it as best they can."

117. See, e.g., M. Osiel, "Modes of Participation in Mass Atrocity," supra note 100, at 815–16.

118. See, e.g., C. Dugger, "Mugabe Aides Are Said to Use Violence to Gain Amnesty," N.Y. Times, April 9, 2009.

119. This fact demonstrates that the fate of an amnesty may in part depend on the strength of the applicable regional human rights system.

120. See, generally, K. Sikkink and C. Walling, "The Impact of Human Rights Trials in Latin America," supra note 97. See also Part II of this volume.

121. R. Slye, "The Legitimacy of Amnesties under International Law and General Principles of Anglo-American Law," supra note 30, at 180; M. Osiel, "Modes of Participation in Mass Atrocity," supra note 100, at 816: "That amnesty will be successfully challenged in

the courts, or reversed by legislation, is a risk with high costs but low probability." See also more generally N. Roht-Arriaza and L. Gibson, "The Developing Jurisprudence on Amnesty" (1998) 20 Human Rights Q. 843.

122. See Section 5, "Amnesties and the ICC."

123. On the jurisprudence of the Special Court for Sierra Leone, see Section 5, "Amnesties and International Law." Concerning the Extraordinary Chambers in the Courts of Cambodia, the 2003 "Agreement between the United Nations and the Royal Government of Cambodia concerning the Prosecution under Cambodian Law of Crimes committed during the period of Democratic Kampuchea," precludes the government from granting a future amnesty or pardon for judged cases. See art. 11: "1. The Royal Government of Cambodia shall not request an amnesty or pardon for any persons who may be investigated for or convicted of crimes referred to in the present Agreement. 2. This provision is based upon a declaration by the Royal Government of Cambodia that until now, with regard to matters covered in the law, there has been only one case, dated 14 September 1996, when a pardon was granted to only one person with regard to a 1979 conviction on the charge of genocide. The United Nations and the Royal Government of Cambodia agree that the scope of this pardon is a matter to be decided by the Extraordinary Chambers."

124. On the inability of such persons to travel freely, see, e.g., E. Lutz and K. Sikkink, "The Justice Cascade: The Evolution and Impact of Foreign Human Rights Trials in Latin America" (2001) 2 Chicago J. Int'l L. 1, at 30–1: "The consequences of this justice cascade are far reaching. With respect to the perpetrators, even if they never face punishment, or even trial, they are finding themselves 'landlocked.' Even where their own government is willing to protect them from the reach of foreign courts, they dare not travel abroad for fear that the country they travel to will extradite them to a country seeking to try them." See also M. Osiel, *Making Sense of Atrocity,* supra note 116, at 230, where the author observes: "The doctrine of universal jurisdiction, permitting foreign prosecution for the most grievous international crimes, much increases the number of states that may choose to disregard national amnesty legislation. This fact may greatly reduce the bargaining value of such legislation to new constitutional rulers. But because universal jurisdiction has been exercised only quite sporadically and many amnesty recipients may have no better options on offer, the deal may still prove appealing, notwithstanding the indeterminacy of its temporal scope."

125. J. Snyder and L. Vinjamuri, "Trials and Errors," supra note 84, at 19.

126. M. Osiel, "Modes of Participation in Mass Atrocity," supra note 100, at 820. Note that as an amnesty reflects domestic balances of power at the time of its enactment, annulling an amnesty may simply reflect changes in the balance of power.

127. On Argentina, see, e.g., C. Nino, "The Duty to Punish Past Abuses of Human Rights Put into Context," supra note 88. On South Africa see, e.g., A. Boraine, "Truth and Reconciliation in South Africa: The Third Way," in *Truth v. Justice: The Morality of Truth Commissions,* ed. R. Rotberg and D. Thompson (Princeton, NJ: Princeton University Press, 2000), at 143.

128. On the differences between these areas of international law see, e.g., M. Freeman and G. van Ert, *International Human Rights Law* (Toronto: Irwin Law, 2004), at chap. 7.

129. Even at the nongovernmental level such unwillingness has arisen. See C. Trumbull, "Giving Amnesty a Second Chance," supra note 63, at 299.

130. Rome Statute of the International Criminal Court (adopted June 17, 1998, entered into force July 1, 2002) 2187 U.N.T.S. 90. See, e.g., R. Wedgwood, "The International Criminal Court: An American View" (1999) 10 European J. Int'l L. 93, at 94–7, where the author explains how discussion of the amnesty issue was so taut at the 1998 Rome Conference that the issue was omitted altogether from the final Rome Statute.

131. Louis Joinet, remarks at a March 2007 seminar in Paris organized by the International Center for Transitional Justice and hosted by the French Ministry of Foreign Affairs.

132. Statute of the International Court of Justice (adopted June 26, 1945, entered into force October 24, 1945).

133. See, generally, M. Freeman and G. van Ert, *International Human Rights Law*, supra note 128, at 63–7.

134. The customary claim would hold more weight if it could be shown that a majority of states believe an amnesty prohibition is already a *jus cogens* norm and thus superfluous to any treaty. However, evidence in support of that claim is difficult to find.

135. Concerning multilateral treaties outside of the human rights realm that explicitly refer to amnesties, see Additional Protocol to the European Convention on Extradition (adopted October 15, 1975), art. 2; and Second Additional Protocol to the European Convention on Extradition (adopted March 17, 1978), art. 4. These treaties allow amnesty to be used as a shield against extradition.

136. Protocol Additional to the Geneva Conventions of August 12, 1949, and relating to the Protection of Victims of Non-international Armed Conflicts (Protocol II), June 8, 1977, 1125 U.N.T.S. 609.

137. N. Roht-Arriaza, "Special Problems of a Duty to Prosecute: Derogation, Amnesties, Statutes of Limitation, and Superior Orders," in N. Roht-Arriaza, ed., *Impunity and Human Rights in International Law and Practice* (New York: Oxford University Press, 1995), at 59.

138. Louis Joinet argues that that the purpose of this article is "to facilitate the reciprocal return of prisoners." See L. Joinet, "Study on Amnesty Laws and Their Role in the Safeguard and Promotion of Human Rights," supra note 40, para. 16.

139. N. Roht-Arriaza and L. Gibson, "The Developing Jurisprudence on Amnesty," supra note 121, at 862–6; L. Mallinder, *Amnesty, Human Rights and Political Transitions*, supra note 33, chapter 5.

140. *Azanian Peoples Organization (AZAPO) and Others v. President of the Republic of South Africa and Others*, Constitutional Court of South Africa, Case No. CCT17/96 (July 25, 1996).

141. Ibid., at para. 31.

142. See, e.g., Human Security Report Project, *Human Security Brief: 2007*, chapter 3 (Trends in Armed Conflict and Coups d'Etat). But also see ibid. at 33: "Interstate wars, though relatively few in number, have been by far the deadliest form of armed conflict since the end of World War II."

143. See, e.g., R. Mani, "Looking Backward and Moving Forward: The Nexus between Development and Transitional Justice" (Paper presented at the "Building a Future on Peace and Justice" conference, Nuremberg, June 25–27, 2007).

144. L. Mallinder, *Amnesty, Human Rights and Political Transitions*, supra note 33, at 20.

145. S. Neff, *War and the Law of Nations: A General History* (Cambridge: Cambridge University Press, 2005), at 2.

146. J. Henckaerts and L. Oswald-Beck, eds., *Customary International Humanitarian Law*, Vol. 1, Rules (Cambridge: Cambridge University Press and International Committee of the Red Cross, 2005), rule 159.

147. See Inter-American Commission on Human Rights, *Lucio Parada Cea and Ors. v. El Salvador* (January 27, 1999), Report No. 199, Case 10,480, para. 115; UN Human Rights Committee, "Concluding Observations of the Human Rights Committee: Lebanon" (January 1, 1997), UN Doc. CCPR/C/79/Add.78, para. 12.

148. L. Mallinder, *Amnesty, Human Rights and Political Transitions*, supra note 33, at 126, 227; C. Bell, *On the Law of Peace*, supra note 56, at 246.

149. L. Mallinder, *Amnesty, Human Rights and Political Transitions*, supra note 33, at 126.

150. A list of the number of states parties to the main treaties discussed herein is found on the website of the UN Office of the High Commissioner for Human Rights.

151. See, e.g., A. O'Shea, *Amnesty for Crime in International Law and Practice*, supra note 3, ch. 7.

152. Darryl Robinson notes it makes more sense to refer to the "duty to bring to justice" than the "duty to prosecute" because a state's *aut dedere aut judicare* ("extradite or prosecute") obligation can be achieved in at least three ways: domestic prosecution, extradition to a willing and competent state, or surrender to an international tribunal. D. Robinson, "Serving the Interests of Justice: Amnesties, Truth Commissions and the International Criminal Court" (2003) 14 European J. Int'l L. 481, at 491.

153. Convention on the Prevention and Punishment of the Crime of Genocide, General Assembly Resolution 260 A (III), adopted December 9, 1948, 78 U.N.T.S. 277.

154. *Reservations to the Convention on the Prevention and Punishment of the Crime of Genocide* (1951) ICJ Reports 15, at 23.

155. Geneva Convention for the Amelioration of the Condition of the Wounded and Sick in Armed Forces in the Field, August 12, 1949, 75 U.N.T.S. 31; Geneva Convention for the Amelioration of the Condition of Wounded, Sick and Shipwrecked Members of Armed Forces at Sea, August 12, 1949, 75 U.N.T.S. 85; Geneva Convention relative to the Treatment of Prisoners of War, August 12, 1949, 75 U.N.T.S. 135; Geneva Convention relative to the Protection of Civilian Persons in Time of War, August 12, 1949, 75 U.N.T.S. 287.

156. Geneva Convention 1, art. 49; Geneva Convention 2, art. 50; Geneva Convention 3, art. 129; Geneva Convention 4, art. 146.

157. Protocol Additional to the Geneva Conventions of August 12, 1949, and relating to the Protection of Victims of International Armed Conflicts (Protocol I), June 8, 1977, 1125 U.N.T.S. 3, art. 85. See also Rome Statute, art. 8.2, which lists 26 "other serious violations of the law and customs applicable in international armed conflict" that the ICC can prosecute.

158. M. Scharf, "The Letter of the Law: The Scope of the International Legal Obligation to Prosecute Human Rights Crimes" (1996) 59 Law and Contemp. Probs. 41, at 43. But see, e.g., D. Newman, "The Rome Statute, Some Reservations Concerning Amnesties, and a Distributive Problem" (2005) 20 Am. U. Int'l L. Rev. 293, at 314: "Yet, if there were an unvariegated duty to prosecute perpetrators of international crimes, the principle of state immunity would seem to be normatively subject to this duty, which it evidently is not, based on the continuing strength of head-of-state immunity in international law."

159. R. Provost, *International Human Rights and Humanitarian Law* (New York: Cambridge University Press, 2002), at 110.

160. Query, however, whether a third state would have an obligation to accept an extradition request from a state that passes an amnesty. This perhaps would be a matter of discretion, not obligation, for the state receiving the request.

161. Convention against Torture and Other Cruel, Inhuman or Degrading Treatment (adopted December 10, 1984, entered into force June 26, 1987) 1465 U.N.T.S. 85.

162. CAT, art. 7(1): "The State Party in territory under whose jurisdiction a person alleged to have committed any offence referred to in article 4 is found, shall in the cases contemplated in article 5, if it does not extradite him, submit the case to its competent authorities for the purpose of prosecution."

163. L. Mallinder, *Amnesty, Human Rights and Political Transitions*, supra note 33, at 127–8.

164. Inter-American Convention to Prevent and Punish Torture (adopted December 8, 1985, entered into force February 28, 1987) OAS Treaty Series, No. 67, arts. 1 and 6.

165. International Convention for the Protection of All Persons from Enforced Disappearance, G.A. Res. A/61/177 (2006), UN Doc. A/61/488. The treaty will enter into force once there are twenty ratifications. As of this writing, that threshold has not been reached.

166. Inter-American Convention on the Forced Disappearances of Persons (adopted June 9, 1994, entered into force March 28, 1996) 33 I.L.M. 1429 (A-60), art. 3.

167. International Convention for the Suppression of Terrorist Bombings (adopted December 15, 1997, entered into force May 23, 2001), U.N.G.A. Res. 52/164, art. 8; International Convention against the Taking of Hostages (adopted December 17, 1979, entered into force June 3, 1983), 1316 U.N.T.S. 205, art. 8. See, more generally, A. O'Shea, *Amnesty for Crime in International Law and Practice*, supra note 3, at 191.

168. Convention on the Prevention and Punishment of Crimes against Internationally Protected Persons (adopted December 14, 1973, entered into force February 20, 1977), 1035 U.N.T.S. 167, art. 7; International Convention for the Suppression of Acts of Nuclear Terrorism (adopted April 13, 2005, entered into force July 7, 2007), art. 11.1: "The State Party in the territory of which the alleged offender is present shall, in cases to which article 9 applies, if it does not extradite that person, be obliged, without exception whatsoever and whether or not the offence was committed in its territory, to submit the case without undue delay to its competent authorities for the purpose of prosecution, through proceedings in accordance with the laws of that State. Those

authorities shall take their decision in the same manner as in the case of any other offence of a grave nature under the law of that State."

169. Convention Concerning Forced or Compulsory Labour (ILO No. 29), 39 U.N.T.S. 55, entered into force May 1, 1932.

170. See, e.g., D. Orentlicher, "Settling Accounts: The Duty to Prosecute Human Rights Violations of a Prior Regime" (1991) 100 Yale L. J. 2537.

171. International Convention on the Elimination of All Forms of Racial Discrimination, G.A. res. 2106 (XX), Annex, 20 U.N. GAOR Supp. (No. 14) at 47, U.N. Doc. A/6014 (1966), 660 U.N.T.S. 195, art. 4.

172. Supplementary Convention on the Abolition of Slavery, the Slave Trade, and Institutions and Practices Similar to Slavery (adopted September 7, 1957, entered into force April 30, 1957), 226 U.N.T.S. 3, arts. 3, 5, 6; International Convention on the Suppression and Punishment of the Crime of Apartheid (adopted November 30, 1973, entered into force July 18, 1976) 1015 U.N.T.S. 243, art. IV; Convention on the Rights of Persons with Disabilities (adopted December 13, 2006, entered into force May 3, 2008) 1144 U.N.T.S. 123, art. 16(5).

173. Rome Statute, arts. 5–8.

174. Universal Declaration on Human Rights (adopted December 10, 1948), UN Doc. A/810, art. 8

175. International Covenant on Civil and Political Rights, General Assembly Res. 2200 A (XXI), adopted December 16, 1966, U.N. GAOR, 21st sess., Supp. No. 16, at 52, UN Doc. A/6316 (1967).

176. European Convention on the Protection of Human Rights and Fundamental Freedoms (adopted November 4, 1950), ETS 5, art. 3; American Convention on Human Rights (adopted November 22, 1969, entered into force July 18, 1978), 1144 U.N.T.S. 123, art. 8; African Charter on Human and Peoples' Rights (adopted June 27, 1981, entered into force October 21, 1986), 1520 U.N.T.S. 217, art. 25.

177. See, e.g, Human Rights Committee, General Comment No. 31 (adopted on March 29, 2004), CCPR/C/21/Rev.1/Add.13, para. 18. See also *Prosecutor v. Kondewa*, supra note 39, para. 40, where the court notes that ICCPR art. 2(3) "does not provide individuals with a right to force a state to prosecute, but does put an obligation on the state to prosecute any suspects who have been credibly accused as a result of the investigation."

178. *Abdülsamet Yaman v. Turkey*, European Court of Human Rights (November 2, 2004), App. No. 32446/96, para. 53.

179. See, e.g., ICCPR arts. 9.5, 14.6; ECHR, art. 5; ACHR, art. 10; Afr CHPR, art. 21.

180. See, e.g., International Convention for the Protection of All Persons from Enforced Disappearance, art. 3; CAT, arts. 6, 12; Geneva Convention 1, art. 49; Geneva Convention 2, art. 50; Geneva Convention 3, art. 129; Geneva Convention 4, art. 146; Inter-American Convention on the Forced Disappearances of Persons, art. 1; Inter-American Convention to Prevent and Punish Torture, art. 8.

181. The concern, however, sometimes is raised that "the main positive effect of truth commissions is to give political cover to amnesties in transitional countries with

strong reform coalitions." J. Snyder and L. Vinjamuri, "Trials and Errors," supra note 84, at 20, 33, 43–4. See also R. Brody, "Justice: The First Casualty of Truth?" *The Nation*, April 30, 2001.

182. G.A. Res. 2391 (XXIII), annex 23 U.N. GAOR Supp. (No. 18) at 40, UN Doc. A/7218 (1968), entered into force November 11, 1970. See also L. Joinet, "Study on Amnesty Laws and Their Role in the Safeguard and Promotion of Human Rights," supra note 40, para. 31.

183. See, e.g., European Commission on Human Rights, *Dujardin and Others v. France* (September 2, 1991), App. No. 16734/90, 72 D.R. 236. In declaring the petitioner's application inadmissible the commission stated, inter alia: "Admittedly, as with any criminal offence, the crime of murder may be covered by an amnesty. That in itself does not contravene the Convention unless it can be seen to form part of a general practice aimed at the systematic prevention of prosecution of the perpetrators of such crimes.... The Commission notes that as a result of the amnesty law adopted in this case in the light of the special circumstances, i.e. the political situation in New Caledonia (France), the prosecution of those suspected of murdering the applicants' close relatives lapsed. Accordingly, the question which arises is whether this infringed the right protected by Article 2 of the Convention. The Commission considers in this connection that the amnesty law, which is entirely exceptional in character, was adopted in the context of a process designed to resolve conflicts between the various communities of the islands."

184. As previously noted, there are examples of amnesties covering crimes committed after the date of enactment. However, there appear to be no examples of amnesties that are completely open-ended in temporal terms in the way that a statutory limitation is.

185. See, e.g., ICCPR, art. 4(1); ECHR, art. 15; ACHR, art. 27(2). These derogation clauses stipulate that the derogating states may not adopt measures that would be inconsistent with their other international legal obligations or that would involve discrimination.

186. See, e.g., ICCPR, art. 4(2). Moreover, certain human rights treaties do not permit derogations at all. For example, derogations are not permitted under the CERD; the CAT; the International Covenant on Economic, Social and Cultural Rights G.A. res. 2200A (XXI), 21 U.N.GAOR Supp. (No. 16) at 49, U.N. Doc. A/6316 (1966), 993 U.N.T.S. 3, entered into force Jan. 3, 1976; or the Convention on the Rights of the Child, G.A. res. 44/25, annex, 44 U.N. GAOR Supp. (No. 49) at 167, U.N. Doc. A/44/49 (1989), entered into force September 2 1990.

187. See *Prosecutor v. Anto Furundzija*, International Criminal Tribunal for the former Yugoslavia, Case No. IT-95-17/1-T (December 10, 1998), para. 155.

188. ICCPR, arts. 7 and 8.

189. UN Human Rights Committee, General Comment No. 29: States of Emergency (article 4) (August 31, 2001), UN Doc. CCPR/C/21/Rev.1/Add.11, para. 14: "[The ICCPR obligation to ensure an effective remedy] is not mentioned in the list of non-derogable provisions in article 4, paragraph 2, but it constitutes a treaty obligation inherent in the Covenant as a whole."

190. ECHR, art. 15.2.
191. Otherwise put, Article 27(2) cannot be used as a pretext for conducting unfair trials. For an interpretation of the meaning and scope of this phrase, see Inter-American Court of Human Rights, *Habeas Corpus in Emergency Situations* (Arts. 27(2) and 7(6) of the American Convention on Human Rights) (January 30, 1987), Advisory Opinion OC-8/87, Inter-Am. Ct. H.R. (Ser. A), No. 8 (1987).
192. But see ibid., where the Court concludes that certain procedural remedies cannot be suspended, including amparo, habeas corpus "and any other effective remedy before judges or competent tribunals (Art. 25(1)), which is designed to guarantee the respect of the rights and freedoms whose suspension is not authorized by the Convention."
193. The focus herein is on nontreaty sources that deal with amnesty as a general issue, and not those dealing with a case-specific situation.
194. On the sources of international law, see Section 4.1, "Treaty sources explicitly related to amnesty."
195. L. Joinet, "Study on Amnesty Laws and Their Role in the Safeguard and Promotion of Human Rights," supra note 40.
196. UN Principles on the Effective Prevention and Investigation of Extra-legal, Arbitrary and Summary Executions (adopted May 24, 1984), ECOSOC Res. 1989/65, UN Doc. E/1989/89 (1989).
197. UN Human Rights Committee, General Comment No. 20: Replaces General Comment 7 concerning Prohibition of Torture and Cruel Treatment or Punishment (Art. 7) (March 10, 1992). It is not clear why the committee did not declare amnesties to also be "generally incompatible" with state duties to prosecute. Compare with the Guidelines to EU Policy towards Third Countries on Torture and other Cruel, Inhuman or Degrading Treatment or Punishment (General Affairs Council, April 9, 2001), which declare that the EU will urge third countries to "ensure to the greatest possible extent that amnesty is not granted in respect of acts of torture, and ensure that amnesties do not deprive individuals of the right to an effective remedy, including compensation and rehabilitation."
198. U.N.G.A. Res. 47/133, UN Doc. A/47/678/Add.2 (1993).
199. See also the UN Working Group on Enforced or Involuntary Disappearances, General Comment on Article 18: WGEID Report 2005 (E/CN.4/2006/56). The group's interpretation on the admissibility of amnesties was not incorporated into the International Convention for the Protection of All Persons from Enforced Disappearance.
200. L. Joinet, "Question of the Impunity of Perpetrators of Human Rights Violations," supra note 39, Principle 25.
201. Principle 18 deals with the duties of states with regard to the administration of justice and provides: "Impunity arises from a failure by States to meet their obligations to investigate violations, to take appropriate measures in respect of the perpetrators, particularly in the area of justice, by ensuring that they are prosecuted, tried and duly punished, to provide victims with effective remedies and reparation for the injuries suffered, and to take steps to prevent any recurrence of such violations. Although the decision to prosecute lies primarily within the competence of the State, supplementary

procedural rules should be introduced to enable victims to institute proceedings, on either an individual or a collective basis, where the authorities fail to do so, particularly as civil plaintiffs. This option should be extended to non-governmental organizations with recognized long-standing activities on behalf of the victims concerned."

202. Principles 33 to 36 concern rights and duties arising out of the reparation obligation, as well as reparation procedures and the scope of the right.

203. D. Orentlicher, "Independent study on best practices, including recommendations, to assist States in strengthening their domestic capacity to combat all aspects of impunity" (February 27, 2004), UN Doc. E/CN.4/2004/88.

204. See, e.g., L. Mallinder, *Amnesty, Human Rights and Political Transitions*, supra note 33, which comprehensively studies general amnesty practices rather than being restricted only to best practices.

205. UN Security Council, "The Rule of Law and Transitional Justice in Conflict and Post-Conflict Societies," UN Doc. S/2004/616 (2004).

206. Ibid., para. 64(c).

207. UN Security Council, "Report of the Secretary-General on the Establishment of a Special Court for Sierra Leone" (October 4, 2000), UN Doc. S/2000/915, para. 22.

208. D. Orentlicher, "Report of the independent expert to update the Set of Principles to combat impunity: Addendum" (February 8, 2005) UN Doc. E/CN.4/2005/102/Add.1. The UN Commission on Human Rights "took note with appreciation" of the Updated Set of Principles but did not adopt them. Resolution 2005/81 on impunity, para. 20.

209. The Updated Set of Principles defines "serious crimes under international law" as encompassing "grave breaches of the Geneva Conventions of 12 August 1949 and of Additional Protocol I thereto of 1977 and other violations of international humanitarian law that are crimes under international law, genocide, crimes against humanity, and other violations of internationally protected human rights that are crimes under international law and/or which international law requires states to penalize, such as torture, enforced disappearance, extrajudicial execution, and slavery." See ibid., "Definitions."

210. Principle 19 provides: "States shall undertake prompt, thorough, independent and impartial investigations of violations of human rights and international humanitarian law and take appropriate measures in respect of the perpetrators, particularly in the area of criminal justice, by ensuring that those responsible for serious crimes under international law are prosecuted, tried and duly punished. Although the decision to prosecute lies primarily within the competence of the State, victims, their families and heirs should be able to institute proceedings, on either an individual or a collective basis, particularly as *parties civiles* or as persons conducting private prosecutions in States whose law of criminal procedure recognizes these procedures. States should guarantee broad legal standing in the judicial process to any wronged party and to any person or non-governmental organization having a legitimate interest therein." This is slightly different from the original Principle 18 referred to in Joinet's Set of Principles but does not affect my argument.

211. D. Orentlicher, "Report of the independent expert to update the Set of Principles to combat impunity" (February 18, 2005) UN Doc. E/CN.4/2005/102.

212. Ibid., "Summary," citing UN Human Rights Commission resolution 2004/72.

213. See, e.g., UN Security Council Resolution 1674 (2006), UN Doc. S/RES/1674/2006, line 8; UN Security Council Resolution 1314 (2000), UN Doc. S/RES/1314/2000, line 2.

214. UN Security Council Resolution 1325 on Women, Peace and Security, UN Doc. S/RES/1325 (2000), line 11: "*Emphasizes* the responsibility of all States to put an end to impunity and to prosecute those responsible for genocide, crimes against humanity, war crimes including those relating to sexual violence against women and girls, and in this regard, stresses the need to exclude these crimes, where feasible from amnesty provisions . . . "; UN Security Council Resolution 1820 on Women, Peace and Security, UN Doc. S/RES/1820 (2008), line 4: "*Notes* that rape and other forms of sexual violence can constitute a war crime, a crime against humanity, or a constitutive act with respect to genocide, *stresses the need for* the exclusion of sexual violence crimes from amnesty provisions in the context of conflict resolution processes, and *calls upon* Member States to comply with their obligations for prosecuting persons responsible for such acts, to ensure that all victims of sexual violence, particularly women and girls, have equal protection under the law and equal access to justice, and *stresses* the importance of ending impunity for such acts as part of a comprehensive approach to seeking sustainable peace, justice, truth, and national reconciliation . . . "

215. L. Mallinder, *Amnesty, Human Rights and Political Transitions*, supra note 33, at 292.

216. Statute of the International Court of Justice, art. 38(1)(d).

217. Ibid., art. 38(1).

218. See, e.g., ibid., art. 59: "The decision of the [International Court of Justice] has no binding force except between the parties and in respect of that particular case." It should be further noted that the principle of stare decisis (i.e., judges must apply the precedents established in earlier decisions) is inapplicable under international law. See also R. Wallace, *International Law*, 5th ed. (London: Sweet and Maxwell, 2005), at 26.

219. See, e.g., *Prosecutor v. Kondewa*, Special Court for Sierra Leone, supra note 39. Although the court acknowledges the obvious point that states continue to practice amnesty, its canvassing of state practice and amnesty scholarship is meager. Nevertheless, the court concludes at paragraph 57 that Article 10 of its own statute "reflects customary international law which nullifies amnesties given to persons accused of bearing great responsibility for serious breaches of international law." The Inter-American Court of Human Rights also has tended to underinvestigate global amnesty practice in its judgments. See, e.g., *Almonacid-Arellano et al. v. Chile* (Preliminary Objections, Merits, Reparations, and Costs), judgment of September 26, 2006, Case No. 12.057.

220. The practice is self-reinforcing when prosecutors adopt the same practice. See, e.g., *Prosecutor v. Radovan Karadzic* (Prosecution's response to Karadzic's submission regarding alleged immunity agreement), August 20, 2008, Case No. IT-95-5/18–1, at para. 4, where the Prosecutor cites precisely this international jurisprudence to assert the existence of a *jus cogens* norm prohibiting the granting of amnesty for "serious violations of international criminal law." The ICTY Trial Chamber ultimately held

only "that any immunity agreement in respect of an accused indicted for genocide, war crimes and/or crimes against humanity before an international tribunal would be invalid under international law." *Prosecutor v. Radovan Karadžić (Immunity Issue)*, Case No. IT-95-5/18-PT (Dec. 17, 2008).

221. See, e.g., *Azanian Peoples Organization (AZAPO) and Others v. President of the Republic of South Africa and Others,* Case No. CCT17/96, at para. 21: "The result, at all levels, is a difficult, sensitive, perhaps even agonising, balancing act between the need for justice to victims of past abuse and the need for reconciliation and rapid transition to a new future; between encouragement to wrongdoers to help in the discovery of the truth and the need for reparations for the victims of that truth; between a correction in the old and the creation of the new. It is an exercise of immense difficulty interacting in a vast network of political, emotional, ethical and logistical considerations. It is an act calling for a judgment falling substantially within the domain of those entrusted with lawmaking in the era preceding and during the transition period. The results may well often be imperfect and the pursuit of the act might inherently support the message of Kant that 'out of the crooked timber of humanity no straight thing was ever made.'"

222. There is, in fact, no inherent reason why international court judgments should be entitled to greater legal weight than those of national courts, especially when one considers the sophistication of many appellate-level national courts. Moreover, when it comes to the issue of amnesty, there may be even greater reason to place equal weight on national judgments. In comparison to their international counterparts, national judges are more likely to understand and take into account the nuances of the local context in which an amnesty has been adopted.

223. See, e.g., "Application of REDRESS to intervene (Amicus Brief on the Legality of Amnesties under International Law)," October 24, 2003, para. 94 and Appendix B. See also the parallel Amicus Brief of the International Commission of Jurists, pp. 30–2 and 36–8.

224. See, e.g., "Application of REDRESS," ibid., para. 94 and Appendix B.

225. See, e.g., ibid., Appendix C.

226. See, e.g., *Abdülsamet Yaman v. Turkey*, App No. 32446/96, Eur. Ct. H. R. (November 2, 2004), para. 55; *Okkali v. Turkey,* App No. 52067/99, Eur. Ct. H. R. (October 17, 2006), para. 76. On the Court's specific jurisprudence on the duty to prosecute, see, generally, S. Van Drooghenbroeck, "Droit pénal et droits de l'homme: le point de vue de la Cour européenne des droits de l'homme," in Y. Cartuyvels et al., eds., *Les droits de l'homme, bouclier ou épée du droit pénal?* (Brussels: Facultés Universitaires de Saint Louis, 2007), at 75–109.

227. But see, e.g., *Oneryildiz v. Turkey*, Eur. Ct. H.R., App. No. 48939/99 (November 30, 2004), which alludes to the question of amnesty in the context of the prohibition on torture: "The Court reaffirms that when an agent of the State is accused of crimes that violate Article 3, the criminal proceedings and sentencing must not be time-barred and the granting of an amnesty or pardon should not be permissible." See also European Commission on Human Rights, *Dujardin and Others v. France*, supra note 183.

228. The first case, *Various Communications v. Mauritania*, African Commission on Human and Peoples' Rights, Communications 54/91, 61/91, 96/93, 98/93, 164/97-196/97, 210/98 (2000), deals with a self-amnesty issued in 1993 (Enactment No. 023-93). The commission found "that an amnesty law adopted with the aim of nullifying suits or other actions seeking redress that may be filed by the victims or their beneficiaries, while having force within Mauritanian national territory, cannot shield that country from fulfilling its international obligations under the Charter" (para. 83). The second case, *Zimbabwe Human Rights NGO Forum v. Zimbabwe*, African Commission on Human and Peoples' Rights, Communications 245/2002 (May 2002), also dealt with a self-amnesty. See also the Commission's Principles and Guidelines on the Right to a Fair Trial and Legal Assistance in Africa, OAU Doc. DOC/OS(XXX)247 (2001), preamble: "The granting of amnesty to absolve perpetrators of human rights violations from accountability violates the right of victims to an effective remedy."

229. Inter-American Commission on Human Rights, 1985/6 Annual Report, chap. 5, https://www.cidh.oas.org/annualrep/85.86eng/chap.5.htm.

230. D. Orentlicher, "Independent study on best practices, including recommendations, to assist States in strengthening their domestic capacity to combat all aspects of impunity," supra note 203, at para. 29. See also S. Canton, "Amnesty Laws," in *Victims Unsilenced: The Inter-American Human Rights System and Transitional Justice in Latin America* (Due Process of Law Foundation, 2007) at 171: "The simplicity with which the Commission has decided such cases contrasts sharply with the thorny debates over amnesty laws that occurred in several countries of the region."

231. *Almonacid-Arellano et al. v. Chile* (Preliminary Objections, Merits, Reparations, and Costs), supra note 219, at para. 171.

232. See, generally, *Barrios Altos Case (Chumbipuma Aguirre et al v. Peru)*, Inter-Am. Ct. H. R. (ser. C) No. 74 (March 14, 2001). The *Almonacid* judgment affirms the following passage from paragraph 41 of the *Barrios Altos* judgment: "all amnesty provisions, provisions on prescription and the establishment of measures designed to eliminate responsibility are inadmissible, because they are intended to prevent the investigation and punishment of those responsible for serious human rights violations such as torture, extra-legal, summary or arbitrary execution and forced disappearance, all of them prohibited because they violate non-derogable rights recognized by international human rights law." Note, however, that the implication of this passage is that an amnesty designed with a different intent – such as the intent to ensure conditions for improved human rights protection in future – may not be prohibited.

233. See, e.g., *Almonacid-Arellano* (Preliminary Objections, Merits, Reparations, and Costs), supra note 219, at para. 85, which highlights the following statements of the Chilean state in the proceedings: "a) to begin with, amnesty or self-amnesty laws are contrary to international human rights law; b) the case law of the higher courts of justice of Chile, traceable from 1998, has established several mechanisms to avoid the application of the Amnesty Decree Law, and so avoid its negative effects regarding the respect for human rights, and c) it endorses the opinion of the Inter-American

Court, which establishes that as a matter of principle, it is desirable that no amnesty laws exist, but in case they do, they must not be an obstacle for the respect of human rights, as established by the Court in the *Case of Barrios Altos.*"

234. See, e.g., B. Martínez, "El Salvador" and S. Canton, "Amnesty Laws," in *Victims Unsilenced*, supra note 230. On a more general note, it should be acknowledged that achievements in the fight against amnesty laws in Latin America are mostly limited to a few countries in the Southern Cone, especially Argentina, Chile, and Peru. Broad amnesties adopted on the rest of the continent, including in Brazil, Nicaragua, El Salvador, and Honduras, remain entrenched. On April 8, 2009, the Inter-American Commission on Human Rights filed an application with the Inter-American Court against Brazil, which will involve an examination of a 1979 amnesty law adopted there: http://www.iachr.org/Comunicados/English/2009/16-09eng.htm.

235. Since the time of his arrest in 2007, Sary has argued that he cannot be tried because he received amnesty in 1994 and a royal pardon in 1996. In its provisional detention order of 14 November 2007, the co-investigating judges of the Extraordinary Chambers found, inter alia, that the 1994 amnesty does not establish a bar to prosecution before the court because it does not cover the offenses within the court's jurisdiction. Provisional Detention Order of the Co-Investigating Judges, Criminal Case File no. 002/14-08-2006, Extraordinary Chambers in the Courts of Cambodia (14 November 2007), para. 13. In the order, the co-investigating judges also found that the 1996 royal pardon does not preclude the prosecution of Sary before the ECCC. Ibid., para. 12. As a whole, the order is provisional and does not bind Cambodia's Trial and Supreme Court Chambers, which will have a chance to rule on the scope of the amnesty and pardon if and when the case eventually proceeds to trial.

236. The Vienna Convention defines *jus cogens* as "a norm accepted and recognized by the international community of States as a whole as a norm from which no derogation is permitted and which can be modified only by a subsequent norm of general international law having the same character." Vienna Convention on the Law of Treaties (adopted May 23, 1969, entered into force January 27, 1980), 1155 U.N.T.S. 331, art. 53.

237. *Prosecutor v. Anto Furundzija*, supra note 187, at para. 155.

238. *Prosecutor v. Morris Kallon and Brima Bazzy Kamara*, Decision on Challenge to Jurisdiction: Lomé Accord Amnesty, Case No. SCSL-2004–15-AR72(E)-2004–16-AR72(E) (Appeals Chamber, March 13, 2004).

239. As the Court itself noted, it was unable to dispute the validity of a provision of its own Statute unless it was void under customary international law. Ibid., para. 62.

240. Ibid., para. 67.

241. Ibid., para. 84.

242. Ibid., para. 82.

243. Ibid., para. 82.

244. See "Application of REDRESS," supra note 223, and "Further Written Submissions on behalf of the Redress Trust, the Lawyers Committee for Human Rights and the International Commission of Jurists," November 21, 2003, http://www.redress .org/casework_and_other_submissions.html.

245. *Prosecutor v. Kondewa*, supra note 39.

246. *Prosecutor v. Augustine Gbao*, Decision on Preliminary Motion on the Invalidity of the Agreement between the United Nations and the Government of Sierra Leone on the Establishment of the Special Court, Case No. SCSL-2004–15-PT-141 (Appeals Chamber, May 25, 2004).

247. *Prosecutor v. Moinina Fofana*, Decision on Preliminary Motion on Lack of Jurisdiction: Illegal Delegation of Jurisdiction by Sierra Leone, Case No. SCSL-2004–14-PT-102 (Appeals Chamber, May 25, 2004).

248. *Prosecutor v. Kondewa*, supra note 39, para. 30.

249. S. Williams, "Amnesties in International Law: The Experience of the Special Court of Sierra Leone" (2005) 5 Human Rights L. Rev. 271, at 307–8.

250. L. Mallinder, *Amnesty, Human Rights and Political Transitions*, supra note 33, at 121.

251. Ibid., 122.

252. Ibid., 329.

253. See, e.g., *Case Concerning Military and Paramilitary Activities in and against Nicaragua*, International Court of Justice, Judgment on Merits (June 27, 1986), at para. 186: "If a state acts in a way *prima facie* incompatible with a recognised rule, but defends its conduct by appealing to exceptions or justifications contained within the rule itself, then whether or not the state's conduct is in fact justifiable on that basis, the significance of that attitude is to confirm rather than to weaken the rule." By corollary, if a state does not defend its conduct by appealing to such exceptions or justifications, the significance would be to weaken the rule, all else being equal. Similarly, policies a state advocates for others but not for itself (e.g., Spain on the issue of amnesty) would also weaken customary claims.

254. In M. Osiel, *Making Sense of Mass Atrocity,* supra note 116, at 234, the author observes, "Still less do neighboring countries condemn such states for violating international legal duties. To the contrary, they often rejoice at the reduced risk of refugee flows into their own territory presented by peace accords in the neighboring state, which is often emerging from civil war. This rejoicing too is pertinent state practice." See more generally T. Franck, "Interpretation and Change in the Law of Humanitarian Intervention," in J. Holzgrefe and R. Keohane, eds., *Humanitarian Intervention: Ethical, Legal, and Political Dilemmas* (New York: Cambridge University Press, 2003), at 204, where the author asserts that it is reasonable to infer one state's acceptance of the legality of another state's actions based on the first's lack of criticism of such actions.

255. See, e.g., Report of the Working Group on the Universal Periodic Review – Algeria, UN Doc. A/HRC/8/29, May 23, 2008, in which only Canada appears to have raised concerns about the impunity created by Algeria's 2006 general amnesty. According to the draft Report of the Working Group on the Universal Periodic Review – Afghanistan, UN Doc. A/HRC/WG.6/5/L.8, May 11, 2009, no state appears to have mentioned, let alone criticized, Afghanistan's 2007 general amnesty.

256. Note that even if a customary anti-amnesty norm crystallized, an amnesty that violated the norm would not, ipso facto, be legally indefensible. As discussion in more detail subsequently, one would still have to determine whether there is a conflicting

customary rule (e.g., an obligation to prevent and suppress international crimes) and then decide how to reconcile the competing rules.

257. UN Doc. A/CONF. 39/27 (1969).

258. See earlier discussion of treaty sources explicitly related to amnesty. See also Section 5, "Amnesties and the International Criminal Court."

259. See, generally, W. Burke-White, "Reframing Impunity: Applying Liberal International Law Theory to an Analysis of Amnesty Legislation" (2001) 42 Harvard Int'l L.J. 467. See also R. Teitel, *Transitional Justice*, supra note 40, at 57.

260. See, e.g., N. Roht-Arriaza and L. Gibson, "The Developing Jurisprudence on Amnesty," supra note 121, at 870–4, where the authors discuss various examples including appellate judgments from El Salvador and South Africa. See also L. Mallinder, *Amnesty, Human Rights and Political Transitions*, supra note 33, chapter 5.

261. *The Case of the S.S. "Lotus"*, Permanent Court of International Justice, PCIJ Ser. A. No. 10 (1927), pages 18–9.

262. N. Roht-Arriaza, "Special Problems of a Duty to Prosecute," supra note 137, at 59: "The debate [on Article 6(5)] also reflects the first major defeat of the argument that amnesty, pardon, and the like are purely domestic matters subject entirely to government discretion and not fit for international regulation."

263. See, e.g., ICCPR, arts. 2, 6–9; Geneva Conventions, art. 1; Protocol I to the Geneva Conventions, art. 1; Supplementary Convention on the Abolition of Slavery, the Slave Trade, and Institutions and Practices Similar to Slavery (adopted September 7, 1956, entered into force April 30, 1957), 226 U.N.T.S. 3, art. 2. See also Universal Declaration of Human Rights (UDHR), General Assembly Resolution 217 A (III), UN Doc. A/810 (1948), arts. 3, 4, 5, 9. There are also regional equivalents to these international sources: e.g., ECHR, arts. 2–5; ACHR, arts. 1, 4–7; AfrCHPR, arts. 4–6; the Inter-American Convention on the Forced Disappearances of Persons, art. 1; the Inter-American Convention to Prevent and Punish Torture, arts. 1 and 6.

264. *Application of the Convention on the Prevention and Punishment of the Crime of Genocide (Bosnia and Herzegovina v. Serbia and Montenegro)*, International Court of Justice, judgment of February 26, 2007, at para. 429.

265. Ibid., at para. 429.

266. See, e.g., ICCPR, art. 2(1); ACHR, art. 1(1).

267. The obligation to prohibit and prevent major human rights violations is also self-imposed by acts of constitutionalization and codification in a majority of states around the world. See, generally, A. O'Shea, *Amnesty for Crime in International Law and Practice*, supra note 3, chapter 9.

268. See, e.g., *Bosnia and Herzegovina v. Serbia and Montenegro*, supra note 264, at para. 64, where the Court holds that genocide prohibition is "assuredly" a *jus cogens* norm. Likewise, when legal scholars refer to a sample list of uncontroversial *jus cogens* norms, they tend to refer not to the prosecution but to the prohibition of acts like torture, war crimes, and genocide. See, generally, U. Linderfalk, "The Effect of *Jus Cogens* Norms: Whoever Opened the Pandora's Box, Did You Ever Think about the Consequences?" (2007) 18 European J. Int'l L. 853.

269. *Bosnia and Herzegovina v. Serbia and Montenegro*, ibid., para. 429.

270. Ibid., para. 430. See also Commentaries to the Draft Articles on State Responsibility, *Yearbook of the International Law Commission*, 2001, Vol. II. (Part 2), UN Doc. A/CN.4/SER.A/2001/Add.1, at 62: "Obligations of prevention are usually construed as best efforts obligations, requiring States to take all reasonable or necessary measures to prevent a given event from occurring, but without warranting that the event will not occur."

271. *Bosnia and Herzegovina v. Serbia and Montenegro*, ibid., at para. 431; Commentaries to the Draft Articles on State Responsibility, ibid., at 62.

272. There may, however, be an implicit hierarchy among these obligations that favors prevention and suppression. Under Article 4(1) of the ICCPR, for example, states may never derogate from ensuring the following: the prohibition on genocide (art. 6), limitations on capital punishment (art. 6), freedom from torture and cruel, inhuman, or degrading treatment or punishment (art. 7), freedom from slavery (art. 8), the right not to be imprisoned for debt (art. 11), the prohibition on ex post facto laws (art. 15), the right to personhood (art. 16), and the right to freedom of thought (art. 18). None of these obligations is remedial whereas several, such as the prohibition of genocide, torture, and slavery, are preventative.

273. See the discussion on the rules of *lex specialis* in Section 4.8, "Reconciling international legal norms."

274. *Velásquez Rodríguez Case*, Inter-American Court of Human Rights, Ser. C (No. 4) (July 29, 1988), at para. 175.

275. See Part II, Section 2.2, "Exhaustion of appropriate options to end the urgent and grave situation."

276. See, e.g., the Vienna Declaration and Programme of Action: "All human rights are universal, indivisible and interdependent and interrelated." World Conference on Human Rights, Vienna Declaration and Programme of Action (adopted July 12, 1993), U.N. Doc. A/CONF.157/23, at para. 5. The indivisibility of human rights implies that a state generally cannot pick and choose which rights it will uphold and which it will not. This characteristic of human rights is also frequently invoked to assert that civil and political rights cannot be divided from or treated as separate or less important than economic, social, and cultural rights.

277. U.N.G.A., Basic Principles and Guidelines on the Right to a Remedy and Reparation for Victims of Gross Violations of International Human Rights Law and Serious Violations of International Humanitarian Law (adopted December 16, 2005), UN Doc. A/RES/60/147 (prepared by C. Bassiouni), para. 3.

278. After all, it is not for nothing that the prohibition (i.e., prevention and suppression) of genocide is an *erga omnes* obligation. See, e.g., *Application of the Convention on the Prevention and Punishment of the Crime of Genocide*, Preliminary Objections, Judgment, I.C.J. Reports (1996), at 595, 615–16, paras. 31–2.

279. See discussion on "Responsibility to protect" herein and in Part II. See also the Commentaries to the Draft Articles on State Responsibility, supra note 270, at 67: "For instance, a State may incur responsibility if it assists another State to circumvent sanctions imposed by the Security Council or provides material aid to a State that uses the aid to commit human rights violations. In this respect, the General Assembly

has called on Member States in a number of cases to refrain from supplying arms and other military assistance to countries found to be committing serious human rights violations. Where the allegation is that the assistance of a State has facilitated human rights abuses by another State, the particular circumstances of each case must be carefully examined to determine whether the aiding State by its aid was aware of and intended to facilitate the commission of the internationally wrongful conduct."

280. Draft Articles on the Responsibility of States for Internationally Wrongful Acts, UN Doc. A/56/10 (2001), art. 16.

281. There is nothing strange about this. "Human rights – like all rights – are also limited between themselves. One person's exercise of her human rights may conflict with the rights of another. Rights to free speech and freedom of the press can, for example, conflict with the right to privacy and the right against injury to reputation": M. Freeman and G. van Ert, *International Human Rights Law*, supra note 128, at 35.

282. See in this regard AfrCHPR, art. 23, which declares the right of peoples to peace and security; UN Declaration on the Right of Peoples to Peace, G.A. Res. 39/11, annex (adopted November 12, 1984), U.N. Doc. A/39/51 (1984); Convention on the Rights of Persons with Disabilities and Optional Protocol (adopted December 13, 2006, entered into force May 3, 2008), UN Doc. A/RES/61/106, art. 11: "States Parties shall take, in accordance with their obligations under international law, including international humanitarian law and international human rights law, all necessary measures to ensure the protection and safety of persons with disabilities in situations of risk, including situations of armed conflict, humanitarian emergencies and the occurrence of natural disasters."

283. See, e.g., N. Roht-Arriaza, "Conclusion: Combating Impunity," in N. Roht-Arriaza, ed., *Impunity and Human Rights in International Law and Practice*, supra note 137, at 299, where the author notes the "international obligation to defend and protect elected democracies is emerging in international law parallel to the obligation to investigate, prosecute, and provide redress." See more generally M. Freeman and G. van Ert, *International Human Rights Law*, supra note 128, at 45–7.

284. As Ruth Wedgwood notes, "The UN Security Council does not sit in daily session to guarantee the institution of democratic rule within the polities of the UN's many non-democratic members. . . . Countries that want to regain democracy are on their own, most of the time." R. Wedgwood, "The International Criminal Court: An American View," supra note 130, at 95–6.

285. International human rights law, of course, allows for rights to be limited as necessary to preserve democracy. See, e.g., ACHR, art. 32. See also *Mendoza et al. v. Uruguay*, Inter-American Commission on Human Rights, Case Nos. 10.029, 10.036, 10.145, 10.305, 10.372, 10.373, 10.374, and 10.375 (October 2, 1992), Report No. 29/92, OEA/Ser.L/V/II.83 Doc. 14, at 154 concerning a 1986 Uruguayan amnesty: "The [Uruguayan] Government pointed out that as with any treaty, the Convention must be interpreted in accordance with the principles embodied in the Vienna Convention on the Law of Treaties, in good faith and in the light of its object and purposes. Accordingly, it pointed out that Articles 8.1 and 25.1 of the Convention should be interpreted in the light of Articles 30 and 32 of the Convention, whereby the enjoyment

and exercise of the rights recognized in the Convention can be restricted when such restrictions are the product of laws enacted for reasons of general interest or when those rights are limited by the rights of others, by the security of all and by the just demands of the general welfare in a democratic society. The Government pointed out that the Caducity Law was enacted in exercise of an authority recognized in international law (Articles 6.4 and 14.6 of the International Covenant of Civil and Political Rights and Article 4.6 of the Convention).”

286. See, e.g., Remarks of Alex Boraine, former vice chair of the South African TRC, Heinrich Boll Conference, February 24, 2007 (Istanbul): “Simply put, it was impossible for the ANC in particular to accept the protection of the security services throughout the negotiating process and then to say to them, ‘Once the election is over, we are going to prosecute you.’ If they had done so there would have been no peaceful election! It is as simple as that. The generals of the old regime had made that abundantly clear.” See also A. Boraine, *A Life in Transition* (Cape Town: Zebra, 2008), at 174.

287. See, e.g., *Almonacid-Arellano*, supra note 219, at para. 121. See also Draft Articles on the Responsibility of States for Internationally Wrongful Acts, supra note 280, art. 14: “The breach of an international obligation by an act of a State having a continuing character extends over the entire period during which the act continues and remains not in conformity with the international obligation.”

288. See, e.g., C. Davenport, *State Repression and the Domestic Democratic Peace* (New York: Cambridge University Press, 2007) See also M. Freeman and G. van Ert, *International Human Rights Law*, supra note 128, at 45: “In modern-day ‘failed states,’ where life resembles nothing so much as Hobbes’ depiction of the state of nature – ‘solitary, poor, nasty, brutish, and short’ – often the chief threat to human rights is not an excess of state power but rather its absence. In such situations, the consolidation and not the curtailment of state power should be the primary objective of human rights supporters. While the international community, via the UN, can do much to protect human rights in some of these extreme situations, it is no substitute for a functioning state. But obviously more than a functioning state is required to ensure adequate human rights protection. Democratic states are widely viewed as the preferred model of protection. Certainly the evidence of human rights practices in democratic states, as compared to non-democratic ones, bears this out in most cases.”

289. See, e.g., K. Sikkink and C. Walling, “The Impact of Human Rights Trials in Latin America,” supra note 97, at 442.

290. The Norwegian negotiator Jan Egeland has observed that “imperfect peace” is often the only realistic alternative to “perfect war.” Cited in C. Bell, *On the Law of Peace*, supra note 56, at 6.

291. See Final Considerations of this volume.

292. Draft Articles on the Responsibility of States for Internationally Wrongful Acts, supra note 280, pt. 1, chap. 5.

293. Ibid., art. 27(2). See also Commentary on Draft Articles, supra note 270, at 71: “The [defenses] do not annul or terminate the obligation; rather they provide a justification or excuse for non-performance while the circumstance in question subsists.”

294. Commentary on Draft Articles, ibid., at 71.
295. Draft Articles on the Responsibility of States for Internationally Wrongful Acts, supra note 280, art. 27. The phrase is "intended to cover situations in which the conditions preventing compliance gradually lessen and allow for partial performance of the obligation." Commentary on Draft Articles, ibid., at 86.
296. Draft Articles on the Responsibility of States for Internationally Wrongful Acts, ibid., art. 26. See also Vienna Convention, art. 53.
297. Examples are provided in Commentary on Draft Articles, supra note 270, at 85.
298. Force majeure is distinguishable from supervening impossibility of performance (Vienna Convention, art. 61). The latter produces treaty termination as opposed to the suspension of the obligation. See Commentary on Draft Articles, supra note 270, at 65.
299. Commentary on Draft Articles, ibid., at 77.
300. Michael Scharf observes that, "while the provisions of the treaties requiring prosecution are nonderogable even in time of public emergency that threatens the life of the nation, the doctrine of *force majeure* can warrant temporary postponement of prosecutions for a reasonable amount of time until a new government is secure enough to take such action against members of the former regime or until a new government has the judicial resources to undertake fair and effective prosecutions." M. Scharf "From the eXile Files" (2006) 63 Wash. & L. Rev. 339, at 373.
301. M. Scharf and N. Rodley, "International Law Principles on Accountability" in M. C. Bassiouni, ed., *Post-Conflict Justice* (Ardsley, N.Y: Transnational Publishers, 2002), at 96.
302. Commentary on Draft Articles, supra note 270, at 78.
303. This language mirrors that of "fundamental change of circumstances" (Article 62 of the Vienna Convention), which provides that such a change must have been unforeseen by the parties at the time the treaty was ratified, and may not be invoked as a ground for terminating or withdrawing from a treaty "unless the existence of those circumstances constituted an essential basis of the consent of the parties to be bound by the treaty . . . and the effect of the change is radically to transform the extent of obligations still to be performed under the treaty." The article further provides that the fundamental change must not have resulted from a breach by the party invoking it.
304. Commentary on Draft Articles, supra note 270, at 78.
305. Ibid., at 78–9.
306. Ibid., at 84.
307. See ibid., at 79–84, citing examples of cases involving fisheries disputes and commercial debts.
308. See, e.g., D. Orentlicher, "Settling Accounts," supra note 170, at 2548; J. Méndez, "In Defense of Transitional Justice," in A. J. McAdams, ed., *Transitional Justice and the Rule of Law in New Democracies* (Notre Dame, IN: University of Notre Dame Press, 1997), chap. 1; A. O'Shea, *Amnesty for Crime in International Law and Practice*, supra note 3, at 85.

309. See, e.g., ICCPR art. 14(1) allows in camera trials "for reasons of morals, public order (*ordre public*) or national security in a democratic society, or when the interest of the private lives of the parties so requires."

310. See also UDHR, art. 29(1).

311. See, e.g., Constitution of the Republic of South Africa, Part II: Bill of Rights (adopted December 4, 1996, entered into force on February 4, 1997), sec. 36(1); Canadian Charter of Rights and Freedoms, Schedule B to the Canada Act 1982 (U.K.) 1982, chap. 11 (entered into force April 17, 1982), sec. 1.

312. "The Siracusa Principles on the Limitation and Derogation Provisions in the International Covenant on Civil and Political Rights" (1985) 7 Human Rights Q. 89, at para. 10. See, generally, M. Freeman and G. van Ert, *International Human Rights Law*, supra note 128, at 33–6.

313. See discussion in Section 4.2, "Treaty sources implicitly related to amnesty."

314. The UN Human Rights Committee asserts that measures taken under ICCPR art. 4 must be of an "exceptional and temporary nature and may only last as long as the life of the nation is threatened." General Comment No. 5: art. 4: Derogation of Rights, Human Rights Committee (13th Sess., July 28, 1981), UN Doc. HRI/GEN/1/Rev.1, at 5 (1994). On derogation in public emergency generally, see J. Fitzpatrick, *Human Rights in Crisis: The International System for Protection Rights During States of Emergency* (Philadelphia: University of Pennsylvania Press, 1994).

315. See, e.g., ICCPR, art. 4(1); ECHR, art. 15; and ACHR, art. 27(2).

316. The specific list of non-derogable rights varies as between the ICCPR, the ECHR, and the ACHR. See discussion in Section 4.2 herein.

317. Commentary on Draft Articles, supra note 270, at 86.

318. See, e.g., "Nuremberg Declaration on Peace and Justice" (annex to the letter dated June 13, 2008, from the Permanent Representatives of Finland, Germany and Jordan to the United Nations addressed to the Secretary-General), UN Doc. A/62/885, sec. III(2): "The most serious crimes of concern to the international community, notably genocide, war crimes, and crimes against humanity, must not go unpunished and their effective prosecution must be ensured.... As a minimal application of this principle, amnesties must not be granted to those bearing the greatest responsibility for genocide, crimes against humanity and serious violations of international humanitarian law." See also sec. IV(2.6): "Amnesties, other than for those bearing the greatest responsibility for genocide, crimes against humanity and war crimes, may be permissible in a specific context and may even be required for the release, demobilization and reintegration of conflict-related prisoners and detainees."

319. "The margin of appreciation concept is an original and defining feature of the jurisprudence of the European Court of Human Rights. It seeks to balance the primacy of domestic implementation and enforcement with the need for supranational supervision. The concept refers to the room of manoeuvre (or degree of deference) that the Court will permit national authorities in fulfilling their obligations under the ECHR. It helps ensure respect for the state's greater knowledge of local conditions and legal culture, as well as accommodation of diverse forms of rights adherence. In deciding

on the applicable margin of appreciation in any one case, the Court will look to the degree of consensus or divergence among member states on the issue." M. Freeman and G. van Ert, *International Human Rights Law*, supra note 128, at 38.

320. It would be otherwise if there were a specific *jus cogens* norm against particular types of amnesty, but there is not.

321. Commentaries to Draft Articles, supra note 270, at 64.

322. Ibid., at 65.

323. International Law Commission, "Fragmentation of International Law: Difficulties Arising from the Diversification and Expansion of International Law," UN Doc. A/CN.4/L.682 (2006) (finalized by Martti Koskenniemi), at para. 5.

324. Commentaries to Draft Articles, supra note 270, at 140.

325. Ibid., at 140.

326. International Law Commission, "Fragmentation of International Law," supra note 323, at para. 24.

327. Ibid., at para. 26.

328. Ibid., at para. 1(4) of the Conclusions.

329. Depending on the body applying the test, respect might take the form of noninterference, and support might take the form of express endorsement or even proactive assistance in enforcement and implementation.

330. M. Arsanjani, "International Criminal Court and National Amnesty Laws" (1999) 93 Am. Soc. Int'l L. Proc. 65, at 66. See also D. Orentlicher, "Swapping Amnesty for Peace and the Duty to Prosecute Human Rights Crimes" (1997) 3 ILSA J. Int'l & Comp. L. 713, at 713. Orentlicher asks whether amnesties represent sound policy and answers her own question as follows: "The answer can only be, 'It depends.' Those who claim to have a universally relevant answer to this question surely overreach the limits of human knowledge."

331. M. Arsanjani, "International Criminal Court and National Amnesty Laws," ibid., at 66. Irrespective of the circumstance, however, it would seem prudential always to undertake efforts to preserve the documentation of past human rights violations as such documentation is crucial for the very operation of future transitional justice mechanisms – whether they be trials, truth commissions, reparation programs, or vetting programs. See, generally, L. Bickford and others, *Documenting Truth*, International Center for Transitional Justice, 2009.

332. Note in this regard Draft Articles on the Responsibility of States for Internationally Wrongful Acts, supra note 280, art. 1: "Every internationally wrongful act of a State entails the international responsibility of that State." An internationally wrongful act may consist of actions, omissions, or both.

333. C. Trumbull, "Giving Amnesty a Second Chance," supra note 63, at 321.

334. Rome Statute of the International Criminal Court, 2187 U.N.T.S. 90 (1998).

335. A provision authorizing the ICC to exercise jurisdiction over the crime of aggression potentially would become a significant factor in the resolution of future amnesty dilemmas, however it is possible that no such provision will ever be adopted.

336. See arts. 11(1) and 24(1).

337. See arts. 11(2) and 12(3).

338. For example, state parties may refuse requests for assistance from the Prosecutor where they concern evidence or documents that relate to national security (art. 93(4)). In the event of noncooperation by a state party, the Court may refer the matter to the Assembly of States Parties, or in the case of a Security Council referral, to the Security Council. The Court does not have independent powers of arrest.

339. P. Seils, "The Impact of the ICC on Peace Negotiations" (Paper presented at the "Building a Future on Peace and Justice" conference, Nuremberg, June 25–27, 2007). (No page numbers in the original.) The ICC Prosecutor himself echoed many of these points in his own address at the same conference. His speech is available at www.iccnow.org.

340. See also, e.g., "Policy Paper on the Interests of Justice," ICC Office of the Prosecutor, September 2007, at 4: "With the entry into force of the Rome Statute, a new legal framework has emerged and this framework necessarily impacts on conflict management efforts. The issue is no longer about whether we agree or disagree with the pursuit of justice in moral or practical terms: it is the law. Any political or security initiative must be compatible with the new legal framework insofar as it involves parties bound by the Rome Statute."

341. G. Young, "Amnesty and Accountability" (2002) 35 U.C. Davis L. Rev. 427, at 474.

342. R. Wedgwood, "The International Criminal Court," supra note 130, at 96.

343. M. Scharf, "The Amnesty Exception to the Jurisdiction of the International Criminal Court" (1999) 32 Cornell Int'l L.J. 507, at 522.

344. C. Stahn, "Complementarity, Amnesties and Alternative Forms of Justice: Some Interpretative Guidelines for the International Criminal Court" (2005) 3 J. Int'l Crim. Just. 695, at 718.

345. A. Seibert-Fohr, "The Relevance of the Rome Statute of the International Criminal Court for Amnesties and Truth Commissions" (2004) 7 Max Planck Y.U.N.L. 553, at 571.

346. Ibid., at 590.

347. It is significant that the phrase appears in the treaty's preamble and not in any operative provision. This makes it difficult to rely on the Rome Statute alone to express the anti-amnesty argument that the duty to prosecute creates a duty not to amnesty.

348. Rome Statute, arts. 53.1.c and 53.2.c. ICC Chief Prosecutor Luis Moreno Ocampo has outlined four main criteria to determine the gravity of crimes under Rome Statute art. 53: the scale of the crimes, their nature, the manner of their commission, and their impact. L. Moreno Ocampo, "Instrument of Justice: The ICC Prosecutor Reflects," *Jurist: Legal News and Research*, January 24, 2007. See also "Letter to Senders Re: Iraq," Office of the Prosecutor, February 9, 2006, http://www.icc-cpi.int, at 8–9.

349. John Dugard, in foreword to A. O'Shea, *Amnesty for Crime in International Law and Practice*, supra note 3, at viii.

350. Ibid., at appendix 1.

351. It also may be noted that, even in the absence of uncertainty about whether and when the ICC will respect a national amnesty, uncertainty as such will remain in the system

of international justice, as foreign courts will continue to have discretion to ignore amnesties and prosecute war criminals under principles such as universal jurisdiction.

352. C. Stahn, "The Geometry of Transitional Justice: Choices of Institutional Design" (2005) 18 Leiden J. Int'l L. 425, at 460. See also P. Seils and M. Wierda, "The International Criminal Court and Conflict Mediation," International Center for Transitional Justice, 2005, at 19.

353. M. Pensky, "Amnesty on Trial," supra note 41, at 15.

354. Note, however, that the Prosecutor's interpretation of his and the Court's role was more diplomatic and less legalistic in the Court's early years. See, e.g., P. Clark, "Law, Politics and Pragmatism: The ICC and Case Selection in Uganda and the Democratic Republic of Congo," in N. Waddell and P. Clark, eds., *Courting Conflict? Justice, Peace and the ICC* (London: Royal African Society, 2008), at 37–46.

355. M. Pensky, "Amnesty on Trial," supra note 41, at 16–17.

356. "Pre-Trial Chamber II commits Jean-Pierre Bemba Gombo to trial," ICC press release, June 15, 2009.

357. "ICC issues a warrant of arrest for Omar Al Bashir, President of Sudan," ICC press release, March 4, 2009.

358. "Warrant of arrest unsealed against five LRA Commanders," ICC press release, October 14, 2005. Announcing the unsealing of the arrest warrants, Prosecutor Ocampo justified the selection of LRA rather than national army cases on the basis of their relative gravity, invoking Article 53 of the Rome Statute. This decision was taken despite extensive documentation, inter alia, "of the occupying Ugandan and Rwandan armies in committing massive atrocities against (DRC) civilians, their tampering with local administrative boundaries, illicit exploitation of Congolese resources, and training of Congolese children for their local and national proxies." S. Baldo, "The Impact of the ICC in the Sudan and DR Congo" (Paper presented at the "Building a Future on Peace and Justice" conference, Nuremberg, June 25–27, 2007).

359. See, e.g., "Ending Zimbabwe's Nightmare: A Possible Way Forward," International Crisis Group, December 2008, which made the following recommendation concerning Zimbabwean despot Robert Mugabe: "Mugabe to be given guarantees against domestic prosecution and extradition, and a similar general amnesty to benefit members of the Joint Operations Command if they accept retirement and do not participate in activities threatening the country's stability."

360. The political label can also stick where an international prosecutor engages in intensive and widespread lobbying and diplomacy behind the scenes.

361. As the South African TRC showed, it is possible to deliver some form of accountability (e.g., public acknowledgement of crimes and public shaming) while also affording amnesty to perpetrators. The two concepts are not inherently mutually exclusive.

362. M. Arsanjani, "International Criminal Court and National Amnesty Laws," supra note 330, at 65.

363. Being under analysis is distinct from, and a legal step prior to, being under investigation. By corollary, it is a legal step after monitoring. As of this writing, there are seven situations under analysis by the OTP: Afghanistan, Chad, Colombia, Ivory Coast, Georgia, Kenya, and Palestine. Of these, Ivory Coast and Israel (regarding Palestine)

are non-states parties. Ivory Coast, however, has accepted the jurisdiction of the ICC under the provisions of Article 12(3) of the Rome Statute.

364. Such a referral will be especially unlikely in a context where a broad and general amnesty contained in a peace accord appears to be contributing to a gradual improvement in public security and governance, such as in Aceh, Indonesia. See, generally, E. Aspinall, "Peace without Justice? The Helsinki Peace Process in Aceh," supra note 106.

365. Despite this significant nonparticipation in the Rome system, it is clear that non–states parties are aware of the risks that the mere existence of the ICC creates for them, and they have begun to adjust some of their practices accordingly. "Armies around the world, even from non-signatory countries, are adjusting their regulations to what is right, avoiding the possibility of their personnel committing acts that would fall under the Court's jurisdiction." Statement of the ICC Prosecutor on the tenth anniversary of the Rome Statute, http://www.iccnow.org/documents/Luis_Moreno_Ocampo_Commemoration_17_July_2008.pdf.

366. See, e.g., A. Liptak, "US Says It Has Withdrawn from World Judicial Body," N.Y. Times, March 10, 2005. In the case of a withdrawal from the Rome system, the ICC would continue to have jurisdiction over crimes committed in the country prior to the effective date of withdrawal. However, in all likelihood, the ICC would lack adequate access to conduct investigations in the country following withdrawal.

367. See, generally, "Sudan: Justice, Peace and the ICC," International Crisis Group, supra note 66.

368. Colombia's unopposed declarations on ratification stated in part: "1. None of the provisions of the Rome Statute concerning the exercise of jurisdiction by the International Criminal Court prevent the Colombian State from granting amnesties, reprieves or judicial pardons for political crimes, provided that they are granted in conformity with the Constitution and with the principles and norms of international law accepted by Colombia.... 5. Availing itself of the option provided in article 124 of the Statute and subject to the conditions established therein, the Government of Colombia declares that it does not accept the jurisdiction of the Court with respect to the category of crimes referred to in article 8 when a crime is alleged to have been committed by Colombian nationals or on Colombian territory." UN Reference, C.N.834.2002.Treates-33 (Depositary Notification), effected August 5, 2002.

369. See, e.g., "African Union in rift with court," BBC News, July 3, 2009, describing an African Union resolution adopted by African states parties to the Rome Statute providing "The AU member states shall not co-operate . . . relating to immunities for the arrest and surrender of Sudanese President Omar al-Bashir to the ICC."

370. See, e.g., M. Struett and S. Weldon, "Why Do States Join the International Criminal Court? A Typology" (Paper presented at the annual meeting of the International Studies Association, 48th Annual Convention, Chicago, February 28, 2007).

371. See, generally, Amnesty International, "International Criminal Court: US Efforts to Obtain Impunity for Genocide, Crimes against Humanity and War Crimes," IOR

40/025/2002 (September 2, 2002), http://www.amnesty.org/en/library/asset/IOR40/ 025/2002/en/dom-IOR400252002en.pdf. The relevance of these agreements appears to have waned in recent years. However, as of December 11, 2006, 46 states parties had signed such agreements with the United States, in many cases under threat of withdrawal of economic or military assistance authorized under U.S. legislation. "Status of US Bilateral Immunity Agreements," Coalition for the International Criminal Court, December 2006: http://www.iccnow.org/documents/CICCFS_BIAstatus_current.pdf.

372. J. Gavron, "Amnesties in the Light of Developments in International Law and the Establishment of the International Criminal Court," supra note 34, at 109.

373. R. Wedgwood, "The International Criminal Court," supra note 130, at 98.

374. See UN Security Council Res. 1422 (2002) and 1487 (2003).

375. Article 18 sets out the procedure for preliminary rulings on admissibility. Article 19 establishes the procedure concerning challenges by a state to the Court's jurisdiction or to the admissibility of a case on the basis that the state is able and willing to investigate or prosecute on its own.

376. As previously noted, Article 20(3) of the statute creates an exception to the principle of *non bis in idem* (double jeopardy), allowing the Court jurisdiction to hear cases previously tried at the national level if the national trials were a sham. Article 20(3) provides: "No person who has been tried by another court for conduct also proscribed under article 6, 7 or 8 shall be tried by the Court with respect to the same conduct unless the proceedings in the other court: (a) Were for the purpose of shielding the person concerned from criminal responsibility for crimes within the jurisdiction of the Court; or (b) Otherwise were not conducted independently or impartially in accordance with the norms of due process recognized by international law and were conducted in a manner which, in the circumstances, was inconsistent with an intent to bring the person concerned to justice."

377. J. Gavron, "Amnesties in the Light of Developments in International Law and the Establishment of the International Criminal Court," supra note 34, at 111–12. Note also that various of the legal defenses described earlier herein (e.g., force majeure) are not dissimilar from the Rome Statute categories of "inability" or "unwillingness," and they potentially could be invoked on similar grounds (e.g., being unable to prosecute when to do so would risk a coup d'état).

378. Ibid., at 110.

379. "Policy Paper on the Interests of Justice," supra note 340, at 8. See also P. Seils, "The Impact of the ICC on Peace Negotiations," supra note 339: "In particular the [OTP] does not consider that the interests of justice is either synonymous with or subsumes the concept of the interests of peace."

380. "Policy Paper on the Interests of Justice," ibid., at 9. Decisions taken in "real situations" include decisions to decline to open investigations (after analysis) into violations alleged to have occurred in Venezuela and Iraq. "Situations under Analysis," ICC Monitor, issue 37 (2009), at 9.

381. The Amnesty Act, 2000 (Uganda), as amended.

382. Of the situations in which it has opened investigations thus far, Uganda is the only one that has involved an amnesty broad enough to encompass ICC crimes. Of the situations under analysis, Afghanistan too has passed an amnesty broad enough to encompass ICC crimes. National Reconciliation Charter, 2007 (Afghanistan). See, generally, H. Chu, "Afghan amnesty shows warlords' clout," Los Angeles Times, April 29, 2007.

383. L. Mallinder, *Amnesty, Human Rights and Political Transitions*, supra note 33, at 287.

384. N. Roht-Arriaza, "Amnesty and the International Criminal Court," in D. Shelton, ed., *International Crimes, Peace and Human Rights: The Role of the International Criminal Court* (Ardsley, N.Y: Transnational Publishers, 2000), at 81. See also D. Robinson, "Serving the Interests of Justice," supra note 152, at 497–8, where the author suggests the following criteria to assess whether deferring to an amnesty arrangement would be "in the interests of justice": "(i) Was the measure adopted by democratic will? (ii) Is the departure from the standard of criminal prosecution of all offenders based on necessity, i.e. irresistible social, economic or political realities? (iii) Is there a full and effective investigation into the facts? (iv) Does the fact-finding inquiry 'name names'? (v) Is the relevant commission or body independent and suitably resourced? (vi) Is there at least some form of punishment of perpetrators (are they identified, required to come forward, required to do community service, subject to lustration)? (vii) Is some form of remedy or compensation provided to victims? (viii) Does the national approach provide or sense of closure or justice to victims? (ix) Is there a commitment to comply with other human rights obligations?"

385. But see P. Clark, "Law, Politics and Pragmatism," supra note 354, at 43: "The author's interviews with government officials indicate that Prosecutor Ocampo approached President Museveni in 2003 and persuaded him to refer the Uganda case to the ICC. The referral suited both parties, providing the ICC with its first state referral of a case and the Ugandan government with another stick with which to beat the LRA."

386. See http://www.icc-cpi.int/cases/UGD/s0204/s0204_b.html.

387. Ordinarily the OTP would review national capacity to determine whether the state was genuinely unable to prosecute ICC crimes, but in the case of Uganda, it applied the doctrine of "uncontested admissibility."

388. International Crisis Group, "Northern Uganda: The Road to Peace, With or Without Kony," December 2008, at 1.

389. See, generally, P. Clark, "Law, Politics and Pragmatism," supra note 354, at 42–3.

390. A. O'Brien, "The Impact of International Justice on Local Peace Initiatives: The Case of Northern Uganda" (Paper presented at the "Building a Future on Peace and Justice" conference, Nuremberg, June 25–27, 2007). Among other things, O'Brien asserts that "the threat of prosecution clearly rattled the LRA military leadership, providing pivotal pressure that propelled the rebels the negotiating table.... Second, the ICC's investigation complicated continued support from Khartoum, the LRA's key foreign ally."

391. M. Okello, "The False Polarisation of Peace and Justice in Uganda," supra note 55, at 2.

392. M. Wierda and M. Otim, "Justice at Juba: International Obligations and Local Demands in Northern Uganda," in N. Waddell and P. Clark, eds., *Courting Conflict?*, supra note 354, at 21 and 23.

393. Even if Uganda decided to challenge admissibility under Articles 17 or 18 of the Rome Statute, the ultimate decision would be for the ICC judges to make.

394. M. Pensky, "Amnesty on Trial," supra note 41, at 5.

395. Ibid., at 27: "The Court has no attractive options. It has itself assumed the role of spoiler in Uganda, but cannot rescind its indictments without losing its credibility."

396. The parties earlier signed an Agreement on Agenda Item 3 on "accountability and reconciliation" (June 29, 2007). The annexure to that agreement (February 19, 2008), which remains unsigned, set out the specific transitional justice mechanisms to be established in Uganda.

397. International Crisis Group, "Northern Uganda: The Road to Peace, with or without Kony," supra note 388, at 4.

398. M. Okello, "The False Polarisation of Peace and Justice in Uganda," supra note 55, at 2. See also "Update Report: Northern Uganda and LRA-Affected Areas," Security Council Report, June 22, 2009: "On 16 January [2009] the Council issued a press statement strongly condemning attacks carried out by the LRA which had resulted in over 500 dead and over 400 abducted. On 17 February Under-Secretary-General for Humanitarian Affairs John Holmes briefed the Council on his visit to the DRC from 6 to 10 February. Holmes said the number of deaths since December 2008 as a result of LRA attacks was believed to have approached 900 while 160,000 were estimated to have fled their homes."

399. See, e.g., A. O'Brien, "The Impact of International Justice on Local Peace Initiatives: The Case of Northern Uganda," supra note 390: "the ICC's attempt to hold the LRA leadership criminally liable for the atrocities they've orchestrated in northern Uganda played a very useful channeling function. The presence of the ICC has embedded accountability and victim's interests in the structure and syntax of the peace process."

400. See "Forgotten Voices: A Population-Based Survey of Attitudes about Peace and Justice in Northern Uganda," International Center for Transitional Justice and the Human Rights Center (University of California, Berkeley), July 2005; and "When the War Ends: A Population-Based Survey on Attitudes about Peace, Justice and Social Reconstruction in Northern Uganda," supra note 80.

401. There is one partial exception. As the Juba talks were ongoing, so was the Ugandan amnesty process. Among others, middle-ranking LRA leaders Sunday Otto and Richard Odong Kau defected at the end of 2007 and received an amnesty from the Ugandan government in early 2008. "With or Without Peace: Disarmament, Demobilisation and Reintegration in Northern Uganda," Justice and Reconciliation Project, February 2008, at 6.

402. As of this writing, the reality of this assertion is most evident in relation to the ICC arrest warrant against Sudanese President Omar al-Bashir. See, generally, International Crisis Group, "Sudan: Justice, Peace and the ICC," supra note 66.

403. Recall that the ICC will not have jurisdiction in respect of any international crimes committed prior to July 1, 2002. Rome Statute, art. 24(1).

404. Presentation by Luis Moreno-Ocampo, December 7, 2008, The Hague, "Conference on 60 Years of the Genocide Convention."

405. Ibid.

406. Office of the Prosecutor, "Report on Prosecutorial Strategy," September 14, 2006, at 4-5. Available at http://www.icc-cpi.int/library/organs/otp/OTP_Prosecutorial -Strategy-20060914_English.pdf.

407. Upon his election, Prosecutor Ocampo declared that an absence of ICC trials "would be its major success." See Statement by Luis Moreno Campo to Assembly of States Parties, April 22, 2003.

408. P. Clark, "Challenging Complementarity: The Role of International Justice in Address- ing Mass Crimes in Africa," presentation at Oxford University conference on "Transitional Justice and International Law," June 23, 2007.

409. See, e.g., Office of the ICC Prosecutor, "Report on Prosecutorial Strategy," September 14, 2006, at 8: "Even in relatively simple cases, the Office will require significant coop- eration; for example, although Thomas Lubanga Dyilo was already in custody in the Democratic Republic of the Congo . . . his transfer to the Court required cooperation not only from the DRC authorities but also from French authorities, who provided an airplane to transport him to The Hague and from the UN Security Council, which quickly lifted the travel ban against him."

410. See, generally, part 9 of the Rome Statute.

411. Although influenced by the adoption of the Rome Statute, the United Nations did not per se need to wait until its adoption to create a position of its own, as earlier treaties such as the Geneva Conventions and the Genocide Convention were already long in place.

412. C. Villa-Vicencio and E. Doxtader, eds., *Pieces of the Puzzle: Keywords on Reconciliation and Transitional Justice* (Cape Town: Institute for Justice and Reconciliation, 2004), at 91.

413. P. Hayner, "Negotiating Peace in Sierra Leone," supra note 95, at 17. The idea of creating UN guidelines on amnesty was proposed as early as 1996 by Professor Dou- glass Cassel: "But the international community can at least refrain from accepting amnesties for serious violations of human rights as valid defenses before international prosecutions. And between the extremes of national amnesties and international pros- ecutions, the United Nations and OAS have a range of options. Even if they cannot compel national prosecutions, they can still repudiate amnesties for human rights violators publicly and diplomatically, undercutting claims of moral legitimacy by the beneficiaries." D. Cassel, "Lessons from the Americas: Guidelines for International Response to Amnesties for Atrocities" (1996) 59 Law & Contemp. Probs. 197, at 203.

414. C. Bell, *On the Law of Peace*, supra note 56, at 248.

415. The full story behind the Sierra Leone amnesty is recounted in P. Hayner, "Negotiating Peace in Sierra Leone," supra note 95, at 6–7.

416. Seventh Report of the Secretary-General on the United Nations Observer Mission in Sierra Leone (July 13, 1999), UN Doc. S/1999/836, para. 54. More generally, see W. Schabas, "Amnesty, the Sierra Leone Truth and Reconciliation Commission and the Special Court for Sierra Leone" (2004) 12 UC Davis J. Int'l L. & Policy 145.

417. P. Hayner, "Negotiating Peace in Sierra Leone," supra note 95, at 33.

418. See "Report of the Secretary General on the Establishment of a Special Court for Sierra Leone," UN Doc. S/2000/915, paras. 22–24.

419. "Report of the Security-General on the Rule of Law and Transitional Justice in Conflict and Post-Conflict Societies," supra note 205.

420. M. Scharf, "From the eXile Files," supra note 300, at 363. The hypocrisy of Brazil on this issue is acute. The broad and general amnesty it adopted to facilitate its own transition to democracy in 1979 remains in force to this day. Lei Concede Anistia e Dá Outras Providências, Law No 6.683/1979 (Brazil).

421. See prior discussion herein on this point in Section 4.3, "Nontreaty sources explicitly related to amnesty."

422. See, e.g., OHCHR, *Rule of Law Tools for Post-Conflict States: Amnesties*, supra note 44, at 11 and 27.

423. Commission on Truth and Friendship, Terms of Reference (March 10, 2005), para. 14(c).

424. "Timor-Leste: UN to boycott truth panel unless it bars amnesty for gross abuses," UN News Center, 26 July 2007.

425. See, e.g., Human Rights Watch, "Selling Justice Short: Why Accountability Matters for Peace," July 2009; "Further Written Submissions on behalf of the Redress Trust, the Lawyers Committee for Human Rights and the International Commission of Jurists," November 21, 2003 (concerning a case before the Special Court for Sierra Leone), http://www.redress.org/casework_and_other_submissions.html.

426. See, e.g., C. Stahn, "United Nations Peace-Building, Amnesties and Alternative Forms of Justice: A Change in Practice?" (2002) 84 Int'l Rev. of the Red Cross 191; L. Joinet, "Question of the Impunity of Perpetrators of Human Rights Violations (Civil and Political)," supra note 26, paras. 1–4. See also OHCHR, *Rule of Law Tools for Post-Conflict States: Amnesties*, supra note 44, at 2, which makes a partial acknowledgment of past UN practice concerning amnesties: "In the past, United Nations mediators have at times encouraged parties to armed conflicts to agree to a broad amnesty with a view to ending the conflicts."

427. See, generally, the Opening Considerations of this volume.

428. See, e.g., C. Sculier, "Négociations de paix au Burundi: une justice encombrante mais incontournable," Centre for Humanitarian Dialogue, May 2008, at 38–9, discussing the risk of UN disengagement in the event of a TRC with authority to amnesty international crimes. See also the earlier discussion on the UN boycott of the Commission on Truth and Friendship set up jointly by Indonesia and Timor-Leste.

429. Promotion of National Unity and Reconciliation Act, 1995 (South Africa), sec. 1(1): "(ix) 'gross violation of human rights' means the violation of human rights through-

(a) the killing, abduction, torture or severe ill-treatment of any person; or (b) any attempt, conspiracy, incitement, instigation, command or procurement to commit an act referred to in paragraph (a), which emanated from conflicts of the past and which was committed during the period 1 March 1960 to the cut-off date within or outside the Republic, and the commission of which was advised, planned, directed, commanded or ordered, by any person acting with a political motive."

430. One of the strongest affirmations of the new norm in fact appears in the "Report of the Secretary-General on the Rule of Law and Transitional Justice in Conflict and Post-Conflict Societies," supra note 205.

431. See, generally, OHCHR, *Rule of Law Tools for Post-Conflict States: Amnesties*, supra note 35, which throughout the text proclaims international law as the basis of the UN's policy.

432. R. Slye, "The Cambodian Amnesties," supra note 105, at 113.

433. See, generally, S. Vandeginste, "Transitional Justice for Burundi: A Long and Winding Road," in K. Ambos and others, *Building a Future on Peace and Justice*, supra note 101, at 409–11.

434. Note also Rome Statute, art. 124, which allows new states parties to postpone ICC jurisdiction for certain crimes for up to seven years.

435. See M. Freeman, "Amnesties and DDR Programs: An Integrated Approach," in A. Patel, P. de Greiff, and L. Waldorf, eds., *Disarming the Past: Transitional Justice and Ex-combatants* (New York: Social Science Research Council, forthcoming 2009). See also L. Mallinder, *Amnesty, Human Rights and Political Transitions*, supra note 33, at 9: "As it is assumed under most legal systems that children are not criminally responsible for their actions, it is usual for child soldiers to not be prosecuted and, instead, be encouraged to participate in rehabilitation programmes."

436. The phrase "those bearing greatest responsibility" appears in the Statute of the Special Court for Sierra Leone (January 16, 2002), art. 1, to signal, inter alia, that the Special Court is responsible for conducting only a limited number of trials.

437. As one author observes (without proposing a different UN position), it would be "unwise to dissuade people from DDR participation based on a threat of prosecution that cannot realistically be fulfilled." See P. van Zyl, "Promoting Transitional Justice in Post-Conflict Societies," in A. Bryden and H. Hänggi, eds., *Security Governance in Post-Conflict Peacebuilding* (Geneva: Geneva Center for the Democratic Control of Armed Forces, 2005), at 220.

438. The Center for Humanitarian Dialogue has established a series of studies on justice and peacemaking, including several in which the UN amnesty position has figured. This will help begin to fill the gap in our knowledge about the actual impact of the UN position. See, generally, http://www.hdcentre.org/publications?filter0=61.

439. In J. Snyder and L. Vinjamuri, "Trials and Errors," supra note 84, at 7, the authors forcefully argue that "the point of departure for justice strategies must be the 'logic of consequences,' in which choices and actions are shaped by pragmatic bargaining rather than by rule following."

440. See OHCHR, *Rule of Law Tools for Post-Conflict States: Amnesties*, supra note 35, Fore-word: "By opposing amnesties that establish impunity for atrocious crimes, United

Nations policy seeks to safeguard a space for justice even when conditions for prose-cutions are not yet adequately established." While UN negotiators must now follow the confidential "Guidelines for United Nations Representatives on Certain Aspects of Negotiations for Conflict Resolution," non–United Nations mediators are not, and it is possible that many of them will take a different position than the UN one.

441. See, e.g., International Council on Human Rights Policy, *Negotiating Justice? Human Rights and Peace Agreements* (2006), at 97 and 120, where it is recommended that mediators and negotiators become more familiar with international law requirements in the area of accountability and have access to human rights advice, including through full-time human rights advisers.

442. See, e.g., E. Aspinall, "Peace without Justice?," supra note 106, at 17, concerning Nobel Prize–winner Martti Ahtisaari's role in the Aceh peace talks. One of the participants at the talks stated as follows: "'GAM [the rebels] at the beginning tended to want to go back to the past more. President Ahtisaari tried to pull the parties back to the present time and encouraged them to forget the past, over and over again. He would tell them that the past has to be dealt with, but now is not the time.'"

443. K. Thorne, "Negotiating Justice" (Paper presented at the Building a Future on Peace and Justice conference, Nuremberg, June 25–27, 2007), at 2.

444. C. Bell, "The 'New Law' of Transitional Justice," in K. Ambos and others, *Building a Future on Peace and Justice*, supra note 101, at 123.

445. See, e.g., L. Kirchoff, "Linking Mediation and Transitional Justice: The Use of Interest-Based Mediation in Processes of Transition," in ibid., at 257. In this context, it is noteworthy that there is no other example to date of another multilateral organization having adopted an official position explicitly on the question of amnesty.

446. Presentation of Diane Orentlicher, Oxford University conference on "Transitional Justice and International Law," June 22, 2007.

447. Louise Mallinder observes: "the impact of this position on the practice of other inter-national actors is debatable . . . since the adoption the UN standpoint in 1999, no clear change in state practice has emerged, possibly because the UN is not involved in all amnesty deliberations, particularly not amnesties offered unilaterally by national governments. Furthermore, the role of the UN as a mediator appears to have declined somewhat in the face of competition from regional intergovernmental bodies, individual states and NGOs all offering mediation services to war-torn states." L. Mallinder, *Amnesty, Human Rights and Political Transitions*, supra note 33, at 339.

448. See Part II, Section 4.4.2.2 "Requirement of nonrecidivism."

449. Diane Orentlicher refers to this as the "local agency critique." Presentation of Diane Orentlicher, Oxford University conference on "Transitional Justice and International Law," June 22, 2007.

450. See, e.g., H. Nassar and L. Maalouf, "Conflict Transformation or Escalation? – The Hariri Tribunal and Its Repercussion on the Conflicts in Lebanon" (Paper presented at the Building a Future on Peace and Justice conference, Nuremberg, June 25–27, 2007), at 4, commenting on the overwhelming public support for the 1991 amnesty that ended the Lebanese civil war at the time it was enacted. At an ICTJ Essentials Course in Paris in March 2008, Louis Joinet noted a similar social and political consensus

in countries like Portugal and Spain when they adopted broad and unconditional amnesties in the 1970s to facilitate returns to democratic rule.

451. S. Ratner and J. Abrams, *Accountability for Human Rights Atrocities in International Law: Beyond the Nuremberg Legacy*, 2nd ed. (New York: Oxford University Press, 2001), at 343.

452. D. Newman, "The Rome Statute, Some Reservations Concerning Amnesties, and a Distributive Problem," supra note 158, at 346. But see L. Kirchhoff, "Linking Mediation and Transitional Justice," supra note 445, at 254, where he argues that "the most fundamental interests of the international community cannot be subject to any deal-making and negotiation – they have an overriding character with regard to all other interests involved."

453. Vienna Convention, art. 27.

454. M. Freeman and G. van Ert, *International Human Rights Law*, supra note 128, at 57.

455. On the tensions that can arise between local and international law in general in transitional contexts, see, e.g., J. Zalaquett, "Confronting Human Rights Violations Committed by Former Governments: Principles Applicable and Political Constraints," in A. Henkin, ed., *State Crimes: Punishment or Pardon* (Queenstown, Md.: Aspen Institute, 1989), at 27.

456. See J. Snyder and L. Vinjamuri, "Trials and Errors," supra note 84, at 42: "Pressed by principled activists and vocal public opinion, democratic leaders often pay lip service to human rights principles and accountability for crimes. These leaders overpromise but underdeliver because they suspect that their publics' underlying preferences are similar to their own: that is, they do not really want to bear the costs and risks that a policy of forceful, unbending application of universal principles would produce."

457. C. Trumbull, "Giving Amnesty a Second Chance," supra note 63, at 316–17. Trumbull also notes, "Essentially, by pursuing this course of action, the international community says: 'We are not willing to risk the loss of our own soldiers in seeking justice, but we are willing to allow more people in the conflict-ridden state to die in order to preserve the right to seek justice on behalf of mankind.' Placing the cost of justice on the most afflicted party is not consistent with the UN's assertion that states have a 'responsibility to protect' populations which are unable to protect themselves": ibid. at 319.

458. D. Orentlicher, "Settling Accounts," supra note 170, at 2548–9: "Because trials secure pre-eminent rights and values, governments should be expected to assume reasonable risks associated with prosecutions, including a risk of military discontent."

459. M. Arsanjani, "International Criminal Court and National Amnesty Laws," supra note 330, at 65.

460. Possible exceptions include Spain, concerning the ongoing conflict with ETA, or the United Kingdom and Northern Ireland, concerning the final resolution of the legacy of the Troubles.

461. Law 46/1977 (Spain); Decree Law 173/74 Political Amnesty, 1974 (Portugal) and Alvor Agreement, 1975 (Portugal/Angola) signed by Portugal and three Angolan nationalist movements, the MPLA, UNITA, and FNLA; Decree No. 62–328 (March 22, 1962) portant amnistie de faits commis dans le cadre des opérations de maintien de

l'ordre dirigées contre l'insurrection algérienne (France). France adopted a total of six amnesty laws between 1962 and 1968 that "wiped out the consequences of the Algerian War." R. Levy, "Pardons and Amnesties as Policy Instruments in Contemporary France," supra note 27, at 563.

462. Note, too, that an act of repeal would not violate the prohibition on ex post facto legislation. No new crime is created, retroactively or prospectively, through the repeal of an amnesty. The repeal merely reestablishes the jurisdiction of courts to try crimes that were criminal at the time when the amnesty was originally issued and for which amnesty was given in the first place. As for any concerns that the repeal of an amnesty would violate the human right to receive the benefit of the lighter penalty (ICCPR, art. 15), there is reason to doubt that the right extends to an amnesty covering acts that were never sanctioned judicially. However, to the extent it is even theoretically applicable to the repeal of an amnesty law, the right expressly excludes acts which at the time of their commission were criminal "according to the general principles of law recognized by the community of nations" (ICCPR, art. 15(2)).

463. See Vienna Declaration and Programme of Action, supra note 276, at para. 60, which affirms: "States should abrogate legislation leading to impunity for those responsible for grave violations of human rights such as torture and prosecute such violations, thereby providing a firm basis for the rule of law."

464. Consider that, unless these states apply the norm to their own prior amnesties for international crimes, the legal value of their diplomatic support of the UN amnesty position is marginal at best. Advocating a norm for others but not for oneself would prove the opposite of *opinio juris*.

465. See Section 4.4.2, "Regional human rights courts and commissions."

466. See P. Aguilar, "The Timing and the Scope of Reparation, Truth and Justice Measures: A Comparison of the Spanish, Argentinian, and Chilean Cases," supra note 101, at 521: "The provisions of the 1977 [Spanish] amnesty law remain intact. In contrast to what has happened in other cases, almost no Spanish judge has invoked national or international norms for the purpose of bypassing the limits of the Amnesty Law."

467. D. Markel, "The Justice of Amnesty? Towards a Theory of Retributivism in Recovering States" (1999) 49 U. Toronto L.J. 389, at 445.

468. See, e.g., C. Bell, "The 'New Law' of Transitional Justice," supra note 444, at 109, where the author refers to "clear instruction" as "the easiest way to ensure that mediators play a normative role."

469. See, generally, Part II, Section 4.4, "Maximum conditions."

470. Consider, too, that the exclusion, ab initio and across the board, of specific international crimes may appear legally presumptuous by implying without any prior legal determination that such crimes had been committed.

471. See, e.g., C. Sculier, "Négociations de paix au Burundi," supra note 428, at 38, on the negotiation of amnesty issues in Burundi, where the United Nations has insisted on its amnesty position and the local government has insisted on a South African approach: "En privilégiant le pardon au detriment d'une responsabilité, l'exemple historique sud-africain, dans lequel l'ONU n'a pas été impliquée, constitue indéniablement un

précedent embarrassant, difficilement compatible avec les préoccupations de celle-ci." It is not surprising, therefore, to see the South African model gradually come under attack by some UN agencies. The fact is that the moral and prudential claims used to justify the UN's amnesty position are undermined by the perceived success of the South African model.

472. The TRC's truth-for-amnesty formula relied on the credible threat of domestic prosecution for its effectiveness – a threat that diminished as the TRC process drew to a close. It is frequently noted that such a threat is rarely present in transitional environments. As such, it is argued, the South African model rarely will work in other countries. M. Freeman, *Truth Commissions and Procedural Fairness,* supra note 24, at 35. However, as already observed, prosecution threats now exist globally via international, hybrid, and foreign courts and therefore a variant of the South African model could possibly work.

473. Of the 7,116 amnesty applications it received, the TRC's Amnesty Committee issued amnesty to only sixteen per cent of the applicants. L. Mallinder, *Amnesty, Human Rights and Political Transitions,* supra note 33, at 132. Yet successive South African governments have made defending the virtue of the TRC amnesty model more difficult by not acting on the factor that differentiated it from a general amnesty, namely prosecuting those who did not apply or qualify for an amnesty. A new national prosecution strategy recently was held to be unconstitutional as an attempted repeat of the TRC amnesty process. See *Ndadimeng et al. v. National Director of Public Prosecutions,* High Court of South Africa (Transvaal Provincial Division), Case No. 32709/07 (December 12, 2008).

474. As Professor Ronald C. Slye notes, "Prior to the case of South Africa, contemporary amnesties added little if anything to public knowledge or acknowledgment about a society's past." "One of the major innovations of the TRC was an amnesty procedure that had as its major purpose revelation." R. Slye, "Amnesty, Truth, and Reconciliation," supra note 115, at 171 and 180. See also K. Greenawalt, "Amnesty's Justice," in ibid., at 197: "Each testimony by a victim and each identification of an offender achieves some portion of the justice of a criminal trial and conviction."

475. Yasmin Sooka, presentation at KU Leuven Faculty of Law seminar, "10 Years After the TRC," November 2008. Further truth – arguably, most truth – was revealed in the TRC process through statement-taking, interviews, hearings, investigation, and research as well as through the power of the commission's Human Rights Violations Committee to subpoena individuals and compel the answering of questions under appropriate guarantees of use immunity. See, e.g., H. Varney, "Research Brief: The use of amnesty in relation to truth-telling: a case study of the South African Truth and Reconciliation Commission," International Center for Transitional Justice, November 2008, para. 4.2.

476. *Azanian Peoples Organization (AZAPO) and Others v. President of the Republic of South Africa and Others,* Constitutional Court of South Africa, Case No. CCT17/96: "The alternative to the grant of immunity from criminal prosecution of offenders is to keep intact the abstract right to such a prosecution for particular persons without the evidence to sustain the prosecution successfully."

477. See, e.g., C. Sculier, "Négociations de paix au Burundi," supra note 471, at 39, describing this consequence of the UN anti-amnesty position in the case of Burundi. An equally dilatory and polarized dynamic between the United Nations and the national government has been visible for nearly two years in Nepal, too, in relation to a proposed national TRC there.

478. As a result of the UN position, debates about new truth commissions have frequently centered on the kind of amnesty-granting power a commission should have, with national authorities tending to favor a broad power along the lines of the South African model and local NGOs and international stakeholders tending to favor a narrower power. This has led to truth commission mandates that end up including amnesty-granting or amnesty-recommending powers for crimes that are of comparatively little significance relative to the atrocities under investigation. See, e.g., An Act to Establish the Truth and Reconciliation Commission of Liberia, 2005 (Liberia), sec. 26(g); The Truth, Justice, and Reconciliation Commission Bill, 2008 (Kenya), Part III. This also has had the result of distracting attention away from a potentially better means of securing the truth from perpetrators of serious crimes, namely, the insertion of a commission subpoena and questioning power combined with a qualified guarantee of use immunity. See Part II, Section 2.3, "Exhaustion of leniency options short of amnesty to end the blackmail."

479. As already noted, the United Nations boycotted the Indonesian-Timorese Commission on Truth and Friendship because the commission had the explicit authority to recommend amnesty for international crimes – a power that it did not exercise in the end. See, e.g., M. Hirst, "An Unfinished Truth: An Analysis of the Commission of Truth and Friendship's Final Report on the 1999 Atrocities in East Timor," International Center for Transitional Justice and others, March 2009, at 26: "The commission made a clear decision not to recommend amnesty or measures for the rehabilitation of anyone wrongly accused of human rights violations. An important reason for this was that the CTF did not establish a fair process open to all for receiving and processing amnesty applications, or a process for investigating individual cases. However in respect of amnesty the CTF also recognized that the alleged perpetrators who appeared in the hearings had not provided 'full cooperation,' reflecting the commission's view that these witnesses had either failed to 'testify truthfully, or had not shown any remorse'."

480. See Section 6.3, "Alternatives to the current UN position."

481. See L. Joinet, "Question of the Impunity of Perpetrators of Human Rights Violations (Civil and Political)," supra note 26, at para. 49: "To those who might be tempted to regard the set of principles proposed here as an obstacle to national reconciliation, I would answer this: these principles are not legal standards in the strict sense, but guiding principles intended not to thwart reconciliation but to avoid distortions in policies so that, once beyond the first stage, which is more 'conciliation' than reconciliation, the foundations of a 'just and lasting reconciliation' may be laid." During a presentation in March 2008 in Paris at an ICTJ Essentials Course, Joinet said that the international position on amnesty should not be unbending but should, instead, be

based on a kind of "relative untouchability," because norms require "oxygen" to be relevant in the real world.

482. D. Cassel, "Lessons from the Americas," supra note 413, at 229, describing a potential application of the policy-oriented approach of the New Haven school of legal theory to the issue of amnesty. As Juan Méndez has similarly noted, "the law provides a framework, not a straightjacket." J. Méndez, "Peace, Justice and Prevention: Dilemmas and False Dilemmas," in M. Bleeker, ed., *Dealing with the Past and Transitional Justice* (Conference Paper 1/2006, Federal Department of Foreign Affairs), at 17.

483. See, e.g., D. Orentlicher, "'Settling Accounts' Revisited: Reconciling Global Norms with Local Agency" (2007) 1 Int'l J. Transitional Justice 1, at 14. See also D. Cassel, "Lessons from the Americas," ibid., at 204: "In Guatemala in 1996, for example, one of the few cards held by amnesty opponents was the argument that the international community would not accept a blanket amnesty for crimes against humanity. While the United Nations' record in Guatemala was far from exemplary, as discussed below, it did not entirely concede this issue. If it had, the amnesty would have been broader. In short, the world and regional community's posture toward amnesties is important on both international and national planes."

484. D. Orentlicher, "'Settling Accounts' Revisited," ibid., at 14 and 22.

485. See C. Trumbull, "Giving Amnesty a Second Chance," supra note 63, at 315.

486. Admittedly, even in the absence of an amnesty prohibition, mediators and negotiating parties only can offer amnesty in the form of immunity from national courts. It is impossible, in the absence of an explicit Security Council resolution, for mediators or negotiating parties to offer or secure immunity from an international, hybrid, or foreign court. However, this does not change the central point about the risk of removing an important bargaining chip.

487. See, e.g., Human Rights Watch, "Selling Justice Short: Why Accountability Matters for Peace," July 2009, at 45: "As agreed during the 2002 Sun City peace talks, the transitional government passed an amnesty law that granted amnesty for engaging in acts of war, but specifically excluded amnesty for war crimes, crimes against humanity, and genocide. Despite setting a marker that such crimes were punishable, individuals with a known record of human rights abuses were integrated into the government and the army, with officials making no serious effort to investigate or prosecute them."

488. For example, Burundi's 2003 provisional immunity law, discussed earlier, explicitly excluded international crimes from its ambit but was used in practice as a pretext for the release of more than three thousand prisoners, many of whom likely were associated with genocidal acts committed in the country. C. Sculier, "Négociations de paix au Burundi," supra note 471, at 36; S. Vandeginste, "Transitional Justice for Burundi: A Long and Winding Road," supra note 433, at 411–3.

489. UN Charter (adopted June 26, 1945, entered into force October 24, 1945) 1 U.N.T.S. 16, art. 2(2): "All Members, in order to ensure to all of them the rights and benefits resulting from membership, shall fulfill in good faith the obligations assumed by them in accordance with the present Charter." See also Vienna Convention, art. 26, which

declares the so-called *pact sunt servanda* principle: "Every treaty in force is binding upon the parties to it and must be performed by them in good faith."

490. *AZAPO and Others v. President of the Republic of South Africa and Others*, supra note 140, at para. 24. See also ibid., at para. 32: "The amnesty contemplated is not a blanket amnesty against criminal prosecution for all and sundry, granted automatically as a uniform act of compulsory statutory amnesia. It is specifically authorised for the purposes of effecting a constructive transition towards a democratic order."

491. See, e.g., G. Meintjes and J. Méndez, "Reconciling Amnesties with Universal Jurisdiction" (2000) 2 Int'l Law FORUM *du droit international* 76, at 85, noting "it is sometimes difficult to ascertain whether the democratic government is operating under coercion or out of its own conscientious beliefs about what the country needs." See also A. Neier, "Emilio Mignone Lecture on behalf of the International Center for Transitional Justice," October 15, 2008, citing Carlos Nino who argued that "what may appear to the international community to be passivity on the part of a government may actually be the active safeguarding against future violations at the cost of forgoing prosecutions."

492. See, e.g., G. Meintjes and J. Méndez, "Reconciling Amnesties with Universal Jurisdiction," ibid., at 95. See also J. Snyder and L. Vinjamuri, "A Midwife for Peace," International Herald Tribune, September 26, 2006: "In a world of failed states and weak institutions – a world where politics in fact often trumps law – prosecutors should show deference to responsible political leaders who have the skills and the mandate to make choices based on prudence and political consequences."

493. W. Schabas, "Amnesty, the Sierra Leone Truth and Reconciliation Commission and the Special Court for Sierra Leone," supra note 416, at 163–4.

494. R. Fisher and W. Ury, *Getting to Yes: Negotiating Agreement without Giving In* (New York: Houghton Mifflin, 1991), at 98: "Having a bottom line makes it easier to resist pressure and temptations of the moment. . . . But the protection afforded by adopting a bottom line involves high costs. It limits your ability to benefit from what you learn during negotiation. By definition, a bottom line is a position that is not to be changed. To that extent, you have shut your ears, deciding in advance that nothing the other party says could cause you to raise or lower your bottom line."

495. Ibid., at 99.

496. Ibid., at 163. It should be noted, however, that even interest-based negotiation and mediation must track, and take place in the shadow of, international law.

497. Note, however, that the flexible approach would still evade the issue of the position's costs. That is because the mere existence of the position shifts how parties negotiate in the first place. In other words, the United Nations does not openly indicate that it is flexible in its application of the position, and therefore parties do not expect such flexibility in practice – and there is nothing about its current practice to augur otherwise.

498. On the general debate about deterrence arguments in this context see, e.g., D. Wippman, "Atrocities, Deterrence, and the Limits of International Justice" (1999) 23 Fordham Int'l L.J. 473; J. Sarkin and E. Daly, "Too Many Questions, Too Few Answers: Reconciliation in Transitional Societies" (2004) 35 Colum. Hum. Rts. L. Rev. 661.

499. For this reason, the Sierra Leone Truth and Reconciliation Commission was "unable to condemn the resort to amnesty by those who negotiated the Lomé Peace Agreement" as too high a price for peace. Witness to Truth, *Report of the Sierra Leone Truth and Reconciliation Commission* (Accra: GPL Press, 2004), at 365.

500. See, e.g., M. Osiel, "Modes of Participation in Mass Atrocity," supra note 100, at 809: "Persuading declining dictators and their minions to part with power is never easy. Their repressive policies are often self-sustaining. Having resorted for so long to sticks, these become sunk costs, as in an experienced cadre of secret police."

501. See, generally, A. Schlunck, *Amnesty versus Accountability: Third Party Intervention Dealing with Gross Human Rights Violations in Internal and International Conflicts* (Berlin: Verlag A. Spitz, 2000), chapter 1 ("The Spoiler Problem").

502. J. Snyder and L. Vinjamuri, "Trials and Errors," supra note 84, at 13.

503. The lack of an amnesty or exile option for the leaders also may have the perverse result of increased violence by middle- and low-level perpetrators. See, e.g., C. Dugger, "Mugabe Aides Are Said to Use Violence to Gain Amnesty," N.Y. Times, April 9, 2009: "President Robert Mugabe's top lieutenants are trying to force the political opposition into granting them amnesty for their past crimes by abducting, detaining and torturing opposition officials and activists, according to senior members of Mr. Mugabe's party . . . now that the opposition has a place in the nation's new government, these strongmen worry that they are suddenly vulnerable to prosecution, especially for crimes committed during last year's election campaign as the world watched. To protect themselves, some of Mr. Mugabe's lieutenants are trying to implicate opposition officials in a supposed plot to overthrow the president, hoping to use it as leverage in any amnesty talks or to press the opposition into quitting the government altogether, ruling party officials said. . . . Mr. Mugabe's lieutenants, part of an inner circle called the Joint Operations Command, know that their 85-year-old leader may not be around much longer to shield them, and they fear losing not just their power and ill-gotten wealth, but also their freedom, officials in the party said."

504. See, e.g., K. Sikkink and C. Walling, "The Impact of Human Rights Trials in Latin America," supra note 97, at 441: "The most crucial ingredient of a rule of law system is the idea that no one is above the law. As such, it is difficult to build a rule of law system while simultaneously ignoring recent gross violations of political and civil rights, and failing to hold past and present government officials accountable for those violations."

505. M. Pensky, "Amnesty on Trial," supra note 41, at 19–20.

506. See, e.g., L. Olson, "Provoking the Dragon on the Patio, Matters of Transitional Justice: Penal Repression vs. Amnesties" (2006) 88 Int'l Rev. Red Cross 275, at 289: "Is not the disquiet caused by grants of amnesty perhaps lessened by the knowledge that the alleged violators are not free from prosecution outside the State (at least for war crimes or other crimes for which States have established universal jurisdiction)?" The growing Latin American jurisprudence on forced disappearances as continuing crimes – according to which an unresolved case of disappearance cannot be the subject of amnesty – is yet another reason to afford more, not less, flexibility in the design of

amnesties. On the same subject, see UN Declaration on the Protection of All Persons from Enforced Disappearances, supra note 198, art. 17.

507. See, generally, Part II, Section 4.4.2, "Conditions for retaining individual grants of amnesty."

508. Dwight Newman argues that a balancing approach ("permissive amnesty rule") "risks some of the gains, but is more sensitive to local circumstances of states in desperate need." D. Newman, "The Rome Statute, Some Reservations Concerning Amnesties, and a Distributive Problem," supra note 158, at 353.

509. M. Pensky, "Amnesty on Trial," supra note 41, at 17: "As a way of beginning an evaluation of the range of arguments justifying the anti-amnesty norm, it's helpful to look first at its opponents. These opponents are just as inappropriately thought of as 'pro-amnesty' as arguments for the limited toleration of abortions are thought of as 'pro-abortion.'"

510. As Alex Boraine, the former vice chair of the South African TRC, rightly argues, "Every attempt should be made to assist countries to find their own solutions provided that there is no blatant disregard of fundamental human rights." A. Boraine, *A Country Unmasked* (Oxford: Oxford University Press, 2001), at 433.

Part II: The Design of Amnesties

1. Professor Michael Scharf similarly describes amnesty as a "bargaining tool of last resort." M. Scharf, "From the eXile Files: An Essay on Trading Justice for Peace" (2006) 63 Wash. & Lee L. Rev. 339, at 347. Discussing the amnesty adopted in the 1999 Lomé Peace Agreement for Sierra Leone, Priscilla Hayner gives the contrasting example of amnesty adopted as a first resort: "Many sources describe the amnesty as the first item agreed on, and note that it was settled quickly as 'a prerequisite for any meaningful negotiation'. One participant reports that the government began the discussions in the first meeting of the political committee by offering a blanket amnesty to the RUF. . . . The amnesty was offered as an incentive, to move things forward." P. Hayner, "Negotiating Peace in Sierra Leone: Confronting the Justice Challenge," International Center for Transitional Justice and Center for Humanitarian Dialogue, December 2007, at 13.

2. L. Mallinder, *Amnesty, Human Rights and Political Transitions: Bridging the Peace and Justice Divide* (Oxford: Hart, 2008), at 239, citing the criterion applied by the Israeli Supreme Court in *Barzilai v. Government of Israel* (Shin Bet Affair) [1986] HCJ 428/86 IsrSC 40(3), 505.

3. A parallel may be drawn with derogation clauses in human rights instruments. Even though derogations must be of a temporary nature, whereas amnesties are usually permanent, such clauses illustrate that international law recognizes the need for deviation from certain norms in circumstances of extreme exigency. See Part I, Section 4.2, "Treaty sources implicitly related to amnesties."

4. Concerning state practice, Louise Mallinder notes, "[M]any amnesty processes seem to have been introduced as a response to a genuine belief that a failure to do so would result in further violence. Substantive grounds for this belief could include

threatening statements or actions by the military or insurgent groups; continuing low-level violence; splintering of extremes away from parties to the peace processes; unwillingness of insurgents to disarm; or a lack of mutual trust among the parties of a transitional government that could cause the political institutions to collapse." L. Mallinder, *Amnesty, Human Rights and Political Transitions*, supra note 2, at 411. See also C. Trumbull, "Giving Amnesty a Second Chance" (2007) 25 Berkeley J. Int'l L. 283, at 321.

5. See, generally, W. Zartman, "The Time of Peace Initiatives: Hurting Stalemates and Ripe Moments" (2001) 1 Global Rev. Ethnopolitics 8. "The concept is based on the notion that when the parties find themselves locked in a conflict from which they cannot escalate to victory and this deadlock is painful to both of them (although not necessarily in equal degree or for the same reasons), they seek an alternative policy or Way Out:" ibid., at 8.

6. T. Friedman, "It's All about Leverage", N.Y. Times, June 1, 2008. The ability to exert pressure or gain leverage varies obviously. It is inherently more difficult to exert pressure on a permanent Security Council member and nuclear power like Russia than on a small and impoverished country like Gabon or Bhutan.

7. G. Evans, *The Responsibility to Protect* (Washington, DC: Brookings Institution Press, 2008), at 114–5.

8. See ibid., at 111–5, where the author provides relevant examples of the use of each of these measures.

9. See, e.g., ibid., at 113, where the author explains how the financial sanctions against South Africa, "involving the cooperation of governments and banks in denying or limiting credit to the South African government and local companies," were successful. "It was conceded outright by (senior ministers and officials) – including the finance minister and the South African Reserve Bank governor – that it was these sanctions, more than any other form of external pressure, that had ultimately forced South Africa to the negotiating table." See also ibid., at 114 concerning the effectiveness of "smart sanctions," which are sanctions targeted against specific individuals, usually political leaders, as opposed to whole countries in order to avoid the collective harms caused by broader sanctions.

10. See, e.g., M. Freeman, *Truth Commissions and Procedural Fairness* (New York: Cambridge University Press, 2006), at 59–62. The case for an inquiry in such a situation can be strengthened by the use of satellite imagery of abuses. See, e.g., J. Page, "Satellite images of Sri Lanka conflict used in war crimes inquiry", The Times, May 22, 2009. "US military satellites secretly monitored Sri Lanka's conflict zone through the latter stages of the war against the Tamil Tigers and American officials are examining images for evidence of war crimes, The Times has learnt. The images are of a higher resolution than any that are available commercially and could bolster the case for an international war crimes inquiry . . . "

11. See, e.g., W. Schabas, *The UN International Criminal Tribunals: The Former Yugoslavia, Rwanda and Sierra Leone* (Cambridge: Cambridge University Press, 2006). See also P. Hayner, "The Challenge of Justice in Negotiating Peace: Lessons from Liberia and Sierra Leone" (Paper presented at the the Building a Future on Peace and Justice

conference, Nuremberg, June 25–27, 2007), at 4: "While certainly not assured in every case, it is clear that in some cases an indictment (such as of Charles Taylor) or arrest (such as rebel leader Foday Sankoh, ten months after the Lomé Accord) can sometimes have a powerful and positive impact on the negotiation or implementation of a peace agreement."

12. See, e.g., "Situation in Darfur: Observations of the United Nations High Commissioner for Human Rights invited in Application of Rule 103 of the Rules of Procedure and Evidence," ICC-02/05 (10 October 2006), Executive Summary: "[T]he High Commissioner has called for an increased visible presence of the International Criminal Court in Sudan, as she believes that carefully tailored strategies can operate effectively to conduct investigations. The International Criminal Court's presence on the ground would also importantly contribute, among other international deployments in the country, to a proactive presence increasing the level of protection perceived and enjoyed by the affected population."

13. See, generally, Part I, Section 5, "Amnesties and the ICC" section. But see also N. Grono, "The Role of the ICC in Peace Processes: Mutually Reinforcing or Mutually Exclusive?" IPPR briefing paper, November 28, 2006: "In Uganda's case, the ICC has received good cooperation from Ugandan authorities, and almost none from the international community. If the international community had provided real assistance in executing the warrants – in the form of intelligence and enhancement of the Ugandan special forces' capabilities – then the LRA leadership may well have been arrested, and it wouldn't be necessary to talk of trading peace for justice."

14. In this regard, see L. Mallinder, *Amnesty, Human Rights and Political Transitions*, supra note 2, at 111–3, where the author discusses the related question of whether individuals are entitled to refuse amnesty and go to court to prove their innocence. See also Article 10 of Law 33/1993 (Djibouti) and Article 43 of Law 53-681/1953 (France), both of which explicitly protect the right of an amnesty beneficiary to seek to establish his or her innocence before a court.

15. See, e.g., E. Aspinall, "Peace without justice? The Helsinki peace process in Aceh," Centre for Humanitarian Dialogue, April 2008, at 19, describing Indonesian Presidential Decree No. 22 of 2005 granting a general amnesty to persons involved in GAM (rebel) activities: "During both the negotiations and the implementation of the MOU, it was never suggested by either party that the amnesty would apply to individuals from the government side. For government officials, doing so would have been an admission of culpability that would have undermined all their previous assertions that government troops had operated lawfully and that a framework for protecting human rights was already in place. That the amnesty applied only to GAM was, perhaps ironically, a sign of the government's strength."

16. In this respect, negotiating stances on prosecutions in the context of peace talks might be best understood as utilitarian strategies rather than positions of principle. See, generally, P. Hazan, *Judging War, Judging History* (Stanford: Stanford University Press, forthcoming 2010), Epilogue.

17. See, generally, C. Bell, *On the Law of Peace: Peace Agreements and the Lex Pacificatoria* (Oxford: Oxford University Press, 2008). Bell observes at 7: "In the early 1990s

mediators often aimed to reach agreement as the endpoint of a peace process, but now the signing of a peace agreement appears as the start of an equally difficult process of social, physical, economic, legal and political reconstruction."

18. On preventive deployment in Macedonia, see G. Evans, *The Responsibility to Protect*, supra note 7, at 56 and 102-3; on South African troops in Burundi, see ibid., at 59.

19. Ibid., at 123: "For most new missions, in fact, Chapter VII mandates have now become routine. These kinds of 'coercive protection' missions are still properly described as peacekeeping . . . rather than peace enforcement operations because . . . they are embarked upon with a reasonable expectation that force may not be needed at all.". However, it remains the case "that there is not a great deal a peacekeeping mission can do when there is no peace to keep": ibid., at 124.

20. On R2P generally, see ibid. At 41, the author explains that R2P entails three interrelated responsibilities, namely, the responsibilities to prevent, react, and rebuild, the former being the most important.

21. But see the African Union's Constitutive Act, which includes a provision for "the right of the Union to intervene in a member state pursuant to a decision of the [AU] assembly in respect of grave circumstances, namely: war crimes, genocide and crimes against humanity," citing a new principle of "non-indifference."

22. Department of Public Information, United Nations, "Secretary-General Defends, Clarifies 'Responsibility to Protect' at Berlin Event on 'Responsible Sovereignty: International Cooperation for a Changed World,'" July 15, 2008, SG/SM/11701.

23. M. Freeman and G. van Ert, *International Human Rights Law* (Toronto: Irwin Law, 2004), at 526–30.

24. "Secretary-General Defends, Clarifies 'Responsibility to Protect'", supra note 22: "Today, the responsibility to protect is a concept, not yet a policy; an aspiration, not yet a reality."

25. See, e.g., G. Evans, *The Responsibility to Protect*, supra note 7, at 26, where he reviews the R2P-like coercive interventions, inter alia, by the British in Sierra Leone, the African Union in Darfur, NATO in Kosovo, and the Australians in East Timor.

26. See, e.g., "Defensive Gestures," The Economist, July 24, 2008: "Mr Obama's message was aimed precisely at countries like Belgium, a small but rich place with almost 40,000 men and women in its armed forces. Only 1,103 Belgian troops are deployed overseas. The largest contingent is with NATO in Afghanistan, guarding Kabul airport. But fearing casualties, the Belgian government has ruled that its troops may not leave the airfield. Another group serves with the United Nations in Lebanon, clearing mines and running a field hospital. Its deployment in 2006 sparked a squabble among Belgium's military trade unions over how dangerous the Lebanese mission might be. A few Belgians also serve in the EU mission in Chad: some 75 soldiers are busily building and repairing EU camps there. Belgium may be an extreme example of Euro-timidity. But Germany also keeps its soldiers well away from Afghan regions with heavy fighting. Spain has some 150,000 men and women in its armed forces. Yet its Socialist government has ruled that no more than 3,000 Spanish troops may serve overseas at any one time (to avoid overstretch, it says). And so it goes on."

27. See, e.g., T. Royle, "How the World's Richest Countries Arm the Poorest," Sunday Herald, June 26, 2005. See also the Control Arms Campaign Web site, at http://www.controlarms.org/en.

28. See, generally, http://www.responsibilitytoprotect.org/, where there is an R2P campaign page for a variety of specific country situations. The inaction on these cases should not, however, obscure the overall 40 percent reduction in conflicts since 1992 and the increase in "activity in conflict prevention, conflict management, negotiated peacemaking, and postconflict peacebuilding activity." G. Evans, *The Responsibility to Protect*, supra note 7, at 234–5.

29. On the history of how and why such failures occur, see, e.g., S. Power, *"A Problem from Hell": America and the Age of Genocide* (New York: Perennial, 2002); B. Valentino, "Still Standing By: Why America and the International Community Fail to Prevent Genocide and Mass Killing" (2003) 1 Perspectives on Politics 565.

30. See, e.g., Sierra Leone Truth and Reconciliation Commission, Final Report, at chap. 6, para. 20: "The Commission subscribes to the general proposition that there will be circumstances where a trade of peace for amnesty represents the least bad of the available alternatives."

31. Admittedly, some governments may refuse to publicly negotiate forms of leniency with groups that they may have characterized, over many years, as unredeemable terrorists. However, the constraints of such positioning would not preclude private negotiations that, as confidence between the parties builds up over time, could eventually generate a softening in the government's characterizations of the armed group, the onset of public negotiations, and ultimately a formal agreement.

32. See, e.g., International Council on Human Rights Policy, *Negotiating Justice? Human Rights and Peace Agreements* (2006), at 96. See also Part I discussion of de facto amnesties.

33. See, e.g., J. Snyder and L. Vinjamuri, "Trials and Errors: Principle and Pragmatism in Strategies of International Justice" (2004) 28 Int'l Security 5, at 8. The full text of the (Bonn) Agreement on Provisional Arrangements in Afghanistan pending the Re-establishment of Permanent Government Institutions (2001) is accessible at www.icrc.org.

34. See, e.g., Human Rights Watch, "Submission to the African Union High-Level Panel on Darfur," June 29, 2009. The full text of the Comprehensive Agreement between The Government of The Republic of The Sudan and The Sudan People's Liberation Movement/Sudan People's Liberation Army is accessible at www.unmis.org.

35. Perpetrators do not necessarily fear an absence of amnesty per se. They primarily fear what an amnesty shields them from, namely domestic prosecution and punishment. Consequently, in the absence of any credible risk of prosecution, they may be prepared to accept an amnesty-less arrangement.

36. See, e.g., C. Bell, *On the Law of Peace*, supra note 17, at 173. Referring to amnesties and trials, Bell notes that "peace agreements rely heavily on 'constructive ambiguity' for the areas of strongest disagreement."

37. Comprehensive Peace Agreement Between the Government of Liberia and the Liberians United for Reconciliation and Democracy (LURD) and the Movement

for Democracy in Liberia (MODEL) and Political Parties, 2003 (Liberia), art. XXXIV.

38. Arusha Peace and Reconciliation Agreement for Burundi, August 28, 2000, Protocol I, chap. 1, arts. 6 and 8.

39. Note that, while reduced sentence schemes typically involve serving sentences in prisons in one's own country, another option may be to serve the sentences in residence but under supervision, or in a prison in a third country. Such options are increasingly visible in criminal sentencing practice internationally.

40. However, the UN Working Group on Enforced or Involuntary Disappearances warns against "imposing insignificant sanctions in order to give the perpetrators the benefit of the right not to be tried twice for the same crime which would in fact result in impunity." Working Group on Enforced or Involuntary Disappearances, General Comments on Article 18 of the Declaration, January 12, 1998, UN Doc. E/CN.4/2006/56, para. 2. The point is that criminal sentences, whether full or reduced, should ordinarily be proportionate to the seriousness of the crime.

41. C. Botero Marino et al., *La ley de alternatividad penal y justicia transicional* (2004), Fundación Social and International Center for Transitional Justice, at 38–40. The relevant legislation provided that complete submission to the Colombian justice system and the confession of at least one crime were requirements for avoiding extradition. Ibid., at 38.

42. Ibid., at 40.

43. R. Uprimny, "Transitional Justice without Transition? Possible Lessons from the Use (and Misuse) of Transitional Justice Discourse in Colombia" (Paper presented at the Building a Future on Peace and Justice conference, Nuremberg, June 25–27, 2007): "So, many paramilitary leaders have been indicted for drug smuggling and requested in extradition by the U.S. government. The Colombian government responded that as long as the paramilitary continued in the [demobilization] process, they would not be extradited."

44. Law 975, June 21, 2005 (Colombia). On the implementation of the law, see, e.g., C Díaz, "Colombia's Bid for Justice and Peace," in K. Ambos, J. Large, and M. Wierda, eds., *Building a Future on Peace and Justice* (Berlin: Springer, 2009), at 491–7.

45. Colombian Constitutional Court, Judgment C-370 (2006).

46. ICTJ website (Colombia page), at http://www.ictj.org/en/where/region2/514.html. The website also states: "The constitutional decision ensures the rights of victims to participate actively in all stages of the criminal process. Paramilitary members not cooperating fully or returning to crime will lose the benefit of reduced penalties and automatically receive substantial prison terms." The alternative sentence consists of "deprivation of liberty" and must be for a minimum term of five years and a maximum term of eight years.

47. The amnesty laws in question are Law 782/2002 (Colombia) and Executive Decree 128/2003 (Colombia).

48. See, e.g., M. Freeman and G. van Ert, *International Human Rights Law*, supra note 23, at 477, where *gacaca* is described.

49. Proyecto de Ley Estatutaria no. 85, 2003 (Colombia).

50. C. Botero Marino et al., *La ley de alternatividad penal y justicia transicional*, supra note 41, at 30–42.

51. See, e.g., M. Freeman, *Truth Commissions and Procedural Fairness*, supra note 10, at 77–8, where the Timor-Leste model is described.

52. B. Garner and H. Black, eds., *Black's Law Dictionary*, 8th ed. (St. Paul, MN: Thomson/West, 2006).

53. See, e.g., ICTY and ICTR Common Rule 90(E). See also "Report of the International Commission of Inquiry on Darfur to the United Nations Secretary-General pursuant to Security Council Resolution 1564 of 18 September 2004," January 25, 2005, UN Doc. S/2005/60, para. 618: "'Use immunity' may be held to be acceptable in international law, at least in the circumstances of a [truth commission]: it contributes to the revelation of truth. Perpetrators are constrained to reveal all, albeit on the limited assurance that their testimonies at the [truth commission] will not be used against them in criminal proceedings. Nevertheless, society can hold them accountable for the crimes they admit to have committed, and they may still be prosecuted, the only evidence not usable against them being the one they gave at the [truth commission] hearings."

54. See, generally, M. Freeman, *Truth Commissions and Procedural Fairness*, supra note 10, at 251–7.

55. M. Scharf, "From the eXile Files," supra note 1, at 343. See also ibid., at 340: "Although the Geneva Conventions and the Genocide Convention require state parties to bring offenders to justice, on the eve of the 2003 invasion of Iraq, President George W. Bush offered to call off the attack if Saddam Hussein and his top lieutenants would agree to relinquish power and go into exile. This was no publicity stunt, as some have characterized it. Working through President Hosni Mubarak of Egypt, the United States actively pursued the matter with several Mideast countries, ultimately persuading Bahrain to agree to provide sanctuary to Hussein if he accepted the deal. When Hussein rejected the proposal, Bush promised that the Iraqi leader would be forced from power and prosecuted as a war criminal."

56. M. Pensky, "Amnesty on Trial: Impunity, Accountability, and the Norms of International Law" (2008) 1 Ethics & Global Politics 1, at 14.

57. As Nick Grono recounts, "In mid-2003, rebel groups were advancing on Monrovia, shelling the city and attempting to starve it into submission. Taylor declared his intention to stay and fight the rebels – but Nigeria's offer of asylum ensured Taylor fled Liberia in July. His departure enabled the deployment of West African peacekeepers, bringing a degree of peace to the country, and saving many lives. Certainly that was the view of Nigeria's President Obasanjo, who claimed[,] 'By giving this one man asylum I have saved thousands of lives. What more does the international community want?'" N. Grono, "The Role of the ICC in Peace Processes: Mutually Reinforcing or Mutually Exclusive?" IPPR briefing paper, November 28, 2006. See also J. Power, "Peacekeeping and Diplomacy: Why Liberia Is a Turning Point for Africa", International Herald Tribune, September 5, 2003.

58. M. Scharf "From the eXile Files," supra note 1, at 341.

59. See, e.g., G. Evans, *The Responsibility to Protect*, supra note 7, at 118 The damage to mediation efforts would have been significantly less if there were more explicit

terms to Taylor's asylum deal (just like there are in an amnesty) and a process for determining whether, when, and how those terms had been broken.

60. Ibid., at 118.

61. Zimbabwe's president, Robert Mugabe, cited the Taylor precedent as a disincentive for his own leaving power. P. Hayner, "Negotiating Justice: Guidance for Mediators," Center for Humanitarian Dialogue and International Center for Transitional Justice, February 2009, at 18. See also G. Evans, *The Responsibility to Protect*, supra note 7, at 118.

62. See, e.g., "Mauritania's ex-leader in Qatar," BBC News, August 22, 2005, describing Qatar's decision to offer asylum to the repressive former Mauritanian president, Maaouiya Ould Sid Ahmed Taya.

63. See, e.g., P. Hayner, "Negotiating Peace in Liberia: Preserving the Possibility for Justice," International Center for Transitional Justice and Centre for Humanitarian Dialogue, November 2007, at 16: "In retrospect, virtually everyone involved in the Lomé talks, or who closely observed them, now agrees without hesitation that an amnesty was necessary for a peace agreement to be reached. Whether some limitation or condition on the amnesty would have been possible, however, is still an open question."

64. In some contexts, though, the courts may have the final say about the interpretation of the amnesty's provisions. See, e.g., L. Vinjamuri, "Trends Regarding Peace Agreements and Accountability from 1980 to 2006" (Paper presented at the Building a Future on Peace and Justice conference, Nuremberg, June 25–27, 2007), at 3: "It is important to note that amnesty provisions are often subject to judicial interpretation and/or modification subsequent to the conclusion of the peace agreement, such that the provision actually implemented may be different from that originally included in the peace agreement."

65. See, generally, J. Klabbers, "The Right to Be Taken Seriously: Self-determination in International Law" (2006) 28 Human Rights Q. 186.

66. See, e.g., C. Trumbull, "Giving Amnesty a Second Chance," supra note 4, at 339–40, on consultation in Colombia; P. Hayner, "Negotiating Peace in Sierra Leone," supra note 1, at 9, on consultation in Sierra Leone.

67. See, e.g., "The Rule of Law and Transitional Justice in Conflict and Post-Conflict Societies: Report of the Secretary-General," UN Doc. S/2004/616 (2004), paras. 16 and 19.

68. P. Vinck and E. Stover, "'Nothing about Us, without Us' Responding to the Needs of Survivors of Mass Violence during and after Armed Conflicts" (Paper presented at the Building a Future on Peace and Justice conference, Nuremberg, June 25–27, 2007), at 3.

69. Donors have a key role to play in making such processes less elite. See, e.g., P. Hayner, "The Challenge of Justice in Negotiating Peace," supra note 11, at 29: "Those willing to provide funds for the talks also largely determine who can attend, and how many. Civil society groups often have to raise funding independently, in order to take part."

70. C. Trumbull, "Giving Amnesty a Second Chance," supra note 4, at 323.

71. Consider in this regard the comments of Donald Steinberg, "Peace Missions and Gender Equality: Lessons from the Ground," speech to OSCE Round Table on Gender

and Security, Vienna, March 11, 2009. Steinberg explains how peace negotiations that exclude women as participants tend to result in inattention to vital issues such as "internal displacement, sexual violence, human trafficking, abuses by government and rebel security forces, and the rebuilding of maternal health care and girls' education." Discussing the 13 amnesties adopted in Angola during and after its civil war, he further notes, "Given the prominence of sexual abuse during the conflict, including rape as a weapon of war, amnesties meant that men with guns forgave other men with guns for crimes committed against women."

72. A good example of this is Uganda's Amnesty Act: "The amnesty process in Uganda was prompted by the Acholi Religious Leaders Peace Initiative (ARLPI), culminating in the Amnesty Act of 2000. . . . Its origins are unique compared to amnesty laws in other situations, as it is based on a consultation among victimized populations. A report by the Refugee Law Project shows that the Amnesty Act continues to enjoy broad popular support in the north, even though the process of reintegrating the perpetrators in the community is not as straightforward as sometimes claimed." See "Forgotten Voices: A Population-Based Survey of Attitudes about Peace and Justice in Northern Uganda," International Center for Transitional Justice and the Human Rights Center (University of California, Berkeley), July 2005, at 46. A key lesson learned from transitional justice is, precisely, that process matters as much as actual outcomes and results.

73. This may have been part of the motivation for the LRA's decision in Uganda to conduct its own victim consultation process during the course of peace talks in 2007. See, e.g., S. O. Egadu, "Uganda: LRA Set to Meet Victims," Institute of War and Peace Reporting, February 11, 2007.

74. P. Vinck and E. Stover, "'Nothing about Us, without Us,'" supra note 68, at 1.

75. See, e.g., "Ex-combatant Views of the Truth and Reconciliation Commission and the Special Court in Sierra Leone," September 2002; "Iraqi Voices: Attitudes toward Transitional Justice and Social Reconstruction," May 2004; "Colombian Perceptions and Opinions on Justice, Truth, Reparations, and Reconciliation," December 2006. All reports can be found at http://ictj.org/en/news/pubs/index.html.

76. See, generally, Freeman and van Ert, *International Human Rights Law*, supra note 48, at 38–9.

77. G. Simpson, "Transitional Justice and Peace Negotiations," unpublished paper, 2008, cited with permission.

78. P. Vinck and E. Stover, "'Nothing about Us, without Us,'" supra note 68, at 1, 3.

79. See, e.g., "Forgotten Voices," supra note 72, at 4, 5: "When respondents were asked whether they would accept amnesty if it were the only road to peace, 29 percent said no." "Sixty-five percent of respondents support the amnesty process for LRA members. However, only 4 percent said that amnesties should be granted unconditionally, and the vast majority noted that some form of acknowledgement and/or retribution should be required of all those granted amnesty."

80. As Professor Ruti Teitel observes, "The amnesty deliberations phase itself advances some of the transitional penal purposes, for these debates often imply legislative hearings and findings relating to past wrongdoing." R. Teitel, *Transitional Justice* (Oxford: Oxford University Press, 2000), 58–9.

81. P. Hayner, *Unspeakable Truths: Confronting State Terror and Atrocity* (New York: Routledge, 2001), at 201, describing the process for adopting South Africa's TRC legislation.

82. This appears to be the case in Burundi, where a process of national consultation on transitional justice options has endured scores of delays and other problems since 2006.

83. This was the case in Uruguay with respect to the Law Nullifying the State's Claim to Punish Certain Crimes (Ley de Caducidad), Law No. 15.848, 1986 (Uruguay). See judgment of Uruguayan Supreme Court (May 2, 1988), concerning the constitutionality of the law. Though not an amnesty law, the Colombian Law on Justice and Peace also was reviewed by the country's Constitutional Court, as noted earlier.

84. Various amnesty scholars list democratic adoption as an indicator of an amnesty's legitimacy. See, e.g., D. Cassel, "Lessons from the Americas: Guidelines for International Response to Amnesties for Atrocities" (1996) 59 Law & Contemp. Probs. 197, at 219; R. Slye, "The Legitimacy of Amnesties under International Law and General Principles of Anglo-American Law: Is a Legitimate Amnesty Possible?" (2002) 43 Va. J. Int'l L. 174, at 245. It should be noted, of course, that an increase in an amnesty's democratic legitimacy makes it less susceptible to subsequent overturning and hence more permanent. That may be a bad result from a perspective of domestic criminal prosecution but not necessarily from a broad human rights perspective, to the extent that the amnesty facilitates the conditions for greater human rights protection going forward.

85. L. Mallinder, *Amnesty, Human Rights and Political Transitions*, supra note 2, at 43.

86. J. Errandonea, "Droits de l'homme et État de Droit: le cas de la loi d'amnistie en Uruguay," in R. Fregosi, ed., *Droits de l'homme et consolidation de la démocratie en Amérique du sud* (Paris: L'Harmattan, forthcoming 2009).

87. N. Valji, "Ghana's National Reconciliation Commission," September 2006, International Center for Transitional Justice and the Centre for the Study of Violence and Reconciliation, at 1.

88. "Algeria: New Amnesty Law Will Ensure Atrocities Go Unpunished," press release of ICTJ and others, March 1, 2006. See also "Myanmar Declares New Constitution Ratified," L.A. Times, May 16, 2008, which describes a referendum in Burma on a new constitution that included a broad self-amnesty provision. The referendum was held only days after a devastating cyclone ravaged the country.

89. L. Mallinder, *Amnesty, Human Rights and Political Transitions*, supra note 2, at 34, discussing the case of Greece in 1973.

90. For example, the Portuguese, Polish, Belgian, Russian, Ukrainian, and Italian constitutions prohibit referenda for clemency measures such as amnesty. F. Paris, "Amnistie, prescription et grâce en Europe," October 2005, UMR 8103 – Paris 1/CNRS, at 92. See also Human Rights Watch, "Selling Justice Short: Why Accountability Matters for Peace," July 2009, at 15: "A number of countries including the Democratic Republic of Congo, Côte d'Ivoire, Croatia, Ethiopia, and Venezuela have adopted legislation or constitutions that prohibit amnesties for the most serious crimes or that contain explicit exceptions to general amnesties for crimes under international law."

91. Working Group on Enforced or Involuntary Disappearances, "General Comment on Article 18 of the Declaration on the Protection of all Persons from Enforced Disappearance," UN Doc. E/CN.4/2006/56, para. 2: "An amnesty law should be considered as being contrary to the provisions of the Declaration even where endorsed by a referendum or similar consultation procedure, if directly or indirectly, as a consequence of its application or implementation, it results in any or all of the following: (a) Ending the State's obligations to investigate, prosecute and punish those responsible for disappearances, as provided for in Articles 4, 13, 14 and 16 of the Declaration. (b) Preventing, impeding or hindering the granting of adequate indemnification, rehabilitation, compensation and reparation as a result of the enforced disappearances, as provided for in Article 19 of the Declaration. (c) Concealing the names of the perpetrators of disappearance, thereby violating the right to truth and information, which can be inferred from Articles 4.2 and 9 of the Declaration. (d) Exonerating the perpetrators of disappearance, treating them as if they had not committed such an act, and therefore have no obligation to indemnify the victim, in contravention of Articles 4 and 18 of the Declaration. (e) Dismissing criminal proceedings or closing investigations against alleged perpetrators of disappearances or imposing insignificant sanctions in order to give the perpetrators the benefit of the right not to be tried twice for the same crime which would in fact result in impunity, thereby violating Article 4.1 of the Declaration."

92. C. Trumbull, "Giving Amnesty a Second Chance," supra note 4, at 323.

93. M. Freeman and G. van Ert, *International Human Rights Law*, supra note 48, at 46: "There is, however, an inherent tension between democracy and human rights. Whereas a primary objective of democracy is to reflect the voice of the majority within the state, a primary objective of human rights is to help protect the individual from the majority and the state. In short, democracy alone is insufficient to ensure human rights; constitutionalism, or the limitation of state power, is the necessary companion of democracy."

94. Consider, however, that if victims constitute a majority of the population, a simple majority should arguably be sufficient. Yet even then complications could arise because there could be a supermajority against amnesty in a country's nonconflict zones and a supermajority for amnesty in its conflict zones.

95. In many postconflict situations, the issue may be moot. Infrastructural and social devastation caused by years of war may make it too difficult to conduct a national referendum.

96. See, e.g., Ghana National Reconciliation Commission Report, October 2004, para. 8.28.

97. C. Trumbull, "Giving Amnesty a Second Chance," supra note 4, at 323: "A truly democratically enacted amnesty requires that the citizens of the country have access to objective information, sufficient to weigh adequately the costs and the benefits of enacting the amnesty legislation. The ability to vote is of little benefit if the state is able to distort or limit the information that is available to the voters."

98. See, by analogy, the influential *Oakes* test, developed by the Canadian Supreme Court. Freeman and van Ert, *International Human Rights Law,* supra note 23, at 199–201. See,

also Draft Articles on the Responsibility of States for Internationally Wrongful Acts, UN Doc. A/56/10 (2001), art. 51, which deals with the principle of proportionality in the context of countermeasures: "Countermeasures must be commensurate with the injury suffered, taking into account the gravity of the internationally wrongful act and the rights in question."

99. Indemnity Act No. 61, 1961 (South Africa); Indemnity Act No. 13, 1977 (South Africa). There were also indemnities in 1990 and 1992. These amnesty processes were individualized, but the TRC omitted to look at the applications submitted through these schemes to verify the accuracy of statements. L. Mallinder, "Indemnity, Amnesty, Pardon and Prosecution Guidelines in South Africa," (Working paper from *Beyond Legalism: Amnesties, Transition and Conflict Transformation* project, Institute of Criminology and Criminal Justice, Queen's University Belfast), February 2009, at 46–7.

100. Surprisingly often, human rights defenders in such situations initially overlook the ongoing application of past amnesties, as I discovered in working on transitional justice issues in places such as Zimbabwe, Colombia, and Sri Lanka.

101. P. Hayner, "Negotiating Peace in Sierra Leone," supra note 1, at 31.

102. United Nations Transitional Administration for East Timor, Regulation 2001/10 on the Establishment of a Commission for Reception, Truth and Reconciliation in East Timor.

103. The community service required under the Timorese truth commission process "usually consisted of a task performed once a week over a set period that was usually no longer than three months. Examples of required tasks included: the repair of public buildings, tree planting, the erection of a village flagpole, and cleaning of church grounds or other facilities." Commission for Reception, Truth and Reconciliation, "Chega! The CAVR Report," chap. 9, para. 112.

104. Roundtable on "Turkey's repentance and amnesty laws," Turkish Economic and Social Studies Foundation, Istanbul, March 8, 2008. See also "Iraq: Allaying Turkish Fears over Kurdish Ambitions," International Crisis Group, January 26, 2005, at 14, where it is recommended that Turkey consider issuing a broader amnesty for the PKK, which would cover the leadership in northern Iraq and not require amnesty applicants to inform on their colleagues; and "Thailand: Political Turmoil and the Southern Insurgency," International Crisis Group, August 28, 2008, at 13, where it is suggested that similiar factors are likely to complicate the implementation of an immunity scheme in Thailand geared toward southern insurgents, according to which eligible individuals could qualify for amnesty upon confessing their wrongdoing and agreeing to undergo six months of "reeducation" under military supervision.

105. Guatemala adopted six amnesties in the 1980s during the civil war. See L. Joinet, "Study on Amnesty Laws and Their Role in the Safeguard and Promotion of Human Rights," UN Doc. E/CN.4/Sub.2/1985/16/Rev.1, paras. 36–7, discussing the first four of these amnesties. By contrast, see "Ruling Palestine II: The West Bank Model?," International Crisis Group, July 17, 2008, at 7, describing an "amnesty understanding" reached between the Israeli government and the Palestinian Authority concerning Palestinian

militants: "In principle, the formula is straightforward: wanted men give up their weapons, promise to refrain from future armed activity and in most cases serve a probationary residency period at a PA installation. In return, Israel removes their names from its wanted list. The amnesty aims to reduce attacks by offering militants a path from resistance to normal lives and has significantly lessened the presence of armed men in Palestinian cities."

106. An alternative or additional option may be to create a defection-oriented amnesty scheme to try to weaken the armed group, and thus to diminish the bargaining position of the leadership. See, generally, Section 4.3.2, "The persons who are expressly eligible or ineligible."

107. Sometimes, however, the incentive is large enough to compensate for the absence of a credible or open threat, as, for example, when the main actors in an armed conflict reach an exhaustion-induced and amnesty-facilitated stalemate and agree to put a permanent end to the fighting. See, generally, W. Zartman, "The Time of Peace Initiatives: Hurting Stalemates and Ripe Moments," supra note 5.

108. See, e.g., M. G. Sesay and M. Suma, "Transitional Justice and DDR: The Case of Sierra Leone," in A. Patel, P. de Greiff, and L. Waldorf, eds., *Disarming the Past: Transitional Justice and Ex-combatants* (New York: Social Science Research Council, forthcoming 2009): "Since this blanket amnesty was a prime factor in enticing the RUF into DDR, its implicit rejection by the mandate of the Special Court and the shift from amnesty to prosecution raised concerns that this would threaten the fragile security situation in the country. The decision to prosecute human rights violators posed great difficulties for the success of any DDR initiatives, as it eliminated one of the incentives for combatants to lay down their arms: that they would not face prosecution for crimes committed during the conflict. Combatants saw the removal of amnesty originally accorded as a betrayal by all parties involved in the peace negotiations and this created huge problems for the NCDDR . . . Despite these setbacks, the public education campaigns of SCWG and other organizations, such as the Post-Conflict Reintegration Initiative for Development and Empowerment, greatly enhanced understanding of the SCSL among ex-combatants and gradually increased their support for the institution."

109. A registration form used by Sierra Leone's National Committee on Disarmament, Demobilization and Reintegration apparently stated in its first term of acceptance that, "in accordance with the Amnesty Conditions[,] you will be exempted from criminal prosecution, with regards to any crimes committed prior to your surrender." See R. Duthie, "Transitional Justice and Social Reintegration" (paper presented at the SIDDR Working Group 3: Reintegration and Peace Building meeting, New York, April 4–5, 2005), at 17–18.

110. See, e.g., "Forgotten Voices," supra note 72, at 40, concerning the case of Uganda: "There has also been much outreach to try to reassure the LRA that they will not be the subjects of revenge killings. Returnees are often required to take part in government organized outreach events. In Gulu, Radio FM Mega runs regular programs for returnees to call upon their former comrades to come out of the bush, and to offer reassurance that they have not been harmed."

111. See, e.g., P. de Greiff, "Theorizing Transitional Justice," in M. Williams, J. Elster and R. Nagy, eds., *Transitional Justice* (New York: NYU Press, forthcoming 2009),where the author contrasts the notions of internal coherence and external coherence. Internal coherence refers to the need to ensure that the different components of a legal or policy measure, in this case, an amnesty, are mutually coherent, aligned, and supportive of one another. The subsequent major section of this chapter addresses this question. External coherence refers to the notion that different policy measures should be maximally conceived and implemented as parts of a single, integrated policy.

112. See, e.g., Law 418, 1997 (Colombia), Title II, chaps. 1–7.

113. See, e.g., 1992 Ghana Constitution, Transitional Provisions, art. 35(2); Law 2003-309 (Ivory Coast), art. 10.

114. See, e.g., Comment by the International Center for Transitional Justice on the Bill Establishing a Truth and Reconciliation Commission in Indonesia (2005), http://www.ictj.org, at 6. See also Presidential Decree 261, 1974 (Greece), an amnesty that expressly precludes the right to compensation for those released from jail, making no exception for those who might have been victims of torture or miscarriages of justice.

115. See, e.g., Ordonnance 06-01 Portant Mise en Oeuvre de la Charte pour la Paix et la Réconciliation Nationale, 2006 (Algeria); International Center for Transitional Justice et al., "Press Release: Algeria: New Amnesty Law Will Ensure Atrocities Go Unpunished," March 1, 2006.

116. See, e.g., Arusha Peace and Reconciliation Agreement 2000 (Burundi), chapter 1, art. 8; Lomé Peace Accord, 1999 (Sierra Leone), arts. IX and XXI; Memorandum of Understanding between the Government of the Republic of Indonesia and the Free Aceh Movement, August 15, 2005, arts. 2 and 3.

117. See Section 4.5, "Maximum viability." See also Law No. 15.848, 1986 (Uruguay), art. 4, which creates an obligation on the state to immediately conduct an investigation into a case of forced disappearance on presentation of a formal complaint against an individual who may be covered under the amnesty law.

118. See, e.g., P. van Zyl, "Promoting Transitional Justice in Post-Conflict Societies," in *Security Governance in Post-Conflict Peacebuilding*, ed. A. Bryden and H. Hänggi (Geneva: Geneva Center for the Democratic Control of Armed Forces, 2005), at 225: "mechanisms such as truth commissions should not be introduced in order to offset decisions to grant amnesty or as efforts to salvage a degree of cosmetic acceptability in an agreement that essentially seeks to bury the past and deny victims their rights to justice, truth, and reparation."

119. Note, however, that achieving external coherence in domestic transitional justice measures is vastly more complicated in the context of a hovering and independent ICC.

120. See, e.g., Office of the United Nations High Commissioner for Human Rights (OHCHR), *Rule of Law Tools for Post-Conflict States: Reparations Programmes* (Geneva: United Nations, 2008); P. de Greiff, ed., *The Handbook on Reparations* (New York: Oxford University Press, 2006).

121. See, generally, R. Rubio-Marín, ed., *What Happened to the Women? Gender and Reparations for Human Rights Violations* (New York: Social Science Research Council, 2006); P. de Greiff and R. Duthie, eds., *Transitional Justice and Development* (New York: Social Science Research Council, 2009). An amnesty might also expressly provide for allocations of development funds to help communities that were particularly victimized in the past. Examples of such amnesties include, for example, Ley 35 por la cual se decreta una amnistía y se dictan normas tendientes al restablecimiento y preservación de la paz, 1982 (Colombia), art. 8: Peace Agreement between the National Committee of Chittagong Hill Tracts and the Parbattya Chattagram Janasanghati Samity, 1997 (Bangladesh); Decree 145-1996: Law of National Reconciliation, 1996 (Guatemala), art. 9.

122. Corrective amnesties tend to provide for the establishment or restoration of such legal rights and freedoms. Examples of such amnesties include Brazil's 1979 Amnesty Act, Law No 6.683, Lei Concede Anistia e Dá Outras Providências (reinstating pensions, providing death certificates to spouses of victims under an expedited process, and reinstating persons to prior positions under expedited process) and the Philippines' 1994 Proclamation No. 347 (restoring civil and political rights, and retirement benefits). In his original UN study on amnesties, Joinet listed the results a corrective amnesty should seek to ensure: immediate release of all political prisoners, right of political exiles to return, "relinquishment of all proceedings, penal or disciplinary," restoration of civil and political rights including "legalization of outlawed parties," "reinstatement in their jobs of persons dismissed for political reasons," and "right of victims of inhuman treatment or their families to compensation" including the family's "right to know." See L. Joinet, "Study on Amnesty Laws and Their Role in the Safeguard and Promotion of Human Rights," supra note 105, para. 81.

123. See, generally, OHCHR, *Rule of Law Tools for Post-Conflict States: Truth Commissions* (Geneva: United Nations, 2006); P. Hayner, *Unspeakable Truths: Confronting State Terror and Atrocity* (New York: Routledge, 2001); M. Freeman, *Truth Commissions and Procedural Fairness*, supra note 10.

124. J. Snyder and L. Vinjamuri, "Trials and Errors," supra note 33, at 20.

125. See, e.g., Lomé Peace Accord, 1999 (Sierra Leone), Part 5, art. XXV; Good Friday Agreement, 1998 (Northern Ireland), chap. 6.

126. See, e.g., Peace Agreement between the Government of El Salvador and the Frente Farabundo Martí para la Liberación Nacional, 1992, chap. 1; Peace Agreement between the Government of Liberia, LURD, MODEL and the Political Parties, 2003, supra note 37, part 4. See also L. Joinet, "Question of the Impunity of Perpetrators of Human Rights Violations (Civil and Political)," UN Doc. E/CN.4/Sub.2/1997/20/Rev1, para. 43: "Disbandment of parastatal armed groups: this is one of the hardest measures to enforce for; if not accompanied by action to reintegrate group members into society, the cure may be worse than the disease."

127. J. Snyder and L. Vinjamuri, "Trials and Errors," supra note 33, at 44: "Above all, external pressure and assistance should be targeted on future-oriented tasks such

as human rights training of police and military personnel, improved human rights monitoring of field operations, reform of military finances and military justice, and punishment of new abuses once the reforms are in place."

128. See, e.g., L. Joinet, "Question of the Impunity of Perpetrators of Human Rights Violations," supra note 126, at para. 43, which lists the following examples: "Repeal of all emergency laws, abolition of emergency courts and recognition of the inviolability and non-derogability of habeas corpus."

129. See, e.g., OHCHR, *Rule of Law Tools for Post-Conflict States: Vetting* (Geneva: United Nations, 2006).

130. See, e.g., International Center for Transitional Justice, *Census and Identification of Security System Personnel after Conflict* (January 2008).

131. See Section 4.4.2 "Conditions for retaining individual grants of amnesty."

132. See, e.g., the proposed Draft Protocol to the Rome Statute in A. O'Shea, *Amnesty for Crime in International Law and Practice* (The Hague: Kluwer Law International, 2002), at 334, where the author lists, inter alia, the following criterion for the United Nations to potentially endorse an amnesty: "Whether the state can give a commitment to prosecute those that do not apply for or do not qualify for amnesty."

133. R. Slye, "Amnesty, Truth, and Reconciliation: Reflections on the South African Amnesty Process," in R. Rotberg and D. Thompson, eds., *Truth vs. Justice: The Morality of Truth Commissions* (Princeton, NJ: Princeton University Press, 2000), at 183.

134. As previously noted, the legacy of the South African TRC's amnesty process has been tarnished unduly by the post-TRC failure to prosecute perpetrators of gross human rights violations who shunned the amnesty process or whose applications were rejected.

135. L. Fletcher and H. Weinstein, "Context, Timing and the Dynamics of Transitional Justice: A Historical Perspective" (2009) 31 Human Rights Q. 163, at 170. Fletcher and Weinstein criticize the assumption "that the 'tool kit' of (transitional justice) interventions is appropriate and productive, if one can only determine which intervention to deploy. Our concern is that this approach relies on the assumption that immediate intervention is necessary – it is assumed that *something* will work – the trick is to find out what."

136. See, e.g., M. Freeman, "Transitional Justice: Fundamental Goals and Unavoidable Complications" (2001) 28 Manitoba L.J. 113. See also L. Huyse, "The Process of Reconciliation," in D. Bloomfield, T. Barnes, and L. Huyse, eds., *Reconciliation after Violent Conflict: A Handbook* (Stockholm: International IDEA, 2003), at 27–32, where Huyse distinguishes among the time, timing, and tempo of reconciliation processes.

137. See, e.g., E. Aspinall, "Peace without Justice?," supra note 15, at 27: "The legal environment for [the MOU's Human Rights Court and Truth and Reconciliation Commission] is very complex and uncertain. At the time of writing, in late 2007, it is more that two years after the signing of the MOU, and little progress has been made in establishing either institution." As of June 2009, neither institution has been established.

138. See, e.g., L. Fletcher and H. Weinstein, "Context, Timing and the Dynamics of Transitional Justice," supra note 135, at 220, where the authors conclude: "Sustained focus on the underlying causes of the conflict is essential so that trials and truth commissions do not become a fetish but an invitation for on-going attention to address the societal fissures."

139. L. Joinet, "Study on Amnesty Laws and Their Role in the Safeguard and Promotion of Human Rights," supra note 105, para. 84.

140. See, generally, M. Freeman, "Amnesties and DDR Programs: An Integrated Approach," in A. Patel, P. de Greiff, and L. Waldorf, eds., *Disarming the Past: Transitional Justice and Ex-combatants* (New York: Social Science Research Council, forthcoming 2009).

141. See, e.g., International Council on Human Rights Policy, *Negotiating Justice? Human Rights and Peace Agreements*, supra note 32, at 72.

142. See, e.g., S. McReynolds, "Land Reform in El Salvador and the Chapultepec Peace Accord" (2002) 30 J. Peasant Stud. 135.

143. See, e.g., C. Manning, "Armed Opposition Groups into Political Parties: Comparing Bosnia, Kosovo, and Mozambique" (2004) 39 Studies in Comp. Int'l Development 1. External monitoring of the ongoing human rights situation also may be important. The UN and other multilateral peace operations now regularly include observation and verification components not only in relation to human rights but also in relation to the holding of elections, prisoner release, and similar peace-building measures. C. Bell, *On the Law of Peace*, supra note 17, at 184–7. "In all these areas international involvement not only reinforces compliance, but enables both detail and controversy to be resolved outside the main negotiations, assisting both the negotiation process and the achievement of substantive agreement": ibid., at 186–7.

144. L. Mallinder, *Amnesty, Human Rights and Political Transitions*, supra note 2, at 58.

145. J. Snyder and L. Vinjamuri, "Trials and Errors," supra note 33, at 33.

146. M. Osiel, *Making Sense of Mass Atrocity* (New York: Cambridge University Press, 2009), at 224. Osiel also cautions: "It is not always easy to assess their *bona fides* in this regard *ex ante*, as the case of Haiti reveals. New democratic rulers may quickly prove no less corrupt or criminally inclined than their undemocratic predecessors": ibid., at 224.

147. See, e.g., C. Sriram, "Conflict Mediation and the ICC: Challenges and Options for Pursuing Peace with Justice at the Regional Level," in K. Ambos, J. Large, and M. Wierda, eds., *Building a Future on Peace and Justice*, supra note 44, at 304, where the author argues that the challenge of pursuing peace with justice is particularly complex in regional conflicts "because mediators are generally authorized to address country-specific causes of conflict and actors, be they state or non-state, and because the design of accountability mechanisms generally focuses upon crimes committed on the territory of (or against the territory of) a particular nation-state." She also notes at 307: "For example, non-state armed groups operating transnationally, whether as mercenaries or as forces with specific socio-political claims, may seldom be the subjects of peace agreements. . . . They may thus become what are sometimes referred

to as 'spoilers': excluded from an agreement, and thus lacking any investment in it, they may seek to undermine it, or alternatively may simply foment conflict in another state."

148. C. Bell, *On the Law of Peace*, supra note 17, at 264: "as we have seen, the signing of a peace agreement does not necessarily mark a post-conflict phase. Processes of peace are not linear with violence often coming and going, in different patterns from that of the conflict."

149. P. Hayner, "The Challenge of Justice in Negotiating Peace," supra note 11, at 1–2. She continues at 3: "In both Sierra Leone and Liberia, as well as in other known cases, there has been a surprising lack of information on reasonable policy alternatives that is both accessible and appropriate to the needs of the mediator and the parties. This prevents a full consideration of all possibilities, in the complicated arena where different justice mechanisms often inter-relate, and issues of sequencing may also have to be taken into account."

150. See, e.g., *Azanian Peoples Organization (AZAPO) and Others v. President of the Republic of South Africa and Others*, Case No. CCT17/96 (July 25, 1996), interpreting the amnesty clause in the Interim Constitution of South Africa.

151. 1992 Ghana Constitution, Transitional Provisions, art. 34.

152. South Africa, Interim Constitution (Act 200 of 1993), Epilogue.

153. Second Amendment to the 1945 Constitution, Retroactivity Amendment 28(I)(1), adopted August 19, 2000.

154. Constitution of the Republic of the Union of Myanmar, 2008 (Burma), chapter XIV, "Transitory Provisions," art. 445: "No legal action shall be taken against those (either individuals or groups who are members of SLORC and SPDC) who officially carried out their duties according to their responsibilities."

155. Sometimes the power is formally shared between the executive and the legislative branches. See, e.g., Constitution of the Philippines, Section 19, Article VII: "[The president] shall also have the power to grant amnesty with the concurrence of a majority of all the members of the Congress."

156. 1996 Abidjan Peace Agreement, art. 14.

157. Linas-Marcoussis Agreement, January 23, 2003 (Ivory Coast), Annex, arts. VI(2) and VII(5).

158. Memorandum of Understanding between the Government of the Republic of Indonesia and the Free Aceh Movement, August 15, 2005.

159. See, generally, C. Bell, "Peace Agreements: Their Nature and Legal Status" (2006) 100 Am. J. Int'l L. 373.

160. See, e.g., C. Bell, *On the Law of Peace*, supra note 17, at 154–5.

161. See, generally, Part I, "Defining amnesty." See also L. Mallinder, *Amnesty, Human Rights and Political Transitions*, supra note x, at 192–7.

162. Such an amnesty could even potentially be treated as a permissible derogation, undertaken in the context of a national emergency, as permitted under a number of human rights treaties. See, generally, Freeman and van Ert, *International Human Rights Law*, supra note 23, at 34–6 and 324–5. A possible attraction of conceiving temporary

amnesty through the prism of permissible derogation is the additional degree of independent oversight it would imply. A state is required to submit to the relevant treaty-monitoring organ its reasons for establishing a state of emergency with respect to the suspension of specific guarantees. That organ then would be required to determine, on an ongoing basis, to what degree such a step was proportional to the emergency in question.

163. This idea "relates to the practice of allowing free passage for negotiators, so as to enable peace talks to occur, except that it stretches the period of immunity from just the duration of the talks to a longer prescribed period, such as the duration of a transitional government. Here, the immunity allows negotiations to occur, but it also aims to ensure some stability whilst the fruits of the negotiations are implemented." L. Mallinder, *Amnesty, Human Rights and Political Transitions*, supra note 2, at 194.

164. R. Slye, "The Cambodian Amnesties: Beneficiaries and the Temporal Reach of Amnesties for Gross Violations of Human Rights" (2004) 22 Wisc. Int'l L.J. 99, at 119–20.

165. R. Slye, "The Legitimacy of Amnesties under International Law and General Principles of Anglo-American Law," supra note 84, at 200: "If we accept the argument that the Pinochets of the world will not give up power without protection against accountability for their past wrongful acts, it is not clear why they would agree merely to postpone accountability as a condition for giving up power."

166. L. Mallinder, *Amnesty, Human Rights and Political Transitions*, supra note 2, at 195: "There are, however, dangers with delayed accountability. For example, temporary immunity is likely to be less attractive to perpetrators than permanent shielding from prosecution, and the uncertainty surrounding their treatment following the end of the transition period may create instability and reduce incentives to establish viable political institutions."

167. Act No. 35/1990, as amended by Indemnity Amendment Act, no. 124/1992 (South Africa), art. 1.

168. L. Mallinder and K. McEvoy, "Article Two Compliant Truth Recovery and Guarantees of Non-Prosecution," Submission to the Consultative Group on the Past, 2008 (copy on file with author and cited with permission), at 20.

169. As of this writing, the law remains in place and the commission of inquiry remains unestablished. The reference to this law is for purposes of citing an example of temporary immunity and is not meant as an endorsement. For an analysis of the law and a series of related legal measures, see S. Vandeginste, "Transitional Justice for Burundi: A Long and Winding Road," in K. Ambos and others, *Building a Future on Peace and Justice*, supra note 44, at 409–18.

170. See, e.g., the U.S. Patriot Act, 115 Stat. 272 (2001), which contains several sunset clauses nullifying parts of the act after a certain time period. These include provisions on wiretapping under a variety of circumstances.

171. See, e.g., Section 33 of the Canadian Charter of Rights and Freedoms, Part I of the Constitution Act 1982, which provides that parliament or the legislature of a province may expressly derogate from various human rights provisions

in the Charter, provided that any law that so derogates may have effect for a maximum of five years after it comes into force, absent an affirmative reenactment of the law by parliament or by the legislature of a province, as the case may be.

172. R. Slye, "The Cambodian Amnesties," supra note 164, at 115.

173. Law No. 18/1994 on Amnesty, November 10, 1994 (Angola).

174. 1992 Ghana Constitution, Transitional Provisions, art. 36(2).

175. See Part I, Section 3, "Amnesties and the fight against impunity."

176. Executive Decree, October 3, 1993 (Haiti).

177. Law on General Amnesty for the Consolidation of Peace, Decree No. 486, March 20, 1993 (El Salvador).

178. Promotion of National Unity and Reconciliation Act, 1995 (South Africa).

179. Law of Civil Harmony, No. 98-08, 1999 (Algeria).

180. Amnesty Act, 2000 (Uganda).

181. Law 4/2002, April 4, 2002 (Angola).

182. An alternative approach in future preambles could be to indicate, in a non-treaty-specific fashion, that the amnesty must be interpreted in a manner consistent with the state's international law obligations. That would encourage a more open-ended canvassing of applicable international law, thus ensuring that the amnesty's normative ends are thoroughly balanced against their full legal limits.

183. Decree 210/1983 (El Salvador).

184. Amnesty Law, October 6, 1994 (Haiti).

185. See, e.g., A. O'Shea, *Amnesty for Crime in International Law and Practice*, supra note 132, at 76: "the rationale for punishment is different for political crimes, as the motivations that inspire their commission can be viewed as selfless, altruistic and in accordance with some perceived 'higher law', rather than being unremittingly bad or evil." See also L. Mallinder, *Amnesty, Human Rights and Political Transitions*, supra note 2, at 95: "In certain cases, amnesty for individuals who commit crimes due to ideological belief has been justified by arguing that such individuals are less in need of punishment than ordinary criminals are, as the former 'are more easily rehabilitated and less of a societal threat, especially in the context of a society that has undergone or is undergoing fundamental political change'."

186. See, e.g., Law 46/1977, October 15, 1977 (Spain), art. 1.

187. Other such purely political crimes include "sedition, subversion, rebellion, using false documents, forgery, anti-government propaganda, possessing illegal weapons, espionage, membership of banned political or religious organisations, desertion, and defamation." L. Mallinder, *Amnesty, Human Rights and Political Transitions*, supra note 2, at 136.

188. Many amnesties, nevertheless, merely declare political offenses as eligible, without further qualifications. See, e.g., Law 212/1992 (Djibouti), art. 1.

189. Cotonou Agreement, July 25, 1993 (Liberia), art. 19.

190. 1994 Lusaka Protocol, November 15, 1994 (Angola), Annex 6, art. 5.

191. Amnesty Law No. 8198, March 11, 1997 (Albania).

192. See Section 4.3.5, "Temporal scope of application."

193. Amnesty Act, Law No. 6.683, Lei Concede Anistia e Dá Outras Providências, August 28, 1979 (Brazil).
194. Decree 62-328, March 22, 1962 (France), art. 1.
195. Presidential Decree 261-1974 – On the Granting of Amnesty (A-211), July 26, 1974 (Greece), art. 1.
196. Décret-loi N° 1/034/90 du 30/8/1990 portant mesure d'amnistie en faveur de prévenus ou condamnés de certaines infractions (Burundi); Décret Loi du 9/9/1993 portant amnistie (Burundi).
197. Amnesty Law, Law 11/1996 (Angola), art. 1.
198. Cited in E. Rekosh, "Romania: A Persistent Culture of Impunity," in N. Roht-Arriaza, ed., *Impunity and Human Rights in International Law and Practice* (New York: Oxford University Press, 1995), at 134–6.
199. Promotion of National Unity and Reconciliation Act, 1995 (South Africa), sec. 20.3: "Whether a particular act, omission or offence contemplated in subsection (2) is an act associated with a political objective, shall be decided with reference to the following criteria:
    (a) The motive of the person who committed the act, omission or offence;
    (b) the context in which the act, omission or offence took place, and in particular whether the act, omission or offence was committed in the course of or as part of a political uprising, disturbance or event, or in reaction thereto;
    (c) the legal and factual nature of the act, omission or offence, including the gravity of the act, omission or offence;
    (d) the object or objective of the act, omission or offence, and in particular whether the act, omission or offence was primarily directed at a political opponent or State property or personnel or against private property or individuals;
    (e) whether the act, omission or offence was committed in the execution of an order of, or on behalf of, or with the approval of, the organisation, institution, liberation movement or body of which the person who committed the act was a member, an agent or a supporter; and
    (f) the relationship between the act, omission or offence and the political objective pursued, and in particular the directness and proximity of the relationship and the proportionality of the act, omission or offence to the objective pursued, *but does not include* any act, omission or offence committed by any person referred to in subsection (2) who acted – (i) for personal gain: Provided that an act, omission or offence by any person who acted and received money or anything of value as an informer of the State or a former state, political organisation or liberation movement, shall not be excluded only on the grounds of that person having received money or anything of value for his or her information; or (ii) out of personal malice, ill-will or spite, directed against the victim of the acts committed." (Emphasis added.)
200. Ibid., sec. 20(3)(f). It was left to the TRC's Amnesty Committee to determine "the relationship between the act, omission or offence and the political objective pursued, and

in particular the directness and proximity of the relationship and the proportionality of the act, omission or offence to the objective pursued."

201. Decree 145-1996: Law of National Reconciliation, 1996 (Guatemala), art. 2.

202. Proclamation 390, September 29, 2000 (Philippines), art. 1.

203. Law 46/1977, October 15, 1977 (Spain), art. 1.

204. Ley 35 por la cual se decreta una amnistía y se dictan normas tendientes al restablecimiento y preservación de la paz, 1982 (Colombia), art. 2.

205. Decreto No. 87-91, January 23, 1991 (Honduras), art. 1.

206. Law of National Reconciliation, Legislative Decree 147, January 23, 1992 (El Salvador), art. 1.

207. Legislative Decree No. 3, January 4, 1990 (Romania), art. 2, extending the amnesty to any crime subject to a sentence of up to three years.

208. Amnesty Law in connection with the events in Aksy District of Southwestern Dzhalal-Abad Region on 17–18 Mar 2002 and the events at the 447 km of the Bishkek-Osh Road, 2002 (Kyrgyzstan), art. 1, which grants amnesty to individuals involved in political unrest as well as envisaging the release of other individuals imprisoned for a wide range of unrelated minor crimes.

209. General Amnesty Law 02/PR/2002 (Chad), art. 2.

210. Convention Relating to the Status of Refugees, Geneva, July 28, 1951, 189 U.N.T.S. 150, entered into force April 22, 1954, arts. 1 and 33.

211. R. Slye, "Justice and Amnesty," in C. Villa-Vicencio and W. Verwoerd, eds., *Looking Back, Reaching Forward: Reflections on the Truth and Reconciliation Commission of South Africa* (London: Zed Books, 2000), at 179–80.

212. See also the 1973 International Convention on the Suppression and Punishment of the Crime of Apartheid, General Assembly resolution 3068 (XXVIII) of November 30, 1973, art. XI.

213. See Part I, Section 6, "The evolving UN position on amnesties."

214. For example, genocide would be an irrelevant, even confusing, exclusion from an amnesty if it did not occur in the particular jurisdiction.

215. See, e.g., 1994 Report on the Situation of Human Rights in El Salvador (OAS Doc. OEA/Ser.L/V/II.85), where the Inter-American Commission on Human Rights asserts that amnesties should exclude the crimes of perjury and other crimes involving deliberate obstructions of justice. See also D. Cassel, "Lessons from the Americas," supra note 84, at 219, where the author lists this as a condition for acceptable amnesties. Note, too, that Rome Statute art. 70(1) sets out an illustrative list of offenses against the administration of justice.

216. Such wording avoids rendering transparent the fact that the amnesty presumptively covers international crimes too.

217. Office of the United Nations High Commissioner for Human Rights, *Rule of Law Tools for Post-Conflict States: Amnesties* (Geneva: United Nations, 2009), at 40. At ibid., the tool concludes: "In this situation, it may be necessary to ensure that the proposed amnesty excludes offences such as 'murder', which might be the only crime under local law that can be used to prosecute perpetrators of genocide."

218. Peace Treaty of Vereeniging, May 31, 1902, art. 4: "No proceedings civil or criminal will be taken against any of the Burghers so surrendering or so returning for any Acts in connection with the prosecution of the War. The benefit of this clause will not extend to certain Acts contrary to the usage of War which have been notified by the Commander in Chief to the Boer Generals, and which shall be tried by Court Martial immediately after the close of hostilities."

219. Amnesty Decree Law, April 3, 1955 (Hungary).

220. Amnesty Law marking GDR's 30th Anniversary, September 25, 1979 (GDR).

221. Declaration of a General Amnesty, March 18, 1980 (Iran) excluded torture.

222. Amnesty Statute No. 6, June 12, 1987 (Uganda) excluded, inter alia, genocide and rape.

223. Ley de Amnistía para. Detenidos por Violación de la Ley de Mantenimiento del Orden y la Seguridad Pública, Ley No. 33, 1987 (Nicaragua) excluded crimes against humanity.

224. Decree 145-1996: Law of National Reconciliation, 1996 (Guatemala) excluded torture, genocide, forced disappearances and "imprescriptible crimes."

225. Amnesty Law No. 8202, 1997 (Albania) excluded crimes against humanity.

226. See Part I, Section 4, "Amnesties and international law." We noted therein that counterterrorism treaties, along with the Genocide Convention, articulate an explicit obligation to prevent alongside the obligation to punish.

227. See L. Mallinder, *Amnesty, Human Rights and Political Transitions*, supra note 2, at 118–35. The reason for its exclusion, however, is more likely due to political considerations than international legal ones.

228. See, e.g., Rome Statute, art. 8(b)(xvi).

229. See, e.g., Law on Amnesty 07-1117/1, March 8, 2002 (Macedonia), art. 3: "The provision of paragraph 1 of this Article does not apply to persons convicted of criminal acts against humanity and international law, illicit production and trafficking of narcotics, psycho-tropic substances and precursors, for enabling the use of narcotics, psychotropic substances and precursors as well as persons sentenced to life imprisonment."

230. M. Freeman, "Lessons Learned from Amnesties for Human Rights Crimes," Transparency International Newsletter, December 2001, at 3.

231. Ibid., at 3.

232. Law of National Pacification, Law No. 22.924, 1983 (Argentina), art. 4, excludes crimes of economic subversion.

233. Law 89-63, July 3, 1989 (Tunisia), art. 1.

234. Décret-loi N° 1/034/90 du 30/8/1990 portant mesure d'amnistie en faveur de prévenus ou condamnés de certaines infractions (Burundi) excludes contractual fraud, criminal corruption, and embezzlement.

235. Legislative Decree No. 3, January 4, 1990 (Romania) excludes bribery.

236. Law on General Amnesty for the Consolidation of Peace – Decree No. 486, 1993 (El Salvador), art. 3, excludes extortion and crimes committed "with a view to profit."

237. General Amnesty Law, March 1999 (Jordan) excludes embezzlement, bribery, and the issuance of bad checks.

238. Proclamation 390, September 29, 2000 (Philippines) excludes crimes committed for personal ends.

239. Clemency Order No. 1, 2000 (Zimbabwe) excludes any offense involving fraud or dishonesty.

240. Rome Statute art. 30(2) provides that a person has intent where "(a) In relation to conduct, that person means to engage in the conduct; (b) In relation to a consequence, that person means to cause that consequence or is aware that it will occur in the ordinary course of events."

241. Ley 35 por la cual se decreta una amnistía y se dictan normas tendientes al restablecimiento y preservación de la paz, 1982 (Colombia), art. 3.

242. Law No. 15.737, 1985 (Uruguay), art. 5.

243. Promotion of National Unity and Reconciliation Act, 1995 (South Africa), s. 20(2)(f).

244. Amnesty Act, Ordinance 3/1979 (Zimbabwe), art. 2; Amnesty (General Pardon) Act, Ordinance 12/1980 (Zimbabwe), art. 3.

245. In Afghanistan, there was religious opposition to a 2007 amnesty in part because the crimes amnestied were viewed as crimes against God and not merely against persons. Interview with Sari Kouvo, ICTJ Afghanistan director, January 2008.

246. See, e.g., Amnesty Law No. 84/91, August 27, 1991 (Lebanon), art. 3.

247. See, e.g., Law No. 26479, June 14, 1995 (Peru), art. 5 (drug trafficking); Law No. 19 on Amnesty, 2008 (Iraq), art. 2 (abductions and trafficking of artifacts); Decree Law 2.191, 1978 (Chile), art. 3 (child abduction). The Iraqi amnesty also excludes, inter alia, incest, rape, homosexuality, embezzlement, and murder. Similarly, the Chilean amnesty also excludes parricide, infanticide, armed robbery, corruption of minors, incest, and drunk driving.

248. See, e.g., Rome Statute, art. 7.1.g.

249. Loi No. 51-18 du 5 janvier 1951 portant amnistie, instituant un régime de libération anticipée, limitant les effets de la dégradation nationale et réprimant les activités antinationales (France).

250. Cited in L. Mallinder and K. McEvoy, "Article Two Compliant Truth Recovery and Guarantees of Non-Prosecution," supra note 168, at 19.

251. Lei Concede Anistia e Dá Outras Providências, Law No 6.683/1979 (Brazil), art. 1.

252. Ley 37 por la cual se declara una amnistía condicional, March 23, 1982 (Colombia), art. 1.

253. Ley 23.492 "Punto Final", December 24, 1986 (Argentina), art. 5.

254. Décret Loi du 9/9/1993 portant amnistie (Burundi).

255. Law on General Amnesty No. 80/96, September 20, 1996 (Croatia), art. 3.

256. Ordonnance no 06-01 du 27 feb 2006 portant mise en oeuvre de la Charte pour la paix et la réconciliation nationale, 2006 (Algeria), sec. 2, art. 10.

257. L. Mallinder, "Exploring the Practise of States in Introducing Amnesties," in K. Ambos, J. Large, and M. Wierda, eds., *Building a Future on Peace and Justice*, supra note 44, at 152.

258. As Professor Ron C. Slye notes, "There exists a continuum of choices, ranging from an amnesty that applies to every individual for all time, to an amnesty that applies to

one individual for one specific event." R. Slye, "The Cambodian Amnesties," supra note 164, at 104.

259. Constitution: Transitional Provisions, art. 4 (Turkey).

260. Décret No. 62-328, March 22, 1962, portant amnistie de faits commis dans le cadre des opérations de maintien de l'ordre dirigées contre l'insurrection algérienne (France).

261. Ley 16595 "Concediendo amnistía e indulto político, en favor de todos los civiles y militares procesados por causas político sociales con motivo de la huelga de Toquepala," 1967 (Peru).

262. Proclamation No. 348, 1994 and Amending Resolution 377, 1994 (Philippines).

263. Law on Amnesty for People Who Committed Crimes during the Counter-Terrorist Operation in the Caucasus, December 13, 1999 (Russia).

264. See, e.g., Law No. 2352 "Due Obedience," 1987 (Argentina).

265. See, generally, C. Nino, "The Duty to Punish Past Abuses of Human Rights Put into Context: The Case of Argentina" (1991) 100 Yale L.J. 2639.

266. See, e.g., Law on Rehabilitation of Persons Repressed for Resistance to the Occupying Regime, May 2, 1990 (Lithuania); Royal Amnesty, July 1994 (Morocco). Other categories of non-self-amnesty include those intended to benefit conscientious objectors in a period of democratic restoration, and those intended to benefit former political opposition leaders who were convicted in absentia so that they can return to their home country in a new era to participate in a transitional government or in reconciliation talks.

267. See supra note 15 concerning the Indonesian army's view of the 2005 Aceh MOU, which contained an amnesty only for the GAM rebels.

268. As Louise Mallinder notes, state actors carry the bulk of obligations under international law but are usually covered by indemnity and state of emergency laws. In that sense, state agents may have less need of amnesties than non-state actors. L. Mallinder, *Amnesty, Human Rights and Political Transitions*, supra note 2, at 85–7 and 113.

269. Law on the Outlawing of the Democratic Kampuchea Group, 1994 (Cambodia). See also R. Slye, "The Cambodian Amnesties," supra note 164, at 102.

270. Law 74/1993 (Djibouti).

271. The Amnesty Act, 2000 (Uganda).

272. Legislative Decree No. 10 with respect to general amnesty for crimes affecting national security, 2001 (Bahrain).

273. L. Mallinder, *Amnesty, Human Rights and Political Transitions*, supra note 2, at 84: "The scale of this result is interesting, as it is perhaps surprising that states are more willing to amnesty their opponents than their own agents, particularly since much of the literature on amnesties focuses on the injustice of governments awarding amnesties to their own agents."

274. See, e.g., M. Osiel, "Modes of Participation in Mass Atrocity" (2005) 39 Cornell Int'l L.J. 793, at 810.

275. Law 46/1977, October 15, 1977 (Spain).

276. Decreto No. 87-91, January 23, 1991 (Honduras).

277. Resolution of the Supreme Assembly of Tajikistan, on Amnesty for Participants in the Political and Military Confrontation in the Republic of Tajikistan, July 1997 (Tajikistan).

278. Law 4/2002, April 4, 2002 (Angola)

279. Order 2007-457, 2007 (Ivory Coast).

280. The 1978 amnesty in Chile often is given as an example of this because there were few opponents of the state who stood to benefit. State forces bore the lion's share of criminal responsibility, as the national TRC later confirmed. See, generally, R. Quinn, "Will the Rule of Law End? Challenging Grants of Amnesty for the Human Rights Violations of a Prior Regime: Chile's New Model" (1994) 62 Fordham L. Rev. 905.

281. See, generally, R. Slye, "The Legitimacy of Amnesties under International Law and General Principles of Anglo-American Law," supra note 84, at 245–7, where the author persuasively argues that the South African amnesty process achieved an unparalleled level of individual accountability compared to any other amnesty process.

282. Law 98-08 on Civil Harmony, 1999 (Algeria).

283. Proclamation 390, September 29, 2000 (Philippines).

284. Townsville Peace Agreement, October 15, 2000 (Solomon Islands), Part Two, section 3.

285. Such specificity is to be contrasted with amnesties that fail to designate particular affiliations. For example, the 1994 and 1996 Angolan amnesties (Law No. 18/1994 and Law No. 11/1996) cover contraventions committed by "soldiers and non-soldiers" in the course of conflict, and the 2000 Angolan amnesty (Law No. 7/2000) covers "all civilians and soldiers, both Angolan and foreign."

286. P. van Zyl, "Promoting Transitional Justice in Post-Conflict Societies," supra note 118, at 220. In this respect, distinguishing beneficiaries by rank represents a principled approach but also a pragmatic one: it can help create divisions between the leadership and the foot soldiers.

287. R. Slye, "The Cambodian Amnesties," supra note 164, at 108. "First, it means that the individual torturer may mingle among his victims with long term consequences. . . . Second, providing amnesty to the torturer undercuts specific and general deterrence": ibid., at 108 and 109.

288. Presidential Decree 261-1974 on the Granting of Amnesty, 1974 (Greece). See, generally, N. Alivizatos and P. Diamandouros, "Politics and the Judiciary in the Greek Transition to Democracy," in A. J. McAdams, ed., *Transitional Justice and the Rule of Law in New Democracies* (Notre Dame: University of Notre Dame Press, 1997), at 36: "[The state] explicitly excluded the 'protagonists' ('those primarily responsible,' or *protaitioi*) of the military regime from the July 1974 amnesty decree and charged the Athens Court of Appeals with the responsibility for investigating, prosecuting, and adjudicating the case."

289. Decreto-Lei No. 758/76, October 22, 1976 (Portugal).

290. Law on the Outlawing of the Democratic Kampuchea Group, July 7, 1994 (Cambodia), art. 6: "For leaders of the 'Democratic Kampuchea' group the amnesty described above does not apply."

291. See, e.g., Rome Statute art. 28: "A military commander or person effectively acting as a military commander shall be criminally responsible for crimes within the jurisdiction

of the Court committed by forces under his or her effective command and control, or effective authority and control as the case may be, as a result of his or her failure to exercise control properly over such forces, where: (i) That military commander or person either knew or, owing to the circumstances at the time, should have known that the forces were committing or about to commit such crimes; and (ii) That military commander or person failed to take all necessary and reasonable measures within his or her power to prevent or repress their commission or to submit the matter to the competent authorities for investigation and prosecution."

292. See, e.g., ibid., art. 33(1): "The fact that a crime within the jurisdiction of the Court has been committed by a person pursuant to an order of a Government or of a superior, whether military or civilian, shall not relieve that person of criminal responsibility unless: (a) The person was under a legal obligation to obey orders of the Government or the superior in question; (b) The person did not know that the order was unlawful; and (c) The order was not manifestly unlawful." See also Article 33(2): "For the purposes of this article, orders to commit genocide or crimes against humanity are manifestly unlawful."

293. See, e.g., *Case Concerning the Arrest Warrant of 11 April 2000 (DRC v. Belgium)* (2002), 41 ILM 536, in which the International Court of Justice held that when abroad, sitting foreign ministers and similar government officials enjoy full immunity from criminal jurisdiction, including for war crimes and crimes against humanity. But the Court held that after a foreign minister ceases to hold public office, the tribunal of one state may – provided it has jurisdiction under international law – try the former foreign minister of another state for any acts committed before or after the minister's period of office and for private acts committed during his time in office. The Court also affirmed that former or incumbent foreign ministers may be tried by international criminal tribunals with jurisdiction over the particular crimes. But see E. Lutz and C. Reiger, eds., *Prosecuting Heads of State* (New York: Cambridge University Press, 2009), analyzing some of the 67 former heads of state or government who have been prosecuted since 1990 for serious human rights or financial crimes notwithstanding such immunities.

294. See also Article 25.3 of the Rome Statute, which makes similar distinctions: "In accordance with this Statute, a person shall be criminally responsible and liable for punishment for a crime within the jurisdiction of the Court if that person: (a) *Commits* such a crime, whether as an individual, jointly with another or through another person, regardless of whether that other person is criminally responsible; (b) *Orders, solicits or induces* the commission of such a crime which in fact occurs or is attempted; (c) For the purpose of facilitating the commission of such a crime, *aids, abets or otherwise assists* in its commission or its attempted commission, including providing the means for its commission; (d) *In any other way contributes* to the commission or attempted commission of such a crime by a group of persons acting *with a common purpose*. Such contribution shall be intentional and shall either: (i) Be made with the aim of furthering the criminal activity or criminal purpose of the group, where such activity or purpose involves the commission of a crime within the jurisdiction of the Court; or (ii) Be made in the knowledge of the intention of the group to commit the crime; (e) In respect of the crime of genocide, directly and publicly *incites*

others to commit genocide; (f) *Attempts to commit* such a crime by taking action that commences its execution by means of a substantial step, but the crime does not occur because of circumstances independent of the person's intentions. However, a person who abandons the effort to commit the crime or otherwise prevents the completion of the crime shall not be liable for punishment under this Statute for the attempt to commit that crime if that person completely and voluntarily gave up the criminal purpose." (Emphasis added)

295. Amnesty (General Pardon) Act, Ordinance 12/1980 (Zimbabwe), art. 3.

296. Decreto-Ley Núm. 33-82, 1982 (Guatemala), art. 1.

297. Law No. 36.934 on General Political Amnesty, April 17, 2000 (Venezuela), art. 1.

298. Amnesty Act 2000 (Uganda), art. 3.

299. See, e.g., L. Mallinder, *Amnesty, Human Rights and Political Transitions*, supra note 2, at 49: "Following the end of the Second World War, national unity was also the justification for amnesties of former collaborators or members of fascist organisations in France, Germany, Italy, Japan and the Philippines. Often, the calls for national unity recognised that the individuals concerned acted in response to social pressure, resulting in the view that there was a need to 'close definitively the file'."

300. Ibid., at 189–92.

301. Decreto-Lei No. 758/76, October 22, 1976 (Portugal).

302. Proclamation No. 390, September 29, 2000 (Philippines).

303. Décret-loi N° 1/034/90 du 30/8/1990 portant mesure d'amnistie en faveur de prévenus ou condamnés de certaines infractions (Burundi).

304. Clemency Order No. 1 (General Amnesty for Politically-Motivated Crimes), October 10, 2000 (Zimbabwe).

305. See Section 4.4.2, "Conditions for retaining individual grants of amnesty."

306. Lei No. 7/00, December 15, 2000 (Angola).

307. Linas-Marcoussis Agreement, April 2003, implemented in La Loi No. 2003-309 portant amnistie, August 8, 2003 (Ivory Coast).

308. See, generally, C. Sriram and A. Ross, "Geographies of Crime and Justice: Contemporary Transitional Justice and the Creation of 'Zones of Impunity'" (2007) 1 Int'l J. Transitional Justice 45.

309. See, e.g., M. Freeman, *Truth Commissions and Procedural Fairness*, supra note 10, chap. 7 ("Publication of findings of individual responsibility").

310. See Part I, Section 5, "Amnesties and the ICC."

311. Law no. 1/1994 (Yemen), art. 1.

312. See A. O'Shea, *Amnesty for Crime in International Law and Practice*, supra note 132, at 69: "The government of Croatia issued a list of individuals covered by the (1996 amnesty) law, while the courts issued lists of those not covered by the law. The minister of justice and Croatian judicial officials have made conflicting statements relating to such lists, and in the circumstances the amnesty has done little to comfort the inhabitants of the region."

313. Ibid., at 268.

314. But see the decision of the Inter-American Court of Human Rights in *Ellacuria v. El Salvador*, Case 10.488, Inter-Am. C.H.R. 136, OEA/ser. L./V./II.106, doc. 6 (1999), at

229: "The Inter-American Court of Human Rights considers that, despite the important contribution that the [Salvadoran] Truth Commission made in establishing the facts surrounding the most serious violations, and in promoting national reconciliation, the role that it played, although highly relevant, cannot be considered as a suitable substitute for proper judicial procedures as a method for arriving at the truth."

315. M. Freeman, *Truth Commissions and Procedural Fairness*, supra note 10, at 79 and 82.

316. See, e.g., N. Roht-Arriaza, "Conclusion: Combating Impunity," in N. Roht-Arriaza, ed., *Impunity and Human Rights in International Law and Practice*, supra note 198, at 301: "In addition in many states access to the evidence necessary to prove liability is available only through the coercive power of the prosecutor – private discovery is much more limited. Indeed, this was part of the basis for the complaints brought against Uruguay and Argentina for enacting de facto amnesties. A civil suit solution would be feasible only if appropriate provisions for access to testimony and documents were part of the package." On the civil law system's approach to civil recovery through criminal prosecutions, see, generally, R. Schlesinger and others, *Comparative Law* (New York: Foundation Press, 1998) at 532–9; M. Glendon and others, *Comparative Legal Traditions*, 2nd. ed. (St. Paul, MN: West, 1999) at 101.

317. As Mark Osiel argues, "To a degree little recognized or acknowledged, amnesty from prosecution is so controversial because monetary compensation, through civil recovery (for wrongful death, battery, infliction of distress, etc.) is virtually unavailable in countries where mass atrocity occurs. If civil litigation were to make such remedies practically accessible, political pressures for prosecution would much diminish, because victims are often content with (even prefer) financial and other redress." M. Osiel, "Modes of Participation in Mass Atrocity," supra note 274, at 812.

318. Law 46/1977 (Spain).

319. Law No. 18/1994 on Amnesty, November 10, 1994 (Angola).

320. Amnesty Law, October 6, 1994 (Haiti).

321. Decree 145-1996: Law of National Reconciliation, 1996 (Guatemala).

322. Amnesty Law, May 7, 2009 (DRC).

323. Law no. 90-19 portant amnistie, August 15, 1990 (Algeria), art. 8.

324. "In some cases, the authority granting amnesty, not content with assuring the criminal impunity of torturers, also seeks to organize a conspiracy of silence by depriving the victims of any possibility of obtaining the material or even moral reparation to which they would be entitled under ordinary law. The purpose is less to avoid a civil sanction such as the possible payment of compensation than to eliminate any possibility of inquiry that might lead to publicity during a civil suit, further confirmation of the fact that publicity is the sanction most feared by persons guilty of serious offences against the human condition." L. Joinet, "Study on Amnesty Laws and Their Role in the Safeguard and Promotion of Human Rights," supra note 105, para. 78. With individualized and conditional amnesties, however, ongoing exposure to civil liability could create a significant disincentive to participation in the amnesty process, thus undermining truth-recovery efforts. See *Azanian Peoples Organization (AZAPO) and*

Others v. President of the Republic of South Africa and Others, Constitutional Court of South Africa, Case No. CCT17/96 (July 25, 1996), at para. 36.

325. Constitution, 1982 (Turkey), provisional art. 15.

326. Law No. 81: General Amnesty and National Reconciliation, 1990 (Nicaragua).

327. Townsville Peace Agreement, October 15, 2000 (Solomon Islands), Part Two.

328. Law No. 26479, 1995 (Peru).

329. Amnesty Law, January 22, 1994 (Mexico), art. 4. See also L. Mallinder, *Amnesty, Human Rights and Political Transitions*, supra note 2, at 78–80: "For example, the 1986 Israeli amnesty was introduced to protect members of Shin Bet, Israel's counter-intelligence agency, and possibly Israeli politicians, from an investigation into the deaths of two Palestinian bus hijackers in 1984. The government justified the amnesty by arguing that any investigation could risk revealing information crucial to state security."

330. The Amnesty Act No. 8/2000 (Solomon Islands), art. 5.

331. But see Part I "Amnesties and the ICC" discussion of Article 98 agreements between the United States and other states. These agreements preclude the surrender or transfer to the ICC of a national of either signatory. See also R. Slye, "The Legitimacy of Amnesties under International Law and General Principles of Anglo-American Law," supra note 84, at 101–7, where the author analyzes two basic principles found in most extradition treaties – namely, the requirement of dual criminality and the political offense exception – and their relation to amnesties for human rights crimes.

332. It already was an issue in the context of the Colombian Law on Justice and Peace, discussed earlier. See, generally, C. Botero Marino et al., *La ley de alternatividad penal y justicia transicional*, supra note 41, at 10–11.

333. See Section 4.4.1.1, "Requirement to submit an individual application."

334. Law No. 23521 ("Due Obedience"), June 4, 1987 (Argentina), art. 3.

335. Law on General Amnesty for the Consolidation of Peace, Decree No. 486, March 20, 1993 (El Salvador), art. 4.

336. Amnesty Act, Ordinance 3/1979 (Zimbabwe), art. 2

337. Decreto No. 87-91, January 23, 1991 (Honduras), art. 3.

338. This is the case of the extraterritorial murder of the former Chilean ambassador Orlando Letelier and his associate Ronni Moffitt. See Decree Law 2.191, 1978 (Chile), sec. 4. Similarly, a 1987 Salvadorean amnesty expressly precludes amnesty for those responsible for the murder of Archibishop Oscar Romero. Ley de Amnistía para el Logro de la Reconciliación Nacional, Decreto No. 805, October 28, 1987 (El Salvador), art. 3.

339. Executive Decree 128/2003 (Colombia), art. 13.

340. B A. Garner and H. C. L Black, eds., *Black's Law Dictionary*, 8th ed. (St. Paul, MN: Thomson/West, 2006).

341. Law No. 11 voiding certain convictions, February 19, 1992 (Hungary), sections 1 and 2.

342. Law on General Amnesty for the Consolidation of Peace, Decree No. 486, March 20, 1993 (El Salvador), art. 4.

343. Amnesty Act, 2000 (Uganda), art. 4.

344. Presidential Decree 261-1974 – On the Granting of Amnesty (A-211), July 26, 1974 (Greece), art. 2

345. Law providing amnesty, January 12, 1955 (Luxembourg), art. 1; Presidential Amnesty, January 16, 1991 (Afghanistan), art. 7. See also Amnesty Law of the People's Assembly, November 18, 1989 (Albania), art. 10, which provides for the pardoning of one-quarter of the accompanying penal fine and the payment of the rest.

346. Law providing amnesty for certain infractions, September 20, 1945 (Belgium), art. 4.

347. Decreto-Ley No. 8-86, 1986 (Guatemala), art. 2.

348. Legislative Decree No. 3, January 4, 1990 (Romania).

349. Law of National Reconciliation, Legislative Decree 147, January 23, 1992 (El Salvador), art. 5.

350. Décret-loi N° 1/034/90 du 30/8/1990 portant mesure d'amnistie en faveur de prévenus ou condamnés de certaines infractions (Burundi).

351. Law of Civil Harmony, No. 98-08, 1999 (Algeria), Chapter III.

352. Promotion of National Unity and Reconciliation Act, 1995 (South Africa), sec. 20(9): "If any person has been granted amnesty in respect of any act or omission which formed the ground of a civil judgment which was delivered at any time before the granting of the amnesty, the publication of the proclamation in terms of subsection (6) shall not affect the operation of the judgment in so far as it applies to that person."

353. Amnesty Act, Ordinance 3/1979 (Zimbabwe), art. 2.

354. The matter is different, however, when the judgment was based on spurious or fabricated allegations and records, or was the product of an unfair trial.

355. Article 7 of Law 46/1977, 1977 (Spain) provides for the elimination of criminal records, including any unfavorable notes in those records.

356. Amnesty by the Council of Ministers, July 24, 1991 (Burkina Faso), art. 3; Law 33/1993 (Djibouti), art. 11. These provisions seem to have emerged out of the French legal tradition. Article 133-11 of the French Criminal Code provides: "Any person who, in the exercise of his functions, has knowledge of criminal convictions, professional or disciplinary sanctions or prohibitions, forfeitures and incapacities erased by an amnesty, is prohibited from recalling their existence in any way whatsoever or allowing an indication of them to remain in any document. However, the original copy of judgments, and judicial decisions are excluded from this prohibition. Furthermore an amnesty does not preclude the enforcement of a publication awarded as compensation." See, generally, R. Levy, "Pardons and Amnesties as Policy Instruments in Contemporary France" (2007) 36 Crime & Justice 551, at 558–9.

357. Promotion of National Unity and Reconciliation Act, 1995 (South Africa), sec. 20(10).

358. See, e.g., ibid., sec. 20(7): "(a) No person who has been granted amnesty in respect of an act, omission or offence shall be criminally or civilly liable in respect of such act, omission or offence and no body or organisation or the State shall be liable, and no person shall be vicariously liable, for any such act, omission or offence. (b) Where amnesty is granted to any person in respect of any act, omission or offence, such amnesty shall have no influence upon the criminal liability of any other person contingent upon the liability of the first-mentioned person."

359. M. Freeman, *Truth Commissions and Procedural Fairness*, supra note 10, at 145–6.

360. Décret loi du 9 septembre 1993 portant amnistie (Burundi).
361. Law of Civil Harmony, No. 98-08, 1999 (Algeria), arts. 3 and 7. In Part I, Section 1, "Defining amnesty," such amnesties were referred to as "hybrid amnesties."
362. Such an approach can be pursued through a single law or through separate laws, as in Colombia, where there are two laws providing amnesty for persons falling below a specific rank (Law 782/2002 and Executive Decree 128/2003) and another law authorizing the prospect of a conditional reduced sentence for those above a specific rank (Justice and Peace Law 975/2005).
363. Though undesirable in principle, some amnesties expressly include crimes committed by citizens outside of national borders. See, e.g., Law on Rehabilitation of Victims of Political Repression, October 18, 1991, as amended (Russia). Naturally, such a clause would not bind courts in the territory where the crimes were committed. See also "Southern African Regional Assessment Mission Reports," International Center for Transitional Justice, October 2007–December 2008, at 102, describing the amnesty process of the South Africa TRC concerning crimes committed beyond the country's borders: "the military hierarchy would not divulge any details regarding cross-border operations, asserting, as others had done, that the Commission was unable to provide a guarantee of international amnesty. Consequently, very few amnesty applications were submitted from members of the military relating to cross-border activities."
364. Presidential Proclamation Formally Ending the Philippine Insurrection and Granting of Pardon and Amnesty, July 4, 1902 (United States/Philippines).
365. Tripoli Agreement (the Government of the Republic of the Philippines and Moro National Liberation Front), December 23, 1976 (Philippines), art. 4(12).
366. Amnesty Law, May 9, 2009 (DRC), art. 1.
367. Decree Law 2.191 (Chile), art. 1.
368. Amnesty Act, Law No. 6.683, Lei Concede Anistia e Dá Outras Providências, August 28, 1979 (Brazil), art. 1.
369. Law No. 81 on General Amnesty and National Reconciliation, March 13, 1990 (Nicaragua), art. 1.
370. Law No. 15/92, 1992 (Mozambique).
371. Amnesty Law No. 8198, March 11, 1997 (Albania).
372. Cotonou Agreement, July 26, 1993 (Liberia); Ceasefire Agreement, July 1, 1999 (DRC).
373. Law Nullifying the State's Claim to Punish Certain Crimes (Ley de Caducidad), Law No. 15.848, 1986 (Uruguay).
374. Law of National Reconciliation, Legislative Decree 147, January 23, 1992 (El Salvador).
375. Proclamation No. 347, 1994 (Philippines).
376. Decreto-Ley Núm. 27-83, 1983 (Guatemala); Amnesty Act, 2000 (Uganda).
377. See Section 3.6.1, "Typology of context and amnesty beneficiaries."
378. L. Mallinder, *Amnesty, Human Rights and Political Transitions*, supra note 2, at 154: "states are increasingly willing to make amnesty beneficiaries more accountable for their crimes by attaching conditions to the amnesty."
379. See Section 4.5, "Maximum viability."

380. L. Mallinder, *Amnesty, Human Rights and Political Transitions*, supra note 2, at 132: "To date, states are increasingly favouring individualised amnesties, although this has not yet formed the majority of cases."

381. Ley 37 por la cual se declara una amnistía condicional, May 14, 1981 (Colombia), art. 5.

382. Decree 210/1983 (El Salvador), arts. 6 and 7.

383. Proclamation No. 347, 1994 (Philippines), sections 4–6.

384. Promotion of National Unity and Reconciliation Act, 1995 (South Africa), sec. 20.

385. Law of Civil Harmony, No. 98-08, 1999 (Algeria), Chapter 5.

386. Amnesty Act, 2000 (Uganda), Part II. Article 4.1 of the law provides: "A reporter shall be taken to be granted the amnesty declared under section 3 if the reporter: (i) reports to the nearest Army or Police Unit, a Chief, a member of the Executive Committee of a local government unit, a magistrate or a religious leader within the locality; (ii) renounces and abandons involvement in the war or armed rebellion; (iii) surrenders at any such place or to any such authority or person any weapons in his or her possession; and (iv) is issued with a Certificate of Amnesty as shall be prescribed in regulations to be made by the Minister."

387. Consider this point in the context of South Africa's application-based amnesty. The fact that senior architects of apartheid crimes mostly did not come forward is usually seen as a defeat for transitional justice and the TRC. However, it could also be seen as a victory for accountability because all those who did not apply for amnesty or who had their applications rejected did not receive amnesty and thus remain liable to domestic prosecution.

388. It is the opposite with the 1996 Guatemalan amnesty (Decree 145-1996: Law of National Reconciliation). There is no application requirement and the burden of proof as to why a person should not get amnesty is on the victim or family. Such a process is inherently less desirable from an accountability perspective.

389. UN DDR Resource Centre Web site (Uganda page), at http://www.unddr.org/countryprogrammes.php?c=37.

390. "Report of the Amnesty Committee," in *Truth and Reconciliation Commission of South Africa Report*, ed. Susan de Villiers (Cape Town: Formeset, 2003), Vol. 6.

391. See Section 4.5, "Maximum viability."

392. An example of an application-based amnesty deadline that was probably too short is that of Ley de Amnistía para el Logro de la Reconciliación Nacional, Decreto No. 805, October 28, 1987 (El Salvador). Article 1.2 of the law gave only fifteen days to apply.

393. See, e.g., L. Mallinder, *Amnesty, Human Rights and Political Transitions*, supra note 2, at 160: "However, problems may arise where an amnesty is frequently extended or renewed, as such activity may create an expectation among insurgents that they can benefit from an amnesty at any time, and can therefore take a 'wait and see' approach rather than engage with the process." See also C. Trumbull, "Giving Amnesty a Second Chance," supra note 4, at 334.

394. See, e.g., R. Slye, "Amnesty, Truth, and Reconciliation: Reflections on the South African Amnesty Process," supra note 133, at 172.

395. G. Meintjes and J. Méndez, "Reconciling Amnesties with Universal Jurisdiction" (2000) 2 Int'l Law FORUM *du droit international* 76, at 90. The authors note that victims have the right to see perpetrators held accountable but not necessarily a right to have the perpetrators punished.
396. Decreto-Lei No. 825/76, November 16, 1976 (Portugal).
397. Amnesty Law, September 20, 1984 (Poland), cited in L. Joinet, "Study on Amnesty Laws and Their Role in the Safeguard and Promotion of Human Rights," supra note 105, para. 34.
398. Law of Civil Harmony, No. 98-08, 1999 (Algeria); Ordonnance 06-01 Portant Mise en Oeuvre de la Charte pour la Paix et la Réconciliation Nationale, 2006 (Algeria).
399. Ibid., art. 10.
400. Decreto-Lei No. 825/76, November 16, 1976 (Portugal), art. 4(3). See also C. Trumbull, "Giving Amnesty a Second Chance," supra note 4, at 337, where the author describes a similar modality used in the Colombian Justice and Peace Law.
401. The priorities are different, however, when the conflict has ended. See, e.g., United Nations Transitional Administration for East Timor, Regulation 2001/10 on the Establishment of a Commission for Reception, Truth and Reconciliation in East Timor, sec. 27.3. It provided that for purposes of reconciliation and truth recovery, the truth commission – in the course of a Community Reconciliation Process hearing – could question the applicant about "the identity of those who organised, planned, instigated, ordered, or participated" in the commission of relevant crimes.
402. See, e.g., C. Trumbull, "Giving Amnesty a Second Chance," supra note 4, at 341, discussing Colombia's Justice and Peace Law: "Ideally, the legislation would require combatants to fully disclose more than their identity and their past crimes. The government may need more information – such as the identity of the rebel leaders, operations strategy, strength of numbers, training bases, etc. – to successfully dismantle the groups. Dismantling the existing groups not only improves the immediate security of the country, but will help ensure that the persons covered by the amnesty do not return to fight upon completion of their sentences. Critics suggest that the administration rejected this full disclosure requirement in order to protect certain government officials or wealthy landowners who might be implicated in the commission of crimes."
403. Ironically, the same process also may expose the state's own complicity in serious violations. See, e.g., R. Uprimny, "Transitional Justice without Transition?," supra note 43, describing the impact of Justice and Peace Law proceedings in Colombia: "Many mass graves have been found, especially because of confessions of some paramilitary that wanted legal benefits. Many revelations have made public about the cruelty of paramilitary groups. Also, some confessions and some judicial decisions (especially some rulings of the Inter-American Court on Human Rights and some investigations carried on by the Supreme Court) have confirmed what human rights NGOs had denounced for several years: the wide complicity of sectors of the Army and the land owners and the political elite with paramilitarism. Many political allies and even some very close collaborators of President Uribe have been accused of complicity with paramilitary groups."

404. The lack of detail may be due to a decision to leave such matters to the discretion of the body responsible for supervising the amnesty process.

405. See, e.g., interview with Howard Varney, *Transitions*, International Center for Transitional Justice, January 2009, at 1: "While the [South African] TRC itself wound up its operations in 1997, the truth-for-amnesty process fumbled along through a time- and resource-consuming process all the way to 2003." In ibid., at 2, Varney adds: "Once [amnesty as a] last resort has been recognized, you then have to assess whether a conditional amnesty program is viable. In other words, is the country capable of operationalizing a complex, resource-draining and time-consuming quasi-judicial process in which there has to be meticulous investigation, verification of the facts, and hearings that accord with procedural fairness?"

406. See, e.g., M. Freeman, *Truth Commissions and Procedural Fairness*, supra note 10, at 35.

407. H. Varney, "Research Brief: The use of amnesty in relation to truth-telling: a case study of the South African Truth and Reconciliation Commission," International Center for Transitional Justice, November 2008, para. 4: "The conditional amnesty was meant to incentivize perpetrators, particularly senior perpetrators, to come forward and speak the truth. This did not happen . . . Very few senior role players came forward. Those that did provided largely sanitized versions of the truth. The bulk of applicants for amnesty were serving prisoners whose crimes were not associated with political objectives. If the amnesty process is to be assessed on whether it was able to incentivize or persuade perpetrators to come forward and speak the full truth, (particularly senior perpetrators), it must be stated that it was an unqualified failure."

408. On South Africa's varied indemnity and amnesty schemes of the early 1990s, see, generally, L. Mallinder, "Indemnity, Amnesty, Pardon and Prosecution Guidelines in South Africa," supra note 99.

409. See, e.g., H. Varney, "Research Brief," supra note 407, at paras. 6 and 7: "The South African model should not be followed unless there is in fact the capacity and the most serious intention to prosecute those who do not qualify for amnesty. . . . It turned out that in South Africa there was very little political will for investigations and prosecutions. Very few resources have been devoted to this task. This is reflected in the stark fact that not a single case from the conflicts of the past is pending before South African courts today."

410. See, e.g., United Nations Transitional Administration for East Timor, Regulation 2001/10 on the Establishment of a Commission for Reception, Truth and Reconciliation in East Timor, which provided that a Community Reconciliation Process hearing panel could recommend, inter alia, a public apology and "other acts of contrition" as a required part of a Community Reconciliation Agreement for a perpetrator to secure future immunity from criminal and civil actions.

411. In the case of the South African TRC, public hearings were mandatory for the most serious crimes. M. Freeman and P. Hayner, "Truth-Telling," in D. Bloomfield et al., eds., *Reconciliation after Violent Conflict: A Handbook* (Stockholm: Institute for Democracy and Electoral Assistance, 2003), at 140–1.

412. R. Slye, "Amnesty, Truth, and Reconciliation," supra note 133, at 173.

413. Ibid., at 177.

414. See, e.g., H. van der Merwe and G. Lamb, "Transitional Justice and DDR: The Case of South Africa," in A. Patel and others, *Disarming the Past*, supra note 140: "The assumption on the part of the ex-combatants was that amnesty would be a vehicle to assist them with the process of reintegrating into civilian life by allowing them to explain their actions and reclaim some sense of dignity while facing the victims of their actions, their communities and society at large. Instead they were subjected to intense cross-examinations about their political motives, the morality of their actions and their honesty, seemingly in an effort to portray them as criminals. Ex-combatants did not feel that they were given the opportunity to explain the full context of their experience under apartheid and the reasons for their specific actions."

415. See, generally, L. Payne, *Unsettling Accounts: Neither Truth nor Reconciliation in Confessions of State Violence* (Durham, N.C.: Duke University Press, 2007). See also M. Freeman, *Truth Commissions and Procedural Fairness*, supra note 10, at chap. 6.

416. See, generally, M. Freeman, *Truth Commissions and Procedural Fairness*, Ibid., at 261–4.

417. See L. Huyse and M. Salter, eds., *Traditional Justice and Reconciliation after Violent Conflict: Learning from African Experiences* (Stockholm: International Institute for Democracy and Electoral Assistance, 2008). In the preface, the report's editors discuss in detail their difficulty in arriving at a term that is sufficiently descriptive without being overinclusive, ethnocentric, or offensive.

418. Ibid., preface, at III.

419. See, e.g., D. Sullivan, ed., *Handbook of Restorative Justice: A Global Perspective* (New York: Routledge, 2008).

420. These were the case studies in L. Huyse and M. Salter, eds., *Traditional Justice and Reconciliation after Violent Conflict*, supra note 417.

421. See ibid., at 194, where the report's editors make the following recommendation: "In the aftermath of regime change or civil war, do not limit the approach adopted and actions undertaken to 'hard reconstruction' (economic stability, disarmament and demobilization, security sector reform and so on), but give sufficient attention to the range of 'soft reconstruction' measures available (restorative justice through informal practices, survivor-oriented programmes, reconciliation, the restoration of local traditional authority)."

422. It should be noted that even the South African TRC process drew inspiration from a tradition-based philosophy known as *ubuntu*. See, generally, M. Battle, *Reconciliation: The Ubuntu Theology of Desmond Tutu* (Cleveland: Pilgrim Press, 1997).

423. See L. Huyse, "Introduction: tradition-based approaches in peacemaking, transitional justice, and reconciliation policies," in L. Huyse and M. Salter, eds., *Traditional Justice and Reconciliation after Violent Conflict*, supra note 417, at 11 and 14. Note also that early in the South African TRC's amnesty process, some commissioners pushed the members of the Amnesty Committee to impose restitution obligations on successful amnesty applicants. However, the committee decided not to do so. Yasmin Sooka, presentation at KU Leuven Faculty of Law, "10 Years after the TRC," November 2008.

424. The Timorese truth commission was responsible for the reception and reintegration of offenders into their communities through the facilitation of community reconciliation agreements (CRAs). As a prerequisite to performing any community service, there needed to be an admission of responsibility by the offender, a voluntary request to perform community service, a public hearing, and a recommendation regarding the proposed content of the service that was proportional to the acts disclosed in the application. If the applicant agreed to perform the recommended service, the CRA was then registered as an order of the court. A person who failed to fulfill his or her obligations could be sentenced, fined, or both, and would not receive immunity from the courts. M. Freeman, *Truth Commissions and Procedural Fairness*, supra note 10, at 77–8.

425. As a condition of eligibility for a reduced sentence, Colombia's Justice and Peace Law, as amended by the country's constitutional court, requires the offender to hand over illegally and legally acquired assets to the state for purposes of ensuring financial compensation to victims. C Díaz, "Colombia's Bid for Justice and Peace," supra note 44, at 489–90.

426. See, e.g, Circulaire du 21 août 1995 relative à l'application de l'article 15 de la loi n° 95-884 du 3 août 1995 portant amnistie (France).

427. See discussion of Colombia's draft Law on Alternative Punishments Section 2.3, "Exhaustion of leniency options short of amnesty to end the blackmail."

428. C. Trumbull, "Giving Amnesty a Second Chance," supra note 4, at 325: "Jail sentences reduce the crime rate by deterring economically motivated criminals and incapacitating violent criminals. Although international prosecutions may not deter potential perpetrators of serious crimes under international law, prosecutions could still be worthwhile based on their incapacitation effect, so long as the benefit from incapacitating criminals outweighs the costs of refusing to recognize amnesties. If amnesties, however, can achieve the same incapacitation effect as prosecutions, the international community can receive the benefit of ensuring that criminals do not commit future crimes, while avoiding the costs that result from rejecting amnesties."

429. See, e.g., Universal Declaration of Human Rights, art. 13; ICCPR, art. 12.

430. See Section 4.5, "Maximum viability."

431. See, generally, Human Rights Committee, ICCPR General Comment 27 (67th sess., 1999), Article 12: Freedom of Movement, A/55/40 vol. 1 (2000) 128, at paras. 11–21 (describing permissible restrictions on freedom of movement).

432. Governor's Island Accord, July 3, 1993 (Haiti), art. 6. See also Decreto No. 87-91, January 23, 1991 (Honduras), art. 3, which provides that foreigners living in the country may benefit from amnesty only if they physically leave the country.

433. M. Scharf, "From the eXile Files," supra note 1, at 340.

434. See Section 2.3, "Exhaustion of leniency options short of amnesty to end the blackmail."

435. See, generally, M. Freeman, "Amnesties and DDR Programs: An Integrated Approach," in A. Patel and others, *Disarming the Past*, supra note 140.

436. Amnesty Law, September 28, 1978 (Mexico), art. 2.

437. Ley 37 por la cual se declara una amnistía condicional, March 23, 1982 (Colombia), art. 3.

438. Decreto-Ley Núm. 27-83, 1983 (Guatemala), art. 2. The same article also requires applicants to disclose locations of other arms deposits.

439. Amnesty Act, 2000 (Uganda), art. 4.

440. Townsville Peace Agreement, October 15, 2000 (Solomon Islands), Part Two, section 3. In "After Baker-Hamilton: What to do in Iraq," International Crisis Group, December 19, 2006, at 20, there is a recommendation for a "far-reaching amnesty" in Iraq that would apply on the condition that eligible individuals surrender their weapons "and, in the case of commanders, instruct fighters under their command to do the same, with the threat of prosecution should they renege on the commitment."

441. Arguably that is the case for Uganda's Amnesty Commission. Between January 1, 2000 and January 19, 2009, 12,503 former LRA combatants received amnesty. Human Rights Watch, "Selling Justice Short: Why Accountability Matters for Peace," July 2009, at 32.

442. See Section 3.6.1, "Typology of amnesty context and beneficiaries."

443. L. Mallinder, *Amnesty, Human Rights and Political Transitions*, supra note 2, at 157.

444. See, generally, M. Freeman, "Amnesties and DDR Programs," supra note 140.

445. Note that the success of DDR may largely depend on the economic benefits available to ex-combatants, not on legal benefits in the form of immunity from adverse legal proceedings. See, generally, E. Harsch, "Reintegration of Ex-Combatants: When Wars End: Transforming Africa's Fighters into Builders," Africa Renewal, October 2005. See also P. Collier, "Demobilization and Insecurity: A Study in the Economics of the Transition from War to Peace" (1994) 6 J. Int'l Development 343.

446. Amnesty Law, September 20, 1984 (Poland), art. 2.

447. Law of Civil Harmony, No. 98-08, 1999 (Algeria), arts. 3 and 7.

448. Amnesty Act, 2000 (Uganda), art. 4.

449. National Reconciliation Charter, 2007 (Afghanistan), art. 4(2).

450. Presidential Decree 124, February 2, 1973 (Philippines), art. 2.

451. See, e.g., Protocol Additional to the Geneva Conventions of August 12, 1949, and relating to the Protection of Victims of International Armed Conflicts (Protocol I), June 8, 1977, 1125 U.N.T.S. 3, arts. 32 and 33. Recall also Protocol Additional to the Geneva Conventions of August 12, 1949, and relating to the Protection of Victims of Non-international Armed Conflicts (Protocol II), June 8, 1977, 1125 U.N.T.S. 609, art. 6(5), concerning the encouragement of amnesty at the end of internal armed conflicts. See also, by analogy, International Convention for the Protection of All Persons from Enforced Disappearance, G.A. Res. A/61/177 (2006), UN Doc. A/61/488, art. 7.2: "Each State Party may establish: (a) Mitigating circumstances, in particular for persons who, having been implicated in the commission of an enforced disappearance, effectively contribute to bringing the disappeared person forward alive or make it possible to clarify cases of enforced disappearance or to identify the perpetrators of an enforced disappearance."

452. Decreto-Ley Núm. 33-82, 1982 (Guatemala), art. 2, which makes the delivery of hostages (in good health) and the return of weapons used for their kidnapping conditions of eligibility for receiving amnesty.

453. Amnesty Law, January 22, 1994 (Mexico), art. 2.

454. Maunikau Accord, 2000 (Fiji).

455. Law of Civil Harmony, No. 98-08, 1999 (Algeria).
456. Decreto-Ley 25499, 1992 (Peru), art. 1.
457. Ley No. 27378 sobre Colaboración Eficaz, 2000 (Peru), Chap. II.
458. Declaration of a General Amnesty, March 18, 1980 (Iran), which provides that if the beneficiary later commits the same or similar crimes, he or she will be punished for both the original and the new crime.
459. Decree-Law 390/1990 (Romania), art. 3.
460. General Amnesty Law No. 84/91, 1991 (Lebanon), art. 2: "L'amnistie ne s'applique pas aux crimes cités ci-dessus, s'ils sont répétitifs et continus, ou dont les auteurs ont persisté à les commettre, ou en firent la récidive, postérieurement à la mise en vigueur de la présente loi, la poursuite reprend dans ce cas là du point où elle fut arrêtée par l'effet de ladite loi."
461. Law No. 18/1994 on Amnesty, November 10, 1994 (Angola), art. 5, which provides that the beneficiary must not commit "any fraudulent crime punishable by a court sentence" for a period of five years.
462. Law No. 19 on Amnesty, 2008 (Iraq), art. 4, which provides that a beneficiary who commits a premeditated crime within five years of the date of the amnesty will be re-sentenced for the original crime and prosecuted for the new one.
463. See, e.g., Memorandum of Understanding between the Government of the Republic of Indonesia and the Free Aceh Movement, August 15, 2005, art. 3.1.4: "Use of weapons by GAM personnel after the signature of this MoU will be regarded as a violation of the MoU and will disqualify the person from amnesty."
464. See, generally, M. Freeman, *Truth Commissions and Procedural Fairness*, supra note 10, at 89–107, concerning procedural and substantive human rights at stake in a non-judicial proceeding that can result in a serious adverse consequence for the subject of the proceeding. See also the extensive literature and standards on lustration, including Council of Europe, Parliamentary Assembly, Resolution 1096 (1996) on measures to dismantle the heritage of former communist totalitarian systems; and Council of Europe Guidelines to ensure that lustration laws and similar administrative measures comply with the requirements of a state based on the rule of law (Doc. 7568).
465. Law 104, December 30, 1993 (Colombia) and Law 418, 1997 (Colombia).
466. R. Teitel, *Transitional Justice*, supra note 80, at 54. See also J. Dorris, *Pardon and Amnesty under Lincoln and Johnson: The Restoration of the Confederates to the Rights and Privileges, 1861–1898* (Chapel Hill: University of North Carolina Press, 1953), at 29–35. The 1863 amnesty issued by President Lincoln required an oath of loyalty to the U.S. Constitution and excluded individuals who treated "colored persons" in a way that violated the laws of war in force at the time. President Johnson issued several subsequent amnesties between 1865 and 1868, which contained the same requirement of an oath of loyalty.
467. *Prosecutor v. Kondewa*, Decision on Lack of Jurisdiction/Abuse of Process: Amnesty provided by the Lomé Accord (Special Court for Sierra Leone), Case No. SCSL-2004-14-AR72 (E) (May 25, 2004), para. 24.
468. See, e.g., L. Mallinder, *Amnesty, Human Rights and Political Transitions*, supra note 2, at 157-8, discussing the example of Northern Ireland: "Under this scheme, prisoners were

released before their organisations had decommissioned, provided their organisations had proclaimed a ceasefire. The early release was conditional on the released individuals refraining from supporting paramilitary organisations, or becoming involved in acts which endanger the public. Furthermore, the releases were designed to occur incrementally with the possibility that they would be halted for members of individual organisations if their organisation breached its ceasefire."

469. On the independence and impartiality of nonjudicial bodies generally, see M. Freeman, *Truth Commissions and Procedural Fairness*, supra note 10, at 132–41.

470. The role of the international community can be vital in building capacity. For example, the United States and the World Bank's Multi-Country Demobilization and Reintegration Programme have provided direct technical and financial support to Uganda's Amnesty Commission.

471. Ley 35 por la cual se decreta una amnistía y se dictan normas tendientes al restablecimiento y preservación de la paz, 1982 (Colombia), art. 9.

472. Such attributes are typical of modern truth commissions. See, generally, M. Freeman, *Truth Commissions and Procedural Fairness*, supra note 10.

473. See Ibid., chap. 2.

474. L. Joinet, "Study on Amnesty Laws and Their Role in the Safeguard and Promotion of Human Rights," supra note x, para. 19c.

475. Proclamation No. 348, 1994 and Amending Resolution 377, 1994 (Philippines), sec. 4, establishing the National Amnesty Commission.

476. Amnesty Law of May 20, 1963 (Rwanda), art. 9.

477. Law of Civil Harmony, No. 98-08, 1999 (Algeria).

478. Amnesty Law, June 8, 1983 (Chad).

479. Law No. 5 on Amnesty, 1973 (Jordan).

480. Ley 35 por la cual se decreta una amnistía y se dictan normas tendientes al restablecimiento y preservación de la paz, 1982 (Colombia), art. 8.

481. But see, e.g., Decree 210/1983 (El Salvador), art. 4, which created an amnesty committee comprising three individuals chosen, respectively, by the national Peace Commission, the Human Rights Commission, and the Ministry of the Interior. Brazil's inter-ministerial Amnesty Commission is located within the Ministry of Justice. Institui Comissão Interministerial para estabelecer critérios e forma de pagamento da reparação econômica aos anistiados políticos de que trata a Lei n° 10.559, de 13 de novembro de 2002, August 27, 2003 (Brazil).

482. But see Proclamation No. 347, 1994 (Philippines), sec. 4, which created a National Amnesty Commission with authority, inter alia, to issue summons and subpoenas and to call on all public institutions "to render assistance in the efficient, effective implementation of its functions." Also, several Colombian amnesty laws have established special victim and witness protection measures with a view to effective implementation of the amnesty scheme. See, e.g., Law 418/1997 (Colombia), Part II, Title 1.

483. See, generally, R. A. Wilson, *The Politics of Truth and Reconciliation in South Africa: Legitimizing the Post-Apartheid State* (Cambridge: Cambridge University Press, 2001); C. Villa-Vicencio, *Looking Back, Reaching Forward: Reflections on the Truth and*

Reconciliation Commission of South Africa (Cape Town: University of Cape Town Press, 2000); J. Sarkin, *Carrots and Sticks: The TRC and the South African Amnesty Process* (Mortsel, Belgium: Intersentia Press, 2004); A. Boraine, *A Country Unmasked* (Oxford: Oxford University Press, 2000).

484. See in this regard *Truth and Reconciliation Commmission v. Colin Cecile Coleman and 36 others and The Chairperson of the Committee on Amnesty*, Case No. 3729/98 (S. Afr. High Court), in which the TRC challenged a collective grant of amnesty by the Amnesty Committee for failure by the applicants to make the necessary disclosures and admissions. The court set aside the grant of amnesty and referred the case back to the committee, which then denied amnesty.

485. The Truth, Justice, and Reconciliation Commission Bill, 2008 (Kenya), Part III.

486. An Act to Establish the Truth and Reconciliation Commission of Liberia (2005), sec. 26(g).

487. See, e.g., M. Freeman, *Truth Commissions and Procedural Fairness*, supra note 10, at 25. See also http://www.ictj.org.

488. See, e.g., "OHCHR-Nepal Raises Concerns about Truth and Reconciliation Commission Bill," Office of the High Commissioner for Human Rights, press release, August 3, 2007.

489. See Part I, Section 6, "The evolving UN position on amnesties."

490. Decision number 006/PUU-IV/2006 regarding the substantiation of the Law on the Truth and Reconciliation Commission. See also Office of the United Nations High Commissioner for Human Rights, *Rule of Law Tools for Post-Conflict States: Amnesties* (Geneva: United Nations, 2009), at 38: "On 7 December 2006 Indonesia's Constitutional Court found article 27 [on amnesty and compensation] unconstitutional and, because it was integral to the Law as a whole, found the Law unconstitutional." But see Amnesty International, 2007 World Report (Indonesia): "In December (2006) the Constitutional Court annulled Law 27/2004 which mandated an Indonesian Commission of Truth and Reconciliation. Rights activists had challenged provisions allowing amnesty for perpetrators of severe human rights violations and limiting victims' ability to obtain compensation. However, the Court ruled that the whole law should be repealed as it was 'illogical,' some articles violated the Constitution, and the annulment of individual articles would render the rest of the law unenforceable. The annulment of the law left victims of past human rights violations without a compensation mechanism."

491. The Head of the Aceh Monitoring Mission (a combined EU and ASEAN body that among its tasks had responsibility for resolving disputed amnesty cases) was empowered to make rulings in disputed cases of individual amnesty. "After the initial release [of 285 GAM members] in August 2005, GAM informed the GoI and AMM that there were still individuals incarcerated throughout Indonesia whom, according to GAM, should be amnestied and released pursuant to the MoU. In order to resolve these cases, a tri-partite working group was established. This group succeeded in facilitating agreement between the parties in a number of cases. However, in an attempt to facilitate further progress, AMM recruited a former Swedish judge internationally experienced in handling amnesty issues. As the parties mutually agreed on cases,

individuals were granted amnesty and released. By way of these facilitation efforts, the parties finally reached consensual agreement on all pending amnesty cases and declared that there were no disputed amnesty cases requiring the decision of the Head of Mission": http://www.aceh-mm.org/.

492. Decree 57-1108, 1957 (France), art. 5.

493. Decree 145-1996: Law of National Reconciliation, 1996 (Guatemala), art. 11. "Article 11 provides that eligibility for amnesty will be determined through expedited proceedings. Cases that involve crimes falling under the law are to be transferred to the appropriate chamber of the Court of Appeals; apparently the idea was to remove pressures on individual judges in these cases by having a panel of judges consider them. Parties must submit their arguments to the Court of Appeals within ten days. Parties may appeal the decision of the Court of Appeals within three days to the Supreme Court, which has five days to rule": N. Roht-Arriaza and L. Gibson, "The Developing Jurisprudence on Amnesty" (1998) 20 Human Rights Q. 843, at 853.

494. Law No. 19 on Amnesty, 2008 (Iraq), art. 5.

495. One interesting example is a 1992 Russian amnesty providing that the issuance of an amnesty certificate can be contested or appealed in court by "interested parties" and "social organizations." Law on Rehabilitation of Victims of Political Repression, October 18, 1991, as amended December 17, 1992 (Russia), art. 10.

496. Amnesty Law, December 3, 1972 (Sudan).

497. Law Nullifying the State's Claim to Punish Certain Crimes (Ley de Caducidad), Law No. 15.848, 1986 (Uruguay), art. 3.

498. Law on the Outlawing of the Democratic Kampuchea Group, July 7, 1994 (Cambodia), art. 7.

499. Proclamation 80, 1987 (Philippines).

500. Ley 37 por la cual se declara una amnistía condicional, May 14, 1981 (Colombia), arts. 3 and 15.

501. Decreto-Ley Núm. 34-82, 1982 (Guatemala), art. 1.

502. Amnesty Act, 2000 (Uganda).

503. "Report of the Amnesty Committee, Section 1, Chapter 2: Administrative Report," in *Truth and Reconciliation Commission of South Africa Report*, vol. 6, paras. 57–9.

504. Victims also had the right to be notified of any decision to grant amnesty in the matter. In the similar case of the Timorese truth commission, which involved plea-bargained immunity, victims had a right to participate at private and public hearings related to their case, a right to obtain a copy of relevant community reconciliation agreements, and a right to protection of their safety, physical and psychological well-being, dignity, and privacy in relation to hearings at which they were present. http://www.cavr-timorleste.org/.

505. R. Mani, *Beyond Retribution: Seeking Justice in the Shadows of War* (Malden, MA: Polity, 2002), at 90. See more generally E. A. Lind and T. R. Tyler, *The Social Psychology of Procedural Justice* (New York: Plenum Press, 1988); B. Frey et al., "Introducing Procedural Utility: Not Only What, But Also How Matters," CREMA Working Paper No. 2003-02.

506. Law on the Outlawing of the Democratic Kampuchea Group, July 7, 1994 (Cambodia), art. 9.
507. In some jurisdictions, access to judicial review is an automatic right; in others, it is limited to cases involving gross procedural irregularities or errors of law. See, e.g., M. Freeman, *Truth Commissions and Procedural Fairness*, supra note 10, at 298–300.
508. Amnesty Law, November 22, 1973 (Yugoslavia).
509. Law on Rehabilitation of Victims of Political Repression, October 18, 1991, as amended December 17, 1992 (Russia), art. 10.
510. Proclamation No. 347, 1994 (Philippines), sec. 4.
511. Promotion of National Unity and Reconciliation Act, 1995 (South Africa), sec. 21.
512. Amnesty Proclamation No. 8, September 7, 1946 (Philippines), cited in A. T. Muyot, "Amnesty in the Philippines: The Legal Concept as a Political Tool" (1994) 69 Philippine L. J. 51, at 70.
513. M. Freeman, *Truth Commissions and Procedural Fairness*, supra note 10, at 251–6.
514. See, e.g., C. Sriram, "Conflict Mediation and the ICC," supra note 147, at 305: "These may include, inter alia, measures to integrate ex-fighters, whether state or non-state, into the security forces, measures to allow former rebels to participate legally in the political process, and even form political parties. It may also include measures to allow all parties to a conflict (or selected ones) a portion of, or a stake in the governance of, the state's economic resources. Finally it may include measures granting a group or groups a degree of territorial autonomy over a particular region."
515. See, e.g., S. Ratner and J. Abrams, *Accountability for Human Rights Atrocities in International Law*, 2d ed. (Oxford: Oxford University Press, 2001), at 154; S. Williams, "Amnesties in International Law: The Experience of the Special Court of Sierra Leone" (2005) 5 Human Rights L. Rev. 271, at 293.

Final Considerations: On the Perennial Contestation of Amnesties

1. The treatment of the subject here is deliberately brief, as there is already abundant comparative scholarship on it. See, e.g., L. Mallinder, *Amnesty, Human Rights and Political Transitions: Bridging the Peace and Justice Divide* (Oxford: Hart, 2008), chapters 5 and 6.
2. Decree Law 2191, 1978 (Chile).
3. In his original study for the United Nations in 1985, Louis Joinet argued that amnesty laws should be narrowly construed by courts because they are tantamount to emergency legislation. "Study on Amnesty Laws and Their Role in the Safeguard and Promotion of Human Rights," UN Doc. E/CN.4/Sub.2/1985/16/Rev.1, para. 21.
4. See Corte Suprema de Justicia [CSJN], 14/6/2005, "Julio Héctor Simón y otros," Colección Oficial de Fallos de la Corte Suprema de Justicia de la Nación [Fallos] (2005-328-2056) (Arg.). This judgment reversed a prior judgment by the same court in which the same laws were ruled constitutional: Corte Suprema de Justicia [CSJN], 22/06/1987, "Camps, Ramón Juan Alberto y otros/Causa incoada en virtud del decreto 280/84 del Poder Ejecutivo Nacional," Colección Oficial de Fallos de la Corte Suprema de Justicia de la Nación [Fallos] (1987-310-1162) (Arg.). For a critical analysis of the

Simón judgment in particular, see, e.g., J. Elias, "Constitutional Changes, Transitional Justice, and Legitimacy: The Life and Death of Argentina's 'Amnesty' Laws" (2008) 31 Hastings Int'l & Comp. L. Rev. 587.

5. Decision of the Indonesian Constitutional Court concerning draft law on a Truth and Reconciliation Commission (December 7, 2006). See, generally, International Center for Transitional Justice press release, "Indonesia: Constitutional Court Strikes Down Flawed Truth Commission Law Decision Presents Opportunity to Address Legacy of Impunity" (December 8, 2006).

6. Corte Suprema de Justicia de Honduras, 27/06/00, 'Petition for Declaration of Unconstitutionality' (No. 20-99), ruling that the amnesties of 1987 and 1991 were unconstitutional to the extent they purported to treat common crimes as political crimes.

7. Corte Suprema de Justicia de El Salvador, 05/10/00, "Ruling on the Constitutionality of the 1993 Amnesty Law", finding that the applicability of a 1993 amnesty to crimes committed by state actors should be assessed on a case-by-case basis.

8. Lomé Peace Accord, 1999 (Sierra Leone), art. IX.

9. Ordonnance 06-01 Portant Mise en Oeuvre de la Charte pour la Paix et la Réconciliation Nationale, 2006 (Algeria).

10. Immunity Decree N.17, 2000 (Fiji).

11. N. Roht-Arriaza and L. Gibson, "The Developing Jurisprudence on Amnesty" (1998) 20 Hum. Rts. Q. 843, at 885. This is all basically akin to the so-called Aylwin doctrine adopted in Chile, according to which courts in that country could refuse to apply a sweeping amnesty law until the facts of the case, including the identity of the presumed authors of the crime, were ascertained. See, e.g., ibid. at 862; M. Freeman, *Truth Commissions and Procedural Fairness* (New York: Cambridge University Press, 2006), at 74. Though it is an important development in the fight against impunity, the doctrine creates a perverse incentive to not search for or find a person's remains.

12. N. Roht-Arriaza and L. Gibson, "The Developing Jurisprudence on Amnesty," ibid., at 884.

13. L. Mallinder, *Amnesty, Human Rights and Political Transitions*, supra note 1, at 235.

14. Ibid., at 206: "national courts changed their position on the amnesties over time, usually being more willing to apply the amnesty unquestionably in the early days of the transition, but becoming more willing to challenge or restrict it as time progresses and the political conditions become more stable.... However, as it has been easier to obtain information on judgments since the 1990s than it has been for the earlier period, these figures may exaggerate these trends."

15. This is the strategy adopted, for example, in the constitutional challenge to Algeria's 2006 amnesty law. Interview with Sofiane Chouiter, Algerian human rights lawyer, February 2008. Concerning the exhaustion of domestic remedies requirement more generally, see M. Freeman and G. van Ert, *International Human Rights Law* (Toronto: Irwin Law, 2004), at 38 and 347.

16. For example, following the order of the Inter-American Court of Human Rights in the *Barrios Altos Case* – the court's first judgment about the compatibility of a specific amnesty law with the American Convention on Human Rights – both the Peruvian

Supreme Court and the Constitutional Tribunal declared the country's 1995 amnesties to be "without any legal effect," and domestic prosecutors and judges have proceeded with trials on the basis of the invalidity of the amnesty legislation. *Barrios Altos Case* (Chumbipuma Aguirre et al *v.* Peru), Inter-Am. Ct. H. R. (ser. C) No. 74 (2001), paras. 41–44. Note, however, that both the Inter-American and European human rights courts have significant case backlogs and thus judgments are not rendered until years after submission.

17. On the rules of reception, generally, see M. Freeman and G. van Ert, *International Human Rights Law*, supra note 15, at 147–8 and 540–1.

18. See Part II, Section 4.1, "Minimum legal entrenchment." See also L. Mallinder, *Amnesty, Human Rights and Political Transitions*, supra note 1, at 224: "In making such determinations, the case law shows that national courts have adopted positions ranging from affording international treaties no weight in domestic legal systems other than as a guide to interpreting the constitution; to declaring that international law is part of domestic law, but with a lesser status than constitutional laws; to finally declaring that international law is hierarchically pre-eminent over domestic laws. Once a court has adopted one of these positions, further variations can occur depending on whether the amnesty is viewed as having constitutional status, and on the date that the relevant treaties were ratified within the domestic legal system."

19. The Law of National Pacification (Law No. 22.924, 1983) was rendered null and void by the Amnesty Nullification Law (Law No. 23.040, 1983). In 2003, both houses of Congress voted to annul two other amnesty laws, in each case with retroactive effect: the Full Stop Law (Law No. 23,492, 1986) and the Due Obedience Law (Law No. 23,521, 1987).

20. The Indemnity Ordinance, 1975 (Bangladesh) was repealed by the Ordinance Repeal Act, Act No. 21, 1996 (Bangladesh). See also D. Orentlicher, "Independent study on best practices, including recommendations, to assist States in strengthening their domestic capacity to combat all aspects of impunity." (February 27, 2004), UN Doc. E/CN.4/2004/88, at para. 30, where the author describes a partial amnesty repeal through the legislature: "[A] Polish law enacted in December 1998 provides that amnesties adopted before 7 December 1989 shall not be enforced in relation to, inter alia, war crimes or crimes against humanity."

21. In addition, as noted in Part I, an act of repeal would not violate the prohibition on ex post facto legislation. No new crime is created, retroactively or prospectively, through the repeal of an amnesty. The repeal merely reestablishes the jurisdiction of courts to try crimes that were criminal at the time when the amnesty was originally issued and for which amnesty was given in the first place.

22. See, e.g., ICCPR, art. 15: "1. No one shall be held guilty of any criminal offence on account of any act or omission which did not constitute a criminal offence, under national or international law, at the time when it was committed. Nor shall a heavier penalty be imposed than the one that was applicable at the time when the criminal offence was committed. If, subsequent to the commission of the offence, provision is made by law for the imposition of the lighter penalty, the offender shall benefit thereby. 2. Nothing in this article shall prejudice the trial and punishment of any person for

any act or omission which, at the time when it was committed, was criminal according to the general principles of law recognized by the community of nations."

23. *Almonacid-Arellano v. Chile* (Preliminary Objections, Merits, Reparations, and Costs), Inter-Am. Ct. H. R. (ser. C) no. 154 (2006), Case No. 12.057, at para. 82(24). As of this writing, no interpretive law has been adopted.

24. As of this writing, there is a plebiscite on the amnesty scheduled to take place during the October 2009 national elections. J. Errandonea, "Droits de l'homme et État de Droit: le cas de la loi d'amnistie en Uruguay," in R. Fregosi, ed., *Droits de l'homme et consolidation de la démocratie en Amérique du sud* (Paris: L'Harmattan, forthcoming 2009).

25. Ghana National Reconciliation Commission Report, October 2004, para. 8.28: "The existence of indemnity clauses under the Transitional Provisions to the 1992 Constitution has remained a sore point with many whose rights were abused by the PNDC government and its appointees. These clauses were not permitted to be debated by the Consultative Assembly in 1992 before insertion into the Draft Constitution. Although the Draft Constitution was later subjected to a referendum, the mode of its handling made it impossible for those who wished for a return to constitutional government, but who disapproved of the clauses, from expressing that preference. A stable constitutional order cannot be founded on injustice and impunity on the part of wrong-doers, matched by a deep sense of grievance by many citizens. The indemnity clauses must be subjected to a referendum once again, so that the democratic mechanisms might assist the nation to resolve this matter for all time."

26. See, e.g., Human Security Report Project, "Human Security Brief: 2007," chapter 3 (Trends in Armed Conflict and Coups d'Etat).

27. See, e.g., A. Puddington, "Freedom in the World 2009: Setbacks and Resilience," Freedom House, at 2–3.

28. L. Mallinder, *Amnesty, Human Rights and Political Transitions*, supra note 1, at 19.

29. Human Security Report Project, "Human Security Brief: 2007," chapter 4 (Targeting Civilians). See also G. Evans, *The Responsibility to Protect* (Washington, DC: Brookings Institution Press, 2008), at 234, where he notes that today "90 per cent or more of war-related deaths are due to disease and malnutrition rather than direct violence."

Index